How to Fast-Track Your Ac

For Susanne, the best publisher an editor could wish for—Adam

For Alessandra—Tony

For my lovely daughters—Joëlle

For my mum Judith—John

How to Fast-Track Your Academic Career
A Guide for Mid-Career Scholars

Edited by

Adam Lindgreen

Professor, Copenhagen Business School, Denmark; Extraordinary Professor, Gordon Institute of Business Science, University of Pretoria, South Africa

C. Anthony Di Benedetto

Professor, Fox School of Business, Temple University, USA

Joëlle Vanhamme

Professor, EDHEC Business School, France

John Nicholson

Professor, Huddersfield Business School, University of Huddersfield, UK

Cheltenham, UK • Northampton, MA, USA

© Adam Lindgreen, C. Anthony Di Benedetto, Joëlle Vanhamme and John Nicholson 2021

All rights reserved. No part of this publication may be reproduced, stored in a retrieval system or transmitted in any form or by any means, electronic, mechanical or photocopying, recording, or otherwise without the prior permission of the publisher.

Published by
Edward Elgar Publishing Limited
The Lypiatts
15 Lansdown Road
Cheltenham
Glos GL50 2JA
UK

Edward Elgar Publishing, Inc.
William Pratt House
9 Dewey Court
Northampton
Massachusetts 01060
USA

Paperback edition 2022

A catalogue record for this book
is available from the British Library

Library of Congress Control Number: 2021933292

This book is available electronically in the **Elgar**online
Business subject collection
http://dx.doi.org/10.4337/9781839101786

ISBN 978 1 83910 177 9 (cased)
ISBN 978 1 83910 178 6 (eBook)
ISBN 978 1 80392 750 3 (paperback)

Printed and bound by CPI Group (UK) Ltd, Croydon, CR0 4YY

Contents

List of figures	viii
List of tables	ix
About the editors	x
List of contributors	xiv

Introduction to *How to Fast-Track Your Academic Career*   1
Adam Lindgreen, C. Anthony Di Benedetto, Joëlle Vanhamme, and John Nicholson

PART 1   GETTING STARTED

1   Becoming a business-to-business marketing scholar   13
Adam Lindgreen and C. Anthony Di Benedetto
In collaboration with *Ko de Ruyter, Lisa Ellram, Christian Grönroos, Michael Hutt, Douglas M. Lambert, Ajay Kohli, Selma Kadić Maglajlić, Matthew Robson, and Michel van der Borgh*

2   Balancing like an academic   38
Adam Lindgreen and C. Anthony Di Benedetto

PART 2   GENERATING IDEAS AND SETTING UP FOR SUCCESS

3   Developing original, courageous ideas   51
Adam Lindgreen, C. Anthony Di Benedetto, and Florian Kock

4   Building research groups   61
Adam Lindgreen, C. Anthony Di Benedetto, Roderick J. Brodie, and Peter Naudé

5   Writing research funding applications   97
Adam Lindgreen, C. Anthony Di Benedetto, Camilla Verdich, Joëlle Vanhamme, Vinod Venkatraman, Steven Pattinson, Ann Højbjerg Clarke, and Zaheer Khan

| 6 | Undertaking cross-disciplinary research
Adam Lindgreen, C. Anthony Di Benedetto, Roderick J. Brodie, and Michel van der Borgh | 118 |
| 7 | Collaborating with practitioners
C. Anthony Di Benedetto, Adam Lindgreen, Marianne Storgaard, and Ann Højbjerg Clarke | 129 |

PART 3 WORKING WITH STUDENTS

| 8 | Guiding Ph.D. students
C. Anthony Di Benedetto, Adam Lindgreen, and Torsten Ringberg
In collaboration with Audhesh Paswan, Laura Peracchio, David Luna, Peter Naudé, Rod Brodie, John Nicholson, Markus Reihlen, Matthew Robson, Ken Peattie, and Hans Baumgartner | 150 |
| 9 | Translating research into teaching
Adam Lindgreen, C. Anthony Di Benedetto, Roderick J. Brodie, and Peter Naudé | 173 |

PART 4 GETTING PUBLISHED

10	Framing a manuscript *Adam Lindgreen and C. Anthony Di Benedetto* In collaboration with Ad de Jong, Luigi De Luca, Heiner Evanschitzky, Michael Mol, Robert Morgan, John Nicholson, and Tobias Schäfers	189
11	Developing conceptual frameworks for business-to-business marketing *Adam Lindgreen, C. Anthony Di Benedetto, Roderick J. Brodie, and Elina Jaakkola*	204
12	Writing a case-study methodology section *Adam Lindgreen, C. Anthony Di Benedetto, and Michael B. Beverland*	225
13	Writing articles for premier academic journals *Peter LaPlaca, Adam Lindgreen, and Joëlle Vanhamme*	236

14	Revising for premier academic journals *Peter LaPlaca, Adam Lindgreen, Joëlle Vanhamme, and C. Anthony Di Benedetto*	257
15	Reviewing manuscripts *Adam Lindgreen and C. Anthony Di Benedetto* *In collaboration with Maja Arslanagić-Kalajdžić, Ad de Jong, Stephan Henneberg, Kristian Möller, John Nicholson, Mark Parry, Audhesh Paswan, Gerrit van Bruggen, Joëlle Vanhamme, and Chun Zhang*	273

PART 5   BEING RELEVANT

16	Getting research cited *Adam Lindgreen, C. Anthony Di Benedetto, Roderick J. Brodie, Julia A. Fehrer, and Michel van der Borgh*	295
17	Defining, identifying, and measuring societal value *Adam Lindgreen, C. Anthony Di Benedetto, Ann Højbjerg Clarke, Majbritt Rostgaard Evald, Niels Bjørn-Andersen, and Douglas M. Lambert*	313

PART 6   OFFERING OUR FINAL THOUGHTS

18	Offering our final thoughts on *How to Fast-Track Your Academic Career* *Adam Lindgreen and C. Anthony Di Benedetto*	349

Appendix 1: Example of charters for research groups: IMP and CMP *C. Anthony Di Benedetto and Adam Lindgreen*	353
Appendix 2: Revising and resubmitting: Go configure: the mix of purchasing practices to choose for your supply base *Adam Lindgreen, Joëlle Vanhamme, Erik van Raaij, and Wesley J. Johnston*	357
Index	388

Figures

3.1	The OBC model as a Venn diagram	53
6.1	Domains of knowledge and levels of theory	120
6.2	Interfaces for theorizing	121
11.1	Role of theory vs. empirical data in developing conceptual frameworks	205
11.2	Domains of knowledge and levels of theory	208
11.3	Styles of theorizing for building conceptual frameworks	211
11.4	Conceptual framework of Du et al. (2013)	212
14.1	The review and revision process	260
14.2	Typical results per 100 submissions (based on 2014 data)	271
A2.1	Four purchasing configurations	369
A2.2	Differences in performance outcomes between purchasing configurations	371

Tables

4.A1	IMP research: selected books and journal articles and number of citations	94
4.A2	CMP research: journal articles and number of citations	95
5.1	Elements of research funding applications	109
9.1	Differences between academics and practitioners	183
11.1	Micro-foundations of dynamic capabilities of for-profit hybrids	216
11.2	Indicators pertaining to purchasing practices	218
11.3	Three styles of developing theoretical frameworks and associated guidelines	222
12.1	Case-study tactics to secure the design tests of validity and reliability	230
14.1	Editors' decision 'rules'	270
17.1	Societal value: activities and measures	318
17.2	Societal value: the societal relevance and societal impact of an individual's research	329
A2.1	Indicators pertaining to purchasing practices	361

About the editors

Adam Lindgreen
After studies in chemistry (Copenhagen University), engineering (the Engineering Academy of Denmark), and physics (Copenhagen University), Professor Adam Lindgreen completed an MSc in food science and technology at the Technical University of Denmark. He also finished an MBA at the University of Leicester. He received his Ph.D. in marketing from Cranfield University. His first appointments were with the Catholique University of Louvain (2000–2001) and Eindhoven University of Technology (2002–2007). Subsequently, he served as Professor of Marketing at Hull University's Business School (2007–2010); University of Birmingham's Business School (2010), where he also was the research director in the Department of Marketing; and University of Cardiff's Business School (2011–2016). Under his leadership, the Department of Marketing and Strategy at Cardiff Business School ranked first among all marketing departments in Australia, Canada, New Zealand, the United Kingdom, and the United States, based upon the hg indices of senior faculty. Since 2016, Adam Lindgreen has been Professor of Marketing at Copenhagen Business School, where he also heads the Department of Marketing. Since 2018, he also is Extraordinary Professor with University of Pretoria's Gordon Institute of Business Science.

Adam Lindgreen has been a visiting professor with various institutions including Georgia State University, HEC Paris, and Melbourne University. His publications have appeared in *Business Horizons*, *California Management Review*, *Entrepreneurship and Regional Development*, *Industrial Marketing Management*, *International Journal of Management Reviews*, *Journal of Advertising*, *Journal of Business Ethics*, *European Journal of Marketing*, *Journal of Business and Industrial Marketing*, *Journal of Marketing Management*, *Journal of the Academy of Marketing Science*, *Journal of Product Innovation Management*, *Journal of World Business*, *Organization Studies*, *Psychology & Marketing*, and *Supply Chain Management: An International Journal*, among others.

Adam Lindgreen's 23 books in business and economics include *A Stakeholder Approach to Corporate Social Responsibility* (with Kotler, Vanhamme, and Maon), *Managing Market Relationships*, *Memorable Customer Experiences* (with Vanhamme and Beverland), *Not All Claps and Cheers* (with Maon,

Vanhamme, Angell, and Memery), *Public Value* (with Koenig-Lewis, Kitchener, Brewer, Moore, and Meynhardt), and *Sustainable Value Chain Management* (with Maon, Vanhamme, and Sen).

The recipient of the "Outstanding Article 2005" award from *Industrial Marketing Management* and the runner-up for the same award in 2016, he serves on the board of several scientific journals; he is Co-Editor-in-Chief of *Industrial Marketing Management* and previously was the joint editor of the *Journal of Business Ethics*' section on corporate responsibility. His research interests include business and industrial marketing management, corporate social responsibility, and sustainability. He has been awarded the Dean's Award for Excellence in Executive Teaching. Furthermore, he has served as an examiner (for dissertations, modules, and programs) at a wide variety of institutions around the world.

Adam Lindgreen is a member of the International Scientific Advisory Panel of the New Zealand Food Safety Science and Research Centre (a partnership between government, industry organizations, and research institutions), as well as of the Chartered Association of Business Schools' Academic Journal Guide (AJG) Scientific Committee in the field of marketing.

Beyond these academic contributions to marketing, Adam Lindgreen has discovered and excavated settlements from the Stone Age in Denmark, including the only major kitchen midden—Sparregård—in the south-east of Denmark; because of its importance, the kitchen midden was later excavated by the National Museum and then protected as a historical monument for future generations. He is also an avid genealogist, having traced his family back to 1390 and published widely including eight books and numerous articles in scientific journals (*Personalhistorisk Tidsskrift*, *The Genealogist*, and *Slægt & Data*) related to methodological issues in genealogy, accounts of population development, and particular family lineages.

C. Anthony Di Benedetto
Dr. C. Anthony Di Benedetto is Professor of Marketing and Supply Chain Management and Senior Washburn Research Fellow at the Fox School of Business, Temple University. He has held visiting professorships at Bocconi University, Politecnico di Milano, Technische Universiteit Eindhoven, Kansai University, Yonsei University, WHU, St. Petersburg State University, Edhec Business School, and IESEG School of Management. In 2010, Anthony Di Benedetto was named the Fulbright-Kathryn and Craig Hall Chair in Entrepreneurship and spent a semester at the Wirtschaftsuniversität Wien.

Anthony Di Benedetto holds a Ph.D. in Administration, an MBA in Marketing, and a BSc in Chemistry, all from McGill University. He taught at the Université du Québec à Montréal (in French) and the University of Kentucky prior to joining Temple. Since arriving at Temple he has taught in Temple's Professional MBA, Executive MBA, International Executive MBA (Singapore, Cali, and Bogotà), Online MBA, and International MBA programs, as well as at the Ph.D., DBA, BBA, and OBBA programs. In 2017, Anthony Di Benedetto taught in the Fox School's Global Immersion program in Vienna; years earlier, in 1992, he was one of the first instructors to teach business classes at Temple's Rome campus. He is a recipient of Temple University's Great Teacher Award, the highest teaching honor bestowed by Temple University. He has also received the Lindback Award for teaching excellence, a Department of Marketing teaching award, and the Lynne A. Cronfeld Research Award/Grant. In 2017, he was selected as Faculty of the Year by students in both the DBA and OMBA programs. In 2015, he received the Musser Excellence in Leadership Award in Research, the highest honor bestowed by the Fox School of Business.

Anthony Di Benedetto is Co-Editor-in-Chief of *Industrial Marketing Management*, and Editor-in-Chief of *Journal of International Consumer Marketing*. He served as Editor of *Journal of Product Innovation Management* for nine years. He is co-author with Merle Crawford of *New Products Management*, the leading textbook in new product development.

Anthony Di Benedetto has been named one of the 50 leading research scholars worldwide in innovation and technology management by the International Association of Management of Technology. He has over 115 refereed academic articles published, in journals including *IEEE Transactions on Engineering Management*, *Industrial Marketing Management*, *Journal of International Business Studies*, *Journal of Operations Management*, *Journal of Product Innovation Management*, *Journal of the Academy of Marketing Science*, *Management Science*, *Strategic Management Journal*, *Columbia Journal of World Business*, and elsewhere. A paper published in *IEEE Transactions on Engineering Management* was named the Best Paper in that journal for 2008. He has been named multiple times to the Dean's Research Honor Roll of the School of Business and Management.

He is a certified New Product Development Professional (NPDP) and is listed in Marquis Who's Who in the World, Marquis Who's Who in America, and Marquis Who's Who in American Education.

Joëlle Vanhamme
Dr. Joëlle Vanhamme is Professor of Marketing at the Edhec Business School. She received her Ph.D. from the Catholic University of Louvain (Louvain School of Management). Joëlle Vanhamme has been Assistant Professor at

Rotterdam School of Management, Associate Professor at IESEG School of Management, and a visiting scholar with Delft University of Technology, Eindhoven University of Technology, Hull University's Business School, Lincoln University, and the University of Auckland's Business School. Her research has appeared in *Business Horizons, California Management Review, Industrial Marketing Management, International Journal of Research in Marketing, Journal of Advertising, Journal of Advertising Research, Journal of Business Ethics, Journal of Consumer Satisfaction, Dissatisfaction and Complaining Behavior, Journal of Customer Behaviour, Journal of Economic Psychology, Journal of Marketing Management, Journal of Retailing, Marketing Letters, Organization Studies, Psychology & Marketing, Recherche et Applications en Marketing*, and *Supply Chain Management: An International Journal*, among others.

John Nicholson

Dr. John Nicholson has a background in the agricultural supply industry, and his first qualification was in agricultural merchanting. He completed his first degree in business studies at the University of Hull in 2000, an MSc in international marketing at the University of Leeds in 2001, and a Ph.D. in Management from the University of Hull in 2009. He is a Senior Fellow of the Higher Education Academy, a Fellow of the Chartered Management Institute, and a Member of the Chartered Institute of Marketing. His academic career began in 2002 as a lecturer in marketing and business strategy at the University of Hull until he left to take up the post of reader in strategy at Sheffield Hallam University in 2015. He joined Huddersfield University as a Chair in Strategic Management in 2017. Over a period of ten years, he has completed twelve doctoral supervisions in diverse areas from change management, SME development and sales management to reverse logistics in waste supply chains. John Nicholson has a variety of research interests, which have included knowledge transfer, supply chains, public–private sector interaction, relational space, entrepreneurship, co-opetition, and regional interaction. He has published in journals such as *Industrial Marketing Management, International Business Review, Journal of Business Research, Journal of Management Inquiry, Marketing Theory, Policy and Politics*, and *Supply Chain Management*. Underpinning his work is a philosophical interest in the agency–structure interaction, and he has published several articles drawing on systems thinking, critical realist, and structurationist ideas. He has also published articles examining the craft of academic writing and doctoral supervision. John Nicholson has served as Associate Editor of *Industrial Marketing Management* since 2017 and is a reviewer for a number of journals.

Contributors

Michael B. Beverland is Professor of Marketing at Sussex University Business School. He also holds an Adjunct Professorship at Copenhagen Business School. He has published in a range of academic journals including *Journal of Advertising, Journal of Business Research, Journal of Consumer Research, Journal of Management Studies, Journal of Product Innovation Management*, and *Journal of the Academy of Marketing Science*. Michael Beverland's research focuses on marketplace authenticity and design driven innovation. His most recent book is *Brand Management: Cocreating Brand Meaning* (Sage, 2018); he has also written *Building Brand Authenticity: 7 Habits of Iconic Brands*.

Niels Bjørn-Andersen is Professor Emeritus in the Department of Digitalization at Copenhagen Business School. He conducts research related to the future of enterprise resource-planning systems, IT in mergers and acquisitions, inter-organizational systems, IT management, and the role of IT in shaping future organizations. Niels Bjørn-Andersen has written or edited 25 books, more than 50 peer-reviewed journal articles, and more than 100 other publications. He has been the principal investigator or co-investigator of more than 30 larger research projects including more recently the €5.9 million ITAIDE research project with IBM and SAP, among others, and the €4 3gERP research project with Microsoft.

Roderick J. Brodie is Professor of Marketing in the Department of Marketing at the University of Auckland. His 120-plus journal articles have appeared in leading international journals including *Industrial Marketing Management, International Journal of Research in Marketing, Journal of Marketing, Journal of Marketing Research, Journal of Service Research*, and *Management Science*, among others. He is an Associate Editor for *Journal of Service Research* and former Associate Editor for *Marketing Theory*. He has served on editorial boards of *Journal of Marketing, International Journal of Research in Marketing*, and other leading international journals. He was the first president of ANZMAC, and in 2004 he was made a founding Fellow. In 2011, Roderick J. Brodie was made a fellow of EMAC.

Ann Højbjerg Clarke is Associate Professor of Marketing and head of Department of Entrepreneurship & Relationship Management, University of

Southern Denmark. She has published in *European Journal of Marketing*, *European Management Journal*, *Industrial Marketing Management*, and *Journal of Business-to-Business Marketing*. Her research interest is in firms' commercialization competences and management of innovation. This includes market segmentation, commercialization, stakeholder involvement, innovation in networks, and innovation ecosystems. In recent years, Ann Højbjerg Clarke has focused more on public private innovation. She has a strong record in fundraising, societal impact, and management of research projects. She has broad management experience including work on advisory boards, steering committees, and head of boards.

Majbritt Rostgaard Evald is Associate Professor of Intrapreneurship and Organization at the Department of Entrepreneurship & Relationship Management, University of Southern Denmark. She has published in the field of entrepreneurship and innovation in journals including *European Management Journal*, *Industrial Marketing Management*, *International Journal of Entrepreneurship and Innovation Management*, and *Journal of Business Venturing*. Currently, Majbritt Rostgaard Evald is co-editing an English textbook *Entrepreneurship Theory and Practice* (Edward Elgar). Her research mainly focuses on intrapreneurship, specifically on how existing firms, alone or together with their external partners, discover and/or create new opportunities and evaluate and organize these based on various governance modes (corporate venturing, corporate incubators, corporate spin-offs, corporate innovation contests, or various forms of collaborations with external partners such as public private innovation). She has considerable experience with externally funded research projects as principal investigator and has received funds from different sources such as the EU Framework Program for Research and Innovation: Horizon 2020 (e.g., Marie Curie), European Regional Development Fund (supplemented by Regional Business Development Funds from the Southern Region), and SDU Strategic Focus Funds.

Julia A. Fehrer is Senior Lecturer in Digital Marketing at the University of Auckland Business School and Research Fellow in Marketing & Service Management at the University of Bayreuth. Her research has been published in *Industrial Marketing Management*, *Journal of Business Research*, *Journal of Service Management*, and *Journal of Service Research*. She has received several international awards including, most notably, in 2019 the Australian & New Zealand Marketing Academy Emerging Researcher of the Year Award. For her innovative approaches to teaching, she received the University of Auckland Business School 2020 Early Career Excellence in Teaching Award.

Elina Jaakkola is Professor of Marketing at Turku School of Economics, University of Turku. Her research focuses on value creation thorough service, addressing topics such as customer/actor engagement, customer experience, service innovation, and knowledge intensive business services. Her research has been published in a wide range of journals and book chapters, for example *AMS Review, Industrial Marketing Management, Journal of Business Research, Journal of Product Innovation Management, Journal of Service Management, Journal of Service Research*, and *Journal of the Academy of Marketing Science*.

Wesley J. Johnston is CBIM Roundtable Professor of Marketing at J. Mack Robinson College of Business at Georgia State University. Johnston's research has been published in journals such as *Journal of Consumer Research, Decision Science*, and *Journal of Marketing*. He is a member of the American Marketing Association, Association for Consumer Research and the Academy of International Business. He has served on the editorial board of several journals and is currently the Editor of *Journal of Business and Industrial Marketing* and the director of the Center for Business and Industrial Marketing.

Zaheer Khan is Professor of International Business at University of Kent's Business School where he heads of the Department of Strategy and International Business. He received his Ph.D. from the University of Birmingham. Zaheer Khan is a visiting professor of international business at the School of Marketing and Communication, the University of Vaasa. His work has appeared in *Global Strategy Journal, Industrial Marketing Management, International Business Review, Journal of International Business Studies, Journal of World Business*, and *Long Range Planning*, among others.

Florian Kock is an Associate Professor of Marketing and Tourism at the Copenhagen Business School in Denmark. Taking a cross-disciplinary approach of cognitive, social and evolutionary psychology, he researches the evolutionary roots of human behavior, and how they materialize in consumption, tourism and education contexts. He publishes in top tier international journals in tourism, hospitality, and marketing, and serves on the editorial board of *Journal of Travel Research*.

Douglas M. Lambert is the Raymond E. Mason Chaired Professor Emeritus at Fisher College of Business and Academy Professor, The Ohio State University. Professor Doug Lambert's research interests include supply chain management, the role of partnerships in achieving a competitive advantage, and measuring and selling the value of logistics. He is Editor of *Supply Chain Management* and co-author of *Building High-Performance Business Relationships, Fundamentals of Logistics Management, Strategic Logistics Management*, and *Management in Marketing Channels*. Doug Lambert has published in *Harvard Business Review, Journal of Business Logistics, Journal* of *Retailing*, and *Transportation Journal*, and he was the co-founder and co-editor of *International Journal of Logistics Management from 1989 to 2007*.

Peter LaPlaca is Emeritus Professor from the University of Connecticut. He was Editor-in-Chief of *Industrial Marketing Management* from 1994 to 2016. He has published in *Industrial Marketing Management, Journal of Business and Industrial Marketing, Journal of Business Research, Journal of Business-to-Business Marketing, Journal of Marketing, Journal of the Academy of Marketing Science*, and *Psychology & Marketing*, among others. Peter LaPlaca has presented a day-long writing workshop *How to Write a World-Class Paper* at over 100 universities on six continents. He is an avid philatelist and has received gold medals at philatelic expositions. He has co-authored (with Anthony Dewey) *The Connecticut Tercentenary Stamp of 1935*, a book detailing the development and use of the stamp celebrating Connecticut's 300th anniversary of its founding. Peter LaPlaca is also an avid photographer and woodworker.

Peter Naudé graduated in marketing from the University of Cape Town and then in operations research from the University of Sussex. After teaching at the Graduate School of Business in Cape Town, he went to Manchester Business School where, after completing his Ph.D., he joined the staff. Between 1999 and 2005, he was Professor of Marketing at the University of Bath's School of Management before returning to Manchester Business School in 2006. Peter Naudé was Deputy Director of Manchester Business School between 2006 and 2012, and he retired in 2017. He currently holds joint appointments at Manchester Metropolitan University Business School and with the Discipline of Marketing at the University of Sydney.

Steven Pattinson is a Senior University Teacher in Strategy at Sheffield University Management School. He received his Ph.D. from Teesside University. He has published in *Industrial Marketing Management, International Journal of Entrepreneurship and Innovation, International Small Business Journal, Journal of Management Inquiry*, and *Management Learning*, among others. Steven Pattinson's main research interests focus on entrepreneurial and innovation processes in science-based, high technology SMEs. He is also interested in social enterprise and social innovation and sits on the academic panel of the FairShares Institute. He serves on the editorial review board of *Industrial Marketing Management*, and he is the case study editor for *International Journal of Entrepreneurship and Innovation*. Steven Pattinson is a senior fellow of the Higher Education Academy.

Torsten Ringberg completed his Ph.D. in Marketing at Penn State University. He is Professor of Marketing at Copenhagen Business School. His work has been published in *Annals of Tourist Research, Journal of Consumer Psychology, Journal of Consumer Research, Journal of Marketing*, and *Journal of Management Studies*, among others. He has won two Best in Practice Awards from the American Marketing Association/Milwaukee (AMA), based on two strategic consulting projects for large US corporations that uncovered managers' and consumers' subconscious mindsets. He is member of the Danish Competition Council that ensures fair competitive market conditions for both online and physical businesses.

Marianne Storgaard is Associate Professor at University of Southern Denmark. She originally graduated in engineering and later was awarded her Ph.D. in management from Aarhus School of Business. Her work has been published in journals such as *Advances in International Management, Global Strategy Journal, Multinational Business Review*, and *Organization Studies*. Her research and teaching interests include international management, change management, and critical management studies.

Erik van Raaij is Professor of Purchasing & Supply Management in Healthcare at Rotterdam School of Management and at the Erasmus School of Health Policy and Management, Erasmus University (Rotterdam). He holds an Engineering degree in Business and a Ph.D. in marketing from the University of Twente. His work has been published in journals such as *California Management Review, Computers & Education, Health Policy, International Journal of Public Administration Research and Theory, Journal of Business Ethics, Journal of Management Studies, Journal of Purchasing and Supply Management, Journal of Supply Chain Management*, and *Organization Science*. Erik van Raaij is Senior Associate Editor of the *Journal of Purchasing and Supply Management*. He is member of the Erasmus Research Institute of Management, member of the Academy of Management, the International Purchasing and Supply Education and Research Association (IPSERA), and the Dutch Purchasing Association (NEVI). Erik van Raaij has received several awards and commendations for teaching excellence. His current research interests include healthcare procurement, buyer–supplier relationships, and empirical research methods.

Michel van der Borgh is an Associate Professor of Marketing at the Department of Marketing at Copenhagen Business School. He received his Ph.D. from Eindhoven University of Technology. He serves as Associate Editor at the *European Journal of Marketing* and is part of the review board of *Industrial Marketing Management*. His research focuses on the management of front-line employees and covers topics like new product selling, ambidexterity, solution sales, and servitization. He has published in several journals including *British Journal of Management*, *Industrial Marketing Management*, *Journal of Service Research*, *Journal of the Academy of Marketing Science*, and *Journal of Product Innovation Management*.

Vinod Venkatraman is an Associate Professor of Marketing, and director of the Center for Applied Research in Decision Making at the Fox School of Business, Temple University. He also holds a secondary affiliation with the Department of Psychology at Temple University. Vinod Venkatraman joined Temple in July 2011 after completing his Ph.D. in psychology and neuroscience at Duke University. His research involves the use of behavioral, eye tracking, neurophysiological, and neuroimaging methodologies to study the effects of context, state, and individual traits on decision preferences. A core emphasis of his research is in the application of findings from the laboratory to real-world decisions in the areas of consumer financial decision making, public policy, and marketing communications. Vinod Venkatraman received the Early Career Award from the Society of Neuroeconomics in 2016 for his contributions to the area of neuroeconomics and decision neuroscience. His research has been published in journals including *Journal of Consumer Psychology*, *Journal of Marketing Research*, *Journal of Neuroscience*, and *Neuron*, and featured in popular media outlets including BBC, *Forbes*, NPR, *LA Times*, and *Newsweek*. Several of his recent research projects have been funded through grants and collaborations with the industry. He is currently pursuing his sabbatical with the Global Science Organization at IPSOS in an effort to bridge the academia–industry gap and make academic research more accessible for business applications.

Camilla Verdich holds a Master's degree in human biology. She received her Ph.D. from the Royal Veterinary and Agricultural University in Copenhagen in 2001. Since 2001, she has worked as research coordinator in the area of health and medical sciences and in interdisciplinary initiatives in the area of lifestyle, obesity, and metabolic diseases, with an increasing focus on supporting researchers in preparing good grant applications and optimizing the fundraising strategies. Camilla Verdich has published on obesity and metabolic research.

'*How to Fast-Track Your Academic Career* provides invaluable insights to mid-career scholars to successfully navigate through the challenges they face in a career in academia. It also addresses the concerns of these mid-career scholars. The book is a must read, not only for mid-career business-to-business marketing scholars but for any scholar who is pursuing an academic career at a business school.'
Daniel J. Petzer, University of Pretoria, South Africa

'We all have memories about "tips" exchanged with colleagues at every stage of our academic life. First, about how to find a supervisor; later, on how to write good articles or answer reviewers' comments? Still later, on how to supervise PhD students or how to use academic research in our teaching. We had the good luck – or not – of having colleagues distilling those very precious pieces of advice. So what a pleasure to find all this advice and these recommendations, orientations, and indications in a single book. Every aspect of our academic lives are dealt with here! I would have loved to read this book when I was a young scholar registering for my first years in a research master. For me, this book is the definitive guide for accompanying you through your life as an academic scholar. Relevant, friendly, and inspiring.'
Catherine Pardo, EMLYON Business School, France

'*How to Fast-Track Your Academic Career* is a highly recommendable book for any marketing scholar, not just for those in the middle or their careers. Becoming successful is important but staying it is even more so. Reading this book will help reflect on one's activities and career but it also provides a very concrete set of tools, which are directly applicable for any scholar. The authors have all made their mark on the field of Industrial Marketing Management and they should be commended for sharing their "secrets to success" with us.'
Gerrit van Bruggen, Rotterdam School of Management, Erasmus University, the Netherlands

'Plenty of guidance exists for early career business school academics but little for mid-career academics. Lindgreen, Di Benedetto, Vanhamme, and Nicholson remedy this deficit by writing a comprehensive book that covers all aspects of the professional life of a mid-career business-to-business researcher – teaching, research, and student supervision. The authors offer useful suggestions on various topics, such as how to create a research group and how to collaborate with practitioners. They share not only their own thoughts and experiences regarding each topic but also the insights of other experienced academics. Overall, I recommend this book for any mid-career business school academic.'
Gloria Barczak, Northeastern University, USA

'How does one become a successful academician? The need to reconcile research, teaching, impact, and service imperatives is a relentless challenge. Equally, balancing professional development and personal lives and responsibilities is a necessary prerequisite to a long and fruitful career. This book, coauthored by a series of successful and internationally regarded academics, provides a very thoughtful exploration of these fundamental, yet challenging questions. The final chapter on societal value provides a holistic synthesis addressing the question of how one defines, identifies, and measures the value one's research to business and wider society. I recommend this book to the doctoral student, tenure-tracker, and mid-career academician.'
Rob Morgan, Cardiff University, UK

Introduction to *How to Fast-Track Your Academic Career*

Adam Lindgreen, C. Anthony Di Benedetto, Joëlle Vanhamme, and John Nicholson

The idea for this book can be traced back to the editor's desk at *Industrial Marketing Management*. The first two authors are the co-Editors-in-Chief of this journal, and they set out to write a series of short editorials aimed at providing guidance on writing and revising research manuscripts to the early- or mid-career business-to-business marketing academic. Working with Peter LaPlaca (former long-time editor of *Industrial Marketing Management*) and some of the leading authors appearing in that journal, a couple of editorials on successfully writing and revising articles appeared in the pages of *Industrial Marketing Management* in 2018. As the idea grew, it was clear that there were many other academic career challenges to be faced, as well as many opportunities specific to the business-to-business marketing scholar, and very few resources available for specific guidance or insight.

We thought about challenges faced by all of us in academia: successfully applying for grants, doing research with colleagues from other departments, supervising Ph.D. students, and even finding a balance between teaching, research, and service. We also considered how many of these challenges are confronted by those specifically in business-to-business marketing. We tend to do very practical research, on topics of great interest to business managers and decision-makers, and many of the research studies published in *Industrial Marketing Management* and other business-to-business marketing journals have immediate, useful managerial implications. Thus, while all career researchers occasionally face the academic–practitioner divide (the familiar "relevance versus elegance" dichotomy), business-to-business marketing researchers have the advantage of working on problems of inherent importance to managers making decisions related to inventory management, supply chain, innovation investment, and similar concerns.

Further, the business community is a source of ideas for future research projects that can be tapped more efficiently by building greater cooperation between academia and management. In addition, since business-to-business marketing academics are frequently working on research projects that directly address business decision issues, some of our most recent publications can potentially be turned into lectures or teaching cases, increasing our effectiveness when we are facing, say, MBA students demanding relevant and timely course content. We tried to incorporate overall issues, as well as specifics that are of relevance to the business-to-business marketing academic community, throughout the chapters of this book.

Ultimately, we have tried to deliver here a book that addresses the concerns and challenges faced by the early- or mid-career business-to-business marketing academic, but which will also add value for our academic colleagues in business schools across the board.

In summary, and originating from our editorials published in *Industrial Marketing Management*, the 18 chapters and two appendices in this book reflect the following main topic parts:

- Part 1: Getting Started.
- Part 2: Generating Ideas and Setting Up for Success.
- Part 3: Working with Students.
- Part 4: Getting Published.
- Part 5: Being Relevant.
- Part 6: Offering Our Final Thoughts.
- Appendices.

PART 1: GETTING STARTED

The first part of the book consists of two chapters. The first chapter, "Becoming a Business-to-Business Marketing Scholar" by Adam Lindgreen and C. Anthony Di Benedetto, asked leading academics in business-to-business marketing to reflect on their careers and to provide advice for doctoral students and early-career academics. Contributors responded to four broad, open-ended questions on this subject: what worked for them in their careers, what did not work, what were the dilemmas they encountered, and what overall advice they would give to junior researchers starting their academic career. This chapter distills the comments and reflections of the contributors into a collective wisdom, organized around the four interview questions, which combine to form a rich set of guidelines for early-career academics.

In the second chapter by Adam Lindgreen and C. Anthony Di Benedetto, "Balancing Like an Academic," the authors describe the academic's tasks as research, teaching, and service. To be successful in one's career, each of these must be kept in balance, and prioritized correctly. This is challenging, as the tasks usually are running in parallel, all are time demanding, and any one task can become overwhelming as deadlines approach. The chapter first takes a deeper look at the various tasks that must be balanced by the academic.

Following that discussion, the authors provide a series of suggestions for how junior academics can become good at prioritization and other skills that help them achieve the desired balance between the tasks of research, teaching, and service, and between work and personal life.

PART 2: GENERATING IDEAS AND SETTING UP FOR SUCCESS

The second part of the book consists of five chapters. Despite evidence of meticulous business-to-business marketing research efforts, and the pleas of editors for truly original, ground-breaking research, there is still a shortage of original, courageous research ideas. To provide guidance to researchers and address this problem, the first chapter, "Developing Original, Courageous Ideas" written by Adam Lindgreen, C. Anthony Di Benedetto, and Florian Kock, applies the OBC model (observe the world, bridge disciplines, and challenge assumptions and theories). The authors discuss the three main and four blended strategies recommended by this model, and illustrate each of these strategies with examples drawn from the marketing literature. The application of the OBC model offers actionable guidelines for generating original research ideas, as well as theoretical grounding for each element of the model. Given the publication pressure felt by young academic researchers, the hope is that the chapter's discussion provides encouragement and guidance, which will result in original, courageous business-to-business marketing research.

In the second chapter, "Building Research Groups," Adam Lindgreen, C. Anthony Di Benedetto, Roderick J. Brodie, and Peter Naudé consider what leads to superior academic research groups. Business school leaders would like to attract and keep the top research talent in order to stay competitive, attract high-potential students, and recruit the most promising young faculty. To accomplish these objectives, a successful research environment for its business academic researchers needs to be established, so that they can produce a sustainable research stream. The authors examine important antecedents including business school research strategy, leadership, governance, and policy, and from these, they develop a set of conditions that are related to long-term success of research programs in academic business institutions. As detailed illustrations, the authors elaborate the experiences of two active research institutions—the Industrial Marketing and Purchasing (IMP) Group and the Contemporary Marketing Practices (CMP) Group—and discuss how each of these groups has implemented the conditions for success. The authors conclude with general observations on the environmental conditions most conducive to sustainable business school research, and present implications regarding the role of the journal editor as a gatekeeper.

Funding applications is the topic of Adam Lindgreen, C. Anthony Di Benedetto, Camilla Verdich, Joëlle Vanhamme, Vinod Venkatraman, Steven Pattinson, Ann Højbjerg Clarke, and Zaheer Khan's chapter "Writing Research Funding Applications." Academic researchers, including those early in their careers, are under intense pressure to write research funding applications and obtain external research funding. Yet relatively little guidance helps them navigate the funding application process. The authors provide insights into the funding writing process, with a special focus on resources available to business-to-business marketing researchers. The practical advice pertains to developing a funding strategy, navigating the funding review process, and providing information that reviewers seek when evaluating funding applications, among others. The authors also highlight the role of university leaders, who must effectively support and reward their faculty's activity of applying for funding, as well as the benefits of university-based research support offices. To conclude, the authors detail two recent successful examples of business-to-business marketing funding applications.

As an applied social science, business-to-business research is inherently cross-disciplinary. The general theories that provide insight into business relationships, systems, and markets have disciplinary foundations in the economics, psychology, sociology, and management disciplines. When conducting cross-disciplinary research, academic researchers, like their counterparts in industry, must overcome functional silos. Depending on the type of research challenge, a multi-disciplinary approach may be required; however, differences in incentives, culture, terminology and jargon, and so forth all can lead to opportunistic and counterproductive behavior. In the fourth chapter, "Undertaking Cross-Disciplinary Research" written by Adam Lindgreen, C. Anthony Di Benedetto, Roderick J. Brodie, and Michel van der Borgh, the authors explore how to undertake cross-disciplinary research that advances knowledge and understanding in the domain of business-to-business research. To achieve this purpose, the authors elaborate on the theorizing processes; they examine how to break cross-disciplinary boundaries; and they provide practical guidelines for undertaking cross-disciplinary research.

C. Anthony Di Benedetto, Adam Lindgreen, Marianne Storgaard, and Ann Højbjerg Clarke offer a meta-perspective on the collaboration between university academics and business practitioners in the fifth chapter "Collaborating with Practitioners." While academics often intuitively and implicitly take an inside perspective, namely a university perspective, in discussing collaborative research and the why, how, and what in collaborating with practitioners, the authors bring to the fore an outside perspective, namely a business perspective, on the same collaboration, which then typically is termed collaborative innovation. Doing this gives the opportunity to mirror the two perspectives against each other and to discuss the differences, difficulties, and learning opportunities in the relationship between universities and businesses. The chapter offers a discussion of how academics can be inspired to engage better with practitioners.

PART 3: WORKING WITH STUDENTS

The third part of the book consists of two chapters. C. Anthony Di Benedetto, Adam Lindgreen, and Torsten Ringberg, in "Guiding Ph.D. Students," discuss the issues and challenges of Ph.D. student supervision. Several academic colleagues with much experience in Ph.D. supervision were asked to contribute their thoughts on this important task. The authors present the tasks of supervision, including how these may be adapted depending on student characteristics such as extent of managerial experience. Then the authors explore the challenges faced by Ph.D. students, and discuss how these can be addressed. Next, they examine the role of the supervisor in helping build student capabilities in publishing and teaching. Furthermore, they address the benefits of taking on supervisory responsibility. In the conclusion, the authors provide retrospectives on their own experiences as Ph.D. supervisors.

At any leading business school, one of the most important goals is to foster an environment of successful academic research. This is especially true at research-intensive business schools where a core of solid, productive researchers leads to recognition and ranking among the top business schools. The second chapter in this section, "Translating Research into Teaching" by Adam Lindgreen, C. Anthony Di Benedetto, Roderick J. Brodie, and Peter Naudé examines how business schools contribute to education by translating their great research into great teaching for graduate business-to-business marketing classes (including MBA programs with such classes). First, the authors present some of the most recent findings on teaching excellence, which pertains to business instructors, as well as to academics in general. Next, they explore the specific opportunities and responsibilities facing the business-to-business marketing academic. The authors then discuss the process by which business-to-business marketing academics can transform our research in meaningful ways and deliver value to our practitioner audience in the classroom.

PART 4: GETTING PUBLISHED

The fourth part of the book consists of six chapters. Even when the research is completed successfully, the authors' job is not done. They must craft the best possible manuscript for submission to a targeted journal, which will put the research into the best possible light and enhance the likelihood of eventual acceptance. This is the process of framing the manuscript. Accordingly, in the first chapter "Framing a Manuscript," the authors Adam Lindgreen and C. Anthony Di Benedetto sought the thoughts and opinions of experienced academic colleagues on how authors should optimally frame manuscripts for journal submission. Each contributor was asked to provide three to five pieces of advice for young scholars on this topic. The objective was to provide some non-obvious recommendations to young scholars that would substantially improve the manuscript from the reviewers' viewpoint. The contributors present guidance on framing each section of the typical academic manuscript, from introduction to conclusion, as well as some suggestions for overall improvement. The authors conclude with summary remarks on the importance of putting in the time and effort to frame the manuscript effectively.

The second chapter "Developing Conceptual Frameworks for Business-to-Business Marketing," co-authored by Adam Lindgreen, C. Anthony Di Benedetto, Roderick J. Brodie, and Elina Jaakkola, considers the issue of robust conceptual frameworks that are essential to building academic knowledge. Theory development involves high-quality conceptualization that integrates and builds on existing knowledge, possibly using a multi-disciplinary approach. Further, especially in an applied research area such as business-to-business marketing, the emerging theory will have meaningful implications for managerial decision-makers. Insightful conceptual framework development advances theory substantially, not incrementally. Theoretical development can be either purely conceptual or based on empirical data. Nevertheless, there are comparatively few guidelines for the process of conceptual framework development. This chapter discusses pathways to develop conceptual frameworks that support academic research, with emphasis on business-to-business marketing research. As guidelines and conventions are available for data-driven approaches such as grounded theory, the authors focus on theorizing processes in which existing theory plays a pivotal role.

Following that, Adam Lindgreen, C. Anthony Di Benedetto, and Michael B. Beverland consider "Writing a Case-Study Methodology Section" in manuscripts. Business-to-business marketing academics study complex phenomena, aiming to describe these phenomena through theoretical frameworks, explaining the relationships among the framework's constructs, and provide guidance and insight to decision-makers. Not surprisingly, often business-to-business researchers undertake qualitative case studies. In this chapter, the authors discuss what they believe could be reported in the write-up of a case-study methodology section. In particular, they consider the issues of selecting cases, crafting instruments and protocols, entering the field, and analyzing the data. How to assess the validity and reliability of qualitative case studies is also discussed. The authors finish the editorial by examining three exemplar case studies that have been published in *Industrial Marketing Management*.

In the fourth chapter, advice follows on "Writing Articles for Premier Academic Journals" by Peter LaPlaca, Adam Lindgreen, and Joëlle Vanhamme. Most of the leading journals in all fields routinely have rejection rates of 80 percent, 95 percent, or higher. All journals prefer articles that make significant contributions to the field. This chapter discusses how authors can improve their publishing success. The authors discuss the up-front end of an article (title, abstract, keywords). Specifically, three types of abstracts are considered: the indicative (descriptive) abstract, the informative abstract, and the structured abstract. Subsequently, the authors discuss the article's introduction that serves four purposes: to focus the reader on the research question or purpose; to establish the proper frame of reference for the reader; to demonstrate the gap in knowledge that the research will fill; and to convince the reader that there is justification for undertaking the research. Then the authors discuss hypotheses and methodology. Regarding the methodology, the authors consider methodological considerations and analysis considerations. The final part of the chapter considers the research findings section and the discussion of these findings, as well as limitations to the research and opportunities for future research. Specifically, the discussion links back to the article's introduction. Dos and don'ts are offered for each of the article's sections. In sum, the chapter presents numerous considerations on how to improve the manuscript and its probability of acceptance.

Revising a manuscript and responding properly to the comments of reviewers and editors often is challenging. The fifth chapter, "Revising for Premier Academic Journals" by Peter LaPlaca, Adam Lindgreen, Joëlle Vanhamme, and C. Anthony Di Benedetto, discusses how to effectively revise a manuscript according to the (minor or major) comments of reviewers and editors for premier academic journals. The authors provide a series of tips for helping the authors in their endeavor, making the process less arduous and improving the possibility of a positive outcome.

Then follows the sixth and final chapter, "Reviewing Manuscripts." The authors, Adam Lindgreen and C. Anthony Di Benedetto, discuss what reviewers are looking for when they make comments and suggestions on the manuscripts they receive for review. Contributors responded to an open invitation to reflect on the review process: what they look for in each part of a manuscript (from introduction to conclusions), what are the mistakes that authors sometimes make, and what advice they would have for authors preparing their manuscripts for submission. Contributors also provided several overall comments on writing style, on making a good first impression, and on the need to address reviewer comments thoroughly in a revision. Thus, the perspectives of several experienced and respected reviewers are gathered and presented in this chapter, providing specific insights on what satisfies or frustrates them when they are reviewing manuscripts.

PART 5: BEING RELEVANT

The fifth part of the book consists of two chapters. In the first chapter, "Getting Research Cited" by Adam Lindgreen, C. Anthony Di Benedetto, Roderick J. Brodie, Julia A. Fehrer, and Michel van der Borgh, the authors discuss the fact that academic success traditionally has been assessed by publications in highly ranked journals. Other measures of research quality such as citations are now available, and these measures offer a wider perspective of academic contribution beyond simple article counting. Citations now are an important consideration when evaluating research impact and quality. Google Scholar, Scopus, and other programs are readily available to provide citation counts; and other measures such as Hirsch's h-index have also been developed. The authors discuss the issue of research citation, focusing on strategies that can be used to ensure that one's research output is read by the intended academic and practitioner audiences. They first examine why articles get cited including a consideration of types of articles and types of citations. They then outline how to set up and present research. This includes a discussion of the research's strong contributions to the field; conceptual and theoretical development; compelling findings; and clear conclusions and implications. Third, the authors provide guidelines to create visibility and understanding of the article's contribution in the offline research community and beyond. Fourth, they examine the critical role of the online environment in creating visibility for an article. Here, after having given an overview of academic search, the authors discuss keywords; design and structure; graphics; metadata and university research repositories; and interactive social media content. They conclude by cautioning about unethical practices to increase citations.

Then follows "Defining, Identifying, and Measuring Societal Value" by Adam Lindgreen, C. Anthony Di Benedetto, Ann Højbjerg Clarke, Majbritt Rostgaard Evald, Niels Bjørn-Andersen, and Douglas M. Lambert. At the same time as the productivity of academics has become more formalized and institutionalized with increasing emphasis on counting publications in high-ranking journals, citations, h-index, and so on, there is an increased demand on academics to contribute to what is referred to as societal value, societal relevance, public value, societal impact, and/or similar phenomena. This chapter is an attempt to provide an overview and hopefully a clarification. The authors propose to use the concept 'societal value' as the overarching concept. This can be achieved only if the research has 'societal relevance' and if it has 'societal impact'. These two sub-components of societal value measure different qualities, but they are dependent on each other and the total absence of one of them results in no societal value. In fact, we shall argue that societal value is the product of societal relevance and societal impact. After defining societal relevance and societal impact, the authors describe how to identify relevant societal value, as well as how to measure the extent to which an individual or an organization might contribute to societal value. Following that, they suggest a number of ways to increase the societal value of academic research. Finally, the authors reflect on the role of academic journals and their editors in the societal value agenda.

PART 6: OFFERING OUR FINAL THOUGHTS

In closing this book, Adam Lindgreen and C. Anthony Di Benedetto conclude with a few final thoughts on several of the key topics addressed in the book's chapters. More specifically, Adam Lindgreen and C. Anthony Di Benedetto discuss the topics of achieving work–life balance, developing courageous ideas, developing strong research groups, pursuing 'good' research funding, undertaking cross-disciplinary research, collaborating with business and the wider society, translating research into teaching, publishing in highly-ranked journals, and achieving societal relevance.

APPENDICES

There are two appendices. An earlier chapter presented the Industrial Marketing and Purchasing (IMP) Group and the Contemporary Marketing Practices (CMP) Group as examples of research groups whose purpose is to support and stimulate high-impact research that is visible in the research community, provide value to practitioners, and influence society. The first appendix, "Example of Charters for Research Groups: IMP and CMP," by C. Anthony Di Benedetto and Adam Lindgreen, takes a closer look at the governance structure of both groups to identify how these goals can be achieved effectively. A business school can choose a governance structure that supports research and education, which again has implications for recruitment, personal development, and retention of faculty. Similarly, a research group is comprised of like-minded academics with a clear vision and research mission, which will impact choices for individual research topics, as well as teaching objectives. Agreement should be reached on numerous initiatives, including publication strategy, funding strategy, impact on university education (focus on research-based or teaching-based education, for example), services to be provided to the academic community, and interaction with society as a whole in terms of delivery of societal value.

The second appendix, "Revising and Resubmitting: Go Configure: The Mix of Purchasing Practices to Choose for Your Supply Base" by Adam Lindgreen, Joëlle Vanhamme, Erik van Raaij, and Wesley J. Johnston, discusses the four rounds of reviews that their article—published in 2013 in *California Management Review* (Vol. 55, No. 2, pp. 72–96)—went through.

CLOSING REMARKS

We extend a special thanks to Edward Elgar and its staff, who have been most helpful throughout this entire process. Equally, we warmly thank our co-authors and contributors with whom we have worked. They have exhibited the desire to share their knowledge and experience with the book's readers—and a willingness to put forward their views for possible challenge by their peers. We hope that this compendium of chapters and themes stimulates and contributes to colleagues who aspire for an academic career. The chapters in this book can help fill some knowledge gaps on important aspects of planning, undertaking, and publishing academic research, while also stimulating further thought and action pertaining to how to 'crack the code' in making an academic career.

We would like to thank our colleagues with whom we co-authored the chapters: Michael B. Beverland, Niels Bjørn-Andersen, Roderick J. Brodie, Ann Højbjerg Clarke, Majbritt Rostgaard Evald, Wesley J. Johnston, Zaheer Khan, Florian Kock, Doug Lambert, Peter Naudé, Steven Pattinson, Torsten Ringberg, Marianne Storgaard, Michel van der Borgh, Erik van Raaij, Vinod Venkatraman, and Camilla Verdich.

Equally so, we give thanks to Gülen Sarial Abi, Selma Kadic-Maglajlic, and Tobias Schäfers with whom we discussed the contents of this book and from whom we received additional themes we could consider in the book.

REFERENCES

Di Benedetto, C.A., Lindgreen, A., & Ringberg, T. (2021), "Editorial: How to guide your Ph.D. students," *Industrial Marketing Management*, Vol. 93, pp. 1–10, https://doi.org/10.1016/j.indmarman.2020.04.006.

Di Benedetto, C.A., Lindgreen, A., Storgaard, M., & Clarke, A.H. (2019), "Editorial: How to collaborate really well with practitioners," *Industrial Marketing Management*, Vol. 82, pp. 1–8, https://doi.org/10.1016/j.indmarman.2019.08.001.

LaPlaca, P., Lindgreen, A., & Vanhamme, J. (2018), "How to write really good articles for premier academic journals," *Industrial Marketing Management*, Vol. 68, pp. 202–209, https://doi.org/10.1016/j.indmarman.2017.11.014.

LaPlaca, P., Lindgreen, A., Vanhamme, J., & Di Benedetto, C.A. (2018), "How to revise, and revise really well, for premier academic journals," *Industrial Marketing Management*, Vol. 72, pp. 174–180, https://doi.org/10.1016/j.indmarman.2018.01.030.

Lindgreen, A. & Di Benedetto, C.A. (2020), "Editorial: How to become a top business-to-business marketing scholar," *Industrial Marketing Management*, Vol. 86, pp. 1–11, https://doi.org/10.1016/j.indmarman.2020.01.014.

Lindgreen, A. & Di Benedetto, C.A. (2020), "Editorial: How to balance like an academic," *Industrial Marketing Management*, Vol. 88, pp. A1–A5, https://doi.org/10.1016/j.indmarman.2020.03.002.

Lindgreen, A. & Di Benedetto, C.A. (2020), "Editorial: How reviewers really judge manuscripts," *Industrial Marketing Management*, Vol. 91, pp. 1–10, https://doi.org/10.1016/j.indmarman.2020.04.002.

Lindgreen, A. & Di Benedetto, C.A. (2021), "Editorial: How authors really frame a top manuscript," *Industrial Marketing Management*, Vol. 92, pp. 1–7, https://doi.org/10.1016/j.indmarman.2020.04.004.

Lindgreen, A., Di Benedetto, C.A., & Beverland, M.B. (2021), "Editorial: How to write up case-study methodology sections," *Industrial Marketing Management*, Vol. 96, pp. 1–4, https://doi.org/10.1016/j.indmarman.2020.04.012.

Lindgreen, A., Di Benedetto, C.A., Brodie, R.J., & Jaakkola, E. (2021), "Editorial: How to develop great conceptual frameworks for business-to-business marketing," *Industrial Marketing Management*, Vol. 94, pp. 1–9, https://doi.org/10.1016/j.indmarman.2020.04.005.

Lindgreen, A., Di Benedetto, C.A., Brodie, R.J., & Naude, P. (2020), "Editorial: How to build great research groups," *Industrial Marketing Management*, Vol. 81, pp. 1–13, https://doi.org/10.1016/j.indmarman.2019.07.009.

Lindgreen, A., Di Benedetto, C.A., Brodie, R.J., & Naude, P. (2020), "Editorial: How to translate great research into great teaching," *Industrial Marketing Management*, Vol. 85, pp. 1–6, https://doi.org/10.1016/j.indmarman.2019.12.014.

Lindgreen, A., Di Benedetto, C.A., Brodie, R.J., & van der Borgh, M. (2020), "Editorial: How to get great research cited," *Industrial Marketing Management*, Vol. 89, pp. A1–A7, https://doi.org/10.1016/j.indmarman.2020.03.023.

Lindgreen, A., Di Benedetto, C.A., Brodie, R.J., & van der Borgh, M. (2020), "Editorial: How to undertake great cross-disciplinary research," *Industrial Marketing Management*, Vol. 90, pp. 1–5, https://doi.org/10.1016/j.indmarman.2020.03.025.

Lindgreen, A., Di Benedetto, C.A., Evald, M.R., Clarke, A.H., Bjørn-Andersen, N., & Lambert, D. (2021), "Editorial: How to define, identify, and measure societal value," *Industrial Marketing Management*, Vol. 97, pp. 1–12, https://www.sciencedirect.com/science/article/pii/S001985012030523X?via%3Dihub.

Lindgreen, A., Di Benedetto, C.A., & Kock, F. (2021), "Editorial: How to develop original, courageous ideas in business marketing research," *Industrial Marketing Management*, Vol. 95, pp. 1–4, https://doi.org/10.1016/j.indmarman.2020.04.011.

Lindgreen, A., Di Benedetto, C.A., Verdich, C., Vanhamme, J., Venkatraman, V., Pattinson, S., Clarke, A.H., & Khan, Z. (2019), "How to write really good research funding applications," *Industrial Marketing Management*, Vol. 77, pp. 232–239, https://doi.org/10.1016/j.indmarman.2019.02.015.

PART 1

Getting started

1. Becoming a business-to-business marketing scholar

Adam Lindgreen and C. Anthony Di Benedetto

In collaboration with Ko de Ruyter, Lisa Ellram, Christian Grönroos, Michael Hutt, Douglas M. Lambert, Ajay Kohli, Selma Kadić Maglajlić, Matthew Robson, and Michel van der Borgh

1. INTRODUCTION

In our graduate studies, we learn to stand on the shoulders of those who have gone before. We seek to make research contributions that advance our theoretical and conceptual understanding of what we are studying. We may not, however, get a chance to learn from the collective learning of our senior colleagues regarding success in our chosen career. This is a twofold issue. First, an early-stage academic needs guidance on how best to use time and resources to prepare for a successful career: what he or she should do, and what should be avoided. Second, what are the specific challenges faced by business-to-business (B2B) marketing researchers, that is, the readership of *Industrial Marketing Management*? What practical advice would the most successful B2B academics provide so that their younger colleagues can get their careers off to a good start? While all of us benefit from the insights of our dissertation chairperson and committee and other thought leaders we may encounter along the way, what if we brought together top B2B academics into a kind of virtual forum? Our objective here is to gather and assemble thoughtful career advice from some of the most published authors in B2B marketing to gain a sense of "how they did it."

To accomplish this objective, we decided to approach some of the most preeminent academic thought leaders in B2B marketing and ask them to reflect on their careers and to provide advice for doctoral students and early-career academics. Each contributor agreed to submit responses via e-mail to four questions in open-ended fashion: what worked for them in their careers, what did not work, what were the dilemmas they encountered, and what overall advice would they give to junior researchers starting their academic career. In the following sections, we have distilled these reflections down into a collective wisdom, organized around the four interview questions. We conclude with a few observations of our own.

2. WHAT WORKS

Our contributors had much advice for young scholars regarding what to do to advance their careers. We have organized their advice on what works into the following five sub-categories, each of which we discuss next:

- Collaborate with academics.
- Collaborate with practitioners.
- Travel off the beaten path.
- Stay focused.
- Have fun and celebrate successes.

2.1   Collaborate with Great Academics

The old saying is that "no man is an island," and that certainly is true for academics. Throughout one's career, there are many opportunities to work with academics who share research interests or have first-hand knowledge about the academic process. Some of these academics we inevitably meet—thesis supervisors, lecturers, and fellow students—early in our careers; others—peers and our own students—at later stages. Further, if we take the initiative to provide service to our colleges and to professional associations, we can increase our contacts exponentially. Ajay Kohli notes:

> I ... had the opportunity to work with very smart and interesting people in my doctoral program and, following that, in my professorial career. I learned an enormous amount about doing research and effective writing from them. It was a blast to work with them and, unsurprisingly, I did my best work with them ... [In addition,] I was very fortunate to have the opportunity to serve in various service roles such as the Associate Dean responsible for launching a new Ph.D. program at Emory University, Editor-in-Chief of the *Journal of Marketing*, AMA Academic Council member, and EMAC VP of Global Relations. These roles brought me in contact with a large number of junior and established colleagues, broadened my intellectual horizons, and provided opportunities for contributing back to the community. (Kohli)

Importantly, we are part of an academic community. Working with a team of collaborators toward a common goal pushes our research agendas forward, and also helps keep us grounded and focused. Ko de Ruyter writes about the value of a collaborative team that includes practitioners, as well as academics:

> My mantra throughout my career has always been to work with a set of collaborators who like to work hard and play hard. I find it very rewarding to work late in the office with a group of people trying to meet a deadline, order pizza in, watch football, and go out for a drink to celebrate whatever milestone (like making the deadline by one minute). I know that some people keep insisting on solo-authored papers, but where is the fun in that? Beyond this, it seems virtually impossible for one person to possess the very wide range of capabilities needed to publish in academic journals these days. This is especially true for B2B research where relationship management goes hand in hand with the latest analysis skills. Also, it is ultimately about the quality (i.e., rigor and relevance) of the research and the way in which it pushes the boundaries of the knowledge base, rather than the composition of a research team or the vita of an individual researcher. Over the years, I have led research teams that tackle specific issues of a grand B2B theme (e.g., technology in industrial marketing). We run these groups, which consist of all academic ranks, in cooperation with companies, trying to solve real-life challenges. Engaging with businesses over longer periods of time in industrial markets is essential for getting access to and being able to collect data. But most of all, pursuing a successful academic career in marketing is really hard at times. It is essential to build in some fun, and perhaps, not take oneself too seriously. (de Ruyter)

We expand on Ko de Ruyter's comments on interaction with practitioners in the next section.

2.2 Collaborate with Great Practitioners

Many of our participants spoke to the importance of closely working with top marketing decision-makers. Practitioner collaboration is especially important to B2B marketing academics, as expressed by Michel van der Borgh and Selma Kadić Maglajlić:

> Academia is a workplace that, we assume, most scholars are in because they are passionate about doing research and teaching others about their insights; that is, they are intrinsically motivated to improve the status quo, either by having impact in academia or by having impact in practice. Interestingly, we observe that top B2B scholars differentiate themselves by acting ambidextrously, conducting rigorous research that helps make this world a better place. This capability is something that can be learned by immersing oneself in the literature *and* engaging with practitioners. Understanding real-life practitioner problems inspires new research projects, but only with sufficient understanding of the extant body of knowledge it is possible for scholars to adequately frame these practitioner problems and develop new research projects and solutions. As such, B2B marketing scholars are not only passive observers of phenomena but also active designers of desired futures. This

approach goes beyond scanning the "future research" section of published articles because it helps to go beyond the thinking frames of other scholars and lead to novel and relevant insights. This implies that B2B scholars have to build close relationships with practitioners directly or indirectly. Building relationships is based on three components: benefits of exchange, costs of exchange, and trust between partners. Therefore, in our experience, scholars should not narrowly focus only on the goal of obtaining data, but also work hard to deliver to companies, for instance via concrete and valuable methodological skills, good ideas, and state-of-the art academic knowledge. Establishing trust is crucial, for instance, by investing a serious amount of time and effort in understanding the company, becoming part of the team, and acting as a good partner. Without this trust, no sensible practitioner will share unique insights and data. The great Michael Jordan was right in claiming that "talent wins games, but teamwork and intelligence win championships." (van der Borgh and Kadić Maglajlić)

A key aspect of the above comment is ambidexterity, and B2B marketing academics are in a unique position to deliver great value to practitioners if they can truly be ambidextrous, that is, to combine their wide knowledge of the extant literature with a clear understanding of the most pressing problems facing decision-makers. How, then, can the academic strengthen these critical ties with practitioners? We begin with Ajay Kohli's actionable recommendations:

Another thing that helped me greatly was interactions with practitioners in the B2B world. These interactions occurred in various ways: (1) a graduate course team, taught with practitioners and other faculty involving, among other things, living cases of their companies, (2) full-time company 'internships' as a junior faculty member, as well as a chaired professor, (3) MSI conferences, and (4) guest speakers in my classes. Through these practitioner interactions, I learned about issues on practitioners' minds, and the language they used to talk about those issues. I also obtained data for research—both in stand-alone ways (e.g., surveys), as well as in more engaged ways (e.g., interviews, focus groups). (Kohli)

A more formal technique, but with great potential research benefit, is the establishment of a corporate research partnership. Michael Hutt speaks to his personal experiences working within such a partnership:

Since strategy research imposes challenging data gathering requirements, corporate research partnerships have assumed a vital role in facilitating numerous studies. My colleagues and I have pursued a research program that explores the interdependencies that surround the formation of strategy across functions, business units, and alliance partners, as well as the embedded patterns of influence that direct organizational buying systems. More recently, we have examined how the tenets of financial portfolio theory can be applied to enrich a firm's market segmentation and customer portfolio decisions. The success of each of these projects hinged on our ability to secure the support and cooperation of a corporate research partner. Each required access to a large number of organizational participants including senior executives. Likewise, others required performance histories of their sales force, access to their alliance team, or several years of data on their entire customer base. These projects are an outgrowth of a corporate research partnership initiative that the Center for Services Leadership at Arizona State University has been pursuing for over two decades. We discovered early on that corporate executives welcome strategy research proposals that combine rigor and relevance to address fundamental problems. Here are a few key lessons that I have learned across more than a dozen studies that were supported by a corporate partner (Hutt, 2008; Hutt & Walker, 2015). First, business marketing executives are far more open to supporting impactful research studies than most faculty researchers expect. Second, the odds of securing company support dramatically increases if key executives are actively engaged in discussing a research topic or domain *before* the research question is sharpened and finalized. Third, drawing on the strategy dialogue with the firm, a short proposal can be developed that describes the value proposition for the partner, specifying the concrete benefits that the study will provide. (Hutt)

Douglas Lambert initiated the International Center for Competitive Excellence (ICCE) in 1992, whose initiatives included a research roundtable of academics and senior executives dedicated to improving managerial practice in supply chain management. He reports on the importance of garnering support from the senior executive community:

[I started the Research Roundtable of ICCE], a team of academics and executives, which became the Global Supply Chain Forum when I moved to The Ohio State University in 1996. The mission of the Forum is to provide the opportunity for leading practitioners and academics to pursue the critical issues related to achieving excellence in supply chain management. The advantage of the Forum was that there was time to work on well-funded, big-idea projects identified by the executive members [such as supply chain partnership] … Since 1996, 36 publications have resulted from Forum research (Lambert & Enz, 2017) including two books, one in its fourth edition (Lambert, 2014), and three supply chain management articles with a total of more than 12,000 Google Scholar citations, one of which is the most cited article published in *Industrial Marketing Management* (Lambert & Cooper, 2000). Fifteen of my 20 most cited publications are from Forum research. But, more important than the citations, the research has influenced management practice and has been delivered in week-long executive education programs on five continents. The Forum research on partnerships and supply chain management was unlike anything I had done before and would not have happened without the business executives identifying the topics as research priorities … If there was any genius associated with my starting the Forum, it was the idea of surrounding oneself with very smart business people and listening to them. (Lambert)

The key takeaways from Hutt and Lambert's comments are that companies are often very willing to support academic research that provides value, and especially willing if senior management is involved early in the process.

2.3 Travel Off the Beaten Path

Academics may occasionally find themselves in a rut, attacking familiar problems with familiar techniques, and not making any progress. At times like these, academics need to find inspiration to make a breakthrough or even to rethink the question they are investigating. Several of our contributors commented on the need to "travel off the beaten path" and to continuously self-renew by bringing in fresh new perspectives. Incidentally, this need does not diminish, even for senior academics. Here is how they do it, starting with Ajay Kohli:

> I focused a reasonable amount on self-renewal, which was very helpful especially later in my career as a chaired professor. I allocated time and energy to learning about new developments periodically—by regularly sitting in on others' classes at various levels, and through self-study … I was very fortunate to have gone to a doctoral program that encouraged thinking outside of one's comfort zones, venturing into unchartered territories, and taking intellectual risks. (Kohli)

Lisa Ellram reminds us of our responsibility, as academics, to keep learning, and that new insights can be gained by looking outside our research discipline:

> My advice is to always keep learning. Read, attend conferences, and talk to people. Ask people in different disciplines questions, learn about how they do research. In what other job do you have the privilege to be paid to learn, and to learn about what you want to learn? If you do not have a curious mind, this may not be the right career for you. (Ellram)

Christian Grönroos suggests ways by which we can travel outside our comfort zone while interacting with decision-makers:

> Asking the interviewees about marketing issues invariably made them talk about traditional marketing activities, whereas they did not understand the meaning of the unconventional themes in a marketing context. Hence, I had to make yet another change. I decided not to use the marketing term, but to ask the interviewees about their thoughts relating to how to get and keep customers, and what it takes to make them satisfied and willing to return. Interestingly, in these conversations the importance of conventional marketing activities, as well as of other activities, unconventional in traditional marketing models, appeared invariably. Later, in my studies of relationship marketing, another new field, I made the same observations. Thus: do not use existing models and frameworks as a starting point for your research, unless you are convinced that they encapsulate the topic you are about to study in its entirety. If they do not, you will probably generate uninteresting results with low or no relevance. (Grönroos)

Grönroos suggests another approach: trying different methodological approaches or conceptual frameworks:

> I am a conceptual researcher. However, as a teaching assistant before I started on my research for a doctoral thesis, I taught quantitative methods and experiments. My Ph.D. thesis was on the marketing challenges of service firms. This field was new and unexplored. I quickly realized that a conventional methodological approach using surveys lead me nowhere. Already then I was interested in theoretical thinking and conceptual work. Conceptually, mainly based on John Rathmell's (1974) thought that the interactions between buyer and seller seemed to have marketing implications, I had developed a tentative framework including both traditional marketing variables and totally new and unconventional themes. When formulating the elements of this framework in the form a questionnaire, I realized that it would be difficult, if not impossible for marketing practitioners to relate to the questions and turned to a case study approach instead. In Scandinavia, such an approach had already developed some interest among marketing researchers. Thus: do not use normally used, 'scientifically' accepted methods, unless you are convinced that they are appropriate for your research. Such methods will probably generate results with low validity and relevance, and of limited or no interest. (Grönroos)

2.4 Stay Focused

Academics need a healthy internal drive to be productive. Sometimes, the most difficult thing to do is to stay motivated, to keep going, and to maintain that internal drive to succeed at research. Matthew Robson provides his insights on the issue of maintaining focus:

> What works the best of all is having a personal research culture and thus letting research truly get under your skin. That way, there is a constant drive to always get back to your research work. To misappropriate a phrase, the paper you are currently working on needs to be no more than two feet away from you at all times, even if at a particular point in time you are carrying it in your mind. Many years ago, as an early career researcher, I read the biography of the renowned Austrian psychiatrist Victor E. Frankl, a Holocaust survivor. One thing that stayed with me from his harrowing account was that when he was first sent to the concentration camp, he had an academic paper on him that was confiscated by the guards. Not realizing what was coming, he was irked by that. He was so into his research that he was not seeing clearly what was going on around him. Victor's drive to get back to his research was misguided. Yet, it is impressive, too. Irrespective of their circumstances, researchers are loath to let the scent go cold. To keep up my drive, I try to find flow in my research by treating a paper as a game that needs finishing—I am a completion nut; varying the roles I perform on papers in order to keep my skills at a high level across the board—it helps with dealing with reviewers; and varying who I work with, finding enthusiastic co-authors and learning from them as I go. I am motivated by being generous with my scholarly activities, and part of this is forging good working relationships with early career researchers. Of course, such researchers have an infectious drive to research, as well as time on their hands, and their enthusiasm and energy boosts my own. (Robson)

2.5 Have Fun and Celebrate Successes

As a final consideration, remember to enjoy the journey and the destination. An academic career will bring some stress and frustration, but also genuine moments of satisfaction and even excitement. As Lisa Ellram writes, it is important to work on projects we enjoy, maintain perspective, and take the time to celebrate the successes and achievements:

> In terms of focusing my research, what has worked best for me is finding real world problems that I am interested in, and that I believe would benefit from some insight, solution, and explanation ... Because research often does not go how we planned, I think it is important to find topics that I am genuinely interested in—things that excite me, and that I want to understand, not just going after a hot topic or joining a project that does not excite me because I was invited. Learn to say no when a project does not feel right for you ... In addition, I think it is very important to keep your perspective. When things do not go as planned, it is rarely the end of the world. Do not worry about how much money other people make, whether they are hitting 'better' journals than you. Compete with yourself in setting goals and focus on those. There are always going to be people doing better or worse than you are. Make your own luck by being engaged, ethical, and a good colleague to work with ... Have fun with what you are doing. Life is short. If being a professor is drudgery for you, you need to change your attitude, your focus, or your job! You will be happier for it, as will everyone around you. (Ellram)

In sum, our contributors provided much guidance to young scholars, gained through their own experiences and successes. In the next section, we review their thoughts and comments on what an early-career academic should avoid.

3. WHAT DOES NOT WORK

We have distilled our contributors' thoughts on mistakes to avoid into the following five sub categories, each of which we discuss next:

- Working with colleagues who lack enthusiasm and aspiration.
- Working on problems with no practical relevance.
- Mimicking other academics.
- Having too little time.
- Handling reviews the wrong way.

3.1 Working With People Who Lack Enthusiasm and Aspirations

We are fortunate as academics in that we usually have much freedom in choosing colleagues with whom to work. As noted earlier, we have many options by which we can connect with colleagues. It makes sense, then, to choose wisely, to increase the chances of successful research output, and also to enjoy the process more. Ajay Kohli's thoughts follow:

> I have tended to work on a variety of topics, simply because I find them interesting, and with a relatively broad set of authors. My experience has been that projects that were fun to do and resulted in impactful outputs were with co-authors who shared my enthusiasm for a topic, aspiration for the work, and work rhythms. Contrarily, when these qualities were absent, the projects tended to flounder. (Kohli)

3.2 Working on Problems With No Practical Relevance

As mentioned earlier, most of our contributors stressed the importance of working on problems of pressing importance to the practitioner audience. Ko de Ruyter writes eloquently about how one can maintain relevance to the practitioner community, while still achieving a high likelihood of academic success. His argument centers around considering the impacts of new developments on practice, rather than simply reporting familiar results. He explains:

> I have found that in the field of B2B marketing, theoretical and practical contributions are required to be balanced. Too many times I have tried out unnecessarily complicated theories in B2B projects, which often resulted in unreadable papers that did not address real-life problems, let alone come up with actionable solutions. A very helpful criterion that I now use is to try to establish a seamless storyline that departs from a real-life B2B challenge all the way to a relevant theoretical paradigm and back. I have found that if this process is seamless, it increases the chance of success. Also, in an extended cooperation with an industrial marketing company I found myself presenting 'flat-line', same old, same old results to the board year after year. I guess that corroboration of findings across time is an important criterion in academic and applied research. However, it is equally important to spice up long-standing research collaborations with new developments or gauging the impact of new technologies alongside it. I have learned that just reporting the same results across time does not work for engaging the interest of stakeholders and, to be honest, journal editors. (de Ruyter)

Another way to ensure that a problem has practical relevance is to get enthusiastic support from senior management. Michael Hutt notes that poor positioning of a research project when seeking practitioner support will leave the impression that the research will have no practical relevance and will result in no management commitment, even in a case where the results are eminently publishable:

> In seeking corporate cooperation and funding for a project, I have encountered far more difficulty in those situations where a research proposal was submitted in the absence of a thorough discussion with key executives in the firm. For example, our research team was enthusiastic about a project that applies modern portfolio theory (from finance) to the customer relationship management process (Tarasi, Bolton,

Hutt, & Walker, 2011). We presented the proposal to a few potential corporate sponsors who politely passed. We failed to nail down the managerial benefits. Upon reflection, we positioned the study in the area of market segmentation and customer profitability, engaged in a lively discussion with a corporate sponsor, and secured support and a high level of cooperation from a large transportation services company. While representing a long journey, each member of our research team views the customer portfolio project as their career article—a Maynard Award winner at the *Journal of Marketing*. (Hutt)

Ko de Ruyter affirms that many early-stage academics may fail to recognize the importance of establishing ties with the practitioner community. While this may be a career mistake for many business academics, it is especially troublesome for B2B marketing researchers, who almost by definition are working on problems of managerial relevance. He also provides a strategy for how one can jump-start a closer relationship with practitioners:

> At the start of my career, I did not spend time talking with senior business marketing professionals. I soon realized that such conversations would have better informed my teaching and my research. Being in a tenure track, I was too focused on research and publishing in international journals. When I did talk to professionals in companies, I realized this was a shortcoming. So, after the first five years or so, I started to actively pursue giving seminars and talks for practitioner audiences. I also volunteered to take on executive teaching, which was frightening at first and very rewarding later. (de Ruyter)

3.3   Mimicking Other Academics

An early-career researcher may be awestruck by a world-renowned academic, or highly impressed by a doctoral seminar lecturer or senior adviser. It is good to try to learn from the success of those that have gone before. One, however, must not fall into the trap of copying them, right down to their teaching styles. We are our own individuals with our own strengths and characteristics; we should recognize these, and build on these, to develop our own individual styles. In the long run, we want to establish our own identities, rather than being a virtual shadow of someone else. Ajay Kohli explains:

> When I was a junior scholar, I admired many of our accomplished colleagues for the way in which they went about their work. I tried to mimic these established scholars in an effort to perform at higher levels. For example, I tried to mimic the teaching style of a senior professor I admired greatly. However, that did not work, and actually was a frustrating and counterproductive experience. I learned the hard way that you have to develop your own style, and be authentic to who you are at your core. (Kohli)

This idea extends to our research as well. Christian Grönroos relates an anecdote about the hazards of using a methodology, which he found to be impractical and, ultimately, not that interesting to him:

> When doing conceptual research, you may still want to ground it empirically as part of the theory development you are doing. For me, attempting to do quantitative studies when working on a conceptual topic has turned out to lead to meaningless results. I remember when I once was determined to do a quantitative study to support a conceptual piece of research on the marketing of consumer and industrial services. I developed a questionnaire, but when I tested it on a former colleague of mine working in business, his reaction was: "Why do you do it like this? Why do you not discuss the themes with people instead?" I followed his advice, and after that, I have stuck to what interests me most, namely conceptual research and theory development and qualitative research. (Grönroos)

3.4   Having Too Little Time

Academics, like everyone else, need to consider time management, which of course is easier said than done. Ajay Kohli suggests making a plan each evening for the next day, and sticking to it, to avoid being distracted by other things that consume our available time:

> I know of several very accomplished scholars who develop a plan for each day, and follow the plan diligently. However, I could never bring myself to do that. I worked hard on a project either because I was thoroughly engrossed in it or because I needed to meet a deadline imposed by co-authors, journals, or promotion systems. I believe it can be useful to develop a plan each evening for the next day, and stick to it. (Kohli)

Matthew Robson notes that we may have less time available, the further we go into our career, due to the many demands on our time, so it is never too early to develop sound time management skills. In fact, the realities of academic writing may require us to set aside—and vigorously defend—lengthy blocks of time to get things done:

> Time management is a tricky issue, and I have seldom got this right. As an early career researcher, it was easy. I recall spending two leisurely days reviewing a paper for a decent journal. If I did that now, all sorts of plates would be crashing onto the floor. One issue is that classroom and administrative duties have short-term deadlines, while journal papers can take as long as they take. Indeed, stronger papers have longer time-frames of development than weaker ones. So it is always the higher-level research work that gets squeezed. Probably, over the years, I should have come up with defensive ways to prioritize top-level research; but that is not exactly commensurate with academia within UK institutions (e.g., TEF, REF, and accreditations) and the best way to nurture and build the marketing academy. Finding a way to devote long blocks of time to papers is incompatible with modern

expectations of presenteeism, and our always available and responsive e-mail culture. A former colleague of mine works on the basis of two-week time blocks on top papers, and he has a set of offensive and defensive mechanisms geared toward carving out these blocks. (Robson)

We can be our own worst enemies if we are unable to say no to a time-consuming responsibility. Project management skills can be adapted to the academic career in order to avoid bottlenecks, keep focused on projects that are consistent with one's objectives, and get papers submitted to top journals. Michel van der Borgh and Selma Kadić Maglajlić explain:

> One of the most challenging aspects of being a scholar is managing your time. These days, junior faculty are asked to be like 'ten-trick ponies', as they need to excel in a multitude of domains including research, teaching, attracting funding, getting international exposure, and being a good citizen. As a result, some junior faculty tend to freeze or decide to pursue a different kind of career. Reflecting on our personal experiences, it became apparent that one tries to navigate the academic landscape, and that it is crucial to learn to prioritize activities, projects, and opportunities without becoming a jerk. Practically, it implies that you need to focus on projects that are intrinsically motivating, build on your strengths, and help you reach your goals. Not doing so will lead to situations where you spend most of your time on projects that are not gratifying, do not help build your profile, and drain energy. A related aspect is that it is important to keep attentional focus and not be occupied with too many things at the same time. Especially with tough or daunting projects and activities, it is easy to procrastinate and flee into new projects or other activities that do not help you move forward. Therefore, it is important to avoid this situation and to ensure to deliver a project before you start a new one. From personal experience, we know that it can happen that projects—although almost finished—stay on the shelf for a long time before being submitted to a journal. Project management skills and applying tools and heuristics from operations management can be useful to prevent this. One such heuristics is to ensure that projects flow to the pipeline as fast as possible and to prevent bottlenecks. If bottlenecks do occur (e.g., projects are not progressing) you need to take action by either killing the project, asking for other scholars to help out, or by prioritizing it yourself. (van der Borgh and Kadić Maglajlić)

Finally, Douglas Lambert reminds us of the scarcity of time, and hence the need to use it on research with maximum impact. This means going slow and steady, always working on top projects, as this strategy will more likely result in academic acceptance and recognition.

> There is growing awareness that the majority of research produced in business schools lacks relevance and benefits no one but the authors who are given pay increases and are promoted for generating research that "infrequently impacts practice, often falls short of standards for credible research, and fails to create a strong return for the investment" (Glick, Tsui, & Davis, 2018). My advice to younger colleagues is to work on fewer, better projects, or as my mentor once said in a Ph.D.

seminar: It is important to "slow down and get it right." Time is the one thing that we all run out of too soon and it happens far faster than most of us ever expect. Why waste such a precious commodity? Rather than focusing on the number of articles and where they are published, Nobel Laureate Bruce Beutler (2017) offered the following advice: "If you do good solid work, consistently, you will be recognized." His colleague, Nobel Laureate Joseph Goldstein (2017) added that: "Any great paper will be found and read." (Lambert)

3.5 Handling Reviews the Wrong Way

All academic researchers experience rejection from top journals; it is impossible to avoid. As with any other kind of setback, what matters is how you handle it and move on. A specific challenge is when a reviewer appears not to understand the research, or whose opinion might just be totally wrong. Lisa Ellram reminds young academics not to be disappointed, but to determine how best to proceed.

> Sometimes I like a project I am working on better than the reviewers. That is frustrating when you cannot find a good home for your research, and you really do not understand why not. Unfortunately, I do not have any insights there except do not let it discourage you from moving ahead … Another issue I have encountered is having inappropriately assigned reviewers who I think do not understand a topic or a method that I have used, and make suggestions that indicate a lack of understanding. A common problem when dealing with case research is reviewers who do not believe that companies are as dysfunctional as they are described ("Why would anyone do this …"—exactly! That is why this is interesting to study …). I have also had reviewers of case research that indicate that my respondents are lying. Clearly, that person should not be assigned to review case research, but they were. In these cases, I want to reach out to the editor and ask him/her to reconsider the reviewer. I have not done this in the past because I do not want to appear to be asking for favors. But it is something that I think I should do that will help other researchers as well. However, as a reviewer or associate editor, I do specifically comment when I see reviewers who appear to not to understand the research, the method, or maybe who have just not read the paper carefully. I will feel free to disagree with them and comment on why and try to do so in the most constructive way possible. I would like to help develop more constructive and thoughtful reviewers. (Ellram)

4. DILEMMAS—AND WHAT TO DO

Our contributors identified a range of dilemmas—difficult situations without a clear solution—that early-career academics face. We have identified several of these dilemmas, and distilled the advice offered by our contributors, in the following section. Our discussion is organized into these sub-categories:

- Sequence of authorship.
- Stand up for what you do.

- Research that does not 'work'.
- Future pipeline.

4.1 Sequence of Authorship

On a co-authored paper, who should be listed first? It is something to consider, especially if author order could be taken as a signal of relative contribution. One simple convention is to use alphabetical order (and noting this in a footnote), but there is no one-size-fits-all solution. Ajay Kohli provides some perspective and recommendations:

> A dilemma to which I have not found a great answer to this day is the issue of author ordering on a co-authored paper. In a well-functioning team, members exchange ideas freely, and the goal is to produce the best ideas and execute on them. In such teams, members tend not to closely monitor who is making what contributions over the multiple years it takes to develop and publish a research project. Indeed, if co-authors spend time and energy on tracking who is contributing what, it is likely to take away from the fun of collaboration, as well as the substance of research. As such, in many cases it is seldom clear who contributed how much to the final product. A solution I settled on early in my career is to work with co-authors I really liked, and who had comparable competences and aspiration levels. We worked on multiple projects, were fully engaged in developing all projects, but alternated lead authorship concurrent with primary responsibilities for developing first drafts of papers, and post-review revisions. This worked quite well. Another approach I used was simply to toss a coin to determine authorship. In yet other cases, I let my co-authors decide the author ordering. (Kohli)

4.2 Stand Up for What You Do

As marketing academics, we understand the value of positioning our research for the intended audience (editors, reviewers, and academic peers). This usually means a clear statement of research objectives in the introduction, a summary of the theoretical and managerial contributions in the conclusion, and an effective abstract. If one is challenging the norm (for example, proposing a very new conceptual model or methodology, or using a conceptual approach in a journal that usually publishes empirical studies), it is especially important to position well, so the reviewers and editor will see and understand the potential contribution, and in some cases to challenge a negative outcome. Christian Grönroos explains, and provides a solution to this dilemma:

> In the field of marketing, journals sometimes claim that they also welcome conceptual papers. However, marketing journals mostly prefer empirical papers using quantitative methods. When doing research on a new topic or approaching a topic in a new way, and especially if you do it conceptually, which I often have done, it is normally more demanding to convince reviewers and editors about the value and

contribution of a paper. Compared to doing empirical papers you have to be more persuasive. Earlier in my career this was less of a problem. I have a feeling that journals were more open-minded then. Once, I had submitted a paper on relationship marketing, which the reviewers turned down. The paper took a new approach to the field, and I honestly considered it solid and its contribution relevant. I wrote to the editor and said that I thought the reviewers did not really understand relationship marketing. The paper was eventually accepted. I had to do that another time, as well with a paper on marketing communication. However, if doing this, you have to be convinced that you have a good case. ... I have also found that submitting papers to special issues may work well. A special issue is focused on a particular theme or field and, in my experience, both editors and reviewers tend to be more open to unorthodox approaches. (Grönroos)

4.3 Research That Does Not Work

What happens if the many months of research yield few interesting and publishable results? As academics, we naturally focus on article publications, yet we may be able to get much mileage out of unsuccessful or marginally successful research in other ways. Lisa Ellram provides some recommendations:

> One dilemma we all face is when we conduct research that does not get the results we hoped for, and the results were not interesting enough to get published anywhere we want to publish. I do not think that can be prevented. I try to use those experiences as examples when I am teaching and have even created case studies or class scenarios from some. I also use these for examples when I give talks. No learning is wasted. (Ellram)

Those results that were just too narrow or uninteresting for the top academic journal in your area might be a great example to use in MBA classes for many years!

4.4 Future Pipeline

Early career academics know the importance of establishing a pipeline. A clear path to future research is always viewed favorably in promotion and tenure decisions, as is a healthy stream of works in process. But what exactly is a pipeline, and what should a young academic be doing to prepare a pipeline for continued success? Matthew Robson suggests taking a broader view of the meaning of academic pipeline:

> An enduring dilemma for me has been which theories, methods, and fields to work in. Making decisions about your academic skill set and how to evolve this logically is crucial. You need to keep updating, but where do you draw the line. Unfortunately, academics are like a flock of birds—feel free to come up with your own collective noun!—in that they move from one hot topic to the next. Substantively, from channels, to entrepreneurship, to services, to digital, to ... Methodologically, from sampling bias, to common method bias, to selection bias, to omitted variable bias,

to ... For sure, being at the vanguard is the best thing for publishing and citations. However, marketing management considerations kind of get left behind. Managers need channels studies (e.g., look at the effect Brexit is having on supply chains and how quickly their arrangements unravel under conditions of uncertainty). Further, they do not want to be fed a diet of marketing papers with the level of methods precision needed to put a rocket on the moon. Our discipline is marketing, and while rigor is important, it has its place! (Robson)

A related question is whether to continue on an established pipeline, or to explore research possibilities in new and trending topics. There is value in both, so how should a young academic allocate time across research streams? What is the trade-off between opening up new research horizons, and jumping onto the hottest new business topic which turns out to be a short-lived fad? Here is some perspective from Michel van der Borgh and Selma Kadić Maglajlić:

> The central dilemma in journalism is that "you don't know what you don't know." Probably this also can be said about the future of academia and our role within this discipline. Practical questions that arise revolve around "what type data will be preferred (i.e., primary survey data versus company data)?," "what methods and data analysis software will become mainstream?," or "which topics should I focus on?" We always reflect on these questions, and it is a never-ending story of which we only understand the answers in hindsight. Indeed, we reflect on whether we should embrace new trends (e.g., big data or social media) or remain loyal to our current research topics and practices, which perhaps are less trendy (salesperson behavior and customer loyalty). Although we cannot predict the future, it is clear that interesting research ideas will remain top priority for journal editors. The same goes for investing in new projects with new co-authors or building upon existing relationships and projects. Although the latter may be more effective and efficient, the former definitely will open up your horizon and enable you to learn new ways of working, irrespective of the outcome of the individual projects. Again, this relates to ambidextrous challenges or trade-offs, but in practice it probably is needed to navigate between both options. (van der Borgh and Kadić Maglajlić)

5. ADVICE TO EARLY-CAREER RESEARCHERS

In this next section, we identify some themes regarding career advice which emerged in our discussions with our collaborators. We organize these themes into the following sub-categories which we explore next:

- Regularity.
- Literature.
- Passion and uniqueness.
- Collaboration.
- Thoroughness.
- Criticism.

5.1 Regularity

Many contributors stressed the importance of having a work routine, and to invest the time required to accumulate a broad knowledge of the literature, especially early in one's career. Ajay Kohli explains the link between routine and research excellence:

> Perhaps the most important thing I would say is to develop a work routine, and stick with it as a matter of priority. Good research requires creativity, and flashes of brilliant insight do not just happen. They require prior preparation and nurturing, which comes much more easily if one has a set work routine. It may be five days a week from 7:00–5:00, six days a week from 8:00–6:00, or seven days a week from 9:00–5:00, or whatever. The important thing is to focus on the work you are doing day in and day out. Research excellence requires regularity. (Kohli)

Matthew Robson notes that a reading routine yields many dividends, especially later in one's career:

> A former dean of mine would come to lunch, and he would ask us if that morning we had "pushed back the boundaries of knowledge." I would answer obsequiously with: "yes, of course professor." But really I would think to myself, 'not quite', as I had spent that morning reading and only two or three papers at that. Yet, it is because of this legwork that ultimately I became an authority in specific fields. So my advice is: do not be in a hurry. Put in the hard yards, as these can keep paying back, even 20 years later. The more senior you are, the more you are pulled in every direction administratively and the less time you have for pure research activities like reading. I seldom read academic work simply for the sake of reading. A department chair I know, when asked the "how can the school better support you?" question in his annual appraisal paperwork, answered: "give me a time machine." So make sure you invest your time well during your formative phases. This ... is your time machine. (Robson)

Having a routine, however, is not the same as being blind to emerging opportunities. As Ko de Ruyter notes, following one's curiosity might lead to a change in research direction that pays off in terms of published output:

> Most importantly, be aware of the fact that life and career tracks may take unexpected turns, and that it is important to recognize opportunities when they present themselves. Equally, it is important to realize that a career path may change because your own interests may change as you grow professionally and personally. Conducting research should ultimately be intrinsically enjoyable, and while people may keep emphasizing that you need to take an agenda-based approach, keep focused on the pursuit of your own curiosity, even if that means changing direction every now and then. Finally, it is important that you celebrate success with your colleagues and your loved ones, because a research career is not a solo journey. (de Ruyter)

Finally, one must never forget that the process from research idea to published paper is a long one. Michel van der Borgh and Selma Kadić Maglajlić provide advice on how to avoid frustration, by setting shorter-term goals, enjoying non-research related activities, and staying positive:

> All in all, it is important that you are happy when doing your work. Every time it is easy to become too occupied with targets and stressed out about not reaching them. Interestingly, we experienced that the situations where targets become less important—for instance because they look unattainable—are often the situations where everything started going smooth and materialized as initially hoped. Although the effect is partly due to the enormous initial investment, it also indicates the importance of relaxing and cheering up. In addition, being a scholar implies that it needs time before projects will land in journals. So, be sure to engage in activities like teaching or mentoring that are rewarding on the short(er) term. It helps to keep sane. (van der Borgh and Kadić Maglajlić)

5.2 Literature

To be successful at research, and to provide value to the practitioner community, it is imperative to stay current with the literature. The number of new articles each year is staggering, and continues to increase. One needs a strategy in order to avoid being inundated. Michael Hutt provides valuable suggestions on how to stay afloat:

> Across a research career, a strategy scholar can secure an edge by developing a habit of regularly scanning important themes and interesting theoretical perspectives across disciplines from psychology and organizational theory to finance and strategic management. Among my favorites are *Administrative Science Quarterly*, *Organizational Science*, and *Academy of Management Review*. By lending a fresh conceptual focus or a novel methodological twist, I can identify several of my published articles where an *Administrative Science Quarterly* article provided a distinctive springboard and differentiating feature that enhanced the contribution. Rather than a targeted search, the approach here is to review article titles, scan through selected articles, and then explore more deeply the one or two articles that relate to your research program, now or potentially in the future. By investing some idle time, say a few hours a month to this exercise and making it a regular habit, a wealth of unique conceptual and methodological ideas accumulate over time and form a portfolio of tools that can be called upon to advance your research program. (Hutt)

While Hutt is writing specifically about strategy research, his comments can be applied to any discipline, and other top journals may be substituted depending on one's research interests.

5.3 Passion and Uniqueness

Many academics choose this career because they are passionate about studying a particular topic. Ajay Kohli reminds us never to lose this passion for one's work, and to pursue research obsessively, saying no to other projects, which we do not feel passionate about:

> Another suggestion I would offer is to work on topics about which you really care. If you have yet to develop a passion for something, explore things that pique your curiosity to see whether you develop a strong interest in it. You are far more likely to develop useful new (publishable) insights on a topic if you are obsessed with it. Learn to say 'no' to working on topics that you do not think you will really enjoy, or are not as high on your list of priorities. The odds are very high that you will have many more ideas than you will have time to work on. So choose well, and dig deep. (Kohli)

Many companies, including Google, allow their employees to work on their own pet projects on company time and provide support for such activities. This practice encourages employee creativity and may result in discoveries that greatly benefit both employee and company. Michel van der Borgh and Selma Kadić Maglajlić suggest that academics can profitably apply a similar policy to their own research:

> Be selective in projects and try to understand what your unique selling point is. For example, Warren Buffett's 5-Step Process for Prioritizing is one way to do this. This prioritization is a continuous process and one that never ends. Following practitioner heuristics, we think it is important—given the current pace of progress in technological advancements and analytics—to reinvent yourself every three years or so. This also implies that you need to take time (say 20 percent) to make this change. Learn from, for instance Google's 20 percent time policy, to allow yourself to work on 'pet' projects for 20 percent of your time. It also helps to stay motivated. (van der Borgh and Kadić Maglajlić)

Christian Grönroos writes about the importance of passion in one's work, and reminds us of the importance of thinking outside of the mainstream:

> In an anthology consisting of career reflections by service marketing pioneers (Fisk, Grove, & John, 2000), I characterized my research approach quoting Frank Sinatra: "I did it my way." In my view, this is a good piece of advice to any young researcher. Dig where no one else has done it before, and you may make a quantum leap. Break out of the box, and you will find that there was no box, only a random construction by the research community. Following the mainstream may be an easier road forward, but probably it will not generate outcomes that are remembered. … In an autobiographical article (Grönroos, 2017, p. 278), I wrote the following, which I have told generations of researchers: "Only if an extant theory or model can be built on in a meaningful way should it be used as a starting point. Only if what

you are studying is known well enough to respondents such that they consistently understand your questions and scale points, and do this in the same way as you intend them to be understood, can you use conventional data-gathering methods and statistical analyses. ... A researcher has to be strong in his or her faith. I always advise students and post docs to believe in themselves and in what they are doing and to listen to comments, but unless they realise there is a better way to do it, never to let themselves be talked out of what they believe in and out of the methodological approach they consider fit for their study. Sometimes, advice from other persons is appropriate, but not at all always." (Grönroos)

As Grönroos says, we need to be passionate in what we do, and to stick with our research ideas which we believe in. Similarly, we need to be able to communicate this passion to our students as well, and this requires that we think about how we can translate our research so it is meaningful and even inspirational for students. Ko de Ruyter provides his perspective:

Learner expectations across different levels seem to be going up continuously. There is much emphasis on delivery, formats (e.g., check all the boxes when it comes to feedback, feedforward, formative and summative assessments) and seemingly less of an emphasis on expertise. Administrators seem very focused on meeting student preferences, rather than shaping them. One of the dilemmas is that this seems to widen the gap between what we do as researchers and as teachers. I stubbornly try to hold on to meaningful and research-driven content, and one of my standard responses to student feedback ("too much theory") has always been: "it's an academic degree" or "it's your last opportunity to learn about this." I am still experimenting with different ways of making our research accessible to students, and I am happy to see that an increasing number of journals develop material for classroom discussion to support this. (de Ruyter)

5.4 Collaboration

Douglas Lambert reminds us of the importance of choosing the right collaborators, which will allow you to build a high-impact research stream:

Our business is a team sport; pick your co-researchers and co-authors well. Choose colleagues who share your work values, build upon your strengths, and offset your weaknesses. Develop research streams instead of working on opportunistic unrelated papers. A research stream is not a collection of unrelated articles on a particular topic, but research that builds upon your prior work. We all know academics who have written many articles on a wide variety of topics, but if you close your eyes and try to picture the person you cannot do so ... What are they known for professionally beyond the fact that they have written a lot of articles? Publish in a small number of outlets directed towards your selected audience(s) so your name appears often enough that people take notice and associate your name with a research stream. Give up short-term gains for bigger payoffs in the long term. (Lambert)

We can also elaborate on effective ways to broaden our reach to collaborate with an exponentially larger number of colleagues. Ajay Kohli recommends offering to review for journals, which is a good way to build visibility and reputation with editors:

> Get involved in reviewing for journals and conferences early in your career. Reach out to journal editors and conference track chairs with an offer to do reviews for them. You learn a lot from the process, and get to contribute back to the community. (Kohli)

Lisa Ellram suggests other effective strategies (building ties with school colleagues and networking at conferences), and reminds us of some of the benefits of getting to know editors and other senior academics:

> If you do not have people to work with, read the work of people in areas you are interested in, go to conferences and meet them, ask them if they would be willing to collaborate, or suggest others with whom you might collaborate on your topics of interest ... Serving as a reviewer can help you understand and improve your own research and help your visibility. Associate editors and journal editors may be asked to do external reviews of your dossier for promotion and tenure purposes. Providing constructive, timely reviews is helpful to create a favorable impression. If you choose to serve as a reviewer, be a gardener, helping the authors improve their work, even if it is weak. Do not view your role as primarily a gatekeeper and critic, to show the associate editor or editor how smart you are. Be reasonable, and help people improve even if they will never know who you are. There are real people behind every paper you review. Have standards, but be kind ... If you have choices in your job opportunities, find work in a collegial, supportive environment. Your life will be more pleasant, and you will not waste so much time dealing with personalities. Find a workplace that values the type of research that you want to do. Find topics that you love to work on, and people you like to work with that do their fair share of work on a timely basis. (Ellram)

5.5 Thoroughness

It is important to have a good start to a research program: to build a conceptual model that will make a theoretical contribution to our research stream. As Michael Hutt notes, it is critical to be thorough at this early stage. Editors and reviewers are likely to be more accepting of a paper addressing a strong and high-potential problem, and more willing to recommend revise and resubmit. He elaborates:

> The essence of a strategy research program revolves around selecting interesting and important research questions that may reveal valuable and significant insights for theory and practice. Importantly, then, the choice of research questions constitutes one of the most important decisions that a researcher makes. Consider the cycle time that an empirical study follows from the idea stage to final acceptance

of a paper at a premier journal. A minimum of two or three years can easily be consumed in designing and executing the study, analyzing results, crafting the paper, and refining the paper through multiple rounds of the review process. To this end, critical attention should be given to the idea phase of the research process and one should insist on choosing only those research ideas that pass a rigorous test of theoretical and managerial significance. If a timely and important problem frames the paper, I find that reviewers and journal editors are more tolerant of some shortcomings (e.g., sample size) and appear more willing to offer the opportunity to undertake a major revision. In reviewing a potential research question, consideration should be given to identifying core hypotheses, assessing the feasibility of developing a vigorous research method for testing them, and, above all, thoughtfully evaluating the degree to which the proposed project fills a gap in the literature and advances marketing theory and practice. Ultimately, the choice of perhaps a dozen or fewer research questions shapes the identity and promise of a scholar's research program in the discipline. (Hutt)

Hutt also acknowledges the importance of coming 'full-circle' in the manuscript, writing a strong conclusion that shows how the research objective stated in the introduction was achieved. Introduction and conclusion thus become bookends for the manuscript, effectively positioning it and reinforcing its contribution to the literature stream. Here is Hutt's view on the benefits of a thorough introduction and conclusion:

An engaging research question simplifies the task of crafting what I believe to be the two most important sections of a manuscript—the introduction and the conclusions sections. If pressed, reviewers and journal editors alike will confess that high-quality papers with publication appeal provide a strong signal of merit that is evident in the first five to six pages of the introduction to a paper. Here, the author has established the importance of the topic, anchored the study in the literature, defined the purpose of the research, and concisely identified the specific contributions, as well as the gaps in the literature that will be filled. Moreover, high-quality papers deliver on the promise that was foreshadowed in the introduction by clearly communicating the contribution of the study in the conclusions/implications section. I believe that the odds of success for a major proportion of the papers submitted to leading marketing journals could be enhanced by devoting special effort to (1) strengthening the value proposition for the paper with a more compelling case in the introduction and (2) offering a detailed closing argument that illuminates the contributions and their significance to theory and practice. (Hutt)

5.6 Criticism

As academics, we need to get used to criticism. Top journals have very low acceptance rates, and reviews can be discouraging. It can be especially disheartening for an early-career academic to receive harsh reviews of their work, and it is not much consolation to learn that it happens to everyone in academia. One strategy to increase chances of success is to get the research 'out there':

present at departmental brown-bag lunches and local conferences, solicit comments from colleagues, present at a national or international conference, and keep improving until the paper is ready for submission to a top journal. Ko de Ruyter offers his thoughts:

> Getting research published is hard, and surely it is not getting any easier. Even though editors keep writing editorials that encourage reviewers to be constructive, the reviewer default position still seems to be to reject papers. Over the years, collaborators from other disciplines have repeatedly told me that they were baffled by some of the harshness of comments that they encountered in marketing journals. My advice therefore to starting academics would be to brace themselves for this and develop a routine that helps you cope with some of the negativity that seems to be related to the review process. Also, try to become an active part of specialist conferences and research groups. You will learn about the discourse that journals expect you to adopt and get a better feel for those ideas, problems and approaches that are appreciated within a specific sub discipline (such as B2B marketing). This will be picked up by review teams and hence your paper will fit in better. (de Ruyter)

6. CONCLUSIONS

Both authors of this chapter were struck by the sage advice offered by the contributors, and were encouraged to reflect on their own careers. A fitting way to conclude, then, is with a brief statement from each of us.

> The role model for my academic career has always been my dissertation chairperson, Roger Calantone. Many of my colleagues' comments reminded me of what I learned from Roger's example as a junior academic. He had a slogan written on the blackboard in his office: "Do things that lead to the top!" This is invaluable advice, as it has led me to stay focused on projects that have advanced my career and to say no to other opportunities, which did not fit. I also learned from Roger that all papers find a home. A blown research project might indeed be a tremendous case example for use in a graduate class—and the students are impressed with the occasional war story from a top company. He also reminded me to keep a drawer of research ideas for which there may not be time today; that way, when the paper I am currently working on is finally sent off for review, I can get started immediately on something else. Roger was also an expert at handling bad reviews. As a very junior academic, sending my first papers off for review, I would become distraught when I received what I thought were brutal comments from reviewers. Roger had this way of looking at the reviews and putting them into perspective, saying something like "Well, Point 1 is valid and we need to fix this. Points 2, 3, 4, and 5 are easy. On Point 6, the reviewer is wrong. No worries. We will get it done." Just hearing these words from a senior person with a seriously impressive research record provided reassurance and confidence to an early-stage academic. Roger also inspired me to do research that has practical significance. He once said that we, as business academics, should be able to take a research conference presentation, make a few positioning changes, and deliver the same presentation to an audience of senior executives, who would feel they learned something of importance. I never forgot this, and this advice has inspired and focused my research in product innovation and

business-to-business marketing. I also learned the value of doing thorough, critical reviews whenever asked. This caught the attention of Tom Hustad, Editor-in-Chief of *Journal of Product Innovation Management* at the time, whose support helped me immensely in my later career. Finally, the comments about not mimicking other academics rang very true for me. I could never be Roger Calantone in the classroom; we have very different teaching styles. Instead, I strove to find my own style which is true to me and my personality. He once told me about what it takes to be a good classroom teacher, and he stressed that I should "be a character." I took this to mean: be yourself, bring your own personality, don't try to be someone you are not, show your human side, and be memorable. (Anthony Di Benedetto)

The single most important piece of advice I can offer is to collaborate with the right people. The reasons are obvious and numerous. You have different skill sets. You encourage each other. You have the same goal of having that d*** paper accepted for publication. And, because you know each other, you won't let each other down; in contrast, you will work hard, and you will celebrate together. In a similar vein, it is equally important not to work with colleagues where you do not 'click' or at universities where research is undervalued. As head of department, I have invested much time and money in setting up an ecosystem that facilitates and supports collaboration between faculty, an ecosystem consisting of supportive and topically driven research clusters that have their own research budgets; brown-bag sessions; visiting academics presenting their research in department meetings; honorary professorships; individual research budgets (for research purposes) that are topped up when individuals publish in prioritized journals; and a research-funding writing club, among other initiatives. I have also considered the composition of the department's faculty and hired faculty to develop new research fields or further strengthen existing ones. When it comes to specific research projects, as a researcher back at University of Auckland and Eindhoven University of Technology, I learned to focus on fewer, but better papers, and also that without a solid introduction that would discuss why this research was worthwhile to undertake (i.e., what do we know, and what do we not know, and why is it important to know—theoretically, methodologically, and/or managerially—what we currently do not know), the chance of having the paper accepted for publication is not high. Indeed, oftentimes, reviewers and editors will not continue reading beyond the introduction when they do not recognize any value in the research. And speaking of papers, the key step is to be invited for a revision. When that is the case, one has (and especially when one has submitted to a good journal) clear comments, suggestions, and directions from the reviewers and possibly the editor that should guide the revision of the paper. Equally important is to have enough creative space for working on one's research. It is no good if you are inundated with teaching, administration, and meetings. I have also often learned much from looking at other colleagues to see what they have done, and what has worked for them. When you compare yourself with others, you realize what you should continue to do, what you should change or stop doing, and what you should start doing. Finally, some colleagues are afraid of reaching out to top scholars. They should not be; top scholars—for the most part—are friendly and interested in collaborating. Thus, the best thing is to approach colleagues with an interesting project (i.e., why is this project worthwhile), and what is in it for you and me (i.e., how will the collaboration be). (Adam Lindgreen)

REFERENCES

Beutler, B. (2017). Interviewed in "The Research Counts, Not The Journal: Views from Nobel Laureates," at: https://www.youtube.com/watch?v=6MQ8R0OyvyQ.

Fisk, R.P, Grove, S.J., & John, J., eds. (2000). *Service Marketing Self-Portraits: Introspections, Reflections, and Glimpses from the Experts*. Chicago, IL: American Marketing Association.

Glick, W.H., Tsui, A., & Davis, G.F. (2018). The moral dilemma of business research. *BizEd*, May/June, pp. 32–37.

Goldstein, J. (2017). Interviewed in "The Research Counts, Not The Journal: Views from Nobel Laureates," at: https://www.youtube.com/watch?v=6MQ8R0OyvyQ.

Grönroos, C. (2017). I did it my way. *Journal of Historical Research in Marketing*, 9(3), pp. 277–301.

Hutt, M.D. (2008). Engaging corporate partners to bridge the theory-practice gap. *Journal of Supply Chain Management*, 44(2), pp. 68–71.

Hutt, M.D. & Walker, B.A. (2015). Bridging the theory-practice gap in business marketing: Lessons from the field—the *JBBM* at 21. *Journal of Business-to-Business Marketing*, 25(1–2), pp. 67–72.

Lambert, D.M. (2014). *Supply Chain Management: Processes, Partnerships, Performance* (4th ed.). Ponte Vedra Beach, FL: Supply Chain Management Institute.

Lambert, D.M. & Cooper, M.C. (2000). Issues in supply chain management. *Industrial Marketing Management*, 29(1), pp. 65–83.

Lambert, D.M. & Enz, M.G. (2017). Issues in supply chain management: Progress and potential. *Industrial Marketing Management*, 62(1), pp. 1–16.

Rathmell, J.M. (1974). *Marketing in the Service Sector*. Cambridge, MA: Winthrop Publishers.

Tarasi, C.O., Bolton, R.N., Hutt, M.D., & Walker, B.A. (2011). Balancing risk and return in a customer portfolio. *Journal of Marketing*, 75(3), pp. 1–17.

2. Balancing like an academic

Adam Lindgreen and C. Anthony Di Benedetto

1. INTRODUCTION

Being an academic requires that the academic performs at an international level in research, delivers excellent education, engages in research dissemination to a variety of stakeholders, and contributes to the department's and wider business school's activities. It also requires that the academic is involved in engagement and internationalization activities, participates proactively in the department's life, undertakes large(r) administrative roles, and is held in esteem in the international research community. At the same time, we have personal lives and responsibilities which cannot be ignored. It is a lot to ask! In this chapter, we explore the realities of this imposing balancing act, and provide some thoughts and guidance to help achieve this balance.

2. THE TASKS OF AN ACADEMIC

The academic's tasks are usually listed in short form as research, teaching, and service. To be successful in one's career, each of these must be kept in balance, and prioritized correctly. This is challenging, as the tasks are usually running in parallel, all are time demanding, and any one task can become overwhelming as deadlines approach. Further, the tasks can all be divided into sub-components: collecting research data and disseminating research results; service to the college and to the professional community; and the varying tasks involved in course delivery. At times, the academic feels like the circus performer balancing several spinning plates on poles, where the challenge is to keep everything spinning at once. This section takes a deeper look at the various tasks that must be balanced by the academic.

2.1 Research

For most academics, research is seen as the "coin of the realm." This is definitely the case at research-intensive business schools. Research is what builds one's reputation, and research is necessary for meeting requirements for tenure and promotion. Probably more than any other task, research is transportable: a strong research record can be attractive to other schools and provide opportunities for career advancement through relocation. Research brings visibility and opportunity: to edit prestigious journals, or run academic institutes. Most career-thinking academics will free up as much time as possible to do research; and the need is never more pronounced than when there is an upcoming tenure or promotion decision. Thus, academics regularly need to publish in highly ranked journals. Some business schools follow the Academic Journal Guide (published by the Chartered Association of Business Schools) or the FT 50 journals (published by *Financial Times*). Other business schools have drawn up their own journal-ranking lists. Depending on the business school, research monographs, edited anthologies, textbooks, and book chapters can be helpful in supplementing high-quality journal articles. Usually, business schools appreciate when academics present their research at one or more of the leading marketing conferences. Research also brings opportunity to work with top Ph.D. students and serve as first supervisor/senior adviser, develop and administer Ph.D. courses, and serve on Ph.D. committees within and sometimes outside the business school.

2.2 Education

Research is what drives research-intensive business schools' other activities, most notably education. Academics must therefore participate in course and program development. For research, academics must publish in high-ranking journals; for education, academics should receive excellent teaching evaluations. In contrast to the somewhat general agreement we see across business schools on the so-called best journals, most business schools have developed their own ways of measuring the quality of education delivery. Often, excellence in education is judged only by how students answer one single question: "this academic was overall a good teacher," or, "I learned a lot in this course." Academics should participate in teaching at all levels (B.Sc., M.Sc., Ph.D., and Executive). Business schools also require that academics demonstrate seriousness in their teaching, and that they adhere to academic integrity and engage in pedagogical initiatives that ensure the students' mastering of the subject taught. Also in education, academics must be willing to participate in department and business school-wide education activities such as study boards. To some extent, academics can combine their activities in research and education. For example, academics could author textbook(s) and case studies for the international market; such textbooks could be general, but they could also be much more aligned with the academics' own research area and perhaps even based more or less on their own published research. Academics could appear regularly as guest speakers outside the academic world on the basis of their educational expertise. For example, they could be involved in relevant professional field(s) in education. They could also be members of book publishers' inspection committees. Academics also often are involved in international accreditation procedures, occasionally as external examiners of study results and theses (M.Sc. and Ph.D.). These last few examples highlight the important gatekeeping responsibility of the academic.

2.3 Funding

Today, most business schools depend (to at least some extent) on external funding. Thus, academics are expected to participate in (large-scale) external funding efforts, sometimes as principal investigator. External funding provides the resources needed to conduct meaningful and relevant research, which can bolster one's academic career in the long run. Many academics are under greater pressure to increase their grant funding, at the same time as state or national funding appropriations are shrinking. Given this fiscal reality, external funding will continue to be a requirement and, increasingly, an expectation for career academics. Business school leaders can create a culture in which significant grant writing success is rewarded, and can provide research support offices and/or local funding committees to assist in increasing the quality of grant applications and the probability of grant success. With a sufficient level of support, academics reasonably could be expected to participate and to benefit. For example, academics can develop and leverage their department's industry contacts, or they can help train junior researchers on how to write successful grants or identify research foundations. By volunteering as the funding committee chairperson of the department, an academic can assist the department head in developing research funding strategy, setting research funding goals, serving as the departmental point person for grant-related issues, forming liaisons with other research institutions, or organizing seminars to assist other faculty in grant writing and fundraising activities.

2.4 Dissemination

Historically, business schools have focused on academic relevance and impact, which has influenced the problems we investigate in academic research. We conduct research into pressing topics affecting decision-makers and society, and our results are potentially meaningful to these audiences. Accordingly, many, if not most, of our leading academic journals insist on a discussion of managerial implications alongside contributions to theory. Today, business schools face growing pressure to produce public value in addition to academic relevance and impact. As a consequence, Cardiff Business School, for example, became the world's first public value business school (Lindgreen et al., 2019). The public value agenda is increasingly important, as society turns to business schools for solutions to global issues, and national governments have begun to use public value as a criterion when they allocate funding (e.g., in the UK REF, which takes place about every six years). Academics should therefore demonstrate how their research brings public value to the wider society. For example, academics could engage in collaborations with business. They could also inform and engage broader audiences through media interviews or workshops with practitioners, or they could sit on research funding bodies.

2.5 Citizenship

A business school should not be a hotel where academics only come in when they teach. Rather, a business school is a community where academics also engage in collaborative research, education, and funding activities and participate in intellectual exchanges related to such activities. Thus, academics should participate actively in research seminars, brown-bag sessions, and the like. They should be active in the promotion of an open and inspiring research debate culture. Academics must also be willing to undertake large administrative roles within the department, as well as represent the department within and occasionally outside the wider business school. They should be willing to serve as a member of their business school's board, research platforms, academic council, and study boards, among others. From time to time, academics must be willing to take on tasks that benefit the department if so required, for example being mentor to more inexperienced colleagues.

2.6 Engagement and Internationalization

A final area in which academics are expected to contribute to is the promotion of the department and the wider business school to external stakeholders (e.g., industry sectors, businesses, government and non-government bodies), the establishment of strategic alliances between the department and the wider business school and other schools and universities, the recruitment of (international) students, and research platforms, among other things. Academics could also work at maintaining relations with alumni. Finally, academics should participate in scouting for and recruitment of academic faculty.

3. THE BALANCING ACT

As academics, we have all been assessed by metrics. We hear from our earliest days in Ph.D. programs that we need to balance among the aforementioned responsibilities, sometimes shortlisted as the 'big three' of research, teaching, and service (i.e., citizenship). For most of us, and particularly early in our careers, we often are told that we are most rewarded for research. Tenure and promotion to associate professor may officially be based on the 'big three,' but, in reality, one needs to be rated as outstanding in research and teaching; satisfactory service is often good enough. It is especially true for junior academics to become good at prioritization and other skills that help them achieve the desired balance. In this section, we review some of these skills and how they can be best implemented.

3.1 To Prioritize Between Importance of Tasks

To be able to prioritize between important and less important tasks is an imperative, and for most career academics, many of the most important tasks often are believed to be related with research. We are constantly performing a balancing act, however, with education responsibilities (including course preparation, delivery, and grading, not to mention the need to consistently upgrade and renew education material), as well as department and school committee tasks, and other services to the community (journal reviewing and editing, participation in business associations, organization of national and international conferences, and so on). If an academic is prioritizing top-level research, for promotion or tenure, career visibility, or whatever reason, then that is the most important task. Especially for tenure-track academics, it is critical not to get sidetracked, and many department chairpersons will be sensitive to this need. The new hire will be given a limited number of course preparations, may be kept away from MBA teaching (or assigned MBA versions of courses which they have already mastered at the undergraduate level), and will try to assign a minimum amount of departmental service. This will vary from school to school, but in a school where research and teaching need to be 'outstanding' and service needs to be 'satisfactory,' the chairperson will ensure that a 'satisfactory' level of service is attained.

We can also address here the issue of balancing research task efforts. With the omnipresent discussion of citations, 'rookies' in the academic world sometimes believe that the more publications they have, the better their chance for a job or a promotion. This, however, is not the case, as most schools will look at the total number of publications in high-rated journals, as well as the number of citations, as evidence of research impact. It is better to have a big article in a top journal than two or three smaller articles in less-known journals. Furthermore, when one starts to 'learn the game,' one should substitute lower-level activities with (fewer) higher-level activities.

3.2 To Prioritize Between Urgency of Tasks

In the preceding section, we noted that academics are responsible for a wide variety of tasks, any of which can climb to the top of the list of priorities at any time, much like the performer with the spinning plates. The dean imposes a real deadline for the development of a new masters' program, or the chairperson needs the merit reviews done in two weeks. At the same time, the departmental secretary requests next semester's syllabi, which will take up more time than usual since one of your courses is a new assignment. Inevitably, teaching and service requirements will inundate academics some weeks, and academics therefore have little choice but to put the research on the back burner. Good performance on these tasks is rewarded in terms of visibility and merit, and may play a role in a tenure or promotion decision. And urgency is a real thing—many of these tasks have real deadlines, while finishing up a research paper could be pushed back a week or two due to circumstances. It is important to always have the research priorities in mind, so that one can return to these priorities quickly when time becomes available. One idea, if possible, is to block a time period of weeks or months, which will be devoted to non-stop (or almost non-stop) research. As editors, we notice an uptick in submissions at the end of the summer and at the end of holiday seasons, since researchers finally found a few weeks of 'me time' to finish up and finally submit the research project that had been pushed aside for too long!

3.3 To Look for Synergies Between the Tasks

As business-to-business marketing academics, our research interests are never too far from managerial practice. We inherently work on projects whose results provide value to middle- and senior-level marketing managers. Thus, there sometimes will be synergy between research and education for us, and it is misleading to think of these as separate silos competing for our time. It may not happen in every case. However, sometimes that case study or those managerial interviews undertaken for an academic research project can turn out to be a great illustrative example that can be pulled out and used in an MBA class. Students like the occasional war story. A career academic may not be able to talk about "those 20 years I spent working at Ford," but certainly many good research studies with meaningful managerial implications can make for just as compelling a classroom story. Incidentally, sometimes a similar interaction can occur between service and teaching. A consulting project may turn out to be a good classroom illustration (with client name and details disguised); an on-site corporate lecture might lead to an insightful discussion that could be used when back on campus.

It might also be possible for academics to set up a research project with their M.Sc. students. Together, the academic and the students identify a relevant research problem and review the literature in order to design the survey questionnaire. After data collection (perhaps undertaken by the students), both parties analyze the data, discuss the findings, and draw up theoretical and managerial conclusions, the result of which could be a journal publication. Obviously, when academics supervise their M.Sc. thesis students, the chances of co-publishing a journal publication is even greater. Sometimes, M.Sc. students have only three months for their thesis, and/or the academic has to supervise a high number of students. In such cases, academics must plan their supervision especially diligently, and there probably will be fewer opportunities for the students to stray off course. Finally, a part of any academic's job is the development of courses and programs. Academics can ponder whether this task presents an opportunity for a research activity that could result in a publication of some sort, too.

3.4 To Manage Time Efficiently

As we have noted, it is important to devote as much time as possible to academic research. However, the allocated time must be used wisely; some projects may not come to fruition, but the goal is a consistent hit rate over several years, and this is where time management comes into play. There are, of course, plenty of time management guidebooks available and rules of thumb to live by, but the reality is that one has to stay focused, and do whatever works to improve time management. Focus is difficult when trying to maintain a balance. Final exams and term projects may take days to grade. Precious hours are diverted away from research during these periods; unlike most research projects, there are real deadlines to submit grades, and inevitably research gets off track. A major business school or department committee assignment can similarly eat away at research time. Additionally, different research projects may be in different stages of completion, so while one is just getting written up for journal submission, another requires questionnaire pretesting, and a third needs more development on the conceptual model. It is important to mobilize every one of the limited hours available per week. One suggestion that has worked well is that when the grading gets tedious, or a standstill is reached in a research project, it is human nature to put it away for a while ... but there should always be something productive to turn to. Academics should always have a 'bottom drawer' of ideas that they can start on, or share with their Ph.D. student. Use that time to get the last cleanup done on a manuscript you are preparing to submit to a journal. Prime-time work hours are not wasted, and the sense of accomplishment, even for a modest achievement, is satisfying. It is better to get back to the heavier lifting after such a break.

3.5   To Manage E-Mails Efficiently

Some academics keep the number of e-mails in their inbox to a minimum. They use the Create Rule feature in Windows Outlook to route non-important e-mails to their junk e-mail inbox. In the same vein, one should only subscribe to important newsletters. When e-mails continue to be received from a particular source, this should be reported as spam. Do not cc in everyone when you answer an e-mail, and ask that your colleagues do not cc you when they answer an e-mail sent to numerous people (unless necessary, of course). If you read an e-mail, you should act upon it immediately (if, of course, you are not required to do some work first), as otherwise you will have to open this e-mail again at a later stage and once again think about what you will have to do. Thus, answer the e-mail and then archive it (if necessary) or delete it. On archiving, one should set up in a logical manner one's e-mail folders that are needed. One could perhaps use a system built around one's tasks (e.g., research, education, funding, dissemination, citizenship, and engagement and internationalization). If one is head of a department, for example, there will be other important folders such as those for individual faculty in the department. Another good rule is to check one's e-mails regularly, at least several times a day and expect the same behavior from the colleagues with whom one works. This is only professional courtesy. The checking of e-mails could be on the way to work, or when one has a natural break from bigger activities during the day. Following this advice, it is possible to have an e-mail inbox that actually becomes one's to-do list.

Now, the reality is that not everyone is so good at managing their e-mails in this way. An old-fashioned to-do list might do just as well. Some academics are veteran list-makers. Everything goes on the list, whether it is research, education, or service related, or even not related to work. It is very useful to have all tasks written down, so there is no need to keep it all in memory. Once the list is written, it is much easier to determine the easy tasks that can be knocked off in an hour, versus those tasks that will be days or weeks. Then, upon completion, scratch it off the list! There is nothing more satisfying than watching the remaining items on the list dwindle down to the last few.

3.6   To Build a Network for Collaboration and Support

It goes without saying that complementarity in research skills will pay off, as in any other line of work. This might mean complementarity in terms of research specialty (a logistics person working with a marketing person on a supply-chain paper, for example), but it might be in other ways as well. Your research collaborator may be able to work on path models until 3:00 am night after night, but may turn to you to write a coherent discussion and conclusions section since he/she knows you are a really good writer. If that works for both of you, great! Another way a colleague can help is in pushing for timely results. As noted above, we often get sidetracked by reality. Having a co-author who actually works faster than you can keep you from getting diverted. A colleague who runs several path models, e-mails them, then checks the next day to see what you thought and whether you had started writing the discussion section yet, can be a not-so-subtle reminder to keep on track!

Being embedded in a network of colleagues, in fact, probably is one of the most important factors to academics' success. When academics collaborate with colleagues from other universities (in other countries), they can tap into these colleagues' ecosystem that could provide additional sources for research funding. It might also suddenly be easier to conduct cross-country data collections. But, networks do not only consist of academics. One should also consider including businesses in one's research and teaching activities. For example, such businesses could offer opportunities for student internships, or they could sit on your program's study board providing input to one's research and teaching agendas.

3.7 To Drop Collaborations That Do Not Work

All through one's research career, but especially when the tenure clock is ticking, one must maintain a focus on the best possible research opportunities. As mentioned before, sometimes one hits a dead-end. (But, a project that may not give rise to a strong research paper might turn out to be an excellent lecture or case study for a graduate class, so indeed all is not lost.) Nevertheless, one wants to minimize the number of true dead-ends. It may turn out that a promising joint project is not going to take off ... or a one-shot research paper together with a new colleague does not have any promise for a later string of papers. If this is the case, it is the time to move on, and to devote research time on projects that have a higher and/or a longer-term payoff!

3.8 To be Sure About an Idea Before Embarking on It

One does not want to spend valuable research time on a topic that ultimately is unpublishable: the topic is too incremental or already over studied; the topic is something that was maybe a hot research topic years ago or uses an outdated analytical technique; the research design is insufficient or fatally flawed. While it is not possible to ensure ultimate acceptance of a research paper at a top journal, there are several things that can be done to screen ideas and to ensure their value. Present the ideas at an informal brown-bag session in front of colleagues; present early versions of the research at local or regional conferences; work with your senior adviser or senior colleagues in your department; read the "directions for future research" in the most recent publications; check the Marketing Science Institute's list of current research priorities or other similar lists, and so on.

3.9 To be Inspired by the Best

You got to know the senior adviser on your dissertation and your committee members. What was their work ethic? How did they come up with good research ideas? What did you learn about the research process from them that potentially can increase your chances of publishing success? They want to see you succeed, and can provide direction for your research career. You can also look at the top names in your field. Who are the people who keep popping up in your literature search? Visit their homepages, and analyze how they have built up their CV. Are they still research active? They might like receiving an e-mail from you or meeting you at a conference. Do not feel intimidated by academics having a big name; most academics still remember how they started in academia and are only happy to meet with more inexperienced staff. They often have research projects that they are too busy to embark on, and they would therefore like to team up with capable and willing colleagues. As Yogi Berra once said, "You can observe a lot by watching." So watch what they do, and observe the kinds of questions they ask that may lead to the next breakthrough research project. They may seem to be miles ahead. They just have more experience and are good at asking the most pertinent research questions! You will be there too at some time, and you will be able to pass on this wisdom to the next generation.

3.10 Find Your Wow Factor

Finding one's wow factor might be a tough call for the new Ph.D. just starting on a tenure track in a new business school. After all, such colleagues think mostly about their recently completed dissertation, how to turn it into an article or two, and how to start up the next big research project. These are all-consuming thoughts! But, in a moment of reflection, it makes sense to think of what it is that you add as a research colleague. Marketing strategists speak of the customer value proposition: what is it that makes this product different, in some important way to customers, from other products offered by competitors? In the same way, it is never too early for a junior academic to brainstorm about what is his/her value proposition. You are one of thousands of marketing academics in the area of business-to-business. What is special about you, and what value do you bring to a research collaboration? What are you really good at? What work or life experiences can you bring to the table that make you stand out? If you want to be a top-10 or top-100 academic in your area in 15 years' time, what should you be doing now?

3.11 How to Achieve an Acceptable Work–Life Balance

Achieving an acceptable work–life balance is a topic that increasingly is discussed in academia and elsewhere. Many academics report that they have a poor work–life balance, leaving them with little time to be with their family and friends or to engage in non-academic activities. As previously discussed, it is true that there is no end to what an academic could do. Academics are evaluated and measured constantly (e.g., student evaluations, paper and funding reviews, citations and h-index measures, and so on). Furthermore, academics often move between universities and indeed countries, and although this may land that coveted job, it creates sources of stress (e.g., selling and buying a house, contracting a moving company, paperwork for immigration and insurances, getting accustomed to the new university and possibly country, and many others). By nature, many academics are ambitious and want to go up through the ranks, which obviously results in pressure, and quite possibly, increased stress. And, when you first have achieved that coveted position, you might realize that the requirements are just too many. Thus, the first thing one should do is to have realistic expectations: do I want to undertake all that it takes to go into academia and, possibly, to get promoted? Going through the Ph.D. process should give an academic a first good idea of what academia is like ... but one should not forget that many Ph.D. students have much more research time than at any other stage later in life! We will suggest some ways of take away the pressure or, at least, to alleviate it from time to time. One could celebrate successes. This could be weekly smaller celebrations after a hard week, or it could be a bigger celebration after the acceptance of a paper or funding or a good student evaluation. However, one should also remember to 'celebrate' during the day: if one works 10 hours a day, one works hard, but not necessarily efficiently. The brain needs to relax, and so you should consider going for a walk or jog during the day. Inspiration can strike at those times! Think of combining research interests with your other interests.

4. CONCLUSIONS

The academic lifestyle is hard to explain to non-academics. While most have heard of the phrase "publish or perish," it is perhaps surprising to some that we are under such time pressure, not just to write, but also to manage our other academic responsibilities, keep up with the developments in our fields, and provide service to the university, our professional associations, and the community. One should not forget to put one's own personal life and responsibilities into the mix. In this chapter, we have detailed some thoughts and personal insights on how to "balance like an academic" and to succeed in spite of these forces tugging us all in many directions. It is manageable, though at times difficult, and we are up to the challenge—after all, if it was easy, anyone could do it!

As a final, final observation, we should not forget that although sometimes we are under stress (addressing seemingly hostile reviewer comments, facing piles of grading, attending boring meetings, writing up reports, or adhering to perplexing administrative rules and regulations), we have the world's best job. When we leave that meeting or send off that report, we are free to pursue the research that gives us the wow factor and that we will want to pass on to our students. A senior colleague once said: "in what other line of work can you change career direction at the start of a new semester?" We are blessed with the opportunity to work with students and help them achieve their personal goals. We were inspired by our own senior advisers, impressed by their contributions to the research community, as well as by our many students, and we strive to make a similar contribution ourselves. As a wise person (probably an academic?) once said, "if you like your job, every weekend is seven days long."

REFERENCES

Lindgreen, A., Koenig-Lewis, N., Kitchener, M., Brewer, J., Moore, M., & Meynhardt, T. (eds.) (2019). *Public Value: Deepening, Enriching, and Broadening the Theory and Practice*. London: Routledge.

PART 2

Generating ideas and setting up for success

3. Developing original, courageous ideas
Adam Lindgreen, C. Anthony Di Benedetto, and Florian Kock

1. INTRODUCTION

Since the inaugural issue of *Industrial Marketing Management* in September 1971, research devoted to business marketing has expanded tremendously. Prior to its introduction, no journal had focused specifically on this academic domain, which clearly represented a gap; by addressing this need, the journal has enjoyed substantial growth on every relevant quantitative measure, including objective submission, page, and citation counts, as well as more subjective indicators such as professional respect. The very number of downloaded articles from *Industrial Marketing Management* suggests that a broad and growing academic community finds its content useful. Furthermore, the research published is impactful, according to the Thomson ISI Impact Factor of citations.

In 2018, *Industrial Marketing Management*'s Two-Year Impact Factor reached 4.779 (its Five-Year Impact Factor was 5.088). Three contributing features have enabled and ensured continued improvements in both quality and influence (Touzani & Moussa, 2010):

1. *Industrial Marketing Management* is read by academics interested in related fields such as strategy, management, innovation, and product development, expanding its influence beyond the narrower field of marketing.
2. The quality of articles published in *Industrial Marketing Management* has increased, leading to more citations in recent years.
3. Research topics covered by the journal have grown in importance.

Such academic prosperity should generate original, courageous research efforts. Instead, we observe the contrary: *Industrial Marketing Management* publishes more articles, but the number of truly original contributions has not increased, which means more relevant knowledge is not necessarily being created. The problem is not limited to this journal. Virtually every publication calls for original manuscripts, and virtually every journal editor worries about the lack of original research being submitted. This gap might reflect the ongoing, extreme pressure on researchers to publish in top-tier journals, yet this explanation actually is paradoxical, because originality and courageousness are essential criteria demanded by the best journals. That is, if researchers encounter both pressures to publish and calls from journals to submit original, courageous research, why do we not see more original, courageous research being published?

The answer may be both obvious and difficult to address. Devising original ideas is difficult in any setting (Smith, 2003), including research, but the underlying, intuitive argument—that originality is the biggest challenge facing researchers—has been ignored in studies that analyze the dearth of original research. Instead, a prevalent assumption seems to predict that if the contextual factors inhibiting originality were removed, original research would naturally follow, like a *deus ex machina*. However, great ideas are the scarcest resource.

Such a situation means that business marketing research and its contributors need help and guidelines for generating original, courageous research ideas. Especially for early- and mid-career researchers, generic advice such as "be more critical," "make sure your topic is relevant," or "think outside the box" simply is not helpful. Furthermore, among the many things that young researchers can learn from reading contributions to top-tier journals, they are unlikely to find detailed discussions of how these authors arrived at their research idea.

In response, we leverage a tripartite model to guide researchers: observe the world, bridge disciplines, and challenge assumptions and theories (OBC) by Kock, Assaf, and Tsionas (2020). Our application of the model includes concrete guidelines for generating original, courageous research ideas, as well as theoretical grounding for each strategic element of the model and a methodology for making them actionable.

2. THE OBC MODEL

The OBC model encompasses three fundamental, strategic elements, reflecting three actions: observe, bridge, and challenge. Each of them can be executed independently or in combination. Our presentation of the application of the OBC model includes a theoretical discussion of the strategies, a methodology for executing it (such that, strictly speaking, the OBC model is a meta-methodology), illustrations with marketing (both business-to-business and business-to-consumer) research examples, and caveats to bear in mind. Adopted from Kock et al. (2020), Figure 3.1 provides an overview of the three strategies (I, II, and III) and their fusions, which also constitute strategies (IV, V, VI, and VII).

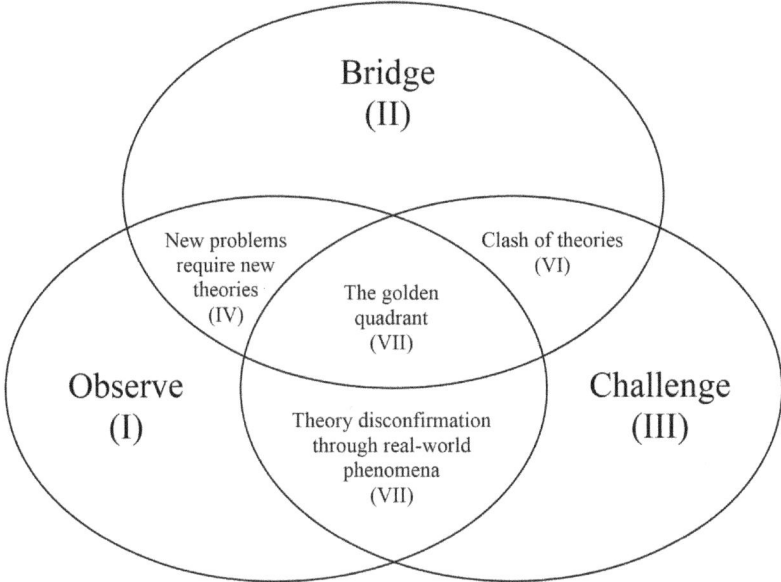

Figure 3.1   The OBC model as a Venn diagram

2.1   Strategy I: Observe the World

To be relevant, concepts and theories must be grounded in compelling, interesting, real-world observations. The importance of a notion is proportional to the vividness and relevance of the phenomena it can explain. Accordingly, original, courageous research ideas might best be gathered from real life rather than inspired by previous publications—yet this source of ideas appears rarely exploited by existing business marketing research. Motivating research from vivid phenomena, instead of doing "research on research," also reflects our goal with this chapter. With this view, we also caution that identifying phenomena can lead to original, courageous research only if the researcher can provide evidence that they are real and pertinent and that studying them is critical to business marketing. Having done so though, researchers will have a clear and obvious foundation for arguing for the motivation, purpose, and contribution of their research, for both peers and non-scientific audiences. This foundation also enables them to establish, elegantly, who will be affected by and benefit from the research findings.

To derive research ideas from observing the world, we emphasize several concrete suggestions made by Kock et al. (2020). First, phenomena generally evident in the world potentially have relevance for business marketing efforts. An example of this 'outside-in' approach is the study by Maon, Lindgreen, and Vanhamme (2009) that examined how disaster relief operations (i.e., a real-world phenomenon of broad significance) affect the design and implementation of commercial supply chain and logistics management operations. Second, some observed phenomena may be more immanent to business marketing, but also extend beyond it, which would evoke an 'inside-out' approach. An example of this is the study that identifies how brands 'dupe' consumers by positioning brands' authenticity through ambiguity in the advertisements of these brands (Beverland, Lindgreen, & Vink, 2008; Dickinson-Delaporte, Beverland, & Lindgreen, 2010). This original idea is inherent and originates from the marketing world. Third, novel phenomena could be internal to conventional business marketing, and studying them could offer insights that are relevant mostly for the discipline, which constitutes an 'inside-in' approach. Thus, although Walley and colleagues' study (Walley, Custance, Taylor, Lindgreen, & Hingley, 2007) offers relevant insights into the role of branding in industrial purchasing of agricultural tractors in the UK, these insights are likely to be of limited interest to other than marketers.

After identifying significant phenomena through one of these approaches, researchers also need a suitable theoretical lens for examining the original ideas. Ideally, the process of identifying important phenomena also reveals which theory is most appropriate. In this process, researchers must consider analysis strategies outside of the business marketing domain, in line with Strategy IV (discussed subsequently), which recognizes that "new problems require new theories." An example is Beverland and Lindgreen (2004) who draw on punctuated equilibrium (a theory that was developed in evolutionary biology by Niles Eldredge and Stephen Jay Gould) when they develop a model of relationship development that explains how firms decide not to invest in relationships or to form and intensify in relationships.

Finally, while observing the world, researchers must keep some caveats in mind. In particular, this strategy can seduce researchers into dedicating themselves to topics and efforts beyond their current capabilities. Particularly for young researchers, diving into a completely new literature stream is risky and difficult; they may not be able to predict the depth accurately. Therefore, in addition to identifying a range of ideas, they should scrutinize the potential of each identified phenomenon, then pursue the one that emerges as most promising or with the highest priority. Furthermore, researchers who observe the world need to avoid getting caught in a phenomenological singularity, focused exclusively on a phenomenon that only appears in a narrow context and is rather exotic, because the resulting research findings will likely have only limited implications for a restricted audience. An example is Hingley, Leek, and Lindgreen (2008) that utilized Morrissey's song lyrics (that concern interpersonal relationships) to analyze interpersonal business-to-business relationships. Although the research was nominated for the Sage Publications-sponsored *The Times Higher Education Research Project of the Year*, this research is exotic and has limited implications. Not surprisingly, according to Harzing's Publish or Perish, the research has attracted but three citations.

2.2 Strategy II: Bridging Disciplines

Academic bridging joins two or more disciplines, through an "intentional effort to draw on the human, theoretical, methodological, and/or empirical resources of a related discipline to shed new light on one's own discipline" (Joireman & Van Lange, 2015, p. 82). Bridging disciplines can reveal original and courageous ideas, as well as produce new theory construction if theories get redesigned to fit the new, combined discipline. However, we tend to immerse ourselves in our own discipline, without looking beyond its boundaries, which can hinder the identification of original ideas. Instead, each domain reproduces its own commonsense theories, mindsets, and assumptions. There are several examples of such discipline-bridging studies in business-to-business marketing: Nicholson and colleagues' application of theory from economic geography to business-to-business competition (Nicholson, Tsagdis, & Brennan, 2013); Wilkinson's (2006) use of an evolutionary approach to building business-to-business marketing theory; and the application of Darwinian theory to understand business-to-business marketing relationships (Johansson & Kask, 2013).

To avoid such insularity, all researchers need to read beyond their own disciplines and pursue greater exposure to other research domains. A challenge for time-pressured researchers is identifying which theoretical or methodological concepts in other disciplines might be relevant to business marketing (Strategy IV: New problems require new theories), enhance or challenge existing business marketing theory (Strategy VI: Clash of theories), or set a foundation for a new business marketing research agenda. The process of recontextualization is relevant here, because it implies redefining or redesigning an original theory to apply to issues in a different discipline.

To illustrate this process, we consider an example that uses theory from neurosciences research. Originating in medical research, neuroscience has been applied successfully in consumer marketing, where researchers understand target customer motivations and behavior by applying neuroscientific tools rather than interviews and focus groups (see, for example, Lee, Broderick, & Chamberlain, 2007). The application of so-called neuromarketing techniques in business-to-business settings, as well as limitations of these techniques, has been discussed recently (Lim, 2018).

Again, a few caveats arise though. The key hurdle to bridging—and a reason for its rare use—is the requirement that researchers become conversant in multiple disciplines. Our advice is to avoid jumping constantly or frivolously across disciplines. Instead, original work demands deep understanding of and extensive training in key domains, so researchers should expand their reading but do so in an intentional and targeted way (Ladik & Stewart, 2008). Nor should they borrow theories carelessly, which actually would constrain theory building for business marketing. The theories must be redesigned or developed particularly for the discipline. Such efforts to derive original business marketing theories in turn can enhance and benefit the originating disciplines from which the theories were derived.

2.3 Strategies III–VII: Challenge Assumptions and Theories

A third path toward courageous research involves pushing the boundaries by challenging the assumptions and theories on which prior studies rely. We find little business marketing research that does so; instead, many studies simply build uncritically on consolidated beliefs and thereby reinforce them. Established, widely accepted methods for arriving at research ideas involve identifying gaps in existing literature (i.e., incremental gap spotting, Alvesson & Sandberg, 2011) rather than challenging existing assumptions. However, hypotheses that are consistent with existing research tend to appear intuitive, prompting the dreaded reviewer question, "so what?" Original, courageous ideas demand that researchers step back from the obvious theoretical layer and identify questionable core assumptions.

Doing so is not, of course, easy. Constant questioning of the assumptions and theories that underlie decades of research requires the ability to think differently and critically, supported by a problematization methodology (Alvesson & Sandberg, 2013). Problematization includes five steps: (1) select a domain, (2) identify its underlying assumptions, (3) evaluate the assumptions critically, (4) develop an alternative grounding, and (5) evaluate and test the alternative. An example of an alternative grounding in networking theory is presented by Peters and colleagues (Peters, Gassenheimer, & Johnson, 2009), who advocate the use of structuration theory to explain the relationship between firm-level and individual learning, and how this learning increases the firm's ability to create value for customers. This perspective differs from a more traditional, reductionist view of the business network, which portrays the network as simply the sum of its member parts (see discussion in Hadjikhani & LaPlaca, 2013).

Following Kock et al. (2020), we believe the most difficult step is the second one because identifying questionable assumptions requires counterfactual reasoning, defined as an ability to conceive of alternatives to existing theoretical assumptions through contrastive questioning (Tsang & Elsaesser, 2011). Two concrete approaches can help in this effort, through links with Strategies I and II. With the clash of theories strategy (Strategy VI in Figure 3.1), researchers pit two (or more) theories with contrasting predictions against one another to highlight a challenge to at least one of them. This approach is consistent with a bridging disciplines strategy, in that contrasting theories often represent or emerge from distinct disciplines. Peters and colleagues (Peters, Pressey, Vanharanta, & Johnston, 2013) take such an approach when discussing the application of two different research traditions (critical realism and constructivism) to the study of business networks. In their empirical study of a specific issue within business networks (novation, or replacement of an obligation between network members), they find managerial value in both theoretical approaches, despite differences in ontological position. Alternatively, theory disconfirmation through real-world phenomena (Strategy VII in Figure 3.1) combines Strategies I and III. Researchers might witness a phenomenon that conflicts with the assumptions and conclusions provided by their research tradition, thereby inspiring an effort to contrast the phenomenon with these existing concepts. Such phenomena are excellent starting points; they offer initial, anecdotal evidence that a particular theory might not hold in all contexts, which should inspire both challenges to existing literature and insightful moderation analyses. For example, examining two empirical datasets in business-to-business networks with multiple buyers and sellers, McCabe, Stern, and Dacko (2013) demonstrate that stochastic modeling based on the Dirichlet stochastic model can be used to predict purchase patterns and loyalty. The authors suggest that their methodology provides a useful tool for decision-makers, but also can be used as a basis for development of integrated theory of network relationship evolution.

2.4 Strategy VII: The Golden Quadrant

As these seemingly separated discussions of the previous strategies reveal, efforts to observe the world, bridge disciplines, and challenge assumptions can be practiced independently, but they also produce synergy effects through combinations. Thus, combining all three strategies might produce a golden quadrant (Strategy VII)—arguably the most difficult approach. It results when a researcher is able to identify and articulate a relevant real-world phenomenon (Strategy I), then examine it across disciplines (Strategy II), and thereby pose pertinent questions to existing ideas and advance the research domain (Strategy III).

An example that fits the golden quadrant is research that has examined managers' assumptions about ecological sustainability and developed an appreciation of strategies that firms may follow (Borland, Ambrosini, Lindgreen, &

Vanhamme, 2016; Borland & Lindgreen, 2013). To achieve this, the authors concentrated on ecological sustainability as discussed in different scientific disciplines (e.g., anthropocentric epistemology and ecocentric epistemology), meaning that the identified ecocentric transformational marketing strategies include not only the business environment, but also the natural environment (e.g., ecological science and, in turn, natural sciences). In doing so, this research questions the premises for marketing strategy. Thus, in addition to achieving a sustained competitive advantage and influencing consumers' preferences, a marketing strategy also must "incorporate the physical environment as the source of physical well-being for all species, as well as the source of all products and services," the authors argue (Borland & Lindgreen, 2013, p. 183). Finally, by proposing universal premises and key principles that ecocentric transformational marketing strategies must adhere to, the research advances knowledge on what constitutes a strategy for sustainability.

3. CONCLUSIONS

Despite evidence of rigorous, meticulous, business marketing research efforts, we find a troubling dearth of original, courageous ideas. In an attempt to provide meaningful, practical advice to help researchers find original ideas and write courageous manuscripts, we apply the OBC model developed by Kock et al. (2020), along with the three main and four blended strategies it recommends. In light of the continuous and growing publication pressures on (especially young) academic researchers, together with desperate pleas from journal editors for original, courageous manuscript submissions, we hope this chapter provides pertinent guidelines and encourages researchers to continue to perform original and courageous research in business marketing.

REFERENCES

Alvesson, M. & Sandberg, J. (2011). Generating research questions through problematization. *Academy of Management Review*, 36(2), 247–271.

Alvesson, M. & Sandberg, J. (2013). *Constructing Research Questions: Doing Interesting Research*. London: Sage.

Beverland, M.B. & Lindgreen, A. (2004). Relationship use and market dynamism: A model of relationship evolution. *Journal of Marketing Management*, 20(7/8), 825–858.

Beverland, M.B., Lindgreen, A., & Vink, M.W. (2008). Projecting authenticity through advertising: Consumer judgment of advertisers' claims. *Journal of Advertising*, 37(1), 5–15.

Borland, H., Ambrosini, V., Lindgreen, A., & Vanhamme, J. (2016). Building theory at the intersection of ecological sustainability and strategic management. *Journal of Business Ethics*, 135(2), 293–307.

Borland, H. & Lindgreen, A. (2013). Sustainability, epistemology, ecocentric business and marketing strategy: Ideology, reality, and vision. *Journal of Business Ethics*, 117(1), 173–187.

Dickinson-Delaporte, S., Beverland, M.B., & Lindgreen, A. (2010). Building corporate reputation with stakeholders: Exploring the role of message ambiguity for social marketers. *European Journal of Marketing*, 44(11/12), 1856–1874.

Hadjikhani, A. & LaPlaca, P. (2013). Development of B2B marketing theory. *Industrial Marketing Management*, 42(3), 294–305.

Hingley, M.K., Leek, S., & Lindgreen, A. (2008). Business relationships the Morrissey way. *British Food Journal*, 110(1), 128–143.

Johansson, T. & Kask, J. (2013). On the promise and premises of a Darwinian theory in research on business relationships. *Industrial Marketing Management*, 42(3), 306–315.

Joireman, J. & Van Lange, P.A. (2015). *How to Publish High-Quality Research*. Washington, DC: American Psychological Association.

Kock, F., Assaf, A.G., & Tsionas, M.E. (2020). Developing courageous research ideas. *Journal of Travel Research*, 59(6), 1140–1146.

Ladik, D.M. & Stewart, D.W. (2008). The contribution continuum. *Journal of the Academy of Marketing Science*, 36(2), 157–165.

Lee, N., Broderick, A.J., & Chamberlain, L. (2007). What is 'neuromarketing'? A discussion and agenda for future research. *International Journal of Psychophysiology*, 63(2), 199–204.

Lim, W.M. (2018). What will business-to-business marketers learn from neuro-marketing? Insights for business marketing practice. *Journal of Business-to-Business Marketing*, 25(3), 251–259.

Maon, F., Lindgreen, A., & Vanhamme, J. (2009). Developing supply chains in disaster relief operations through cross-sector socially oriented collaborations: A theoretical model. *Supply Chain Management: An International Journal*, 14(2), 149–164.

McCabe, J., Stern, P., & Dacko, S.G. (2013). Purposeful empiricism: How stochastic modeling informs industrial marketing research. *Industrial Marketing Management*, 42(3), 421–432.

Nicholson, J., Tsagdis, D., & Brennan, R. (2013). The structuration of relational space: Implications for firm and regional competitiveness. *Industrial Marketing Management*, 42(3), 372–381.

Peters, L.D., Gassenheimer, J.B., & Johnson, W.J. (2009). Marketing and the structuration of organizational learning. *Marketing Theory*, 9(3), 341–368.

Peters, L.D., Pressey, A.D., Vanharanta, M., & Johnston, W.J. (2013). Constructivism and critical realism as alternative approaches to the study of business networks: Convergences and divergences in theory and in research practice. *Industrial Marketing Management*, 42(3), 336–346.

Smith, D.C. (2003). The importance and challenges of being interesting. *Journal of the Academy of Marketing Science*, 31(3), 319–322.

Touzani, M. & Moussa, S. (2010). Ranking marketing journals using the search engine Google Scholar. *Marketing Education Review*, 20(3), 229–247.

Tsang, E.W.K. & Elsaesser, F. (2011). How contrastive explanation facilitates theory building. *Academy of Management Review*, 36(2), 404–419.

Walley, K., Custance, P., Taylor, S., Lindgreen, A., & Hingley, M.K. (2007). The importance of brand in the industrial purchase decision: A case study of the UK tractor market. *Journal of Business and Industrial Marketing*, 22(6), 383–393.

Wilkinson, I.F. (2006). The evolution of an evolutionary perspective on B2B business. *Journal of Business and Industrial Marketing*, 21(7), 458–465.

4. Building research groups
Adam Lindgreen, C. Anthony Di Benedetto, Roderick J. Brodie, and Peter Naudé

1. INTRODUCTION

For business researchers, establishing a solid research track record is a prerequisite to success. Business schools often have lofty publication expectations of their newly hired assistant professors before considering promotion and tenure. It is often in the best interest of the junior researcher to play it safe and pursue research in well-established research streams, at least until achieving tenure, when it may be possible to take more chances on more groundbreaking (and riskier) research. In fact, a promotion and tenure committee may be interested in seeing not just a number of publications in top journals, but two or three established research streams where the researcher has made contributions to the literature. Business schools also benefit greatly from the success of their top academics. More big research grants, and more A-level journal publications, lead to a solid research reputation, which in turn makes it easier to hire junior professors from top research institutions, attract top graduate and doctoral students to their programs, and offer chairs to big-name senior academics looking for a career change. It is in the interest of business school managers to know how to build an environment conducive to academic research at the highest level.

We examine the factors that have led to the establishment of a successful environment for business academic researchers. More particularly, we examine issues including business school research strategy, leadership, governance, and policy, and from this framework, we develop a set of conditions that are closely related to long-term success of academic research programs in business schools. We then present a brief history of two active research institutions, the Industrial Marketing and Purchasing (IMP) Group and the Contemporary Marketing Practices (CMP) Group, and discuss how each of these has implemented the conditions for success in their own particular settings. We conclude with general observations and implications for the environmental conditions most conducive to sustainable business school research, and briefly discuss the role of the journal editor as a gatekeeper in the process of supporting radically new research streams.

Throughout our discussion, we focus on the creation of the research stream as the desired outcome. Business school managers would like to invest efficiently, in terms of both their financial outlay and human resources. If a large investment is made, say, to funding a research center or institute, hiring faculty from top schools and recruiting the best junior researchers, the expectation would be to have a stream of research as an output from this investment. That is, the researchers would be able to conduct high-level research that results in sustainable research output in terms of published articles, additional outcomes that further the research stream in the pipeline, as well as other research planned and/or seeking funding approval.

Before continuing, we would like to make a distinction between a research stream and a school of thought. Consider, for example, the innovation literature (Di Benedetto, 2013) that shows the emergence from the first few articles through growth and now maturity. In the early years, there was a narrow range of research streams: new product process, R&D–marketing interface, organizational issues, accelerated time to market, and a few other research streams. Twenty years later, as the innovation discipline matured, more academics had decided to be 'innovation scholars,' the research field became more multidisciplinary and multinational, construct measures were more fully developed, and a wider range of methodologies were used. By this time, new research streams had emerged that were not even on the radar screen 20 years earlier: organizational learning, product architecture, mass customization, open innovation, entrepreneurial innovation, transformational leadership, information technology in innovation, and many other research streams. We define each of these as 'research streams' within the innovation 'school of thought.' Although scholars in a group are all innovation scholars, they have narrower and deeper research expertise. That is, research streams emerge through time, as scholars raise new questions for academic research. One could even subdivide this further if one considers that a research stream, which was originally, say, case-based or qualitative research, then attracts survey or experimental research, or vice versa.

The importance is that the scholars taking the chances and doing research, which is not business-as-usual, need to be supported and recognized, and encouraged to take changes, and this can come from their own institution, as well as their chosen research organization. As an example, years ago, we saw the first few Ph.D. graduates in innovation; earlier, a typical concentration would be a mainstream choice such as marketing or management. By the early 2000s, the first few assistant professors had been promoted and tenured based on an innovation publication record (many articles in *Industrial Marketing Management, Journal of Product Innovation Management*, and so on) rather than mainstream marketing or management. This was a significant turning point because it meant that one could pursue a career in innovation management per se. As such, it is probably a significant milestone in the recognition of innovation as a school of thought.

2. STRATEGIES FOR RESEARCH SUCCESS

A goal of business school administration is to foster an environment of successful academic research. Especially in the case of the most research-intensive business schools, having a core of solid, productive researchers leads to recognition and ranking among the top business schools. This scholarly recognition attracts new Ph.D. graduates eager to establish careers in a strong research environment, as well as mid-career academics looking for a chaired position. It also ensures the school is on the shortlist for the best students applying for Ph.D. programs in business. But this is more easily said than done. What, indeed, is successful academic research? Those of us who do business research know that we intend to make contributions that will resonate with the practitioner community and aid their decision-making skills. Yet, we must also please the editors and reviewers in the academic community, and preferably place our research in the highest-rated journals in our field. It is easy for business school managers to establish quantitative goals for hiring, promotion, and tenure such as number of articles published in A-level journals. However, what can managers do to facilitate their faculty's achievement of their publication goals? In this section, we review issues such as business school research strategy and policy, leadership and governance issues, as well as choice of assessment metrics, which will aid in identifying the conditions most conducive to long-term research program success.

2.1 Strategy, Leadership, and Policy

At research-intensive business schools, the aim of the research strategy should most probably be to conduct demonstrably impactful research that influences society; can be deployed usefully in developing education; and can be communicated to and used by practitioners. Fulfilling this aim starts with publishing research with a high impact on the research community, which generally means publishing in influential journals.

This ambitious goal demands great performance expectations of faculty members, in the form of high-quality world-class research. Faculty members must be committed to rigorous, theory-driven, empirical research and theory development—outcomes that are central goals for any reputable business school.

A business school's leadership can seek a governance structure that reflects and supports key areas including research and education. The governance structure also should support the recruitment, retention, and expansion of faculty members, in line with support for personal development. Equally important is to set up research groups. Faculty members choose that (those) research group(s) that is (are) organized around themes they want to research and teach. Less important to a research group is the range of methodological approaches that researchers employ.

When developing its policies, a research group could be considering a range of initiatives including the following:

- Which publication strategy should the research group follow? When the group wants to be proactive in both academia and society, the group will need to contribute to the ongoing debate about present and future societal challenges to which its research and education are relevant. Such dissemination often results in dialogue, interaction, and reflection that can fertilize further research and identify new challenges. It also provides awareness, which can strengthen the position of the group in competition for research funding. We will discuss the issue of publications in more details in section 2.2, "Assessing for success."
- What will be the research group's funding strategy that will allow the group to undertake its research projects? To increase the number and quality of funding applications, the group could set up a funding committee to develop and leverage industry contacts. Colleagues who have been involved with research funding bodies could give feedback on outgoing funding applications. Another possibility is to form a writing club; this could involve peer reviews of funding applications, and it could, in the longer term, result in further collaboration between faculty members. This institution of brown-bag seminars and seminars with world-class researchers constitutes another avenue for discussing research ideas, detailing the funding landscape, and considering future developments, among others. For further ideas, such as building strategic alliances with key research centers, we refer to Lindgreen et al. (2019b).
- How will the research group contribute to the school's education? The group could contemplate offering research-based education; for example, when faculty members collaborate with students on research projects, those students become co-authors of conference papers or journal articles. Alternatively, the group claim a teaching-based approach, acknowledging that they discuss research-based issues with, say, executive students and thus gain inspiration for their research through their teaching.
- Which services will the research group offer to the wider academic community? Such services should demonstrate impact on the research commu-

nity. It could include reviewing for conferences and journals, participating in international networks, starting collaboration with international scholars, and arranging workshops, sessions, or panels at conferences. It might also include being journal editor, member of influential journal advisory/editorial review boards, or at least being a reviewer for such journals.
- How will the research group interact with the wider society and, most importantly, deliver societal value? In the context of public life, value is an important measure on the contribution to business and social good of activities for which strict financial measures are inappropriate or fundamentally unsound. The group could demonstrate the ability to inform and engage broader audiences through media interviews or workshops with practitioners. For further ideas about possible actions pertaining to the multiple aspects surrounding public value, we refer to Lindgreen et al. (2019a).

2.2 Assessing for Success

Increasing academic success is assessed not only on the journals that work is published in, but also by the scholarly impact of the work. Journal rankings such as the Association of Business Schools' Academic Journal Guide (AJG; formerly ABS) and the Australian Business Deans Council's ranking (ABDC) often are employed. The AJG ranking, for example, is compiled by a scientific committee comprised of 58 subject area expects spanning 22 research fields. Although the subject area expects do not act as representatives of their relevant learned societies in that research field, these experts do solicit advice from both learned societies and eminent scholars to judge the quality of a journal. Other important inputs include a journal's impact factor, submission and acceptance rates, age of journal, the journal's editor, reviewing process including the editorial review board, authors publishing in the journal, and the inclusion of the journal in other rankings, among others.

While the ranking of the journal is still an important indicator, other indicators of research quality are emerging that provide a broader view of innovation and academic contribution. Thus, there is a need for a meaningful portfolio of measures. As discussed by Brodie, "one size does not fit all," rather what is needed is a dashboard of metrics coupled with qualitative judgment. The question then arises: which metrics should be used to judge research quality?

Citations increasingly provide an important measure of the research quality. Google Scholar, Scopus, and Web of Science are among the many software programs that retrieve and analyze academic citations. In addition to the number of publications and the number of citations, it is possible to include measures such as average citations per publication, Hirsch's h-index, Egghe's g-index, the hg-index (to retain the advantages of both h and g measures, as well as to minimize their disadvantages; cf. Soutar, Wilkinson, & Young,

2015), and the i10-index. The so-called Field-Weighted Citation Impact takes into account the differences in research behavior across different research disciplines, meaning that citations are compared with the average number of citations by all other similar publications (in the Scopus database). Another means of judging research quality is to set up an effective benchmarking, that is, to identify a pertinent group of scholars or research groups that are committed to maintaining the very best research, for example, the Russell Group universities in the UK or the Group of Eight universities in Australia.

And yet, research is more than just publishing in influential journals. Research should have an impact that establishes the reputation of scholars or research groups among multiple stakeholder groups: scholars, the business community, and students, to name a few. PlumX Metrics, another software program, provides information about how scholars interact with articles, books, conference papers, and book chapters, among others. In addition to citations, categories include usage (e.g., clicks, downloads, views, and library holdings), captures (e.g., bookmarks, favorites, and reference managers), mentions (e.g., blogs, news articles, comments, reviews, and Wikipedia links), and social media (e.g., likes, shares, and tweets). Other measures include, for example, an article being included on doctoral seminar reading lists or awarded best paper awards.

It also becomes important to assess the contribution that research makes to influence practice. To make this assessment, there needs to an understanding of how research is used by both academics and practitioners. This requires paying explicit attention to the socialization of knowledge and the role academic research can play in these processes (Brodie & Peters, 2019; Nenonen, Brodie, Storbacka, & Peters, 2017). Therefore, faculty members also seek to publish in reputable practitioner-oriented journals (e.g., *Harvard Business Review*, *California Management Review*, and *MIT Sloan Management Review*, all on the FT 50 journal ranking) and to publish with well-respected publishers monographs and research anthologies that may contribute significantly to establish the reputation of scholars or research groups. This effort also is evidenced when popular media report on research findings and when government-sponsored research networks, in collaboration with scholars or research groups, communicate pertinent knowledge to industry and the wider public.

Methods for assessing research quality continue to be debated and developed. Aguinis and colleagues (Aguinis, Cummings, Ramani, & Cummings, 2020) argue that the use of journal rankings comes "with negative effects on the field's research methods, knowledge generation, and social dynamics." For example, the San Francisco Declaration on Research Assessment (DORA) movement advocates, among others, that research be evaluated on its scientific content rather than publication metrics of the journal in which that research was published. This could include some of the above measurements, for example, the research's influence on policy and practice. To illustrate, Cardiff Business School, a leading UK business school and one of only two business schools to be ranked in the top 10 of the UK government's five research assessment exercises since 1992, now envisions itself as a school that improves social and economic conditions. The school's approach is interdisciplinary teaching and research that addresses grand challenges; also, the school has chosen to operate a progressive approach to its own governance (Kitchener, 2019a, 2019b).

3. CONDITIONS FOR SUCCESS FOR A RESEARCH STREAM

Recently, Brodie and Juric (2018) reflected on the conditions that led to the successful development of a new research stream on customer engagement. Two seminal articles published in 2011 and 2013 initiated the research stream. The first article established the conceptual domain of customer engagement (Brodie, Hollebeek, Juric, & Ilic, 2011a), and the second refined this conceptualization with empirical research (Brodie, Ilic, & Hollebeek, 2013). As of July 2019, each article has had over 1,700 citations in Google Scholar. These two articles have led to a stream of influential publications that have broadened the research stream (Breidbach & Brodie, 2017; Brodie, Fehrer, Jaakkola, & Conduit, 2019; Storbacka et al., 2016). The first academic book on customer engagement (Brodie, Hollebeek, & Conduit, 2016) and three special issues of journals (*Journal of Marketing Management*, *Journal of Service Theory and Practice*, and *Journal of Strategic Marketing*), which involved contributions from over 100 authors from North America, Europe, and Australasia, have played important roles in establishing this research stream. Building on this work, other special issues of journals, other articles, and book chapters are all contributing to what is now a substantial international stream of research. Scopus and Google Scholar have reported a steady increase in the number of articles using the concept of customer engagement and related concepts since 2011.

Drawing on the initial reflections by Brodie and Juric (2018) about the conditions that led to the development of the customer engagement research stream, we propose that there are five necessary initial conditions that determine the success of a research stream, and, additionally, five key conditions that build on these initial conditions and also impact the success of a research stream. The five initial conditions are:

1. *Research problems leading to research opportunities*: The first initial condition is to have the capability to identify an important research

problem, which is of practical and academic interest that creates future research opportunities.

2. *Initiating research stream*: The second initial condition that builds on the first is to have the capability to initiate the research stream by bringing together talented groups of scholars to realize research opportunities. Key attributes include having scholars with creative curiosity, the ability to spot new opportunities, a passion to publish in the best journals, an ability to work cohesively as a team, and having complementary abilities.

3. *Clarity in expression*: The third initial condition is to have the capability to provide clarity in academic arguments that provide foundations for the emerging research stream. Academic scholarship requires an understanding of academic conventions, especially for written expression and theoretical framing. However, innovative new research streams are often challenging the status quo, meaning that careful consideration needs to be given as to why established academic conventions need to be challenged.

4. *Teamwork within a network of scholars*: The fourth initial condition is to have the capability to develop a network of talented scholars who continue to embrace research opportunities. The network starts with a core group that provides leadership to facilitate an international network and broaden the stream of research. Workshop forums and special sessions at conferences targeted at special issues of journals and books play an important role. Having well-known international scholars can play an important role in adding credibility to the emerging network. Central to the success of this formation and operations of teams is openness and honesty, as well as respect for the variety of skills, abilities, and roles different researchers can play. The network needs to build on mutual trust, and that can be enhanced by not only collaborating on research projects, but also socializing together.

5. *Platform to consolidate knowledge*: The fifth initial condition is that the network of scholars needs to produce research that consolidates the knowledge in the area. This provides foundations for further innovative research. For example, in 2016, the customer engagement research stream produced the first academic book on customer engagement, which took stock of the development of the research area (Brodie et al., 2016). The book consisted of 16 review chapters, and 39 authors from Europe, North America, and Australasia who have gone on to produce journal articles to further advance the research area.

The five key conditions that build on the initial conditions and impact the success of the research stream are:

1. *Role of theory and theorizing*: The first key condition is the need for fresh thinking about the role of theory and theorizing that leads to new approaches (Brodie & Peters, 2019). We suggest greater emphasis needs to be given to the process of theorizing rather than to the focus on theory. Being "stuck in the middle, neither being firmly based in real-world data, nor reaching a sufficient level of abstraction" should be avoided (Gummesson, 2004, p. 317).
2. *Sustaining leadership and innovation*: The second key condition is to put a process in place to sustain leadership and innovation. The group who provides the leadership to initiate the research stream needs to broaden as the research stream expands. With the research stream developing, the network needs to embrace distributed leadership that will generate empowerment to propagate new initiatives and to keep the momentum in the research stream. Eventually, when the network has achieved its research ambitions, it might embrace broader challenges in the field or, more drastically, reinvent itself by identifying a new important research problem and thus initiating a new research stream.
3. *Getting research accepted*: The third key condition is that scholars within the research stream have the persistence to get research accepted in high-quality journals. Innovative research that challenges conventional thinking can meet barriers in the review process because of 'similarity bias' of reviewers. Similarity bias occurs when research does not fit norms and practices that reviewers are familiar with. Editors have an important role in recognizing and supporting innovative research that challenges conventional thinking.
4. *Getting research recognized*: The fourth key condition is that the research stream needs to become visible and understood by other researchers. Workshops, forums, and special sessions at conferences where leading scholars outside the research stream participate can play an important role in creating visibility and understanding for the research stream. In addition, online platforms such as Google Scholar, Mendeley, Academia, and publishers' platforms are playing an increasingly important role in creating recognition. Acceptance is more short term and micro (i.e., individual); in contrast, recognition is more long term and macro (i.e., collective). Individual authors get their manuscripts accepted for inclusion in high-quality journals. The research gets recognition when the research stream starts to head toward maturity with more manuscripts accepted for such journals and the authors start to influence later scholars to pursue research in the stream.

5. *Tenacity and resilience*: The fifth key condition is for the researchers to have tenacity and resilience. Research that challenges conventional thinking can be expected to meet resistance, and it is tempting to give up. However, if the group of scholars believes strongly in what they want to achieve there usually is a way to succeed. Innovative manuscripts take time to develop, and the review process based on rigorous critique can play an important role in improving manuscripts, leading to clarity in expression. Researchers in a new research stream that challenge conventional wisdom need the conviction to stick with the stream, even in the face of rejection at high-quality journals. It is easy just to give up and focus on writing something more conventionally accepted. That is, rather than making the radical contribution (which is risky, as reviewers or editors may not recognize the contribution), researchers can settle for making an incremental contribution, which still builds theory and is publishable, but at lower risk of rejection. A researcher with the required tenacity and resilience can overcome this rejection. Winston Churchill's famous speech at Harrow School in 1941 is of relevance here: "Never give in, never give in, never, never, never, never – in nothing, great or small, large or petty – never give in except to convictions of honour and good sense." Senior, tenured academics might find it easier to take chances later in their academic career and include a more radical research direction in their project portfolio. However, when senior, tenured academics have to deliver X number of articles in high-quality journals (this is, for example, the case in the UK where research assessments have been conducted since 1986), such academics will hesitate before pursuing radical research.

4. REVIEW OF THE IMP AND CMP RESEARCH PROGRAMS

In this section, we first give a short history of the activities of the Industrial Marketing and Purchasing (IMP) Group and then of the Contemporary Marketing Practices (CMP) Group.

4.1 Industrial Marketing and Purchasing Group (IMP)

Coming together in 1976, researchers from five different countries formed the IMP Group (Turnbull, Ford, & Cunningham, 1996). The aim was to "make a comparative analysis of operations, strategies and organization structures of companies involved in export marketing to, and international purchasing from France, Germany, Italy, Sweden, and the United Kingdom" (Cunningham, 1980, p. 322). The scale of the research project was enormous, based on 876 interviews, with the focus always on the interactions between the parties involved.

A basic starting point of the research project was the recognition of the interdependencies that exist in buyer–supplier relationships; something that the more traditional American approaches to understanding organizational buyer behavior had ignored (Robinson, Faris, & Wind, 1967; Sheth, 1973; Webster & Wind, 1972). The researchers' view, based on understanding buyer–supplier relationships as an interaction approach, rejected the traditionally accepted '4Ps' approach. Instead, the researchers believed that "the great majority of business purchases do not exist as individual events and hence cannot be fully understood if each one is examined in isolation" (Turnbull et al., 1996, p. 45). The researchers challenged the prevailing view of understanding organizational buying behavior on four different grounds (see Cunningham, 1980; Håkansson, 1982; Turnbull et al., 1996).

The first was to challenge the prevailing view in which the industrial buyer behavior literature concentrated on analyzing discrete purchasing decisions. Instead, based on some of the researchers' earlier work, their view was of the buyer–supplier interaction based on relationships, which often varied in length, complexity, and dynamism (Cunningham & White, 1973; Håkansson & Östberg, 1975; Ford, 1978, 1980). Such relationships were influenced not only by the different technological capabilities of the companies involved, but also by the roles of the different individuals involved in the buying and selling process, which was far more complex than 'a buyer' and 'a salesperson.'

A corollary of this was the second ground, which refuted the idea that business-to-business marketing involved the manipulation of the 'marketing mix' variables so often applied in more traditional business-to-consumer marketing. Rather than segmenting a market into different passive segments, each of which then could be targeted by an optimally designed set of the 4Ps, the interaction approach demanded a more insightful understanding of what each party wanted from the relationship.

The third ground laid down challenged the adoption of the traditional view derived from the economic theory that saw markets as consisting of an atomistic structure with numerous buyers and sellers, with buyers moving freely between competing suppliers. Instead, the researchers' earlier work had identified the fact that business-to-business marketing was typified by a high degree of stability in buyer–supplier relationships, accentuating the importance of understanding the relationship management mechanisms utilized by both parties (Ford, 1978; Håkansson, Johanson, & Wootz, 1976).

The final ground of the early IMP researchers concerned the traditional separation in studying either the approaches adopted by industrial purchasing agents or industrial marketers. Instead, seeing them as opposite sides of the same coin, the researchers emphasized the similarity of the tasks, with both parties "involved in the search for suitable trading partners. Both parties recognize the costs of change and the benefits and risks involved in becoming dependent upon the other" (Cunningham, 1980, p. 323).

Having set out their grounds, the IMP Group proceeded with their program of research. Since we were not involved in this early process, it is not clear to us whether or how agreement was reached on the methodology to adopt. Cunningham (1980, p. 324) argues that, given the diverse theoretical backgrounds of the individuals involved, it was clear that "no single theoretical model could be imposed." Rather, he suggests that an incremental process of accommodating different ideas eventually resulted in the interaction model adopted. In order to understand buyer–seller interaction, it was argued that four sets of variables had to be studied simultaneously: the elements and processes of the interaction itself; characteristics of the individuals and organizations involved; the environment within which the interaction occurs; and the atmosphere affecting and affected by the interaction. This model "draws upon inter-organizational theory, the 'new institutional, economic theory' in addition to concepts such as risk reduction, power and dependence, interpersonal and distribution channel power, industrial buying behaviors and the internationalization process of the firm" (Cunningham, 1980, p. 324).

This original study, termed the 'IMP 1' study to distinguish it from subsequent rounds of additional data collected, focused exclusively on industrial products, ignoring services. As explained in both Cunningham (1980) and Håkansson (1982), a 'choice matrix' was developed that categorized suppliers' product technology into raw materials, parts, and equipment; and distinguished between the customers' manufacturing technology as to whether it involved unit production, batch, and mass production, or process manufacture.

An extraordinary amount of data was then collected. The 876 interviews were conducted with companies in France (260), Germany (161), Italy (117), Sweden (180), and the United Kingdom (158) (Cunningham, 1980, p. 330). Approximately half of these were marketing study interviews, and half were purchasing study interviews. Due to the complexity, and the strategic sensitivity of the relationships being studied, only personal interviews were used. Care was taken that only those with direct involvement in and experience of the relationship were interviewed. There were often multiple interviews in the same company, covering different customers or suppliers.

The objective at this early stage clearly was on theory building, not theory testing. As argued by Cunningham, "the development of a better theoretical understanding of the process of interaction between companies across different national and cultural barriers is a major academic objective. The research is not intended to test a model but rather to lead to the formulation of a model which integrates industrial marketing and organizational buying behavior" (1980, p. 337).

This early work of the IMP Group resulted in two books, which set much of the scene for the work that was to come: Turnbull and Cunningham (1981) and Håkansson (1982). Instrumental in encouraging the group was the Annual IMP Group Conference, held every year since 1984 (apart from 1987 in which no conference was held). This conference has been supplemented in some years with an additional 'IMP Asia' conference being held. The 'membership' of the IMP Group always has been seen as a very flexible concept: while there certainly are the core team of the original researchers, there are many others who remain connected to varying degrees. Membership of the group has always been free, and the IMP Group website currently shows a total of 403 people registered as members (www.impgroup.org). While this may be seen as evidence of success, it also has a natural disadvantage in that it is almost impossible to keep to the tight focus that categorized the IMP 1 study, with the conferences now increasingly general in scope, dealing with some topics or methodologies that some core members would see as peripheral distractions. This view is counter-balanced by others calling for more inclusion of different topics and methodologies (Cunningham, 2008). However, one developmental theme that has consistently stayed within IMP thinking is the extension of the area of study from relationships and interactions between buyers and suppliers to see such relationships as being embedded within a broader network (Håkansson & Snehota, 1989).

The annual conference has resulted in a significant amount of published work: from some different sources (Henneberg, Jiang, Naudé, & Ormrod, 2009; Wuehrer & Smejkal, 2013; see also the IMP Group's website), we can calculate that over 4,000 papers have so far been presented at the annual IMP conferences. Since the conference held in Turku in 1998, a special issue of *Industrial Marketing Management* has been dedicated to highlighting the best papers from the conference. To date, there have been 19 such special issues of *Industrial Marketing Management*, and 2 special issues of the *Journal of Business and Industrial Marketing*. There have also been another 22 special issues of *Industrial Marketing Management* that have been edited by members of the IMP Group (for an excellent understanding of the co-creation activities that have taken place between *Industrial Marketing Management* and the IMP Group, see Möller & Halinen, 2018). Researchers from the IMP Group have contributed significantly to the academic debate over the years. Appendix Table 4.A1 lists notable publications along with their number of Google citations as of November 2018.

4.2 Contemporary Marketing Practices Group (CMP)

In contrast to the IMP Group, the CMP Group operated on a far smaller scale involving a network of fewer than 30 scholars. The research in the fullest sense only lasted for not much more than a decade, but the timely nature of the research meant it had made an important contribution. Of note, the CMP research is still being cited. For example in the last three years the *Journal of Marketing* article (Coviello, Brodie, Danaher, & Johnston, 2002) has averaged over 30 Google Scholar citations per year. As with the IMP program, the CMP program was initiated by concern that the mainstream marketing management approach was failing to reflect the changes taking place. Since the 1980s, a fragmentation of mainstream marketing has occurred. Greater emphasis was now placed on marketing processes, relationships with customers, and relationships with other stakeholders including suppliers, channel intermediaries, and other market contacts. To reflect this change, the term "relationship marketing" was coined back in 1983. Relationship marketing had gained support in the literature to the point where some researchers (e.g., Grönroos, 1990; Sheth, Gardner, & Garrett, 1988) suggested it as a "new marketing paradigm."

While the arguments for a paradigm shift in marketing were persuasive, there was a lack of research to understand the nature of the changes in marketing practices. This motivated a research group at the University of Auckland's Business School to establish an international investigation into marketing practices. The program's original objective was to profile marketing practices in a contemporary environment and to examine the relevance of relational marketing in different organizational, economic and cultural contexts. The research was initiated by seminal articles by Coviello, Brodie, and Munro (1997), which outlined the conceptual framework, and Brodie, Coviello, Brooks, and Little (1997), which reported empirical research undertaken in New Zealand.

Over the next decade, the research from the CMP group has grown to include a core group of researchers in New Zealand, the USA, the UK, and Argentina with a broader network of researchers in countries such as Canada, Finland, Holland, Germany, Ireland, Spain, Russia, Thailand, Malaysia, Ghana, Ivory Coast, China, and Australia who replicated and expanded the original research undertaken in New Zealand. The CMP research program resulted in over 50 published research articles (Brodie, Coviello, & Winklhofer, 2008). These included an article in the *Journal of Marketing* (Coviello et al., 2002). Appendix Table 4.A2 lists the most highly cited articles.

Central to the CMP research program was the development of a typology of market and marketing practices. This was developed into the survey instrument that served as a basis for the research in the different countries. The CMP typology was informed by six general theoretical frameworks that relate to economic and social processes. These frameworks are services marketing, inter-organizational exchange relationships, channels, networks, strategic management, and the value chain and information technology within and between organizations (Coviello et al., 1997). In parallel with its process of drawing on general theories, the typology also was informed by applied theory and empirical research about marketing practices. This included research undertaken with middle managers, who acted as participant observers for their organizations. In addition to responding to a structured questionnaire, survey participants were required to reflect on the practices in their organizations. This provided qualitative assessments of the organization's marketing practices, changes to marketing practices in general, and any influences on these practices. When analyzing the results, researchers moved between statistical analysis of the quantitative data and the qualitative analysis of individual responses and groups of cases. Thus, the mid-range theorizing process was characterized by abductive reasoning, where conceptual work is intertwined with empirical research (Brodie & Peters, 2019; Dubois & Gadde, 2002).

The CMP typology recognizes concepts associated with the market activity and concepts associated with management activities. The five concepts or dimensions relating to external or market activity are the purpose of exchange, nature of communication, type of contact, duration of exchange, and formality of exchange. The four concepts or dimensions relating to management activity are managerial intent, managerial focus, managerial investment, and managerial level of implementation. Having identified the dimensions that distinguish between market and managerial practices, the literature was then re-analyzed based on those dimensions to identify various ideal types of practice. For the initial classification scheme, four practices subsequently were identified (Coviello et al., 1997). The three most relevant practices to contemporary marketing are:

Transactional practice is the traditional managerial approach. It is defined as a practice using the '4P' transactional approach to attract customers in a broad market or specific market segment.

Traditional relationship practice is the relationship approach articulated since the 1980s and which has its roots in service marketing and business-to-business marketing. It is defined by the development of personal interactions between employees and individual customers.

Network practice is characterized by the development of relationships with customers and companies within the network and has its roots in the IMP Group. (Axelsson & Easton, 1992)

With the emergence of e-business and the internet in the 1990s, it became necessary to revise and expand the original CMP framework to include another generic type of practice. The framework now recognized the powerful influence that information and communication technologies were having in facilitating change in business and marketing. As with the development of the original CMP typology, an extensive content analysis was undertaken of the marketing, management, and information systems literature to conceptualize the emerging practice. Consistent with the original typology, attention was given to the five market-related dimensions and the four management-related dimensions that distinguish this practice from other practices. This led to an additional practice (Coviello, Milley, & Marcolin, 2001; see also Lindgreen, Palmer, & Vanhamme, 2004).

> *Interactive practice* is defined as "using interactive information and communication technologies to create and mediate dialogue between the firm and identified customers". (Brodie, Saren, & Pels, 2011b, p. 83)

Importantly, the mid-range theorizing process used by the CMP research program enabled the development of a comprehensive typology that could investigate multiple practices empirically. Rather than a simple either/or dichotomous classification of practices (transactions versus relationships), the typology assumes alternative types of practices within companies are not assumed to be mutually exclusive. Thus, empirical research can identify companies with different combinations of transactional, relational, network, and interactive practices. Some companies may have practices with a stronger transactional emphasis, while others have practices with a strong relational emphasis, and yet other companies may have practices that are pluralistic. This broader view of markets and marketing means the typology can be used to investigate a comprehensive range of relevant empirical phenomena and then to classify these phenomena that are not mutually exclusive.

The survey phase of the CMP research led to generalizations about contemporary marketing practice, which challenged the view that a new paradigm for marketing was emerging based on relationships:

- While there is some support for consumer goods companies being more transactional, and business and service companies being more relational, there are many exceptions.
- Companies can be grouped equally into those whose marketing practices are predominantly transactional, relational, or a transactional/relational hybrid. Each group includes all types of companies (consumer goods, consumer services, business-to-business goods, and business-to-business services).
- Marketing practices tend to be pluralistic in that all types of practice are in evidence, and managerial practice has not shifted from transactional to relational approaches per se.
- Companies that adopted pluralistic practices tend to perform better.

In parallel to the survey-based investigations undertaken in the first phase of CMP research, some qualitative studies also were conducted. The qualitative research evidence considered the influence of context on the implementation of relational marketing. It also offered insight into managers' perceived challenges and barriers to implementing relationship marketing. Other case study investigations were undertaken to understand specific sectoral influences. Examples include studies in wine (Beverland & Lindgreen, 2004; Lindgreen, 2001; Lindgreen, Antioco, & Beverland, 2003), the distribution of dairy products and online shopping (Lindgreen, 2008), and the automotive industry (Lindgreen, 2008). Such studies considered industry context more closely than did earlier CMP research, while others extended the early focus on marketing practices to encompass more specific topics such as innovation in marketing (Palmer & Brookes, 2002) and managerial perspectives specific to business-to-business marketing (Palmer, 2002). These extensions complemented the findings of other qualitative research and identified key trends impacting marketing practice (Brodie, Brookes, & Coviello, 2000; Brookes & Brodie, 2000; Lindgreen, 2001).

5. REFLECTIONS ON CONDITIONS FOR SUCCESS

Earlier, in section 3, we identified five necessary initial conditions that determine the success of a research stream, and an additional five key conditions that build on the initial conditions and also contribute to success. At this point, we review and assess how both IMP and CMP groups achieved the conditions and established successful research streams.

5.1 Initial Condition 1: Research Problems Leading to Research Opportunities

The first necessary initial condition is the capability to identify an important research problem that is of practical and academic interest that creates the research opportunities.

IMP: Given the remarkable success of the IMP Group in terms of both the number of articles published and the citations achieved, it is clear that a research problem with opportunities was indeed identified. It seems as if the source was a critical examination of the current theories to understand industrial marketing, which simply did not match with the reality that the early researchers saw around them. A number of these early articles clearly showed the importance of longer-term relationships rather than an approach of optimizing individual sales through systematic manipulation of the marketing mix variables (see, for example, Cunningham & White, 1973; Ford, 1978; Håkansson & Östberg, 1975). The identification of the research problem itself was laid down beautifully and emphatically in the four challenges identified above (see Cunningham, 1980; Håkansson, 1982; Turnbull et al., 1996).

CMP: The CMP research program was initiated by practical problems that also were of academic interest. As discussed in the previous section, from the 1980s, relationship marketing gained support in the literature to the point where some researchers (e.g., Christopher, Payne, & Ballantyne, 1991; Grönroos, 1990; Sheth et al., 1988) were suggesting it as a new marketing paradigm. While the arguments for a paradigm shift in marketing were persuasive, there was lack of research to support the case. This led to the CMP program's objective to profile marketing practices in a contemporary environment, and to examine the relevance of relational marketing in different organizational, economic, and cultural contexts. Of note is that the CMP research aligns with the research agenda by Day and Montgomery (1999) who in their *Journal of Marketing* article "Charting New Directions for Marketing" identified "How do firms relate to their markets?" as one of the four most important issues for academic research in the marketing discipline in the twenty-first century.

5.2   Initial Condition 2: Initiating Research Stream

The second initial condition is to be able to initiate the research stream by bringing together talented groups of scholars to realize research opportunities.

IMP: As discussed in detail in the previous section, the IMP Group was formed by some researchers from five different countries coming together in 1976 (Turnbull et al., 1996). The aim was to "make a comparative analysis of operations, strategies and organization structures of companies involved in export marketing to, and international purchasing from France, Germany, Italy, Sweden, and the United Kingdom" (Cunningham, 1980, p. 322).

CMP: The program was initiated by a group of researchers at the University of Auckland consisting of Nicole Coviello, Richard Brookes, Vicki Little, and Rod Brodie. The group's research was characterized by a creative curiosity, an ability to spot opportunities, a passion to publish in the best journals, and an ability to work cohesively as a team to take advantage of the different members' complementary abilities. As discussed, the two seminal articles by Coviello et al. (1997) and Brodie et al. (1997) created international recognition, and an international research group subsequently was formed.

5.3   Initial Condition 3: Clarity in Expression

The third initial condition is to be able to provide clarity in academic arguments and provide foundations for the emerging research stream.

IMP: One way in which the IMP Group supported its members in achieving this clarity was through the annual conference submission process. This helped authors to tighten their logic and clarity before ultimate submission to a journal after the conference. Full papers would be submitted some months before the conference itself took place. This meant that there was a period available in which the papers could be sent for review and then returned to the authors for improvement before being finally accepted. The papers were subsequently uploaded to the Group's website. It is therefore lamentable that external network pressures have forced a change in this practice: in spite of the conference never claiming copyright of the uploaded papers, several journal editors started rejecting submissions on the basis that the papers already had been published on the website. This has led to a change in procedures, whereby an extended paper is submitted and reviewed, but which is not made more widely available.

CMP: The seminal articles by Coviello et al. (1997) and Brodie et al. (1997) provided the foundations for the emerging research stream. The subsequent sequence of articles by Coviello, Brodie, and others led to the refinement of the core academic arguments that CMP was based on (see Appendix Table 4.A2). This sequence of articles clarified the importance of the research, and this led to the *Journal of Marketing* article by Coviello et al. (2002) that established the CMP perspective within the mainstream literature of the marketing discipline. As with IMP, CMP ran some workshops and forums, and, in addition, there was a sequence of conference papers that also led to the clarity in expression. Peer review played an important role in this process, as did the rigorous reviews for the leading journals where the research was published.

5.4 Initial Condition 4: Teamwork Within a Network of Scholars

The fourth initial condition is to be able to develop a network of talented scholars who embrace research opportunities.

IMP: The IMP Group excelled in creating, maintaining, and developing a network of scholars. Since its inception in 1976, the researchers involved managed to pull together a tightly knit and academically cohesive team that negotiated the way forward in terms of how to get a number of different academics from different countries and different theoretical backgrounds (Cunningham, 1980) to agree a common way forward to study business relationships in an international context. The argument is put forward that "it is also important to include leading scholars who add credibility." Interestingly, this was not the approach initially taken by the IMP Group. The (perhaps apocryphal?) story goes that one of the early 'rules' of the group was "no professors to be included," based on the assumption that leading scholars had made it to the top by adopting the prevailing approach to studying marketing as the manipulation of the marketing mix variables, and that they would not be willing/able to contribute to a radical new interpretation of industrial marketing.

CMP: The publication of the conceptual article by Coviello et al. (1997) and the empirical article by Brodie et al. (1997) generated interest from the UK and other European scholars who were attracted to the common sense practical aspects of the research. These scholars approached the University of Auckland group to join the research program. The network was enhanced by some Ph.D. studies. This included Adam Lindgreen (Cranfield University, 2000), Roger Palmer (Cranfield University, 2001), Mairead Brady (Strathclyde University, 2001), and Vicky Little (University of Auckland, 2004). CMP research was presented at the International Colloquium on Relationship Marketing, initiated by David Ballantyne in the 1990s, and participants of this colloquium became part of the network. The network started to meet on an annual basis to discuss future directions for research. These meetings focused on openness and honesty, as well as respect for the variety of skills, abilities, and roles of the members of the network.

5.5 Initial Condition 5: Platform to Consolidate Knowledge

The fifth initial condition is that the network of scholars needs to produce research that consolidates the knowledge in the area that provides the platform for further innovative research.

IMP: The IMP Group has been extraordinarily proficient at providing a platform in a variety of ways. First, until the process was forced to change (as discussed above), the conference papers were always uploaded onto the website and made freely available, acting as a resource for all the researchers. Second, David Ford put considerable effort into editing a number of books that sought to consolidate the existing best research (Ford, 1990, 1997, 2002). Third, there have been the special issues of *Industrial Marketing Management*, with 19 special issues being based on the best conference papers and a further 22 special issues based on other topics of particular interest. These special issues have acted to consolidate knowledge of both what was discussed in the particular year's conference and also to consolidate thinking of other topics of special interest. The final consolidation approach has been via other books. This has taken different forms. First, before the conference was allocated a special issue of *Industrial Marketing Management*, an attempt was made to consolidate knowledge from the conference by producing edited books based on selected papers (see, for example, Naudé & Turnbull, 1998; Walter, Ritter, & Gemünden, 1997). Secondly, Ford and Håkansson have worked with a range of different IMP members over the years to produce a number of books on their latest thinking (see, for example, Ford et al., 1998, 2002; Håkansson, Ford, Gadde, Snehota, & Waluszewski, 2009). The most recent attempt to consolidate the IMP Group's thinking can be found in Håkansson and Snehota (2017). This book was based on work done in 2015 and 2016, during workshops "at which researchers presented original research papers on three topics, namely (a) managerial, (b) policy and (c) research implications of the IMP research findings" (Håkansson and Snehota, 2107, p. x). These three themes were then integrated into a further workshop in 2016, which resulted in the book.

CMP: The most focused effort to consolidate knowledge about CMP was in the special issue of the *Journal of Business Research* in 2008 that was edited by Brodie and Brady (2008). This special issue included seven articles that examined theoretical, empirical, and educational issues. Brodie et al. (2008) provided the overview in their "Contemporary Marketing Practices Research Program: A Review of the First Decade." Other research that consolidated knowledge included books by Brookes and Palmer (2004) and Lindgreen (2008) and over 10 book chapters.

5.6 Key Condition 1: Role of Theory and Theorizing

The first key condition that builds on the initial conditions is to have fresh thinking about the role of theory and theorizing.

IMP: As mentioned above, a core objective of the original IMP 1 research project was indeed "the development of a better theoretical understanding of the process of interaction" (Cunningham, 1980, p. 337), based upon not only a broad understanding of different academic fields, but also a keen understanding of the practicalities of practicing managers. In this way, IMP researchers have attempted to bridge the gap that can exist between general theory on one hand and empirical observation on the other.

The IMP Group has been fortunate to have at its core some extremely competent and original thinkers whose very starting point was to reconceptualize our understanding of how business-to-business markets function. This continual reconceptualizing and refining has continued, with notable contributions being made in terms of the ARA Model (Håkansson & Johanson, 1992) and also the expansion of the original thinking of the importance of interactions and relationships to include the study of the networks within which interactions and relationships are embedded (Håkansson & Snehota, 1989).

CMP: The CMP approach was informed simultaneously by theory and practice work with managers, attempting to work with managers to develop a mutual understanding of how to operationalize mid-range theories (Brodie, 2013) using abductive reasoning (Brodie & Peters, 2019). The abductive reasoning process led research that theorized with managers (Nenonen et al., 2017). The theorizing approach led to multi-method research designs. The CMP group initially used sequential designs with alternative methods being employed in stages, that is, using results from one stage to feed into the next stage in the sequence. The preferred CMP approach now, however, is to use a 'parallel design' where methods are carried out in parallel, with results feeding into each other simultaneously. For example, most CMP surveys are undertaken with middle managers, who act as participant observers for their organizations. In addition to responding to a structured questionnaire, middle managers are required to reflect on the practices in their organizations and, in so doing, provide qualitative assessments of their marketing practices, changes to marketing practice, and influences on these practices. When analyzing the results, CMP researchers move back and forth between the statistical analysis of the quantitative data and the qualitative analysis of individual responses and groups of cases.

5.7 Key Condition 2: Sustaining Leadership and Innovation

The second key condition that builds on the initial conditions is to have ways to sustain leadership and innovation to keep the momentum in the research stream.

IMP: Assessing the level of innovation attained is a multi-dimensional construct, and there are a number of areas in which the IMP Group has excelled. These include the number of books published, the number of conference papers and journal articles published, the number of *Industrial Marketing Management* (and other) special issues published, and the number of citations (some of which are shown in Appendix Table 4.A1), all of which point to a very high level of sustained innovation indeed. One aspect of innovation is the focus of that innovation: to what extent should it be encouraged to be kept narrow, or allowed to broaden? It is interesting that almost from the start of the IMP 1 research project, the level of innovation was kept extremely narrow and deep. Cunningham argues that in the original research project envisaged, the focus was to be on understanding "managers' perceptions of, and attitudes to, the buying and marketing behavior of their customer and suppliers," and also on "an analysis of how companies interact" (1980, p. 328). With the subsequent almost 40 years of work on developing our understanding of interactions, relationships, and networks, a lot of extremely innovative work has emerged.

However, two areas identified by Cunningham largely have been ignored, the first of which is developing our understanding of the international dimension of how relationships are managed. As anyone attending the more recent IMP conferences will acknowledge, this international aspect is not a prominent theme. Second, a specific area of interest of the original work was to study "the education, experience and cultural backgrounds of marketing and purchasing executives in the five countries" (Cunningham, 1980, p. 328). To date, this examination of the composition of the different actor groups involved in the buying and selling process has largely been absent. The third area of potential innovation concerns the introduction of new research approaches and methodologies beyond the more traditional case study approach that has typified so much of the IMP Group's work. Over the years, this discussion has provided a natural tension between those researchers who want to maintain the traditional methodological focus, and those researchers who seek to introduce more methodological and analytical variance.

CMP: The founders of the CMP group provided the hub for innovation with other members of the CMP group. As discussed in the previous section, the CMP typology evolved to include IT-enabled interactivity. This ensured that CMP's conceptual foundations were redeveloped to remain contemporary. An important aspect of the CMP research that kept it contemporary was to apply action research with "living case studies" where the executive students were treated as participant observers of the marketing practices in the organization they worked for (Little, Brookes, & Palmer, 2008). From the mid-2000s, some members started to undertake research within the broader service-dominant logic perspective (Vargo & Lusch, 2008) that was superseding the narrower relationship marketing perspective. As discussed by Brodie, Loebler, and Fehrer (2019), service-dominant logic is becoming a unifying paradigm, which hopes to provide the foundations for a general theory of the market and value cocreation. The CMP research with its focus on the theory–practice interface to develop mid-range theory (Brodie et al., 2011b) provided fresh thinking for empirically grounding service-dominant logic research (Brodie & Loebler, 2018; Lusch & Vargo, 2014; Vargo & Lusch, 2017). Hence, the innovation associated with the CMP research stream was subsumed into the broader service-dominant logic research stream.

5.8   Key Condition 3: Getting Research Accepted

The third key condition that builds on the initial conditions is that scholars within the research stream have the persistence to get research accepted in high-quality journals.

IMP: As noted above, the IMP Group has had considerable success in getting its work published via numerous conference papers, journal articles, and a large number of books. It has a sustained record of getting its research accepted across a wide range of channels. Special thanks in reaching a wider audience must go to the previous editor of *Industrial Marketing Management*, Peter LaPlaca, who regularly attended the conferences and gave the IMP Group access to so many special issues over the years, covering both the conference papers and other, more focused issues (see the review by Möller & Halinen, 2018). This tradition has been continued by the journal's current editors-in-chief, Adam Lindgreen and Tony Di Benedetto. Three articles, in particular, deserve mention—Bengtsson and Kock (2000), Walter, Ritter, and Gemünden (2001), and Ritter, Wilkinson, and Johnston (2004)—that are all among the top-10 most cited articles in the journal since 2000, with 1,995, 1,166 and 859 citations respectively.

It is a moot point as to whether the IMP Group's introduction of the IMP Journal was a good idea or not. The journal was launched in February 2006, but ceased to exist as an independent journal in December 2014. As of 2018, the journal was combined with the *Journal of Business and Industrial Marketing*, in which it was given its own special subsection. On the one hand, for the IMP Group to have its own journal could be interpreted as being too internally focused, with there being a need to reach an audience wider than just the IMP Group itself if it was to continue to influence the broader marketing community. An equally valid interpretation of events is that it was done too hastily, and that the journal should have been given more time to be nurtured and grow (Purchase, 2018).

CMP: As with all new research streams that challenge conventional thinking, there are initial problems in getting the work accepted. For example, an article, which outlined the CMP typology, was rejected in 1996 from a special IMP issue of the *International Journal of Research in Marketing* on markets as networks. However, this rejection led to an improved version that had great clarity of expression that was accepted for the *Journal of Marketing Management* (Coviello et al., 1997). As discussed above, there was a sequence of CMP articles, which refined the academic arguments about CMP that led to the submission to the *Journal of Marketing* (Coviello et al., 2002). While this article eventually was accepted, there were some challenges that needed to be overcome. One of the most controversial demands was that the editor required that a sample of US companies be collected, even though the research had samples of companies from Scandinavia, New Zealand, and Canada. A key factor for the *Journal of Marketing* article getting accepted, and also the other CMP work getting accepted, was very clear communication to the editors about the important contribution of the research. This was particularly important when resubmitting revisions to overcome the similarity bias of reviewers and editors.

5.9 Key Condition 4: Getting Research Recognized

The fourth key condition is that the research stream that builds on the initial conditions needs to become visible and understood by other researchers.

IMP: There is no doubt that the IMP Group has extremely high visibility. It has a well-attended conference each year, and it also has some additional workshops/seminars each year to which some people are invited. A good recent example is the book by Håkansson and Snehota (2017), which was the output of four such workshops. While these are all evidence of visibility and the research being understood by others, there is certainly incontrovertible evidence for its success in being cited. As shown in Appendix Table 4.A1, a number of the articles and books have received very high citations indeed.

Given the Group's close cooperation with *Industrial Marketing Management* over the years, this journal is the one that is most aspired to by many within the IMP Group. This raises the issue not just of where the work is published, but also where it is cited, in that citations on their own are good, but citations in the top journals are better. The conclusion reached by Di Benedetto and colleagues is that "The citations patterns show very low citation rates for IMM in the top-tier marketing journals ... indicating that IMM's share of knowledge imported by top marketing journals remains relatively small" (Di Benedetto, Sarin, Belkhouja, & Haon, 2018, p. 14). The journal citing most articles in *Industrial Marketing Management* is overwhelmingly *Industrial Marketing Management* itself. There is, however, clear evidence pointing to the increasing impact factor of *Industrial Marketing Management* over recent years, in spite of a "decreasing emphasis being placed on marketing strategy research in general (and consequently business-to-business/industrial marketing research)" in the top journals (Di Benedetto et al., 2018, p. 15). The overall picture painted, therefore, is that the IMP Group's work, along with other articles in the business-to-business area, struggle to be cited in the top journals.

CMP: The two initial seminal articles and the *Journal of Marketing* article play pivotal roles in getting the CMP research recognized. This led to high visibility and high citations for about 20 articles (see Appendix Table 4.A2). The recognition for the CMP work is because of its unique contribution in bridging theory and practice in a way, which provided practical implications. As discussed above, further recognition came from the books and book chapters.

5.10 Key Condition 5: Tenacity and Resilience

The fifth key condition, which draws on all of the other nine conditions, is for the researchers to have tenacity and resilience. Research that challenges conventional thinking can be expected to meet with resistance, and it is tempting to give up.

IMP: The importance of this condition in determining the success of the IMP Group's work does not seem particularly applicable. This is for two reasons. The first is that right in the beginning when launching the IMP 1 research study, a number of the researchers had already had their work published in the mainstream literature, and hence were both accepted by the academic community and knowledgeable about the process of getting published. Secondly, from an early stage, the group worked hard to support itself; as the Group expanded in numbers, so running the annual conference on a shoe-string demanded hard work and commitment from the organizing committee each year, but it did build a wonderfully internal supportive network for older and newer members alike.

CMP: As discussed above, the importance of this condition in determining the success of the CMP Group's work was in getting the two initial CMP articles accepted and then getting the *Journal of Marketing* article accepted. In these cases, the researchers' tenacity and resilience played an important role in getting through the review processes. However, as with IMP, once the visibility and recognition were achieved, this condition did not play such an important role.

6. CONCLUSIONS

Business school managers would like to build, and maintain, their research portfolios; individual researchers working within a business school framework would like to keep adding to their publication track record at leading journals. To accomplish these goals, managers need to consider how to invest effectively in research such that they can nurture sustainable research streams. We identified five initial conditions, as well as five key conditions, which are most conducive to a sustainable and productive academic research environment. We also presented detailed examples of these conditions in practice, in two successful research institutions, the IMP and CMP Groups. Our examination of the IMP Group presented evidence showing how this group has made significant research contributions. Similarly, the examination identifies unique aspects of the CMP research stream that led to its success for over a decade. We assess that the 10 conditions are robust and identify the essence of what has led to the success of two research streams.

Of the 10 conditions, the condition of "sustaining leadership and innovation" requires further consideration. The IMP Group has grown considerably over time. This raises the issue as to the ideal size of a research group in order to sustain innovative research. If there are too few members, there may not be enough variance in ideas to sustain the innovation. If there are too many members, the innovation may become too diffuse and lack focus. Within the IMP Group, the rapid increase in the number of members has led naturally to this debate. The discussions center around whether the IMP research should stay focused, or whether it should welcome a fragmentation in focus and acceptance of a wider range of methodological approaches. In contrast, the CMP group always was small, so the question did not arise. However, perhaps the CMP group did not grow enough to sustain leadership in innovation.

Having its beginnings in the 1970s, the IMP Group has had a head start of almost 20 years over the CMP Group. As IMP became developed, the research published has increased, but the cohesiveness of its brand position has become less clear, as different topics and methodologies are adopted. In contrast, the main research thrust of the CMP group only lasted a decade, where there was a singular focus based on the original research objective to profile marketing practices in a contemporary environment and to examine the relevance of relational marketing in different organizational, economic and cultural contexts. Rather than expand with a broader range of topics and methodologies, the CMP researchers migrated into other research streams, as the research had served its purpose. The pioneering CMP research that developed a typology of marketing practices based on mid-range theory using abductive reasoning is now playing a major role in service-dominant logic (Brodie & Loebler, 2018). Another research stream built upon the CMP research to develop an instrument to measure companies' use of purchasing practices and identified four configurations of practices ranging from transactional over interpersonal dyadic and interpersonal network to integrative relational configurations (Lindgreen, Vanhamme, van Raaij, & Johnston, 2013).

As a final thought, one must also consider the substantial role of the journal editor(s) in supporting emerging research streams. An editor may on occasion see some promise in a radical new research study that has received reject reviews due to its being "too different" or "too challenging." The editor may overrule the reviewers and make a major revision recommendation instead, thereby giving the author with the promising, but radical new research idea another chance to make a contribution. This editorial decision requires vision or insight on the part of the editor and is highly idiosyncratic. If the paper has been rejected from several A journals for being "too different," it might be a good idea for the author to try a good lower-level journal. The editor may be willing to take a rider on a paper if the editor is convinced of the promise in the research, and especially so if the editor is looking to boost the profile of the journal. After all, not all of the influential articles in marketing or other business disciplines were published in the A journals. If anything, the highest-profile journals may sometimes be quite conservative in their selection decisions, depending on the editor at that given time.

REFERENCES

Aguinis, H., Cummings, C., Ramani, R.S., & Cummings, T.G. (2020). "An A is an A": The new bottom line for valuing academic research. *Academy of Management Perspectives*, 34(1), pp. 170–172.

Anderson, J., Håkansson, H., & Johanson, J. (1994). Dyadic business relationships within a business network context. *Journal of Marketing*, 58(4), pp. 1–15.

Axelsson, B. & Easton, G. (Eds.) (1992). *Industrial Networks: A New View of Reality*. London: Routledge.

Bengtsson, M. & Kock, S. (2000). 'Coopetition' in business networks: To cooperate and compete simultaneously. *Industrial Marketing Management*, 29(5), pp. 411–426.

Beverland, M.B. & Lindgreen, A. (2004). Relationship use and market dynamism: A model of relationship evolution. *Journal of Marketing Management*, 20(7/8), pp. 825–858.

Brady, M., Saren, M., & Tzokas, N. (2002). Integrating information technology into marketing. *Journal of Marketing Management*, 18(5/6), pp. 555–578.

Breidbach, C. & Brodie, R.J. (2017). Engagement platforms and value cocreation in the sharing economy: Conceptual foundations and research directions. *Journal of Service Theory and Practice*, 27(4), pp. 761–777.

Brodie, R.J. (2013). Future of theorizing in marketing: Increasing contribution by bridging theory and practice. In Moutinho, L., Bigné, E., & Manrai, A. (Eds.), *Companion to the Future of Marketing*. London: Routledge, pp. 88–104.

Brodie, R.J. & Brady, M. (2008). Introduction to the special issue on contemporary marketing practices. *Journal of Business and Industrial Marketing*, 23(2), pp. 81–83.

Brodie, R.J., Brookes, R.W., & Coviello, N.E. (2000). Relationship marketing for consumer products. In Blois, K. (Ed.), *Oxford Textbook on Marketing*. Oxford: Oxford University Press, pp. 517–533.

Brodie, R.J., Coviello, N.E., Brooks, R.W., & Little, V. (1997). Towards a paradigm shift in marketing? An examination of current marketing practices. *Journal of Marketing Management*, 13(5), pp. 383–406.

Brodie, R.J., Coviello, N.E., & Winklhofer, H. (2008). Investigating contemporary marketing practices: A review of the first decade of the CMP research program. *Journal of Business and Industrial Marketing*, 23(2), pp. 84–94.

Brodie, R.J., Fehrer, J.A., Jaakkola, E., & Conduit, J. (2019). Actor engagement in networks: Defining the conceptual domain. *Journal of Service Research*, 22(2), pp. 173–188.

Brodie, R.J., Hollebeek, L.D., & Conduit, J. (Eds.) (2016). *Customer Engagement: Contemporary Issues and Challenges*. London: Routledge.

Brodie, R.J., Hollebeek, L.D., Juric, B., & Ilic, A. (2011a). Customer engagement: Conceptual domain, fundamental propositions, and implications for research. *Journal of Service Research*, 14(3), pp. 252–271.

Brodie, R.J., Ilic, A.J.B., & Hollebeek, L.D. (2013). Consumer engagement in a virtual brand community: An exploratory analysis. *Journal of Business Research*, 66(1), pp. 105–114.

Brodie, R.J. & Juric, B. (2018). Customer engagement: Developing an innovative research that has scholarly impact. *Journal of Global Scholars of Marketing Science*, 28(3), pp. 291–303.

Brodie, R.J. & Loebler, H. (2018). Advancing knowledge about service-dominant logic: The role of midrange theory. In Vargo, S.L. & Lusch, R.F. (Eds.), *The SAGE Handbook on Service-Dominant Logic*. London: Sage Publishing, pp. 564–579.

Brodie, R.J., Loebler, H., & Fehrer, J. (2019). Evolution of service-dominant logic: Towards a paradigm and metatheory of the market and value cocreation? *Industrial Marketing Management*, 79, pp. 3–12.

Brodie, R.J. & Peters, L.D. (2020). New directions for service research: Refreshing the process of theorizing to increase contribution. *Journal of Services Marketing*, 34(3), pp. 415–428.

Brodie, R.J., Saren, M., & Pels, J. (2011b). Theorizing about marketing and the SD logic: Exploring the bridging role of middle range theory. *Marketing Theory*, 11(1), pp. 75–91.

Brodie, R.J., Winklhofer, H., Coviello, N.E., & Johnston, W.J. (2007). Is e-marketing coming of age? An examination of the penetration of e-marketing and firm performance. *Journal of Interactive Marketing*, 21(1), pp. 2–21.

Brookes, R.W. & Brodie, R.J. (2000). Introduction to marketing strategies. In Cravens, D., Merrilees, B., & Walker, R. (Eds.), *Strategic Marketing*. New York: Irwin McGraw-Hill, pp. 1–20.

Brookes, R.W., Brodie, R.J., Coviello, N.E., & Palmer, R.A. (2004). How managers perceive the impacts of information technologies on contemporary practices: Reinforcing, enhancing or transforming? *Journal of Relationship Marketing Management*, 3(4), pp. 7–26.

Brookes, R.W. & Palmer, R.A. (2004). *The New Global Marketing Reality*. Basingstoke: Palgrave Macmillan.

Christopher, M., Payne, A., & Ballantyne, D. (1991). *Relationship Marketing: Bringing Quality, Customer Service and Marketing Together*. London: Butterworth.

Coviello, N.E. & Brodie, R.J. (1998). From transaction to relationship marketing: An investigation of managerial perceptions and practices. *Journal of Strategic Marketing*, 6(3), pp. 171–186.

Coviello, N.E. & Brodie, R.J. (2001). Contemporary marketing practices of consumer and business-to-business firms: How different are they? *Journal of Business and Industrial Marketing*, 16(5), pp. 382–400.

Coviello, N.E., Brodie, R.J., Brookes, R.W., & Palmer, R.A. (2003). Assessing the role of e-marketing in contemporary marketing practice. *Journal of Marketing Management*, 9(7), pp. 857–881.

Coviello, N.E., Brodie, R.J., Danaher, P.J., & Johnston, W.J. (2002). How firms relate to their markets: An empirical examination of contemporary marketing practice. *Journal of Marketing*, 66(3), pp. 33–46.

Coviello, N.E., Brodie, R.H., & Munro, H.J. (1997). Understanding contemporary marketing: Development of a classification scheme. *Journal of Marketing Management*, 13(6), pp. 501–522.

Coviello, N.E., Brodie, R.J., & Munro, H.J. (2000). An investigation of marketing practice by firm size. *Journal of Business Venturing*, 15(5/6), pp. 523–545.

Coviello, N.E., Milley, R., & Marcolin, B. (2001). Understanding IT-enabled interactivity in contemporary marketing. *Journal of Interactive Marketing*, 15(4), pp. 18–33.

Coviello, N.E., Winklhofer, H., & Hamilton, K. (2006). Marketing practices and performance of small service firms: An examination in the tourism accommodation sector. *Journal of Service Research*, 9(1), pp. 38–58.

Cunningham, M.T. (1980). International marketing and purchasing of industrial goods: Features of a European research project. *European Journal of Marketing*, 14(5/6), pp. 322–338.

Cunningham, M.T. (2008). Pictures at an exhibition of business markets: Is there a case for competition? *The IMP Journal*, 2(1), pp. 46–59.

Cunningham, M.T. & White, J.G. (1973). The behaviour of industrial buyers in their search for suppliers of machine tools. *Journal of Management Studies*, 7(3), pp. 189–202.

Day, G. & Montgomery, D. (1999). Charting new directions for marketing. *Journal of Marketing*, 63 (Special issue), pp. 3–13.

Di Benedetto, C.A. (2013). The emergence of the product innovation discipline and implications for future research. In Kahn, K.B. (Ed.), *The PDMA Handbook of New Product Development*. Hoboken, NJ: John Wiley & Sons, pp. 416–426.

Di Benedetto, C.A., Sarin, S., Belkhouja, M., & Haon, C. (2018). Patterns of knowledge outflow from industrial marketing management to major marketing and specialized journals (1999–2013): A citation analysis. *Industrial Marketing Management*, 69, pp. 13–17.

Dubois, A. & Gadde, L.E. (2002). Systematic combining: An abductive approach to case research. *Journal of Business Research*, 55(7), pp. 553–560.

Ford, D. (1978). Stability factors in industrial marketing channels. *Industrial Marketing Management*, 7(6), pp. 410–422.

Ford, D. (1980). The development of buyer-seller relationships in industrial markets. *European Journal of Marketing*, 14(5/6), pp. 339–353.

Ford, D. (Ed.) (1990). *Understanding Business Markets: Interactions, Relationships and Networks*. London: Academic Press.

Ford, D. (Ed.) (1997). *Understanding Business Markets*, 2nd ed. London: Dryden Press.

Ford, D. (Ed.) (2002). *Understanding Business Marketing and Purchasing*, 3rd ed. London: Thompson Learning.

Ford, D., Berthon, P., Brown, S., Gadde, L.-E., Håkansson, H., Naudé, P., Ritter, T., & Snehota, I. (2002). *The Business Marketing Course: Managing in Complex Networks*. Chichester: John Wiley & Sons.

Ford, D., Gadde, L.-E., Håkansson, H., Lundgren, A., Snehota, I., Turnbull, P., & Wilson, D. (1998). *Managing Business Relationships*. New York: John Wiley & Sons.

Grönroos, C. (1990). *Service Management and Marketing: Managing the Moments of Truth in Service Competition*. Lexington, MA: Lexington Books.

Gummesson, E. (2004). Qualitative research in marketing: Road-map for a wilderness of complexity and unpredictability. *European Journal of Marketing*, 39(3), pp. 309–327.

Håkansson, H. (Ed.) (1982). *International Marketing and Purchasing: An Interaction Approach*. Chichester: John Wiley & Sons.

Håkansson, H. (1987). *Industrial Technological Development: A Network Approach*. London: Croom Helm.

Håkansson, H. (1989). *Corporate Technological Behaviour: Co-operation and Networks*. London: Routledge.

Håkansson, H. & Ford, D. (2002). How should companies interact in business networks? *Journal of Business Research*, 55(2), pp. 133–139.

Håkansson, H., Ford, D., Gadde, L.-E., Snehota, I., & Waluszewski, A. (2009). *Business in Networks*. Chichester: John Wiley & Sons.

Håkansson, H., Johanson, J., & Wootz, B. (1976). Influence tactics in buyer-seller processes. *Industrial Marketing Management*, 4(6), pp. 319–332.

Håkansson, H. & Johanson, J. (1992). A model of industrial networks. In Axelsson, B. & Easton, G. (Eds.), *Industrial Networks: A New View of Reality*. London: Routledge, pp. 28–34 (reprinted in Ford, 2002).

Håkansson, H. & Östberg, C. (1975). Industrial marketing: An organizational problem? *Industrial Marketing Management*, 4(2/3), pp. 113–123.

Håkansson, H. & Snehota, I. (1989). No business is an island: The network concept of business strategy. *Scandinavian Journal of Management*, 5(3), pp. 187–200.

Håkansson, H. & Snehota, I. (Eds.) (2017). *No Business is an Island: Making Sense of the Interactive Business World*. Bingley: Emerald Publishing.

Henneberg, S.C., Jiang, Z., Naudé, P., & Ormrod, R.P. (2009). The network researchers' network: A social network analysis of the IMP Group 1984–2006. *The IMP Journal*, 3(1), pp. 28–49.

Johanson, J. & Mattsson, L.-G. (1987). Interorganizational relations in industrial systems: A network approach compared with the transaction-cost approach. *International Studies of Management & Organization*, 17(1), pp. 34–48.

Johanson, J. & Mattsson, L.-G. (2015). Internationalisation in industrial systems: A network approach. In Forsgren, M., Holm, U., & Johanson, J. (Eds.), *Knowledge, Networks and Power*. Basingstoke: Palgrave Macmillan, pp. 111–132.

Kitchener, M. (2019a). Cardiff Business School: The public value business school. https://www.cardiff.ac.uk/__data/assets/pdf_file/0008/572732/Cardiff-Business-School-Public-Value.pdf (accessed May 22, 2019).

Kitchener, M. (2019b). The public value of social science: From manifesto to organizational strategy. In Lindgreen, A., Koenig-Lewis, N., Kitchener, M., Brewer, J., Moore, M., & Meynhardt, T. (Eds.), *Public Value: Deepening, Enriching, and Broadening the Theory and Practice*. London: Routledge, pp. 301–315.

Lindgreen, A. (2001). An exploration of contemporary marketing practices in the New Zealand wine sector: Evidence from three cases. *International Journal of Wine Marketing*, 13(1), pp. 5–22.

Lindgreen, A. (2008). *Managing Market Relationships: Methodological and Empirical Insights*. Aldershot: Gower Publishing.

Lindgreen, A., Antioco, M.D.J., & Beverland, M.B. (2003). Contemporary marketing practice: A research agenda and preliminary findings. *International Journal of Customer Relationship Management*, 6(1), pp. 51–72.

Lindgreen, A., Davis, R., Brodie, R.J., & Buchanan-Oliver, M. (2000). Pluralism in contemporary marketing practices. *International Journal of Bank Marketing*, 18(6), pp. 294–308.

Lindgreen, A., Di Benedetto, C.A., Verdich, C., Vanhamme, J., Venkatraman, V., Pattinson, S., Clarke, A.H., & Khan, Z. (2019a). How to write really good research funding applications. *Industrial Marketing Management*, 77, pp. 232–239.

Lindgreen, A., Koenig-Lewis, N., Kitchener, M., Brewer, J.D., Moore, M., & Meynhardt, T. (Eds.) (2019b). *Public Value: Deepening, Enriching, and Broadening the Theory and Practice*. London: Routledge.

Lindgreen, A., Palmer, R., & Vanhamme, J. (2004). Contemporary marketing practice: Theoretical propositions and practical implications. *Marketing Intelligence & Planning*, 22(6), pp. 673–692.

Lindgreen, A., Palmer, R., Vanhamme, J., & Wouters, J.P.M. (2006). A relationship-management assessment tool: Questioning, identifying, and prioritizing critical aspects of customer relationships. *Industrial Marketing Management*, 35(1), pp. 57–71.

Lindgreen, A., Palmer, R., Wetzels, M., & Antioco, M. (2008). Do different marketing practices require different leadership styles? An exploratory study. *Journal of Business & Industrial Marketing*, 24(1), pp. 114–126.

Lindgreen, A., Vanhamme, J., van Raaij, E.M., & Johnston, W.J. (2013). Go configure: The mix of purchasing practices to choose for your supply base. *California Management Review*, 55(2), pp. 72–96.

Little, V., Brookes, R., & Palmer, R. (2008). Research-informed teaching and teaching-informed research: The Contemporary Marketing Practices (CMP) living case study approach to understanding marketing practice. *Journal of Business and Industrial Marketing*, 23(2), pp. 124–134.

Lusch, R.F. & Vargo, S.L. (2014). *Service-Dominant Logic: Premises, Perspectives, Possibilities*. Cambridge: Cambridge University Press.

Möller, K. & Halinen, A. (2018). IMP thinking and IMM: Co-creating value for business marketing. *Industrial Marketing Management*, 69, pp. 18–31.

Naudé, P. & Turnbull, P.W. (Eds.) (1998). *Network Dynamics in International Marketing*. Oxford: Pergamon Press.

Nenonen, S., Brodie, R.J., Storbacka, K., & Peters, L.D. (2017). Theorizing with managers: How to achieve both academic rigor and practical relevance? *European Journal of Marketing*, 51(7/8), pp. 1130–1152.

Palmer, R.A. (2002). Managerial understanding of contemporary industrial marketing issues. *Qualitative Market Research: An International Journal*, 5(2), pp. 135–143.

Palmer, R.A. & Brookes, R.W. (2002). Incremental innovation: A case study analysis. *Journal of Database Marketing*, 10(1), pp. 71–83.

Pels, J. (1999). Exchange relationships in consumer markets. *European Journal of Marketing*, 33(1/2), pp. 19–37.

Pels, J., Brodie, R.J., & Johnston, W.J. (2004). Benchmarking business-to-business practices in emerging and developed economies: Argentina compared to the USA and New Zealand. *Journal of Business and Industrial Marketing*, 19(6), pp. 386–396.

Pels, J., Coviello, N.E., & Brodie, R.J. (2000). Integrating transactional and relational marketing exchange: A pluralistic perspective. *Journal of Marketing Theory and Practice*, 8(3), pp. 11–20.

Purchase, S. (2018). Personal communication.

Ritter, T., Wilkinson, I.F., & Johnston, W.J. (2004). Managing in complex business networks. *Industrial Marketing Management*, 33(3), pp. 175–183.

Robinson, P.J., Faris, C.W., & Wind, Y. (1967). *Industrial Buying and Creative Marketing*. Boston: Allyn & Bacon.

Sheth, J. (1973). A model of industrial buyer behaviour. *Journal of Marketing*, 37(4), pp. 50–56.

Sheth, J.M., Gardner, D.M., & Garrett, D.E. (1988). *Marketing Theory: Evolution and Evaluation*. New York: John Wiley and Sons.

Snehota, I. & Håkansson, H. (Eds.) (1995). *Developing Relationships in Business Networks*. London: Routledge.

Soutar, G.N., Wilkinson, I., & Young, L. (2015). Research performance of marketing academics and departments: An international comparison. *Australasian Marketing Journal*, 23(2), pp. 155–161.

Storbacka, K., Brodie, R.J., Böhmann, T., Maglio, P.P., & Nenonen, S. (2016). Actor engagement in service ecosystems: Directions for further research. *Journal of Business Research*, 69(8), pp. 3008–3017.

Turnbull, P.W. & Cunningham, M.T. (1981). *International Marketing and Purchasing*. London: Macmillan.

Turnbull, P., Ford, D., & Cunningham, M. (1996). Interaction, relationships and networks in business markets: An evolving perspective. *Journal of Business and Industrial Marketing*, 11(3/4), pp. 44–62.

Vargo, S.L. & Lusch, R.F. (2008). Service dominant logic: Continuing the evolution. *Journal of the Academy of Marketing Science*, 36(1), pp. 1–10.

Vargo, S.L. & Lusch, R.F. (2017). Service-dominant logic 2025. *International Journal of Research in Marketing*, 34(1), pp. 46–67.

Wagner, R. (2005). Contemporary marketing practices in Russia. *European Journal of Marketing*, 39(1/2), pp. 199–215.

Walter, A., Ritter, T., & Gemünden, H.-G. (Eds.) (1997). *Relationships and Networks in International Markets*. London: Pergamon Press.

Walter, A., Ritter, T., & Gemünden, H.-G. (2001). Value creation in buyer-seller relationships: Theoretical considerations and empirical results from a supplier's perspective. *Industrial Marketing Management*, 30(4), pp. 365–377.

Webster, F.E. & Wind, Y. (1972). A general model for understanding organizational buying behaviour. *Journal of Marketing*, 36(2), pp. 12–19.

Wilson, D.T. (1995). An integrated model of buyer-seller relationships. *Journal of the Academy of Marketing Science*, 55(2), pp. 133–139.

Wuehrer, G.A. & Smejkal, A.E. (2013). Diversity in homogeneity: A longitudinal bibliometric review of Industrial Marketing and Purchasing (IMP) Group Conferences from 1984 to 2012. *The IMP Journal*, 7(3), pp. 140–158.

APPENDIX

Table 4.A1 IMP research: selected books and journal articles and number of citations

Author(s), title, and details	Number of citations
Anderson, J., Håkansson, H., & Johanson, J. (1994). Dyadic business relationships within a business network context. *Journal of Marketing*, 58(4), pp. 1–15.	3,078
Bengtsson, M. & Kock, S. (2000). 'Coopetition' in business networks: To cooperate and compete simultaneously. *Industrial Marketing Management*, 29(5), pp. 411–426.	1,995
Ford, D. (1980). The development of buyer-seller relationships in industrial markets. *European Journal of Marketing*, 14(5/6), pp. 339–353.	1,748
Ford, D. (Ed.) (1990). *Understanding Business Markets: Interactions, Relationships and Networks*. London: Academic Press.	1,506
Ford, D., Gadde, L.-E., Håkansson, H., Lundgren, A., Snehota, I., Turnbull, P., & Wilson, D. (1998). *Managing Business Relationships*. New York: John Wiley & Sons.	2,298
Håkansson, H. (Ed.) (1982). *International Marketing and Purchasing: An Interaction Approach*. Chichester: John Wiley & Sons.	4,164
Håkansson, H. (1987). *Industrial Technological Development: A Network Approach*. London: Croom Helm.	2,067
Håkansson, H. (1989). *Corporate Technological Behaviour: Co-operation and Networks*. London: Routledge.	1,301
Håkansson, H. & Ford, D. (2002). How should companies interact in business networks? *Journal of Business Research*, 55(2), pp. 133–139.	1,725
Håkansson, H. & Johanson, J. (1992). A model of industrial networks. In Axelsson, B. & Easton, G. (Eds.), *Industrial Networks: A New View of Reality*. London: Routledge, pp. 28–34.	1,284
Håkansson, H. & Snehota, I. (1989). No business is an island: The network concept of business strategy. *Scandinavian Journal of Management*, 5(3), pp. 187–200.	2,130
Johanson, J. & Mattsson, L.-G. (1987). Interorganizational relations in industrial systems: A network approach compared with the transaction-cost approach. *International Studies of Management & Organization*, 17(1), pp. 34–48.	1,672
Johanson, J. & Mattsson, L.-G. (2015). Internationalisation in industrial systems: A network approach. In Forsgren, M., Holm, U., & Johanson, J. (Eds), *Knowledge, Networks and Power*. Basingstoke: Palgrave Macmillan, pp. 111–132.	2,824
Snehota, I. & Håkansson, H. (Eds.) (1995). *Developing Relationships in Business Networks*. London: Routledge.	4,812

Author(s), title, and details	Number of citations
Walter, A., Ritter, T., & Gemünden, H.-G. (2001). Value creation in buyer-seller relationships: Theoretical considerations and empirical results from a supplier's perspective. *Industrial Marketing Management*, 30(4), pp. 365–377.	1,166
Wilson, D.T. (1995). An integrated model of buyer-seller relationships. *Journal of the Academy of Marketing Science*, 55(2), pp. 133–139.	3,182

Table 4.A2   CMP research: journal articles and number of citations

Author(s), title, and details	Number of citations
Brady, M., Saren, M., & Tzokas, N. (2002). Integrating information technology into marketing. *Journal of Marketing Management*, 18(5/6), pp. 555–578.	152
Brodie, R.J., Coviello, N.E., Brooks, R.W., & Little, V. (1997). Towards a paradigm shift in marketing? An examination of current marketing practices. *Journal of Marketing Management*, 13(5), pp. 383–406.	544
Brodie, R.J., Winklhofer, H., Coviello, N.E., & Johnston, W.J. (2007). Is e-marketing coming of age? An examination of the penetration of e-marketing and firm performance. *Journal of Interactive Marketing*, 21(1), pp. 2–21.	224
Brookes, R.W., Brodie, R.J., Coviello, N.E., & Palmer, R.A. (2004). How managers perceive the impacts of information technologies on contemporary practices: Reinforcing, enhancing or transforming? *Journal of Relationship Marketing Management*, 3(4), pp. 7–26.	58
Coviello, N.E. & Brodie, R.J. (1998). From transaction to relationship marketing: An investigation of managerial perceptions and practices. *Journal of Strategic Marketing*, 6(3), pp. 171–186.	339
Coviello, N.E. & Brodie, R.J. (2001). Contemporary marketing practices of consumer and business-to-business firms: How different are they? *Journal of Business and Industrial Marketing*, 16(5), pp. 382–400.	188
Coviello, N.E., Brodie, R.J., Brookes, R.W., & Palmer, R.A. (2003). Assessing the role of e-marketing in contemporary marketing practice. *Journal of Marketing Management*, 9(7), pp. 857–881.	58
Coviello, N.E., Brodie, R.J., Danaher, P.J., & Johnston, W.J. (2002). How firms relate to their markets: An empirical examination of contemporary marketing practice. *Journal of Marketing*, 66(3), pp. 33–46.	660
Coviello, N.E., Brodie, R.H., & Munro, H.J. (1997). Understanding contemporary marketing: Development of a classification scheme. *Journal of Marketing Management*, 13(6), pp. 501–522.	660
Coviello, N.E., Brodie, R.J., & Munro, H.J. (2000). An investigation of marketing practice by firm size. *Journal of Business Venturing*, 15(5/6), pp. 523–545.	343

Author(s), title, and details	Number of citations
Coviello, N.E., Milley, R., & Marcolin, B. (2001). Understanding IT-enabled interactivity in contemporary marketing. *Journal of Interactive Marketing*, 15(4), pp. 18–33.	245
Coviello, N.E., Winklhofer, H., & Hamilton, K. (2006). Marketing practices and performance of small service firms: An examination in the tourism accommodation sector. *Journal of Service Research*, 9(1), pp. 38–58.	123
Lindgreen, A., Davis, R., Brodie, R.J., & Buchanan-Oliver, M. (2000). Pluralism in contemporary marketing practices. *International Journal of Bank Marketing*, 18(6), pp. 294–308.	123
Lindgreen, A., Palmer, R., & Vanhamme, J. (2004). Contemporary marketing practice: Theoretical propositions and practical implications. *Marketing Intelligence & Planning*, 22(6), pp. 673–692.	105
Lindgreen, A., Palmer, R., Vanhamme, J., & Wouters, J.P.M. (2006). A relationship-management assessment tool: Questioning, identifying, and prioritizing critical aspects of customer relationships. *Industrial Marketing Management*, 35(1), pp. 57–71.	209
Lindgreen, A., Palmer, R., Wetzels, M., & Antioco, M. (2008). Do different marketing practices require different leadership styles? An exploratory study. *Journal of Business & Industrial Marketing*, 24(1), pp. 114–126.	53
Pels, J. (1999). Exchange relationships in consumer markets. *European Journal of Marketing*, 33(1/2), pp. 19–37.	172
Pels, J., Brodie, R.J., & Johnston, W.J. (2004). Benchmarking business-to-business practices in emerging and developed economies: Argentina compared to the USA and New Zealand. *Journal of Business and Industrial Marketing*, 19(6), pp. 386–396.	51
Pels, J., Coviello, N.E., & Brodie, R.J. (2000). Integrating transactional and relational marketing exchange: A pluralistic perspective. *Journal of Marketing Theory and Practice*, 8(3), pp. 11–20.	98
Wagner, R. (2005). Contemporary marketing practices in Russia. *European Journal of Marketing*, 39(1/2), pp. 199–215.	71

5. Writing research funding applications
Adam Lindgreen, C. Anthony Di Benedetto, Camilla Verdich, Joëlle Vanhamme, Vinod Venkatraman, Steven Pattinson, Ann Højbjerg Clarke, and Zaheer Khan

1. INTRODUCTION

Industrial Marketing Management aims to promote the best research, with relevant implications for academics and practitioners—a goal that similarly has gained widespread attention in recent years (Bartunek & Rynes, 2014; Carton & Mouricou, 2017; Kieser, Nicolai, & Seidl, 2015; Toffel, 2016), such that both governments and research funding bodies (e.g., strategic research councils) offer funding only for research that has relevance to consumers, practitioners, or policy makers. Universities increasingly demand that their faculty obtain research funding (Blume-Kohout, Kumar, & Sood, 2015). Attracting such research funding can be significant for academics, in terms of developing impactful research, enhancing their career prospects, and closing the research–relevance gap (Bloch, Graverson, & Pedersen, 2014; Gerritsen, Plug, & van der Wiel, 2013). Along with this increasing pressure on faculty to seek external research funding, many countries have cut their funding of higher education, sometimes dramatically (Tandberg, 2010), drastically limiting the amount of funding available.

The combination of these trends increases competition and rejection rates for research funding, with potentially detrimental effects on funding efforts and research funding income for the future. Considering the current climate surrounding business schools, or universities in general, external research funding will remain an important priority and qualification for most researchers. In this crucial, competitive, challenging setting, very little guidance exists to help researchers develop effective research funding applications, however. Although some broad literature suggests general guidelines, we also note the lack of insights into research funding efforts related to business-to-business marketing management. With this chapter, we attempt to establish a comprehensive set of guidelines to assist researchers in this field, by addressing some key topics.

First, we examine the importance of leadership (department, school, or university level) for creating a culture in which researchers regard applying for research funding as one of their primary tasks. Relatedly, we outline strategies and action plans that leaders can implement to encourage, develop, support, and reward researchers who actively pursue funding. Second, we explore the benefits of exploiting various relationships and networks to identify funding opportunities. Third, we consider research support offices, which many schools feature and which offer a range of services related to strategic and practical aspects of applying for research funding. Fourth, we scrutinize actual research funding applications to explicate both the evaluation process and the elements in an application that reviewers seek from research funding applications. Fifth, and finally, we review two successful funding applications to gain a broader perspective. Throughout the chapter, we reflect on typical challenges for early-career researchers.

2. LEADERSHIP

Many business schools and universities set ambitious goals of increasing their research funding exponentially in coming years. Researchers who attract research funding should be rewarded, and leaders should offer realistic, in-kind support to contribute to the feasibility of the proposed research project and demonstrate the support of the host organization. When successful funding applications become a prerequisite for tenure or promotion (Fischer & Zigmond, 1998), early-career researchers must balance the demand that they publish articles in top journals with their need to write successful research funding applications (Lindgreen, Vallaster, & Vanhamme, 2001). Thus, the start of an academic career can be a very stressful period, requiring careful consideration of ways to deal with the varying demands, some of which we discuss next.

At university level, when research funding is on the agenda, senior management might be willing to send all the incoming funds to the successful departments (or applicants) or supplement that funding, insofar as charging no overhead costs. Such forms of support encourage departments and their faculty to seek funding.

At the department level, the head might organize seminars to instruct early-career researchers in how to write good applications or identify relevant research foundations (Porter, 2011). The seminars also could outline key questions that every application should answer, detail the funding landscape, and predict future developments. With sufficient knowledge about different research foundations and research funding elements, the head of the department can assess whether a particular researcher or research group is likely to be successful in attracting a specific research funding. Based on these insights, the head of department can encourage good combinations of research ideas, researchers, and funding agencies.

A series of research seminars also can encourage faculty members who might feel discouraged or are having trouble receiving funding. They should cover various question topics, including the following:

- How did you get the idea for your research?
- How did this idea become an actual research project on which you worked?
- Do you ever get discouraged?
- How do you motivate yourself when discouraged?
- Have you changed any scholarly habits to become even more productive?

Furthermore, research seminars allow visiting academics to meet with individual faculty members who share similar research interests and want to discuss their research in progress. These visiting academics then can expand the department's existing relationships and networks, as well as encourage new perspectives and ideas. Furthermore, visiting academics can help early-career researchers take stock of their efforts and likelihood of garnering funding. Similarly, informal brown-bag seminars allow faculty members to present their projects in progress to their peers and ask for advice, comments, and suggestions.

Considering their many responsibilities, heads of department might establish a research funding committee and delegate responsibility to this committee to promote the quality and quantity of funding applications. Such committees also help lower barriers to applying for research funding, spread knowhow and information about research funding opportunities, and supplement centrally coordinated efforts by the university's research support office. In addition, formal training should be available by the research support office to suggest a structured approach to crafting a successful application. Some schools maintain dedicated programs to support early-career researchers; others provide specific suggestions for drawing up research budgets or administering research funds.

A chairperson of a research funding committee should receive credit for work hours devoted to tasks such as (see also Porter, 2011):

- Chairing departmental research funding committee and leading its meetings.
- Maintaining ongoing, direct contact with the research support office.
- Assisting the head of department in formulating a research funding strategy.
- Working toward meeting the department's research funding goals.

- Answering research funding-related queries from top management.
- Serving as the first point of contact for research funding-related issues.
- Coordinating obligatory or voluntary internal peer reviews of applications.
- Establishing strategic alliances with other research-intensive institutions.
- Organizing seminars, such as department meetings to present various aspects of fundraising, selective meetings for faculty members actively seeking research funding, or writing clubs to read and comment on one another's ideas and applications.
- Establishing subgroups that investigate research funding from industry actors.

With regard to incentives at the individual level to increase submissions of successful funding applications, the head of the department might award applicants work hours to application writing, as well as buy-out time if they receive the funding and the inclusion of research funding as a criterion for promotion. Heads of department should establish these optimal conditions. For example, to incentivize research funding efforts, heads of department might send a strong signal by giving early-career researchers explicit time to work on promising research applications (judged by the quality of the research topic, rationale, and strength of the applicant). The overhead costs for successful funding applications also could be channeled back to funding holders; obtaining funding should be evaluated positively in personnel reviews. Highly ranked research publications resulting from a research project could be awarded with money deposited in the individual researcher's account, which then could be used to facilitate new funding applications.

During annual reviews, heads of departments should discuss detailed research plans with faculty members, including how they plan to develop successful research funding applications. This information should detail the likely applications to be submitted in the next one, three, and five years. Successful research funding then would be important elements to inform recruitment and promotion decisions.

Faculty members also should discuss their research plans with mentors, because research plans are intrinsically connected to funding applications. In fact, each faculty member should have an opportunity to work with a mentor (internal or external to the department), especially if they plan to apply for big research funding. The purpose of a mentoring system is not solely for mentors to work with mentees on particular research projects; rather, it is to offer a framework for discussing pertinent issues. Support from an experienced mentor, who has attracted external funding and been involved in assessing grant applications, is invaluable to early-career researchers. Some supervisors also might have their own funding that allows them to support their students and projects by early-career colleagues (Lindgreen, Palmer, Vanhamme, &

Beverland, 2002). With mentors, early-career researchers should discuss a strategy for seeking realistic research funding, as well as ways to optimize the proposed research project to reflect the available foundations and instruments.

Individual faculty members might want to form their own funding application writing club, though most projects should be presented in a brown-bag seminar before being entered into the writing club. Considering the variety of research interests within any given department, more than one writing club could form. To support them, departments could invite a leading academic in the field to attend writing club meetings—an initiative that also could lead to longer term collaborations between faculty members and leading academics. Writing clubs offer several key opportunities. First, when scholars are considering whether to devote significant time and effort to a funding application, they can draw on other colleagues' previous experience to help make their determination. Second, other early-career researchers can contribute to and co-author research funding applications. Funding writing skills require training to develop, and obtaining even small funding can provide early-career researchers with a sense of independence, as well as a new entry for their CVs. Third, writing club members can discuss research funding, to specify which investment strategies they might match (i.e., a project could respond to calls for different funding, interdisciplinary research, post doc and mobility research funding, excellence funding, or industrial collaboration).

Departments likely regard larger funding amounts as more important; the production and transaction costs are proportionally higher for projects with smaller funding. At research-intensive universities, departments also prioritize research projects that lead to academic publications, rather than consultancy tasks. In such settings, consultancy-based funding applications should be minimized, along with empirical analyses that do not meet the requirements for potential publication in influential academic journals. Yet to the frustration of academics, government-backed funds often focus on research activities designed to aid businesses or enterprises. Thus researchers face a dilemma: Academic journals prioritize micro-analyses that lead to new theoretical insights, but government-backed research funding supports aggregated, cross-disciplinary analyses at the macro or meso level.

The ongoing challenge is to find government-funded projects that also lead to findings that can be published in influential academic journals. For example, a disconnect often arises between research objectives and research funding opportunities, but rather than trying to build tenuous connections, researchers need to find funding opportunities that already reveal synergies with their own research agenda. Research funding applications that pertain to the researchers' area of expertise also provide them with an opportunity to kill two birds with one stone: complete the application and receive funding, then potentially publish the findings of the funded research project in peer-reviewed journals.

If it leverages his or her existing research expertise, the funding application also gains credibility, because reviewers take researchers' curriculum vitae (CV) into consideration in their evaluations. The quality of the CV can be as important as the promise of the research project, because it can demonstrate a match among the proposed research project, the competences of the researcher, and the goals of the funding agency.

3. RELATIONSHIPS AND NETWORKS

No researchers are alone in their funding writing, though it may seem that way sometimes. Thus another option for the department is to seek strategic alliances with key research institutions to increase the quality of its research funding applications (e.g., inviting renowned scholars to join the applications), as well as the number of large-scale research projects in which the department serves as a partner (e.g., linking to other research institutions with potential synergistic effects). Even early-career researchers have personal networks that they should leverage to develop their research grant applications. Partaking in cross-disciplinary strategic alliances with other institutions can be effective, because government agencies often prefer aggregated, cross-disciplinary projects. Beyond the strategic alliances, networking and faculty members' ability to produce attractive applications are key outcomes of such efforts. Networks provide access to nationally and internationally dispersed colleagues, who might have complementary research expertise or interests, as is often required by funding agencies. For example, the Global Challenges Research Fund requires grant applications to include at least one partner organization from the DAC List of ODA Recipients (OECD, 2018), a list that identifies all countries and territories eligible to receive official development assistance.

Willing partners are available among the network of working relationships that researchers develop, and some funding agencies prioritize such research support, which in turn may reveal funding opportunities. Academic institutions also provide support for preparing applications or even internal funding for cross-disciplinary projects. An industry association could be looking to fund a certain number of research projects per year.

Many national and international research funding bodies invest in individual and collaborative funding. Collaborative funding offers opportunities to strengthen networks. In some cases, a researcher needs to take the lead on a large-scale application; in other cases, an effective strategy is to join applications led by other researchers. It is important to maintain an ongoing dialogue with close collaborators to discuss upcoming opportunities and options to participate in others' applications.

To find funding in creative ways, researchers can search publications by industry associations, which may offer funding or access to databases. Many universities have their own research institutes, such as the Institute for the Study of Business Markets (www.isbm.org), headquartered at Pennsylvania State University. In addition, business-to-business marketing management researchers should check the current list of research priorities by the Marketing Science Institute (www.msi.org). A priority research topic is more likely to produce a successful research funding application.

Researchers also should be prepared to move beyond their traditional networks or comfort zones. Many collaborative research funding call for interdisciplinary or intersector approaches, so scholars should identify researchers from other disciplines who might provide complementary competences. They could even prepare a short pitch, explaining how others might contribute and what the impact of their contribution would be. For example, a researcher working on business-to-business product innovation might want to find a colleague from the engineering school who can offer product development insights; industrial designers could be good collaborators for research projects studying the functionality, aesthetics, or ergonomics of new products.

Learning from colleagues also can be an inspiration. Early-career researchers should identify colleagues who have succeeded in obtaining similar funding, because they can offer advice about how they prepared their application or review a new application. They might even share a copy of their own successful application for inspiration. Furthermore, they likely will reveal where they obtained support and resources. A funding writing specialist in the research support office will have extensive experience writing big proposals and can contribute to ensure all the paperwork is in order and deadlines are met.

The hosting university also might offer research funding or funding-in-aid, providing seed money for exploratory research or pilot tests. These application processes tend to be less daunting, and promising early results based on this funding can be beneficial for subsequent, external applications. In this effort, early-career researchers still need to identify research priorities; if the dean of research introduces a new initiative to support cross-functional research, faculty members may be more likely to get funding to work with colleagues in other departments, so business-to-business researchers might study big data analytics with a management information systems scholar or distribution logistics with a transportation or supply chain management researcher.

Finally, researchers should attend conferences and seminars devoted to research topics that match the requirements of funding agencies. National and international conferences feature works in progress by relevant colleagues, which may help researchers refine their own research plans. Internally, brown-bag seminars with visiting professors are critical to attend, especially those that range beyond business-to-business marketing. A consumer behavioral researcher presenting on the wisdom of crowds or the effectiveness of social media marketing might stimulate interesting ideas for business-to-business marketing applications. The avenues for further research that appear at the end of most published articles also offer good sources of inspiration.

4. RESEARCH SUPPORT OFFICE

As noted, most universities have a research support office that offers services related to strategic and practical aspects of applying for research funding. Whether at a central university or department level, this office will have thorough experience with the general techniques of funding writing, as well as with specific funding instruments. Yet even with these helpful services, many researchers use the research support offices only at the last minute and for mandatory aspects, such as gaining approval of a research budget or obtaining signatures on formal documents. We recommend that early-career researchers get in touch with the research support office as soon as they consider applying for a research funding, then exploit all of its available services and advice (e.g., outlining the fundraising strategy, obtaining invitations to funding writing workshops and information meetings, obtaining templates for elements of the application, contacting other research funding holders willing to share their experience). In addition, research support office personnel may be available to read and provide feedback on draft versions of applications. They likely are already in contact with key funding bodies, so they can provide pertinent advice. Starting early and involving support staff enables researchers to complete the administrative elements of the application easily, then obtain feedback about how to fine-tune the scientific and technical elements of the application.

Larger private research foundations and national funding agencies also represent sources of advice, information, and support. Researchers should not hesitate to contact research foundations; they often appreciate the dialogue and are interested in attracting as many strong applications as possible. The research foundations might agree to check the formalities of incoming applications, such as whether they meet the overall scope. However, they rarely are involved in the actual evaluation or selection of successful applications. For EU funding, researchers can obtain guidance from their national contact point, who can be identified by a search on the EU website, often functioning within national agencies tasked with encouraging research and innovation.

5. RESEARCH FUNDING APPLICATION

A good research funding application provides reviewers with all the relevant information in a clear and accessible manner, allowing them to become excited and assess the proposal according to the evaluation criteria established by the research foundation. The evaluation criteria might vary somewhat, but key questions usually revolve around what, why, how, who, and where queries. That is, reviewers assess:

- What—the research idea;
- Why—the extent to which the research addresses an important problem or challenge in a novel and groundbreaking manner and to whom it is important;
- How—the objectives and methods and its potential impact, in terms of how the research might change science or the world;
- Who—including the research profile and competences of the applicants; and
- Where—reflecting the research environment with respect to both access to appropriate infrastructures and the intellectual setting.

More concrete evaluation criteria likely are available on the research foundation's website. Researchers should pay close attention to these criteria while developing their funding applications, to ensure they provide reviewers with easily accessible answers and meet all the listed criteria in a logical, clear manner. In addition, the project description must follow the exact instructions listed in the research call. We describe some generic elements of nearly all project descriptions in the following sections.

Writing a research funding application is not the same as writing a doctoral research proposal. The writing style for a funding application, for example, should differ from the traditional style required by academic writing. Porter (2007) summarizes key differences: The writing should be persuasive and personal, selling the research idea and conveying excitement in accessible language with short sentences, supported with bullet points and key phrases. A funding application should focus on demonstrating that the proposed project matches the goals set by the research foundation, as well as describing its objectives, proposed activities, and expected outcomes. This future-oriented description of the actions to be taken also should detail the important problem that the project will address. Verbosity and incomprehensible text, with unexplained abbreviations, poor grammar, or spelling errors, will have negative influences on evaluations.

Furthermore, writing a doctoral research proposal usually means starting from scratch, without having conducted any research or collected any data to test the hypotheses. Some doctoral students do not even have specific hypotheses when they write their doctoral research proposals. An application for a research funding differs significantly. Most funding applications refer to projects that researchers partly have conducted or started. The findings from their preliminary studies suggest the need for additional, follow-up studies, and such needs represent the foundation for a logical application that can appeal to research funding agencies.

Yet researchers cannot get caught in 'autopilot mode' when developing their funding applications. Early-career researchers often acquire, mostly unconsciously, routines and practices during their doctoral training, which they continue to apply in various settings, reflecting a sort of unconscious competence (Luft & Ingham, 1955) or heuristic reasoning (Ippoliti, 2015). For example, researchers might unthinkingly apply existing routines and practices to craft research questions, design their empirical studies, or write methodology sections. Yet such routines and practices might not be standard in other domains and fields. Therefore, the ways that researchers need to write, justify, and explain their research pursuits for one funding application may be very different from what they need to do for another (Porter, 2007).

In particular, a key goal is to find a balance between using technical jargon (to convey subject matter expertise) and simplicity (to appeal to a broad audience of unknown research funding reviewers) when writing an application. That is, researchers must write well enough for everyone on the review panel to understand their applications, but also convey specific details about the proposed research project in a sufficiently technical manner.

The target readers of a research funding application are its evaluators; the researcher's aim is to prompt the best possible evaluation from these reviewers. Understanding reviewers and the evaluation process thus is critical. Typical reviewers are scientists who might not have expertise within the researcher's particular research area. They often conduct their evaluations outside regular work hours, donating their efforts and time voluntarily. In addition, they may be responsible for reviewing dozens of applications, on a long list of predefined evaluation criteria. Thus, the best funding applications are easy to follow, convey excitement about the project, and provide all the information the reviewer might need. Some reviewers develop an impression of the quality of the application quickly; the rest of the time they devote to the review (whether 15 minutes or several hours) involves identifying relevant information that confirms (or contradicts) their initial view and completing the assessment forms.

Due to the vast number of applications a reviewer will assess, using predefined evaluation criteria (to make a good first impression), the application structure must follow the exact guidelines listed in the call for proposals. Reviewers should be able to get a sense of the project from the abstract and accompanying illustrations, so that they read more detailed parts more closely to gain insights into particular details, rather than desperately searching for the overall meaning. According to the Danish Agency of Science and Higher Education (2018), reviewers skim funding applications to obtain an overview and familiarize themselves with the proposed project. The abstract is key; it gives the reviewer an idea of the underlying idea and can convey excitement and enthusiasm. Researchers should regard the abstract of their application like a 'movie trailer' that captures readers' interest and offers a solid argument for embracing the overall research project. After having read the abstract, the reviewer should be excited about the research project, understand the main idea, and agree that, overall, it matches the research foundation's goals. In this case, the reviewer will look forward to reading the rest of the application, anticipating that it will be exiting and a pleasure to read and evaluate.

Another useful element is the estimation of the time needed to conduct a research project, although this is not an easy task. It becomes even more difficult when we realize that reviewers with one funding agency might reject an application as insufficiently ambitious (e.g., if the project will take X years, the research should do more), even as reviewers from another funding agency reject the same application for the opposite reason (e.g., a research project that lasts the same X years could not possibly achieve all that the application proposes). This ambiguity and the ultimate review response often depends on whether the review panel is familiar with the type of research and methodology proposed. Thus, applicants must justify their workload, as well as why the time scale they propose is appropriate. They also need to adjust their predictions to the agency; funding applications funded by public institutions versus industry actors differ greatly in the expected timelines. Compared with public institutions, industry agencies often require significantly shorter time scales and expect funded research projects to be completed faster, so that the findings can be used while the topic is still relevant and timely. Industry funding sources also tend to care little about researchers' academic schedules (e.g., exam periods, heavy teaching periods), so applicants might find themselves devoting much of their time to working on their research project. Such demands require that they confirm they can fit the research project into their work agenda, perhaps with innovative solutions (e.g., moving some teaching responsibilities to another semester).

The layout of the application, including its illustrations and graphics, are useful elements. Key illustrations should explain the overall concept and methodology; the time scale could be represented in a Gantt chart, revealing the organization of the project. Guidelines for graphical abstracts are available from Elsevier (https://www.elsevier.com/authors/journal-authors/graphical-abstract) and other publishers. An ideal approach would be to prepare four or five simple, high-quality illustrations designed to present the research project to a broad audience, then incorporate these illustrations into the application with appropriate titles and legends. The illustrations should capture the essence of what the research foundation wants, such as interdisciplinary approaches or applications of knowledge to achieve societal impacts. A good graphic is easier to recall than several pages of text when evaluating applications.

Budget predictions are critical, with several effects on funding applications. To derive a research budget for a funding application, researchers must identify different categories that require funding, such as personnel, graduate student support, equipment, materials, and supplies. Then they can delve deeper into each category. For example, graduate student support budgets must include students' fringe benefits (e.g., health insurance) and tuition, in addition to their stipends. Beyond these categories, funding applications should account for indirect expenses, which typically are a percentage of research funding, charged by universities for administering them. Some funding agencies impose restrictions on which budget items they will support and the amount of indirect expenses they are prepared to pay. Thus researchers must discuss with and gain approval from their university for their budgets, prior to submitting their application.

The ultimate success of an application requires nearly unanimous approval from a sizable group of reviewers (Porter, 2007). After having read an application, the primary and secondary reviewers need to be passionate about the research project and should be equipped with strong arguments to convey their support to the rest of the review panel and overcome any concerns. Here again, the abstract and illustrations are important assets, easily accessible to review panel members who might not have read the full application. A video entitled *NIH Peer Review Revealed* (https://www.youtube.com/watch?v=fBDxI6l4dOA) provides a front-row seat to an NIH peer review meeting, in which real scientists review fictional but realistic funding applications for their scientific merit. As this video shows, the reviewers discuss their evaluation criteria, including the need for them to feel excited and enthusiastic, rather than concerned or struggling with the information.

Therefore, a good funding application achieves the following outcomes (Porter, 2005): Reviewers immediately recognize the interesting, innovative ideas contained in the proposal and how those ideas will contribute to addressing the objectives put forth by the research foundation in the call for research proposals, as well as to moving the research field forward. Then the reviewers can devote their attention to the concrete aims, hypotheses, and methods, as well as their consistency (Porter, 2005). The contribution to the state of the art, the presence of some preliminary data, appropriate identifications of potential risks, and solid contingency plans all can help eliminate potential concerns and affirm that the research project will be feasible. Table 5.1 summarizes elements of a typical research funding application.

Table 5.1   *Elements of research funding applications*

Elements	Description
Abstract	The abstract is the first thing reviewers read; in some cases, it is the only thing all reviewers read. Thus, the abstract must offer a solid argument for the proposed research and leave reviewers excited and interested in reading the rest of the application. The abstract should give a clear picture of the objectives, why the project is important, what the expected outcomes are, and how these outcomes will be accomplished.
Introduction	A short introduction can present the central problem, challenge, or question that the research proposal aims to address, thereby allowing reviewers to recognize why the research project is important and how it promises to solve a problem, challenge, or question.
Background and state of the art	The background section should provide an overview of the current state of the art and demonstrate the researcher's solid foundation and contributions to this research area. Many researchers try to pack too many details into this section, offering reviews of the entire research field. In contrast, the goal should be to provide a brief, educational summary of the background that is pertinent for the particular research project, clearly demonstrating knowledge gaps or methodological weaknesses that have limited progression and setting the scene for how the proposed research project will advance the field.
Preliminary results	The presentation of preliminary results should demonstrate the soundness of the research idea, hypotheses, and proposed approach. Researchers should avoid offering a rash of data that seem to imply that the research project is already completed.
Objectives and hypotheses	This section gives direction to the whole research proposal. It might present an overarching goal or objective, in addition to more concrete objectives. Some pitfalls to avoid include presenting only vague overall goals or confusing the objectives with the tasks and deliverables. The objectives are concrete steps toward accomplishing the goal of the research project. In some cases, this section follows right after the introduction, whereas in others, the background section is necessary to set the foundation for understanding the objectives and hypotheses.

Elements	Description
Work plan and methodological approach	This next section contains the plan for achieving specific objectives. It should start with a description of the research strategy, reflecting insights into knowledge gaps and the preliminary results. Then it can provide an overview of the studies that will constitute the project. With this information, reviewers can gain an overview of the project and its elements. Furthermore, this section should refer to the Gantt diagram, which provides a graphic overview of the methodological approaches, deliverables, and milestones.
	Then each study or work package should be presented within dedicated subsections. These subsections might repeat specific objectives, present hypotheses, and summarize the background and rationale for each part of the study. The description of the concrete research approach then should contain the appropriate level of detail and, when relevant, deliverables and milestones. Each subsection should conclude with a summary of the outcome and interpretation—that is, one or two sentences to describe what will be available at the end of this stage and how it will feed into the rest of the research project. It is not appropriate to present a detailed protocol for each study; reviewers instead need to be convinced that the objectives can be achieved and understand how, so too many details can be overwhelming.
	Finally, a separate section should summarize the risks and contingency plans to demonstrate a complete sense of the research project, including potential difficulties and solid strategies for handling them. A short section on ethical considerations also may be relevant.
Organization and feasibility	This section supports reviewers' evaluations of the research environment, project leadership, and feasibility. In collaborative projects, it should summarize the roles, contributions, experiences, and competences of each partner. The research budget and time scale can be cited briefly, to highlight the feasibility of the proposed project. The contributions from the host organization also might be mentioned here, to underline its commitment and the feasibility of the project. Researchers must make sure to provide clear information about who will lead any collaborative research projects.
Dissemination and communication of results	In describing plans for disseminating the findings, this section should cite specific conferences and journals, as well as options for sharing the information with stakeholders such as industrial partners, policy makers, and the general public. The details in this section should match the research foundation's emphasis and priorities.

Elements	Description
Originality, significance, and expected impacts	Finally, the funding application needs to emphasize the novelty and originality of the proposed project, its potential to advance the field, and the expected societal impacts. This section thus offers an important link back to the introduction, describing the problem to be solved or question answered. The expected societal impacts or key performance indicators may be more prominent, depending on the focus of the research foundation. Many private research foundations (and the EU) prioritize societal impact considerations.
Additional elements	Moreover, some application packages should include CVs from any co-applicants, publication lists, a letter of commitment from the host institution, collaboration agreements, and research budget information. These documents meet the guidelines established by the research foundation; they also should be revised and optimized to match the evaluation criteria. For example, researchers might expand their CVs to include a section on leadership and a summary of previous research, highlighting aspects that demonstrate they are appropriate recipients of research funding.

6. TWO CASES

Two cases of successful research funding offer a broader perspective on our recommendations. One case involved a consortium of researchers applying for Danish regional research funding; the other case sought funding from a leading UK agency.

6.1 Case 1: Danish Regional Research Funding

As a researcher at a research intensive university, the principal investigator (located at the University of Southern Denmark) has driven or actively participated in 12 successful funding applications to Danish and European funding agencies, earning funding that totals close to 4 million euro. The applications pertain to public–private innovation, design, and business model innovation. A team of researchers and anywhere from three to 12 consortia partners participated in these funding applications.

Started in 2015 and scheduled to finish in 2019, the research project received a total of 7.4 million euro; the partnering university (i.e., University of Southern Denmark) received 1.2 million euro of the total. The purpose of the research project is to strengthen the growth and innovation capacity of regional small- and medium-sized companies by developing increased use and competences for design, including design thinking, strategic design, and design-driven innovation. Furthermore, the research project aims to increase innovation cooperation between companies and knowledge institutions, as well as the total number of innovative companies in the region (i.e., southern Denmark). The research project consists of nine subprojects; the University of Southern Denmark leads three of them ("Reframe the Future," "Value Chain Innovation," and "Accumulation of Knowledge and Reporting across the Work Packages").

The research project was not broken down into subprojects initially, and there was not sufficient discussion of the collaboration among consortium partners or the integration and interactions of the different subprojects. This gap resulted in several challenges, which required revisions to the funding application. Forming the consortium and writing the funding application was a long and political process. As the partners sought to agree on core ideas and align their roles, other research projects spun out.

The process began in 2014, when the Region of Southern Denmark announced plans to bring together and support design activities and actors in the region. The initial consortium consisted of three public incubators, four municipalities, four educational institutions, and the design-cluster office. In numerous meetings among the consortium partners and leading administrators and politicians from various municipalities, the purpose was to align the partners around a common vision and understanding of the core idea and concept of the funding application, as well as determining the roles of the different partners and the administration of the project. This stage ended with the realization that the interests of the initial consortium partners were too diverse for a collective agreement. Therefore, three municipalities, three incubators, and University of Southern Denmark's entrepreneurship institution left the consortium (but continued in a separate collaboration, which earned funding for another research project focused on entrepreneurship and growth among design and creative companies).

The reduced consortium, consisting of two educational institutions (Design School Kolding and University of Southern Denmark), the publicly funded design cluster Design2innovate (located in southern Denmark), the Capital of Children (an innovation unit formed by Billund municipality and the LEGO foundation), and Kolding municipality continued and completed the funding application. With a reduced consortium, the work progressed faster. The research application eventually included nine subprojects. To support cooperation, the consortium had to agree on a common vision and understanding, as well as establish trust among the partners and recognition of one another's skills. The consortium partners realized that understanding other partners' motivations and competences would help them develop a research project that matched their own goals.

To write the funding application, the first step was to understand the strategy and plans of the Region of Southern Denmark's fund. The consortium partners studied the regional fund's strategy and previously funded projects. Next, the consortium partners discussed the overall purpose of their proposed research project, then shaped their arguments according to various steps of the research project. The administrative managers from the partnering institutions reached agreement. The planning and description of some subprojects started immediately after the consortium partners had agreed on the overall research purpose, which further improved understanding and agreement among the partners. Some subprojects emerged later in the process; the partners entered into dialogues with the regional fund to understand how it perceived the relevance of these subprojects. This feedback helped ensure that the funding application and subprojects matched the regional fund's scope.

When writing the application for three subprojects led by the University of Southern Denmark, the consortium partners pondered research questions they wanted to publish in academic journals, yet the application never explicitly mentioned these research questions. Rather, it described the problem that companies in the region were seeking to address. Consortium partners had to look for evidence that this problem also was of academic interest, using academic sources and a report from the Danish Industry Association. These sources together convinced the regional fund that the research questions were both legitimate and relevant.

The chairperson of the board of the design-cluster office facilitated two meetings with groups of companies potentially interested in participating in the research project, designed to understand the companies' needs and get their commitment to participate. Part of the process planning the different subprojects also involved finding ways to integrate them, even though different partnering institutions would conduct the subprojects.

The outcome was that the regional fund selected all subprojects for funding. Of interest is that the regional fund initially rejected one public–private innovation subproject involving Kolding municipality, arguing that this project was too distant from design, and that the regional fund already supported this type of research in other programs. The rejection led to the formation of a new subproject among the three municipalities and public–private innovation researchers from the University of Southern Denmark. The municipalities identified essential challenges in their welfare services that they had not been able to solve and sought a consortium of companies to address. The regional fund eventually chose to fund this research project.

The research consortium also discussed the integration of subprojects and the involvement of the partnering institutions. This part of the research project remains challenging. The consortium plans to seek collaboration with companies at a much earlier stage for its future funding applications, which is particularly feasible because it has established close working relationships with many companies.

Perhaps the most interesting learning outcome of working with a regional fund is the access it provides to exceptional empirical data. The researchers collaborate closely with both public institutions and private companies. In addition, to ensure the academic quality of the research, it may be necessary to apply for research funding from other places.

6.2 Case 2: Funding From a Leading UK Funding Agency

This research project involves colleagues from two universities (Birkbeck College University of London and University of Kent), dedicated to examining the relational and absorptive capabilities of service sector companies for co-creating radical or incremental innovations with supply chain partners. The research project is funded by the British Academy of Management's competitive research funding. With a multiple case study approach, the research project seeks to make important contributions to both extant literature and key stakeholders, reflecting both the service sector's important role in local economic development and the lack of sufficient knowledge about how companies operating in service sectors co-create innovations in service supply chains.

Some similarities and differences arise from a comparison of this research project with the Danish regional fund-supported project. In a similar sense, this research project featured clear planning, designed to identify potential problems and challenges to service sector companies, particularly after the Brexit vote. The principal and co-investigators started discussing initial ideas, seeking to understand network- and company-level capabilities and their role in innovation. The initial idea was developed and reviewed at the department level, followed by a solicitation of feedback from the director of research. The final proposal was then developed in accordance with the requirements and guidance of the British Academy of Management. Unlike the Danish project though, the investigators did not develop any subprojects but instead focused on understanding the role of relational and internal capabilities in a wider supply chain context. As such, the investigators did not work in a consortium setting, though they identified relevant companies from two different regions that could be interviewed as part of the research project.

The investigators also identified a clear research question and linked it to the methodology. The research project description featured sound justifications, as well as information about the sampling strategy and potential respondents. Finally, the investigators spent much time fine-tuning the impact and dissemination strategies.

The research project was evaluated on the following criteria:

- Content: quality of potential contribution to the field.
- Potential significance for theory and/or practice.

- Originality: methodology/research design/knowledge of the field.
- Relevance for British Academy of Management Grant Scheme 2017–2018.
- Quality of application: organization, structure, and clarity.

The investigators' experience with developing this application, as well as working on and reviewing several other funding applications, leads the investigators to offer the following suggestions and strategies for securing research funding:

- Understand the funding bodies' requirements and align the proposal with those requirements.
- Recognize the importance of project planning and addressing a research problem.
- Align the research questions with the proposed methodology.
- Keep the target audience and potential reviewers in mind; get peer feedback and adjust the proposal by integrating experienced colleagues' suggestions and removing any mistakes.
- Identify the potential impact and dissemination strategies for a range of stakeholders, both academic and non-academic.

7. CONCLUSIONS

Academic researchers face increased pressure to write funding applications and obtain external funding. University administrators see successful research funding applications as a source of funding, an opportunity to gain recognition, and a means to boost their rankings. Scholars who write successful research funding proposals, then produce research that is relevant to managers and policy makers, can help close the research–relevance gap. However, as research funding continues to be cut, and rejection rates for funding proposals rise, the ever-increasing pressure on academics demands that they write better funding applications. With this chapter, we seek to help them do so, focusing on the context of business-to-business marketing academic research and the particular challenges for early-career researchers.

Specifically, we provide practical advice for developing funding strategies. This chapter also highlights that leadership at every level within the university is critical for establishing a culture that places a high priority on funding writing. Various strategies and plans can help university leaders and heads of department support and reward funding writing activity by faculty members. Furthermore, no academic researchers should feel alone in their quest to write proposals and obtain funding; they can rely on relationships and networks to identify and pursue fundable research opportunities. In turn, we offer some practical guidance for preparing the actual application. The funding review process may seem mysterious to especially early-career researchers, so we attempt to remove some of the mystery by exploring attributes that most funding reviewers seek. In turn, and leveraging our own experiences with seeking funding, we provide details about each element of a successful funding application. We conclude by outlining two recent, successful business-to-business marketing research funding applications, which can serve as starting points for future proposals.

Considering the complexity and difficulty of writing grant applications, a successful application might seem like an end goal, but really, receiving a research grant is only the beginning. The research project needs to be completed successfully, so researchers should immediately seek out their research support office to ensure the transfer of funds between the agency and the university. Most universities have well-established processes to facilitate this transfer. The researcher, as the principal investigator, is responsible for all activities related to the grant, including budgets, personnel management, data collection, periodic progress updates, and submissions of findings to the funding agency. In many cases, continuing to receive funding may be contingent on meeting intermediate objectives in a timely manner.

Research funding writing is a daunting task, and the chances of obtaining funding often are slim. Yet the pressure to produce persists. Luckily, there are many resources available, including university-led research institutes or research support offices whose employees have expert knowledge about application processes and experience managing all the details of an application. Researchers also might apply for seed money from their university or a government agency. It may not be enough to fund years of research, but such initial funding can get the research off the ground and permit scholars to conduct some exploratory work, develop and pretest surveys, or initiate the first stage of a multi-phase research initiative.

REFERENCES

Bartunek, J.M. & Rynes, S.L. (2014). Academics and practitioners are alike and unlike: The paradoxes of academic-practitioner relationships. *Journal of Management*, 40(5), pp. 1181–1201.

Bloch, C., Graversen, E.K., & Pedersen, H.S. (2014). Competitive research grants and their impact on career performance. *Minerva*, 52(1), pp. 77–96.

Blume-Kohout, M.E., Kumar, K.B., & Sood, N. (2015). University R&D funding strategies in a changing federal funding environment. *Science and Public Policy*, 42(3), pp. 355–368.

Carton, G. & Mouricou, P. (2017). Is management research relevant? A systematic analysis of the rigor-relevance debate in top-tier journals (1994–2013). *M@n@gement*, 20(2), pp. 166–203.

Danish Agency of Science and Higher Education (2018). *Evaluations and Evaluators in Horizon 2020: Report on an Analysis among Danish Evaluators*. Copenhagen: Danish Agency of Science and Higher Education.

Fischer, B.A. & Zigmond, M.J. (1998). Survival skills for graduate school and beyond. *New Directions for Higher Education*, 101, pp. 29–40.

Gerritsen, S., Plug, E., & van der Wiel, K. (2013). Up or out? How individual research grants affect academic careers in the Netherlands. *CPB Discussion Paper 249*, CPB Netherlands Bureau for Economic Policy Analysis.

Ippoliti, E. (2015). Reasoning at the frontier of knowledge: Introductory essay. In Ippoliti, E. (Ed.), *Heuristic Reasoning* (pp. 1–10). Heidelberg: Springer.

Kieser, A., Nicolai, A., & Seidl, D. (2015). The practical relevance of management research: Turning the debate on relevance into a rigorous scientific research program. *Academy of Management Annals*, 9(1), pp. 143–233.

Lindgreen, A., Palmer, R., Vanhamme, J., & Beverland, M.B. (2002). Finding and choosing a supervisor. *Marketing Review*, 3(2), pp. 147–166.

Lindgreen, A., Vallaster, C., & Vanhamme, J. (2001). Reflections on the PhD process: The experiences of three survivors. *Marketing Review*, 1(4), pp. 505–529.

Luft, J. & Ingham, H. (1955). The Johari window: A graphic model for interpersonal relations. *Proceedings of the Western Training Laboratory in Group Development*. Los Angeles: University of California.

OECD (2018). *DAC List of ODA Recipients*. http://www.oecd.org/dac/financing-sustainable-development/development-finance-standards/daclist.htm.

Porter, R. (2005). What do grant reviewers really want, anyway? *Journal of Research Administration*, 36(2), 47–55.

Porter, R. (2007). Why academics have a hard time writing good grant proposals. *Journal of Research Administration*, 38(2), 37–43.

Porter, R. (2011). More paper out the door: Ten inexpensive ways to stimulate proposal development. *Research Management Review*, 18(1), pp. 64–72.

Tandberg, D.A. (2010). Politics, interest groups and state funding of public higher education. *Research in Higher Education*, 51(5), pp. 416–450.

Toffel, M.W. (2016). Enhancing the practical relevance of research. *Production and Operations Management*, 25(9), pp. 1493–1505.

6. Undertaking cross-disciplinary research

Adam Lindgreen, C. Anthony Di Benedetto, Roderick J. Brodie, and Michel van der Borgh

1. INTRODUCTION

As an applied social science, business-to-business research is inherently cross-disciplinary. This is because the general theories that provide insight into business relationships, systems, and markets have disciplinary foundations in the economics, psychology, sociology, and management disciplines. Commonly used general theories are, among others, Social Exchange Theory, Organizational Economics (Transaction Cost Economics, Agency Theory, and Plural Form Institutional Theory), Commitment-Trust Theory of Relationships, Structuration Theory, Actor-Network Theory, Corporate Social Responsibility, Stakeholder Theory and, more broadly, Systems Theory, Complexity Theory, and Evolutionary Psychology Theory. Different disciplines in business-to-business research make use of these general theories in varying degree. For example, Transaction Cost Economics provides a framework for researchers seeking to explain and guide decision-makers as to how to organize transactions, while Evolutionary Psychology Theory offers a framework for researchers trying to explain how consumers make their decisions.

Recently, Brodie and Peters (2020) propose a theorizing process that explicitly considers the use of cross-disciplinary research. The theorizing process takes into account multiple theoretical pathways and recognizes how different general theoretic perspectives lead to the development of midrange theory and empirical research.

A major barrier that needs to be overcome when undertaking cross-disciplinary research comes from a parallel with organization structures, where there is a path from start-up to functional (silo) structure, to matrix structure, and to customer/project-based teams. Depending on the type of research challenge, the organization structure may relate to whether a multi-disciplinary or monodisciplinary approach is necessary. Differences in incentives, culture, terminology and jargon, and so forth all can lead to opportunistic and counterproductive behavior.

The purpose of this chapter is to explore how to undertake cross-disciplinary research that advances knowledge and understanding in the domain of business-to-business research. To achieve this purpose, we first elaborate on the theorizing processes. Second, we examine how to break cross-disciplinary boundaries. Third, we provide practical guidelines for undertaking cross-disciplinary research.

2. THEORIZING PROCESSES FOR CROSS-DISCIPLINARY RESEARCH

The theorizing process developed by Brodie and Peters (2020) provides guidelines for undertaking cross-disciplinary research by integrating general theoretic perspectives and contextual research to develop midrange theory. A distinction is made between the theoretical domain of knowledge and the empirical domain of knowledge; and, as depicted in Figure 6.1, midrange theory bridges these two domains. Fundamental to the domains of knowledge is the paradigmatic perspective. The paradigmatic perspective provides the outer ring for the recursive theorizing process between general theory, midrange theory, and applied research. A paradigm (e.g., positivism, pragmatism, or subjectivism) is the generally accepted perspective of a particular discipline at a given time and provides philosophical consensus on how to understand reality and conduct research (Kuhn, 1962). While a theory explains something, a paradigm does not explain something, but exists before theory. We explore a paradigmatic perspective that is not based on a single discipline, but one that is cross-disciplinary.

Figure 6.1 distinguishes between three levels of theory, which we discuss next.

General theories: These theories are conceptions and perspectives utilizing theory that is framed at the highest conceptual level and provides a perspective or logic of explanation for a domain. The theories are broad in scope, integrative, and context-free, and thus do not directly lead to empirical investigation. The theories provide the foundations for understanding and explanation.

Midrange theories: Midrange theories are context-specific. Hence, these theories provide frameworks that can be used to undertake empirical observation and models to guide managerial practices. Most of the theories currently used in business-to-business research have these characteristics.

Applied theory: Applied theory is embedded in empirical research and context. While the focus of applied theory traditionally has been with empirical research, 'theories-in-use' can play an important role (see, for example, Beverland, 2004; Zeithaml et al., 2020). Theories-in-use recognize that prac-

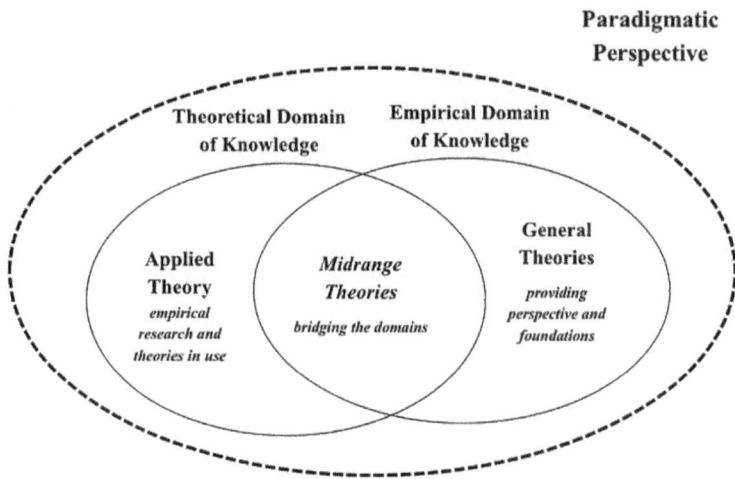

Figure 6.1   Domains of knowledge and levels of theory

ticing managers, customers, and other stakeholders in a service system use theory. Theories-in-use are context-specific and can be based on tacit mental models.

The theorizing process outlined in Figure 6.1 recognizes there are multiple pathways to develop midrange theory and hence undertake empirical research. An important distinction is made between the focal general theoretic perspective and other general theories. The marketing discipline traditionally has been based on a dyadic buyer–seller perspective, and the focal general theoretic perspectives are based on general theories either from microeconomics or psychology. In contrast, within contemporary business-to-business research, a network perspective is adopted where focal general theoretic perspectives inherently are cross-disciplinary and broadened, drawing on sociological and institutional foundations and the management disciplines. For example, the focal general theoretic perspective provided by S-D logic is cross-disciplinary and is a synthesis of general theories including institutional theory, systems theory, complexity theory, complexity economics, and evolutionary theory (Vargo & Lusch, 2017). Specific examples where authors have interfaced other general theory with S-D logic to develop midrange theory include practice theory (Kjellberg & Helgesson, 2006), actor-network theory (Chandler & Vargo, 2011), and systems and ecosystems theory (Frow et al., 2014).

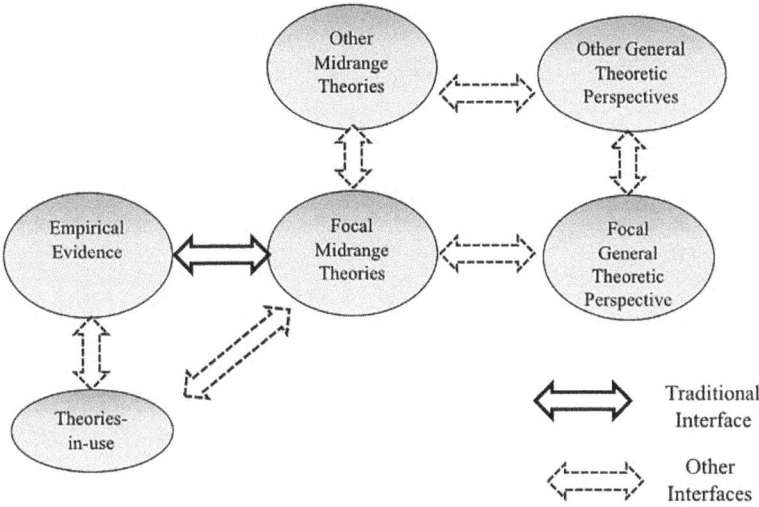

Figure 6.2   Interfaces for theorizing

As outlined in Figure 6.2, the focal general theoretic perspective can interface directly with midrange theory, but other general theoretic perspectives can also provide pathways that can lead to other midrange theories, which then leads to a focal midrange theory that can be used in business-to-business research. For example, when defining the conceptual domain for customer engagement, Brodie and colleagues (Brodie, Hollebeek, Juric, & Ilic, 2011) adopted a focal general theoretic perspective from S-D logic, but also drew extensively on general and midrange theory from psychology, sociology, political science, and organizational behavior literatures to develop midrange theory. The theorizing process also drew on research, which can serve as an input for developing and refining a focal midrange theory. Applied theory drawing on theories-in-use provided valuable input to ensure the cross-disciplinary theorizing resonated with practice.

In summary, to undertake cross-disciplinary research, we suggest that there first needs to be a paradigm shift. Second, explicit attention needs to be given to the process of theorizing, rather than just focusing on theory as an outcome (Weick, 1995). Our approach meets the challenge by paying attention to both (1) theoretical frameworks and their cross-disciplinary foundations and (2) managerial practices to inform research processes. The recursive theorizing process leads to multiple pathways to develop midrange theory and hence undertake empirical research.

A somewhat different, but complementary perspective comes from design science research (Simon, 1969). Design science research is the standard paradigm in engineering disciplines such as mechanical engineering, chemical engineering, and information systems, but also common in medicine and law. By relying on a philosophy of pragmatism, design science researchers use any method, technique, and procedure to improve "the human condition by developing knowledge to solve field problems, i.e. problematic situations in reality" (Denyer, Tranfield, & Van Aken, 2008, p. 394). Being an applied social science, business-to-business marketing inherently can be typified as a design science.

Design science considers different types of design artifacts (Romme, 2016) including values (e.g., increase welfare of all stakeholders), concepts (e.g., customer engagement), models (e.g., S-D logic), design rules (e.g., to achieve Y do X), and instantiations (e.g., customer management system implemented in a company). The order in which these artifacts can be created are multitude. For instance, based on theories-in-use, practitioners can create instantiations, which then are studied by scholars to create midrange theories. In contrast, academics also can create design rules and instantiations from theoretical models. The creation and justification of all these artifact types belongs to the work domain of both academics and practitioners and can cross many disciplines.

Design science research centers on classes of problems, which refer to problems that share a set of commonalities and as such are considered generalizable across organizational settings (e.g., decision-making under uncertainty; allocation of marketing resources). Different framing of the problem (i.e., using a different theoretical lens or paradigm) may lead to different solution outcomes. As such, design science scholars acknowledge that there are no universal solutions to problems, but instead advance that multiple solution artifacts can coexist within a class of problems. Operating in an interdisciplinary research team can be especially valuable, as it may help to identify the most promising research approaches and solutions.

3. CROSS-DISCIPLINARY RESEARCH

3.1 Barriers to Breaking Cross-Disciplinary Research

Although many university administrators may call for 'interdisciplinary research,' they often do not really know what to expect. It may be true that the biggest and most lucrative research topics may require a big-picture perspective, and the participation of researchers from several disciplines. This does not mean, however, that interdisciplinary research will necessarily come about organically. Next, we will discuss some barriers to breaking cross-disciplinary boundaries.

First, it is clear that a research team does not need to be made up of 'interdisciplinary people' (however that is defined), but rather by experts in their own areas who have enough familiarity with the research problem, and understanding of the basics of each other's discipline so that they can communicate effectively. A business-to-business marketing strategy person does not have to be an expert in big-data analytics to co-author a research grant proposal, or to work effectively on a research team (or vice versa). The construct 'imported' from the other discipline should be well-defined, well-measured, and already well-published, making it easier to use in the new context. Some initial, intuitive, basic understanding of the concept by all involved in the research team would also help, but encyclopedic understanding is not required. This consideration has research team composition and even hiring implications. It would be better for the research team to be composed of these two (monodisciplinary) experts who have a good combination of skills and good communication abilities, rather than two interdisciplinary researchers who lack experience or expertise.

Incidentally, this same issue arises in industry as well. New-product teams are typically multidisciplinary in nature, with representation from marketing, R&D, engineering, design, manufacturing, and others all playing a part. In cases where a specific technical expertise is critical, say for example in the development of a new business-to-business product requiring state-of-the-art fluid dynamics, it would be better for the leading engineers on the new-product team to be experts on this topic. High levels of functional expertise are most valuable, and would be the expected contribution of these engineers (Ulrich & Eppinger, 2000, pp. 28–29). Their time away from the laboratory is better spent keeping up with the latest technological advances and going to top meetings in their field than learning about new-product launch strategy.

Another barrier to effective interdisciplinarity is that academic research usually is very monodisciplinary. An interdisciplinary research grant application might falter because the reviewers are likely to be monodisciplinary experts who may not understand the cross-disciplinary aspects, or who may fail to see the value of the joint research. Similarly, it is generally harder to get interdisciplinary research conducted, peer-reviewed, and published since the same reviewers will be gatekeepers in this process as well. Due to these factors, researchers under pressure from university administrators to conduct interdisciplinary research may fall back on opportunities in closely related fields (marketing can easily reach out to research partners in strategic management or organizational studies, for example), rather than stretching to riskier, but potentially lucrative partnerships with researchers in very different silos: engineering, mathematics, hard sciences, or medicine, for example.

University administration's efforts to support and reward interdisciplinary research may be misguided at times: interdisciplinary research should not be the end in and of itself! Forcing some vaguely defined interdisciplinary agenda on researchers can lead to wasted effort or, at best, research projects that are difficult to get funded or published for reasons stated above. A better approach would be to start with the research problem, identify to which problem class it belongs, and if the research problem is big or complicated enough to warrant interdisciplinary work, and questions arise that require input across multiple disciplines, then the contacts are made and the joint research is initiated. Also, university administration should resist the temptation to reward interdisciplinary research for its own sake. It would be far more beneficial to create a research environment where researchers are doing quality work in their own disciplines, but rewarded for taking on the bigger interdisciplinary research challenges on occasion.

3.2   Suggestions for How to Undertake Cross-Disciplinary Research

In this section, we provide some action-oriented guidelines that can serve as a starting point for breaking down the above identified silo barriers and fostering a research workplace environment that encourages and values cross-disciplinary work.

A great idea for researchers is to collaborate with colleagues from other departments inside their university or outside their university. For instance, researchers should try to join initiatives within their university that target big themes (e.g., sustainability, digitalization, or sharing economy). As an example, the Fox School at Temple has an Innovation and Entrepreneurship Institute (IEI), and faculty from all areas who are interested in innovation research (marketing, strategic management, entrepreneurship, and so on) can work jointly in this space. One of the goals of this institute is to collaborate with like-minded members of the business community, for example, by partnering with the Product Development & Management Association. Copenhagen Business School has conceptualized Business-in-Society platforms so that its researchers can engage in knowledge production based on "context-driven, problem-focused and interdisciplinary research that deals with complex societal and business problems." These platforms are funded for five years with regular evaluation of performance and success criteria after which research teams can apply for funding to set up new platforms. At this time, there are the following platforms: Diversity and Difference Platform, Inequality Platform, Digital Transformations Platform, and Maritime Platform.

Researchers should consider working with colleagues outside their domain, as this will increase the size of the audience coming across their research—and could open entirely new research fields. A marketing department with strong interest in business-to-business and/or innovation may effectively collaborate with the engineering or medical schools. Try to profit from opportunities to present your work outside your area, as this leads to increased visibility, novel insights, and possibly future collaborative opportunities.

Researchers could connect with practitioners. Their requests for help are often interdisciplinary in nature and require input from other people. Important here is to have an open mind and be open for input from these other people. Ensure that you engage in research publishable in high-quality journals, though, at least eventually. Your business school may be pushing for closer ties with the business community, so these efforts may be seen as worthwhile service contributions at annual review time. A previous editorial recommended that universities provide incentives to foster an intellectual environment in which academics are encouraged to question assumptions and revisit their academic contributions, so that they can have greater relevance and offer more meaningful solutions to the business community (Di Benedetto, Lindgreen, Storgaard, & Clarke, 2019).

Make sure you search for cross-disciplinary topics that have your personal interest, that is, what do you value? Think outside of the box about who might be interested in cross-disciplinary work, or which department might provide insights for your research. As an example, your marketing department may have several researchers who are doing quantitative consumer research based on big-data analysis, or applying neuroscience techniques to understand consumer response to advertising. Could some of those concepts be equally applied in a business-to-business setting in a novel way?

Positioning cross-disciplinary research in monodisciplinary top journals is difficult. When targeting such journals, it is important to frame your own part of the research in terms of your own field. This will be a balancing act, as you do not want to lose your co-authors along the way. Be clear about your expectations and make sure that your collaborators understand what you want to get out of the research, and that your objective is indeed to collaborate—not to take over or usurp the co-authors' projects or ideas. This issue can possibly be addressed with a statement of research objectives that clearly positions the research in terms of what contribution it makes to the business-to-business literature stream.

Start with a clear and carefully constructed research question, which defines the precise problem class and knowledge gap. This will demonstrate the need for expertise from more than one scientific discipline, as the problem will require interdisciplinary collaboration to tackle properly. We mentioned earlier a possible collaboration with a research partner in neurosciences. One may identify a research gap, for example in managerial decision-making that could benefit from joint work with a neuroscience expert. It makes sense to hone this gap into a specific research problem that can pique interest among potential collaborators and can provide context and direction for the collaborative work.

Senior faculty in your department may have worked on cross-disciplinary projects in the past, and might have access to mentors in other departments. Reach out to these potential research partners. They may be able to identify possible collaborators for you, based on your research interests, and may know of available funding. A research partner from outside your department might even write an influential reference letter for an impending promotion of tenure decision. Look at your colleagues' university web pages, get to know their research agendas, and see what they are currently working on. If a cross-disciplinary institute exists, such as Temple's IEI or Copenhagen Business School's Business-in-Society platforms, it may be easy to reach out to researchers whose work is surprisingly close to yours, or who may want to work jointly with you in organizing outreach meetings or seminars with the business community.

Be sure there is a clear vision for the research. If two or more departments are involved, it may not be clear who is responsible for providing guidance. The right solution might be to establish a leadership team, which can call in other members to provide expertise to the team on an ad hoc basis. The leader, or leadership team, should set team objectives and timelines, and hold regular meetings, to ensure the project maintains momentum. It is also up to the leader(s) to make sure that all team members' voices are heard, including junior members and part-time members whose available time may be limited.

And here are a few additional thoughts for motivation:

Visit networking events, for example, for funding opportunities that are cross-disciplinary in nature. Here, you often can connect with people from other domains and practitioners.

Read topics outside of your main research area, not only scientific articles, but also books. Be inspired by people like Bill Gates and Warren Buffett who read a lot.

Working with someone outside your discipline means that you will not need to know this literature in as much depth as otherwise. After some preliminary work to scope out mutual research interests, a good partner should be able to provide some direction regarding the most relevant articles and authors with which you should become familiar.

4. CONCLUSIONS

Academic institutions know the value of cross-disciplinary research. The bigger, and more relevant, the problem is, the more likely it will require experts from many different research areas to provide their expertise to help solve the problem. We see cross-disciplinary teams, such as new-product teams hard at work in industry, with members contributing their own expertise to reach a common goal. But, as in industry collaboration, effective academic collaboration is not always easily achieved. Functional silo thinking may be difficult to overcome, and reward structures may be unproductive or may backfire if not well planned. Academic administrators should resist the temptation to push for cross-disciplinary research for its own sake, allowing cross-disciplinary bonds to form if deemed necessary for the research problem being undertaken.

We presented a theorizing process (Figure 6.1) that provides guidelines for cross-disciplinary research by focusing on midrange theory, integrating general theoretic perspectives and contextual research to develop midrange theory. Explicit attention needs to be given to the process of theorizing, not theory, as an outcome. The process we present is recursive in the sense that it considers both theoretical frameworks and their cross-disciplinary foundations, as well as managerial practices to inform these research processes. The process thus provides multiple possibilities for development of midrange theory. If it is decided that cross-disciplinary research is required to tackle a particularly challenging problem, researchers are incentivized to reach outside their comfort zone and work with collaborators from an unfamiliar part of the university, or from industry. We need to remind ourselves of the fact that all of us—designers and practitioners across different fields—are designers working collaboratively to solve a problem or address a challenge via the creation of artifacts.

With this process in mind, we proposed several practical steps that can be undertaken to facilitate effective cross-disciplinary research. These steps include: establish a clear vision for the research project, carefully construct a clear research question, work with senior colleagues who have access to mentors in different parts of the university, take advantage of institutes within your school that are problem-focused and are cross-disciplinary in nature, and develop a positioning strategy for your cross-disciplinary research that will interest the top academic journals.

REFERENCES

Beverland, M. (2004). Uncovering "theories-in-use": Building luxury wine brands. *European Journal of Marketing*, 38(3/4), 446–466.

Brodie, R.J., Hollebeek, L.D., Juric, B., & Ilic, A. (2011). Customer engagement: Conceptual domain, fundamental propositions, and implications for research. *Journal of Service Research*, 14(3), 252–271.

Brodie, R.J. & Peters, L.D. (2020). New directions for service research: Refreshing the process of theorizing to increase contribution. *Journal of Services Marketing*, 34(3), pp. 415–428.

Chandler, J.D. & Vargo, S.L. (2011). Contextualization and value-in-context: How context frames exchange. *Marketing Theory*, 11(1), 35–49.

Denyer, D., Tranfield, D., & Van Aken, J.E. (2008). Developing design propositions through research synthesis. *Organization Studies*, 29(3), 393–413.

Di Benedetto, C.A., Lindgreen, A., Storgaard, M., & Clarke, A.H. (2019). Editorial: How to collaborate really well with practitioners. *Industrial Marketing Management*, 82, 1–8.

Frow, P., McColl-Kennedy, J.R., Hilton, T., Davidson, A., Payne, A., & Brozovic, D. (2014). Value propositions: A service ecosystems perspective. *Marketing Theory*, 14(3), 327–351.

Kjellberg, H. & Helgesson, C.-F. (2006). Multiple versions of markets: Multiplicity and performativity in market practice. *Industrial Marketing Management*, 35(7), 839–855.

Kuhn, T.S. (1962). *The Structure of Scientific Revolutions*. Chicago, IL: University of Chicago Press.

Romme, A.G.L. (2016). *The Quest for Professionalism: The Case of Management and Entrepreneurship*. Oxford: Oxford University Press.

Simon, H.A. (1969). *The Sciences of the Artificial*. Cambridge, MA: MIT Press.

Ulrich, K.T. & Eppinger, S.D. (2000). *Product Design and Development*, 2nd ed. New York: McGraw-Hill.

Vargo, S.L. & Lusch, R.F. (2017). Service-dominant logic 2025. *International Journal of Research in Marketing*, 34(1), 46–67.

Weick, K.E. (1995). What theory is not, theorizing is. *Administrative Science Quarterly*, 40, 385–390.

Zeithaml, V.A., Jaworski, B.J., Kohli, A.K., Tuli, K.R., Ulaga, W., & Zaltman, G. (2020). A theories-in-use approach to building marketing theory. *Journal of Marketing*, 84(1), 32–51.

7. Collaborating with practitioners
C. Anthony Di Benedetto, Adam Lindgreen, Marianne Storgaard, and Ann Højbjerg Clarke

1. INTRODUCTION

A recent editorial of *Industrial Marketing Management* (Lindgreen & Di Benedetto, 2018) noted that too often an article's managerial implications consist of "a simple rewording of the results section and little else" (p. 2). We offer insights to the explicit collaboration between academics and practitioners from the outset of a research undertaking. That is, research that is of interest to academics, but also clearly has meaning and importance to the practitioners involved. This is the 'rigor versus relevance' argument: rigorous articles that provide significant theoretical insight are influential and highly cited, but relevance means a real contribution to both academics and practitioners.

Inspired by Chesbrough's (2003) seminal work on open innovation, the principles of collaboration and the idea of working with many different partners and sources in order to innovate in a sustainable manner (Laursen & Salter, 2006) are prevalent in most organizations (Hernandez-Espallardo, Osorio-Tinoco, & Rodriguez-Orejuela, 2017). As no one organization is likely to possess all the resources needed to operate successfully and solve all problems it faces (Pera, Occhiocupo, & Clarke, 2016), collaboration is used as a means to solve complex and diverse problems among individuals, teams, and organizations.

The basic aim of collaboration is to pursue goals collaboratively that otherwise would be difficult to pursue. Collaboration is described as situations where individuals or teams work together and share learning across disciplinary or organizational boundaries (Hibbert, Siedlok, & Beech, 2016; Huxham & Vangen, 2005). The idea is that while individuals lack adequate experience, context, and expertise to solve complex and diverse problems, collaboration offers greater epistemic authority, as collaboration allows the organization to solve problems that require capabilities based on inputs from multiple specialties (Beaver, 2004).

Although research historically has revolved around innovation (Desai, 2018), debate currently focuses on why and how academics should engage in university–business collaboration (Clauss & Kesting, 2017). Although university–business collaborations have increased markedly in relevance over the past decade, little remains known about these collaborations (Perkmann et al., 2013). For example, academics often intuitively and implicitly take an inside perspective (i.e., that of the university) when discussing 'collaborative research,' but this is just one side of the coin in university–business collaborations. The outside perspective (i.e., that of the business) is the other side of the coin in university–business collaborations, which then typically are termed as 'collaborative innovation' (e.g., Hernandez-Espallardo et al., 2017; Lakemond, Bengtsson, Laursen, & Tell, 2016; Najafi-Tavani et al., 2018). We contribute to literature by identifying the similarities between, and the differences in, these two types of university–business collaborations. To this end, we draw on past literatures including that on academic–practitioner collaboration (Bartunek, 2007), collaborative theorizing (Nenonen, Brodie, Storbacka, & Peter, 2017), critical engagement (Bridgman, 2007), engaged scholarship (Van de Ven, 2007), and impact scholarship (Antonacopoulou, 2009).

The remaining parts are organized as follows. First, we describe how universities and businesses often have very different motivations for, and expectations of, engaging in university–business collaborations. Next, we outline typical challenges that each of the partners face when engaging in university–business collaborations. Finally, we suggest how insights and advice given to practitioners about how to engage in university–business collaborations could serve as an inspiration for academics aspiring to engage really well in such collaborations. A place to start is for academics to recognize that practitioners are not a homogeneous group, and that it is important to develop competences that permit ongoing learning and continuous improvement in collaboration skills.

2. MOTIVATIONS FOR, AND EXPECTATIONS OF, ENGAGING IN UNIVERSITY–BUSINESS COLLABORATIONS

2.1 Business Perspective

From a business perspective, collaboration, involving a wide range of external partners and sources, has long been an important part of business *modus operandi*. The meeting of people with different logics, mindsets, skills, and ideas spurs innovative thinking and allows room for radically new ideas (Beaver, 2004). Studies find that organizations generally benefit from collaborating with other organizations (e.g., Cruz-González, López-Sáez, & Navas-López, 2015; Feller, Parhankangas, Smeds, & Jaatinen, 2013) and from involving external partners including suppliers, customers, and competitors (e.g., Najafi-Tavani et al., 2018). For example, collaborative innovations have been shown to expand the knowledge base and the innovation capability of an organization (Alexiev, Volberda, & Van den Bosch, 2016; Heirati, O'Cass, Schoefer, & Siahtiri, 2016).

Collaborative innovation, however, is characterized by being complex and risky and by involving highly unpredictable outcomes. Therefore, collaborative innovation comes with many potential sources of conflict (e.g., De Araújo Burcharth, Knudsen, & Søndergaard, 2014). As a result, collaborative innovation efforts often are described as "troublesome arrangements" (Hibbert et al., 2016, p. 26) and as "highly resource-consuming and often painful" processes (Huxham & Vangen, 2004, p. 200), with no clear criteria for a common approach. It is therefore not surprising that collaboration presents difficult problems that can lead to misunderstanding and ineffective learning (Hibbert et al., 2016, p. 26). Recent studies describe how collaboration can be inhibited by cognitive barriers (Skippari, Laukkanen, & Salo, 2017), problematic power dynamics (Chicksand, 2015), and differences in relational norms (Zhou, Zhang, Zhuang, & Zhou, 2015), among others.

Universities present particular important collaborative partners for businesses (Etzkowitz, 2010; Perkmann & Walsh, 2007; Winkelbach & Walter, 2015) because universities spur and enable both technical development, as well as product and organizational development in businesses (Shaw & Allen, 2006). Universities promote real problem solving and continuous improvement (Pecas & Henriques, 2006) and act as co-producers of innovation (Muller & Doloreux, 2009). As research per se typically is not the goal of university–business collaborations when seen from a business perspective, businesses sometimes regard universities as advisers or consultants in the innovation processes. This perspective underscores a traditional assumption that businesses mostly are interested in finding quick and efficient solutions to their immediate problems (Pasmore et al., 2008, p. 12) and in prescriptive knowledge immediately applicable in the organization.

Recent findings, however, that managerial interest in university–business collaborations is not limited to prescriptive knowledge, as managers equally are interested in using theoretical knowledge both conceptually and symbolically, challenge this traditional assumption (Åge, 2014). Following this perspective, businesses have ample reasons to engage with academic consultants rather than commercial or practice-based consultants. Academic consulting goes beyond the mapping stage (of benchmarking and comparative research); ideally, academic consulting challenges current practice and existing benchmarks (Docherty & Smith, 2007, p. 277). Furthermore, in contrast to commercial or practice-based consultants, businesses perceive academic consultants to be neutral. Rather than concerning themselves with the issue of 'repeat business', academics are preoccupied with maintaining academic rigor while at the same time providing publicly accountable results (Docherty & Smith, 2007, p. 278). Businesses therefore know that they receive honest and direct advice from their university partners.

2.2 University Perspective

Most academics, basically, collaborate with practitioners in order to collect data that can give grounds for new academic knowledge. Academics ultimately are evaluated by their publication performance (Lindgreen, Di Benedetto, Brodie, & Naudé, 2019). This is what grants academics legitimacy, and publishing in prestigious journals, therefore, is what typically drives academics. During the past decades, academia has witnessed an increasing heterogeneity in research designs. There is a tendency that academics within business and social science turn to more collaborative research designs through which they engage with external partners (Antonacopoulou, 2010; Godin & Gingras, 2000; Pettigrew, 2003). Questions have been raised about the role that universities play in society and the relevance, or the societal impact, that universities have (Pettigrew & Starkey, 2016). This issue has been described as the 'rigor–relevance gap' (Hodgkinson & Rousseau, 2009) or the 'theory–practice gap' (Van de Ven, 2007).

University research typically is criticized for being too distant from practice to have a real meaning for society. A one-sided focus on academic impact, therefore, can threaten the legitimacy of academics (Aguinis, Shapiro, Antonacopoulou, & Cummings, 2014). As a result, academics are expected to be more innovative and collaborative (Darabi & Clark, 2012) in the way they do research. There is increasing acknowledgment that research within business and social science—in order to stay relevant—requires that academics transcend boundaries between communities and perspectives, and that academics form productive collaborations with practitioners (Antonacopoulou, 2010). Therefore, academics achieve knowledge generation through collaboration, as mutual engagement is a necessary stepping-stone to, and the most important enabler of, societal impact (Pera et al., 2016). Societal impact is increasingly an important motivation for academics to engage in university–business research collaborations. There is a wealth of studies debating research relevance, using different concepts such as 'applicability' (Barge, 2001), 'usefulness' (Learmonth, Lockett, & Dowd, 2012), 'impact' (Leahrey, Beckman, & Stanko, 2017; Smith, 2018), and 'relevance' (Vicari, 2013). Research projects are designed with specific regard for the nature and objectives of co-produced knowledge and the different ways that different audiences consume it (Nenonen et al., 2017).

Another widespread motivation for academics to engage in university–business research collaborations is based on economic considerations. Internationally, there has been a continuous decline in public funding of research activities, which has led many universities to search for new ways of generating income and to commercialize their skills and research (Darabi & Clark, 2012; Heckscher & Martin-Rios, 2013). This development has spurred an increasing motivation for universities to engage with businesses and to create stable relationships with businesses. Furthermore, due to rapid changes in the general competition and speed of innovation, universities aim for stronger links with businesses (Plewa, Quester, & Baaken, 2005). Arguably, a paradigm shift is underway shifting the role of universities from primarily research and education towards also involving the role of "creating collaborative and innovative opportunities through engagement with industries" (Darabi & Clark, 2012, p. 478).

However, while establishing new funding streams is important for universities, few academics engage in collaboration with businesses only for financial gain. Academics assume, "or at least hope, that academia and practice are compatible" (Bartunek & Rynes, 2014, p. 1195). Walker (2010) questions the feasibility of close university–business collaborations, however, and points to problematic issues in the collaboration process such as: who owns the right to define the problems to be researched, who has the knowledge to state the questions, and whose language and forms of expression dominate. The question, therefore, is whether academics should engage only in weak versions of collaborations, that is, little more than conversations between academics and practitioners (Walker, 2010, p. 206). Similarly, the scientific value of collaborative research sometimes has been questioned: while collaboration may be a sensible activity to undertake, it does not necessarily lead to improved research (Kieser & Leiner, 2009, p. 528). Academics should hold their cognitive and emotional distance to their research object(s) in order to fulfill their genuine function of generating knowledge characterized by critical reflections on current practices (Kieser & Leiner, 2009).

2.3 Discussion

Searching for answers to the question of how academics can engage really well with practitioners, a first relevant issue to address would be the differing motivations and expectations between universities and businesses for entering university–business collaborations. Businesses typically collaborate with their surroundings to challenge their own existing practices, to expand innovative thinking, and to use the knowledge to come up with new perspectives and ideas that could spur product, technical, and organizational development.

Universities, in contrast, tend not to search for challenging unexpected input, but rather to look for answers to problems they often have specified in advance. Publishing is a clear priority on academics' agenda, and too much improvisation and creative change of direction in the collaboration process often is hard for academics to handle. Therefore, academics need to acknowledge this gap of motives and expectations, ensuring that the university–business collaboration is useful and relevant for both parties. This means that academics should have in-depth knowledge about why their practitioner partners choose to collaborate with them, and what these practitioners expect to gain from the collaboration. It is important to consider the needs for, and commitments to, the collaboration from both parties. The academic collaboration leader should thus be able to excel in management of expectations.

Practical relevance of university–business collaboration often is limited because much theory becomes "lost in translation" (Shapiro, Kirkman, & Courtney, 2007, p. 249) due to the lack of coherence between the problems investigated by academics and the actual problems that practitioners face. Academics sometimes assume that a theory is 'right,' and needs to be properly disseminated to practitioners, for the theory to gain relevance. It may, however, be better to assume that the theory itself can be improved through interaction with the practitioner community (Jarzabkowski, Mohrman, & Scherer, 2010, p. 1193). Traditionally, only academics have taken the role of defining research questions, but many practitioners are very well educated, some have obtained Ph.D. degrees themselves, and therefore certainly are able to develop researchable research questions with meaningful theoretical contributions and managerial implications (Nenonen et al., 2017, p. 1136). For their part, academics increasingly are aware that they must engage in research that is useful to practitioners, as this will ensure trust between universities and businesses (Santini et al., 2016, p. 1841). The expectations from both parties about the outcomes of the collaboration, therefore, need to be managed in order to build trust within the relationship (Vangen & Huxham, 2003).

By continuously collaborating with practitioners within their research field, it becomes much easier for academics to engage and embed their research in ways that makes it relevant for both parties. This has led scholars to call for increased contact and interaction between universities and businesses (Bartunek, 2007; Heckscher & Martin-Rios, 2013). The role of the academic leading a university–business collaboration thus calls for a certain professional outlook. The academic needs to be in touch with, and to join the conversation of the practice field investigated. Through involvement in different collaborative research projects, academics build a common ground and a bridging position in the business environment, which then can serve as building blocks and antecedents to larger research projects (Spekkink & Boons, 2016).

As a final observation, through collaborations the involved parties get the opportunity to connect with previously unconnected partners and, along the way, trusting relationships between them may develop (Inkpen & Tsang, 2005). Academic research needs to return to pragmatism in the sense that not only should research produce relevant academic knowledge; there is also a need for research to be socialized (Fendt, Kaminska-Labbe, & Sachs, 2008). Practitioners should be included in research processes as active, reflective, and empowered participants. Similarly, criticizing that most discussions about including practitioners in research still revolve around an 'if' question, discussing whether or not it is possible to produce valuable research knowledge in collaboration with practitioners, it would be relevant to rather ask 'how' collaborative research can be managed in order to yield both theoretical and practical value (Nenonen et al., 2017).

3. CHALLENGES IN UNIVERSITY–BUSINESS COLLABORATIONS

3.1 Business Perspective

Questions remain whether collaborating with universities actually is an advantage for businesses in terms of innovation performance (Du, Leten, & Vanhaverbeke, 2014). For example, practitioners are not likely to turn to academic journals and seek out research studies on management strategy or practice, when making business decisions (Rynes, Bartunek, & Daft, 2001). Practitioners experience that collaborations often turn out as unsuitable outputs that do not meet the needs of their businesses (Pertuzé, Calder, Greitzer, & Lucas, 2010; Marzo-Navarro, Pedraja-Iglesias, & Rivera-Torres, 2009). A literature review of university–business collaborations identifies that many businesses join collaborations with high expectations in terms of benefiting from these collaborations (Yassi et al., 2010). Yet, practitioners often are disappointed to find out that academics are most concerned about their own interests (obtaining data for publication purposes, obtaining research funding, or getting academic promotions), and not necessarily focusing on the practitioner's needs (Yassi et al., 2010). Practitioners thus find the common university–business platform often utilized for the sole purpose of serving the academic's interests.

From the outset of a business–university collaboration project, most businesses expect the collaboration to show feasibility and practical usefulness of the businesses' innovative ideas. Characteristically, however, universities work at a slower pace, and one that businesses may not be able to influence during the collaboration process (Lazzarotti, Manzini, Nosella, & Pellegrini, 2016). Businesses, therefore, sometimes find it almost painful to work with universities that focus on long-term academic endeavors (Darabi & Clark,

2012). Businesses find the bureaucratic system and the slow-motion culture of universities stifling of any kind of innovative progress (Darabi & Clark, 2012). Furthermore, "peculiar features" characterize academics and challenge practitioners (Lazzarotti et al., 2016, p. 144): academics, for example, operate with more autonomy and freedom than practitioners do. For academics, the potential societal or monetary benefits of a collaborative outcome are less interesting than their own scientific publications and reputation. In general, studies identify how cultural differences between academia and business can result in differing attitudes and objectives of collaborations (Arvanitis, Kubli, & Woerter, 2008; Ylijoki, 2003). Additionally, the lack of trust between academics and practitioners can be a barrier to collaboration. Practitioners may fear outsiders and be unwilling to provide information to academics who may share it with competitors (Darabi & Clark, 2012, p. 487). While businesses traditionally have opposed the sharing of innovations by claiming exclusiveness in non-disclosure agreements (Lee, 2000), collaborations call for careful alignment of joint development agreements (Mehlman et al., 2010).

3.2   University Perspective

In academia, much debate is going on concerning what good research is and, ultimately, which approaches the academic society favors in terms of publishing. In focusing on how to theorize with managers, Nenonen et al. (2017) note that collaborative university–business research relies heavily on creative abductive approaches. Abduction may be defined as an approach where innovation and creativity play a role in the scientific method (Mingers, 2014, p. 53). Using an abductive approach, however, may cause problems for the academic in the reviewing process, because most journal reviewers are more comfortable with deductive and inductive reasoning (Nenonen et al., 2017). Proponents of collaborative approaches such as action research would argue that abductive action research provides results that practitioners may need, but academics may not value (Gustavsen, 2003, p. 93). Such collaborative research often is deemed of minor, less valuable importance than other scientific approaches. Consequently, despite its potential, action research is still very much underrepresented, especially in the A-level journals (Kieser & Leiner, 2012).

Collaborative research typically is somewhat more time consuming than more classic approaches to research. For example, the effort of recruiting practitioners for collaboration is a lengthy process (Nenonen et al., 2017). Academics easily can end up in situations wondering whether engaging in a university–business collaboration is worth the effort. Well-publishing academics may feel that there is not much to gain by collaborating with practitioners (Shapiro et al., 2007). Yet, few studies have sought to measure the effect of collaborative research and whether this assumption is true. The studies available suggest that researchers undertaking collaborative research do not necessarily compromise their other academic objectives by doing so (Godin & Gingras, 2000).

There also is the problem of objectivity. Collaborative, interventionist researchers do not simply observe and collect data, they also offer solutions to the organization's problems, and the fact that they are conducting their research within an organizational environment indeed alters that environment (Arnaboldi, 2013). Such an approach raises concerns about the quality of a study's theoretical contribution because researchers might be so absorbed in finding the optimal organizational solution that they do not sufficiently reflect on the theoretical implications of the findings (Arnaboldi, 2013).

Engaging in collaborative research and "socializing new knowledge" (Nenonen et al., 2017, p. 1146), comes with a cost because it challenges certain academic conventions. While the demand for more societal impact and relevance draws researchers towards more collaborative approaches, academics often are discouraged to follow such approaches because such efforts are often not adequately recognized by universities or included in their key metrics (Nenonen et al., 2017, p. 1146). Incentive systems currently dominating the universities result in scholarly work that may indeed be irrelevant, except to other academics (Bartunek & Rynes, 2014, p. 1187). The choice of whether and how to engage with businesses is often contingent on the particular management philosophy at the university. Local faculty attitudes are central in determining whether the university is willing to aim for impact beyond academia (Pettigrew & Starkey, 2016). If, from a faculty perspective, impact outside the realms of academia is of secondary concern, it could potentially widen the gap between academics' focus on publication and the expectation of outside stakeholders (Pettigrew & Starkey, 2016, p. 659).

Academics engaging in collaborative research also have to be aware of how their work could serve certain business interests and influence current business practices. Clearly, relevant academic knowledge can strongly upset the organizational power balance (Jarzabkowski et al., 2010, p. 1193). Academics must therefore reflect on who the recipient of academic insight should be: the powerful businesses and practitioners, or more marginalized decision-makers who lack power (Jarzabkowski et al., 2010, p. 1193). Although there is a strong argument that research should stay relevant to the externally generated demands coming from the practitioner's world (Vicari, 2013, p. 173), this approach can result in ethical dilemmas. Yassi et al. (2010) suggest that while universities should engage in service learning and participatory action research, they should also protect the professional integrity of their faculty who are engaging in such research with their practitioner partners (Yassi et al., 2010, p. 485). The ethical dilemmas that academics face when engaging in university–business collaborations can be considerable when participating businesses have invested significant amounts of money in the collaborative research. Indeed, Nenonen et al. (2017) hold that university–business collaborations may face scrutiny for ethical misconduct, especially in the case where private sector research funding is a significant component in the university's faculty metrics and incentives (p. 1147).

3.3   Discussion

In its essence, university–business collaboration represents a collision of logics and a clash of different perspectives and challenges. As very different actors, with very different agendas and dilemmas, participate equally to find answers to a shared problem, a great deal of epistemic reflexivity is called for from the academic collaboration leader, acknowledging that no one partner in the collaboration—not even the collaboration leader—has all the answers in advance. The involved partners collaborate to reach common reflection and cognition, not only in defining the research problem, but also throughout the research process. This means that the academic collaboration leader will need to approach the collaboration with an open mind and a willingness to learn. This is, however, a central challenge for many academics because this requires that they open the door to external constituencies and stakeholders and invite open discussion of their research purposes and objectives (Heckscher & Martin-Rios, 2013, pp. 137–138). Only a revolutionary change in mindset will enable academics to do this.

Collaboration fosters opportunities for co-poiesis, which Bouncken (2008) defines as "the joint birth of knowledge" (p. 43). Distinguishing between knowledge combination, learning, and co-poiesis, Clauss and Kesting (2017) regard co-poiesis as a two-way phenomenon that leads to a synergetic combination of knowledge, which provides benefit for all participants in the collaboration (Clauss and Kesting, 2017, p. 188). By combining different perspectives on problem solving in intense interaction, co-poiesis have considerable potential for joint innovative generation of new insights.

In a similar vein, Hibbert, Siedlok, and Beech (2016) distinguish between two modes of engagement, namely instrumental collaborative exchange and curiosity-driven dialogue. While a rather limited approach in which knowledge is borrowed from partners for the purpose of a particular project characterizes the former mode of engagement, the latter mode of engagement enables a process of self-change and learning through engaging with others. In a curiosity-driven dialogue, people are reflectively aware of how disciplinary specialization is a constraint for learning. Therefore, the curiosity-driven dialogue is based on an acceptance of less certainty about the issue being studied, the outcomes that might emerge, and the costs and benefits that may be accrued (Hibbert et al., 2016, p. 38). Curiosity-driven dialogue opens the arena for new discussions and allows for deeper understanding of the knowledge and perspectives of others; there must exist a willingness to learn from those participants who may benefit from these discussions (Bartunek, 2007, p. 1328). Such relational attitude serves as an alternative to the more traditional linear attitude, in which the researchers sometimes tend to bring not only the questions, but also the answers when interacting with practice.

Following this line of thought, the collaboration leaders must carefully evaluate their own practices and be aware of their own limitations and constraints. A single, specialized researcher will lack the required experience, context, or expertise to solve a sufficiently complex problem; collaboration allows the solution of complex problems, the solutions for which will not reside within the boundaries of any one academic specialty (Beaver, 2004, p. 403).

4. CONCLUSION: HOW TO ENGAGE REALLY WELL IN UNIVERSITY–BUSINESS COLLABORATIONS

While most articles would end up suggesting a number of managerial implications, we consider here the implications that the preceding discussions might have for academics or, to be more specific, academic collaboration leaders engaging in university–business collaborations. In searching for answers to the question of how academics engage really well with practitioners, we acknowledge that there are no simple or easy answers or quick-fix solutions.

A wealth of studies have focused on systemic issues such as the need for the academic system to expand a culture of relating to, and collaborating with, businesses and to recognize and support those individuals who excel at developing relationships with the practitioner community (Darabi & Clark, 2012, p. 490). It is important for the university system to learn from collaborating business partners, as these have shown an ability to engage with multiple stakeholders and to mobilize diverse knowledge sources in creating positive and practical results responding to complex problems (Heckscher & Martin-Rios, 2013). Although it would require tremendous changes in the university system to develop such collaborative capabilities, it is required in order to spur changes to current practice (Heckscher & Martin-Rios, 2013, p. 139). University faculties are central when it comes to setting a course of collaboration (Pettigrew & Starkey, 2016) and, therefore, there is widespread demand for the scientific community to rethink the metrics used to evaluate scholarship such that academics are encouraged to attempt interdisciplinary research (Leahrey et al., 2017, p. 132). Also at an individual level, there seem to be important issues that academics—with the ambition of engaging in collaboration with practitioners—could benefit from considering. In the following, we suggest three such issues: conversation with practitioners, collaborative competences, and constant learning.

4.1   Conversation With Practitioners

Most academics are busy with research, education, and funding applications. With a chronic lack of time, developing relationships with businesses risks becoming academics' lowest priority (Darabi & Clark, 2012). For some academics, relating to businesses is a rather exotic endeavor, which is much more challenging than the classical tasks of research, education, and funding applications. However, personal relationships and social networking are key requirements in collaborative relationships, and in order to generate that academic collaboration leaders need to join the conversation of the field of practice that they want to engage in (Darabi & Clark, 2012).

To 'socialize research' (Fendt et al., 2008), academics need to engage in long-term relationship with practitioners. Successful collaboration typically is the culmination of a long-term relationship (Benneworth, 2001). Indeed, the real benefits of collaborations tend to arise in dealing with problems occurring during the collaboration process. That way, the collaboration impacts both the university and the business, possibly in unforeseeable ways, by affecting the social relationships that actually produce and use knowledge (Benneworth, 2001, p. 226). This implies that both building long-term relations, and following an open-minded approach to the collaboration, are important.

Academics, however, tend to be protective of their resources and traditions, having perhaps a perception that dealing with external parties such as practitioners can be unpleasant, time-consuming, and frustrating (Heckscher & Martin-Rios, 2013, p. 139). Recent studies speculate why collaborative approaches often are deprioritized. Power dynamics, a need for security, and egoistic individualism are some of the possible factors explaining why people avoid collaborations (Raelin, 2018). In a similar vein, decision-makers in businesses tend to suppress their use of collaborative engagements with external stakeholders when their legitimacy is at risk, for example, when the business's actions are perceived to be controversial (Desai, 2018, p. 220). While these studies do not focus specifically on university–business collaborations, they might serve as inspiration here. For example, is the reason why academics refrain from university–business collaboration that they might find themselves challenged by lacking experience in leading such collaborations or that they experience little or no control of the collaborative research?

A collaboration leader needs to be appreciative that practitioners are far from being a homogeneous, uniform group of collaborative partners. Often, academics tend to treat practitioners as a kind of 'black-box group', for example by using the term 'business' when referring to any non-university organization

(Clauss & Kesting, 2017, p. 186). By regarding and treating all practitioners as one, academics risk overlooking the specificities of the very diverse group of practitioners from various sectors, businesses, and professional environments, and how they might represent very different approaches to, and aspirations for, the collaboration with universities. Maybe more sensitivity and reflexivity in discussing specifically how particular businesses can benefit from collaborating with universities would be of value.

Clauss and Kesting (2017) argue that most university–business collaborations are driven by academics who only are decision-makers within the universities. Therefore, practitioners should know the particularities of working with academics and understand how they react. The question could be turned around: what should academics be aware of when collaborating with practitioners? A starting point would be to recognize that practitioners are not a homogeneous or uniform group of potential collaborative partners.

4.2   Collaborative Competences

Academics who hope to improve practitioner collaboration need to develop a skill set that will serve them effectively. Collaborative research leaders often take on a role as the challenger, a role that involves "challenging, re-conceptualizing and generally thinking innovatively about practitioner agendas" (Pollitt, 2006, p. 261). The ability to challenge and question a business's taken-for-granted assumptions is a key competence that academics must have, but it requires both comprehensive professional knowledge and professional authority to engage in such a way. Universities that incentivize an intellectual environment in which assumptions are questioned and challenged obtain a unique competitive advantage and can substantially and positively influence the practitioner community (Paton, Chia, & Burt, 2014, p. 269).

Indeed, the role of academics should not be to offer immediate solutions of practical problems. Rather, academics must be prepared to open up the field of possible actions, shedding light on the situation itself, as well as on the problems to be solved (Jarzabkowski et al., 2010). An important element of this academic role is the capability to 'relevate' (Paton et al., 2014), meaning to expand the range of issues under consideration, or to include issues previously thought irrelevant, into the decision process. Paton et al. (2014, p. 267) suggest that academics are, interestingly, in an ideal position to accomplish these changes, due to their ability to offer different and challenging viewpoints to practicing managers and decision-makers. These authors note, however, that academics are more likely to contribute value to practitioners if they seek to challenge conventional wisdom and familiar decision-making mindsets, rather than simply focusing on decision-makers' immediate concerns. It is the act of creating dissonance on the part of managers that leads to the consideration of new and previously ignored decision-making possibilities.

Taking part in and leading university–business collaborations calls, however, for a careful awareness of a particular set of competences. Studies have stressed the importance of culture and competences among individual collaboration partners, as this determines the execution of the collaboration process (Del Giudice & Maggioni, 2014). While some academics might be naturals in leading collaborative processes, some would argue that "the pressures on universities around funding and near market commercial activities are such that many academics are being forced into such activities when they are perhaps not suited to the task" (Docherty & Smith, 2007, p. 275). Academics will need competences that stem from the fields of, for example, facilitation, consultancy, and project management, which are not part of the classic academic training (Docherty & Smith, 2007, p. 275).

For example, studies have shown that inter-organizational collaborations call for appropriate socio-psychological features and mindsets and a high propensity to interact and share knowledge (Jolink & Dankbaar, 2010; Lazzarotti et al., 2016). Bartunek (2007) points to the relational attitude of academics when arguing that "bringing one's whole self to an engagement with others, being genuinely interested in their experience, demonstrating trustworthiness, and seeking feedback from them represent crucial relational attitudes that create high-quality connections" (p. 1328).

In a similar vein, a genuine interest in the practitioners' life world is important. The concept of 'interactional expertise' is the competence that an academic can draw on when interacting with people whose practices and relationships the academic wants to study in a meaningful way (Collins, 2004). Interactional expertise involves the ability to understand and communicate about a domain that the academic does not practice. Academics who possess this interactional expertise have learned how to work with specialists, with their own particular knowledge and interests. That is, they encourage specialists to share this knowledge and discuss technical content and context. Thus, the academic not only accesses and becomes familiar with the specialist's knowledge, but develops a real appreciation for it (Langley, Smallman, Tsoukas, & Van de Ven, 2013, p. 6). Kieser and Leiner (2009) often are cited for their skepticism towards collaborative research yielding valuable academic output, but they address the value in academics facilitating collaboration where research is not the intended output. From that point of view, these authors point to the competences of being bilingual and bi-competent facilitators who are "able to speak the language of practice and science but also be able to transfer schemas between the two contexts" (p. 528).

4.3 Constant Personal Learning

To engage in fruitful collaborations with practitioners, academics must be willing to learn from their collaboration partners. There cannot be any collaborative research unless all participants share a fundamental interest in learning and in reflexively examining and questioning the shared work (Pasmore et al., 2008). In addition, academics should learn throughout the research process, through interaction with practice (Jarzabkowski et al., 2010). Theories are approximations of the real world, and new information results in better understanding, better theory, and ultimately, frameworks, which are more useful for application in practical settings. Therefore, every time an academic is involved in a practical application of an organizational theory, it is an opportunity to improve or modify the theory (Jarzabkowski et al., 2010, p. 1196).

While some studies on collaborative innovation highlight the concept of absorptive capacity when discussing "the ability of a firm to recognize the value of new, external information, assimilate it, and apply it to commercial ends" (Cohen & Levinthal, 1990, p. 128), these studies typically do so in evaluating the learning capacity of the practitioners (e.g., Najafi-Tavani et al., 2018; Wu, 2014). Following the idea that academics have to learn on equal terms as practitioners, it is relevant to discuss the concept of absorptive capacity on the academic side of the collaboration. As noted by Gioia (2013, p. 135), academics often call for organizational change and may sometimes complain that practitioners are slow to change their organizations; however, academics themselves may not "practice what they preach" in this regard.

Thus, instead of placing the locus of learning and change solely with the practitioners, as academics often do, the collaboration leaders might benefit from applying what has been called a practice orientation to research. According to this view, academics are seen as practitioners themselves, who collectively have accepted the implication that their own practice is incomplete and in a constant state of change (Antonacopoulou, 2010, p. 221). Antonacopoulou points to the potentials in practice-relevant scholarship, which focuses critically on the research practice itself and calls for research practitioners to engage in 're-search' and in "reflexive critique about the ways in which they perform their research practices" (p. 220). This highlights the idea that academics engaging in university–business collaboration have to be open-minded, ready to learn, and willing to change the course of direction of the collaboration if new relevant discoveries appear along the way. In the end, that is what university–business collaboration is all about.

Overall, we argue that we need to look for learning potential in the way academics engage with their surroundings, and we call for greater sensitivity and reflexivity in the way academics collaborate with practitioners. Importantly, to improve collaboration, academics can themselves use some of the advice that they dispense to management. The practitioner community is not homogeneous and time and effort must be taken to open the lines of communication and foster a collaborative environment. And despite the attractiveness of providing a 'quick fix' to an imminent decision-maker's problem, the greatest value (to academic and practitioner) occurs when the academic challenges conventional wisdom and traditional decision-making mindsets.

REFERENCES

Åge, L.-J. (2014). How and why managers use conceptual devices in business-to-business research. *Journal of Business & Industrial Marketing*, 29(7/8), pp. 633–641.

Aguinis, H., Shapiro, D.L., Antonacopoulou, E.P., & Cummings, T.G. (2014). Scholarly impact: A pluralist conceptualization. *Academy of Management Learning & Education*, 13(4), pp. 623–639.

Alexiev, S.A., Volberda, W.H., & Van den Bosch, A.J.F. (2016). Interorganizational collaboration and firm innovativeness: Unpacking the role of the organizational environment. *Journal of Business Research*, 69(2), pp. 974–984.

Antonacopoulou, E.P. (2009). Impact and scholarship: Unlearning and practising to co-create actionable knowledge. *Management Learning*, 40(4), pp. 421–430.

Antonacopoulou, E.P. (2010). Beyond co-production: Practice-relevant scholarship as a foundation for delivering impact through powerful ideas. *Public Money & Management*, 30(4), pp. 219–226.

Arnaboldi, M. (2013). Consultant-researches in public sector transformation: An evolving role. *Financial Accountability & Management*, 29(2), pp. 140–160.

Arvanitis, S., Kubli, U., & Woerter, M. (2008). University-industry knowledge and technology transfer in Switzerland: What university scientists think about co-operation with private enterprises. *Research Policy*, 37(10), pp. 1865–1883.

Barge, J.K. (2001). Practical theory as mapping engaged reflection, and transformative practice. *Communication Theory*, 11(1), pp. 5–13.

Bartunek, J.M. (2007). Academic-practitioner collaboration need not require joint or relevant research: Toward a relational scholarship of integration. *Academy of Management Journal*, 50(6), pp. 1323–1333.

Bartunek, J.M. & Rynes, S.L. (2014). Academics and practitioners are alike and unlike: The paradoxes of academic-practitioner relationships. *Journal of Management*, 40(5), pp. 1181–1201.

Beaver, D.D. (2004). Does collaborative research have greater epistemic authority? *Scientometrics*, 60(3), pp. 399–408.

Benneworth, P. (2001). Academic entrepreneurship and long-term business relationships: Understanding 'commercialization' activities. *Enterprise and Innovation Management Studies*, 2(3), pp. 225–237.

Bouncken, R.B. (2008). Autopoiesis: The conception of joint learning. *European Journal of Management*, 8(4), pp. 40–46.

Bridgman, T. (2007). Reconstituting relevance: Exploring possibilities for management educators' critical engagement with the public. *Management Learning*, 38(4), pp. 425–439.

Chesbrough, H. (2003). *Open Innovation: A New Imperative for Creating and Profiting from Technology*. Boston, MA: Harvard Business School Press.

Chicksand, D. (2015). Partnerships: The role that power plays in collaborative buyer-supplier exchanges. *Industrial Marketing Management*, 48(5), pp. 121–139.

Clauss, T. & Kesting, T. (2017). How businesses should govern knowledge-intensive collaborations with universities: An empirical investigation of university professors. *Industrial Marketing Management*, 62(3), pp. 185–198.

Cohen, W.M. and Levinthal, D.A. (1990). Absorptive capacity: A new perspective on learning and innovation. *Administrative Science Quarterly*, 35(1), pp. 128–152.

Collins, H. (2004). Interactional expertise as a third kind of knowledge. *Phenomenology and the Cognitive Sciences*, 3(2), pp. 125–143.

Cruz-González, J., López-Sáez, P., & Navas-López, J.E. (2015). Absorbing knowledge from supply-chain, industry and science: The distinct moderating role of formal liaison devices on new product development and novelty. *Industrial Marketing Management*, 47(4), pp. 75–85.

Darabi, F. & Clark, M. (2012). Developing business school/SMEs collaboration: The role of trust. *International Journal of Entrepreneurial Behaviour & Research*, 18(4), pp. 477–493.

De Araújo Burcharth, A.L., Knudsen, M.P., & Søndergaard, H.A. (2014). Neither invented nor shared here: The impact and management of attitudes for the adoption of open innovation practices. *Technovation*, 34(3), pp. 149–161.

Del Giudice, M. & Maggioni, V. (2014). Managerial practices and operative directions of knowledge management within inter-firm networks: A global view. *Journal of Knowledge Management*, 18(5), pp. 841–846.

Desai, V.M. (2018). Collaborative stakeholder engagement: An integration between theories of organizational legitimacy and learning. *Academy of Management Journal*, 61(1), pp. 220–244.

Docherty, I. & Smith, D. (2007). Practicing what we preach? Academic consultancy in a multi-disciplinary environment. *Public Money & Management*, 27(4), pp. 273–280.

Du, J., Leten, B., & Vanhaverbeke, W. (2014). Managing open innovation projects with science-based and market-based partners. *Research Policy*, 43(5), pp. 828–840.

Etzkowitz, H. (2010). *The Triple Helix: University-Industry-Government Innovation in Action*. London: Routledge.

Feller, J., Parhankangas, A., Smeds, R., & Jaatinen, M. (2013). How companies learn to collaborate: Emergence of improved inter-organizational processes in R&D alliances. *Organization Studies*, 34(3), pp. 313–343.

Fendt, J., Kaminska-Labbe, R., & Sachs, W. (2008). Producing and socializing relevant management knowledge: Re-turn to pragmatism. *European Business Review*, 20(6), pp. 471–491.

Gioia, D. (2013). Editor's choice introduction. *Journal of Management Inquiry*, 22(1), pp. 2–3.

Godin, B. & Gingras, Y. (2000). Impact of collaborative research on academic science. *Science and Public Policy*, 27(1), pp. 65–73.

Gustavsen, B. (2003). Action research and the problem of the single case. *Concepts & Transformation*, 8(1), pp. 93–99.

Heckscher, C. & Martin-Rios, C. (2013). Looking back, moving forward: Toward collaborative universities. *Journal of Management Inquiry*, 22(1), pp. 136–139.

Heirati, N., O'Cass, A., Schoefer, K., & Siahtiri, V. (2016). Do professional service firms benefit from customer and supplier collaborations in competitive, turbulent environments? *Industrial Marketing Management*, 55(4), pp. 50–58.

Hernandez-Espallardo, M., Osorio-Tinoco, F., & Rodriguez-Orejuela, A. (2017). Improving firm performance through inter-organizational collaborative innovations: The key mediating role of the employee's job-related attitudes. *Management Decision*, 56(6), pp. 1167–1182.

Hibbert, P., Siedlok, F., & Beech, N. (2016). The role of interpretation on learning practices in the context of collaboration. *Academy of Management Learning & Education*, 15(1), pp. 26–44.

Hodgkinson, G.P. & Rousseau, D.M. (2009). Bridging the rigour–relevance gap in management research: It's already happening. *Journal of Management Studies*, 46(3), pp. 534–546.

Huxham, C. & Vangen, S. (2004). Doing things collaboratively: Realizing the advantages or succumbing to inertia? *Organizational Dynamics*, 22(2), pp. 190–201.

Huxham, C. & Vangen, S. (2005). *Managing to Collaborate*. London: Routledge.

Inkpen, A.C. & Tsang, E.W. (2005). Social capital, networks, and knowledge transfer. *Academy of Management Review*, 30(1), pp. 146–165.

Jarzabkowski, P., Mohrman, S.A., & Scherer, A.G. (2010). Organization studies as applied science: The generation and use of academic knowledge about organizations. Introduction to the special issue. *Organization Studies*, 31(9/10), pp. 1189–1207.

Jolink, M. & Dankbaar, B. (2010). Creating a climate for inter-organizational networking through people management. *International Journal of Human Resource Management*, 21(9), pp. 1436–1453.

Kieser, A. & Leiner, L. (2009). Why the rigour-relevance gap in management research is unbridgeable. *Journal of Management Studies*, 46(3), pp. 516–533.

Kieser, A. & Leiner, L. (2012). Collaborate with practitioners: But beware of collaborative research. *Journal of Management Inquiry*, 21(1), pp. 14–28.

Lakemond, N., Bengtsson, L., Laursen, K., & Tell, F. (2016). Match and manage: The use of knowledge matching and project management to integrate knowledge in collaborative inbound open innovation. *Industrial and Corporate Change*, 25(2), pp. 333–352.

Langley, A., Smallman, C., Tsoukas, H., & Van de Ven, A. (2013). Process studies of change in organization and management: Unveiling temporality, activity and flow. *Academy of Management Journal*, 56(1), pp. 1–13.

Laursen, K. & Salter, A. (2006). Open for innovation: The role of openness in explaining innovation performance among UK manufacturing firms. *Strategic Management Journal*, 27(2), pp. 131–150.

Lazzarotti, V., Manzini, R., Nosella, A., & Pellegrini, L. (2016). Collaborations with scientific partners: The mediating role of the social context in fostering innovation performance. *Creativity and Innovation Management*, 25(1), pp. 142–156.

Leahrey, E., Beckman, C.M., & Stanko, T.L. (2017). Prominent but less productive: The impact of interdisciplinarity on scientists' research. *Administrative Science Quarterly*, 62(1), pp. 105–139.

Learmonth, M., Lockett, A., & Dowd, K. (2012). Promoting scholarship that matters: The uselessness of useful research and the usefulness of useless research. *British Journal of Management*, 23(1), pp. 35–44.

Lee, Y.S. (2000). The sustainability of university-industry research collaboration: An empirical assessment. *The Journal of Technology Transfer*, 25(2), pp. 111–133.

Lindgreen, A. & Di Benedetto, C.A. (2018). Continuous improvement at *Industrial Marketing Management*: Suggestions from the Editorial Review Board. *Industrial Marketing Management*, 71, pp. 1–4.

Lindgreen, A., Di Benedetto, C.A., Brodie, R.J., & Naudé, P. (2019). How to build great research groups. *Industrial Marketing Management*, 81, pp. 1–13.

Marzo-Navarro, M., Pedraja-Iglesias, M., & Rivera-Torres, P. (2009). The marketing approach in relationship between universities and firms. *Journal of Relationship Marketing*, 8(2), pp. 127–147.

Mehlman, S.K., Saucedo, S.U., Taylor, R.P., Slowinski, G., Carreras, E., & Arena, C. (2010). Better practices for managing intellectual assets in collaborations. *Research Technology Management*, 53(1), pp. 55–66.

Mingers, J. (2014). *System Thinking, Critical Realism and Philosophy: A Confluence of Ideas*. Abingdon: Routledge.

Muller, E. & Doloreux, D. (2009). What we should know about knowledge-intensive business services. *Technology in Society*, 31(1), pp. 64–72.

Najafi-Tavani, S., Najafi-Tavani, Z., Naudé, P., Oghazi, P., & Zeynaloo, E. (2018). How collaborative innovation networks affect new product performance: Product innovation capability, process innovation, and absorptive capacity. *Industrial Marketing Management*, 73(6), pp. 193–205.

Nenonen, S., Brodie, R.J., Storbacka, K., & Peter, L.D. (2017). Theorizing with managers: How to achieve both academic rigor and practical relevance? *European Journal of Marketing*, 51(7/8), pp. 1130–1152.

Pasmore, W.A., Stymne, B., Shani, A.B., Mohrman, S.A., & Adler, N. (2008). The promise of collaborative management research. In Shani, A.B., Mohrman, S.A., Pasmore, W.A., Stymne, B., & Adler, N. (Eds.), *Handbook of Collaborative Management Research* (pp. 7–31). Thousand Oaks, CA: Sage Publications.

Paton, S., Chia, R., & Burt, G. (2014). Relevance or 'relevate'? How university business schools can add value through reflexively learning from strategic partnerships with business. *Management Learning*, 45(3), pp. 267–288.

Pecas, P. & Henriques, E. (2006). Best practices of collaboration between universities and industrial SMEs. *Benchmarking: An International Journal*, 13(1/2), pp. 54–67.

Pera, N., Occhiocupo, N., & Clarke, J. (2016). Motives and resources for value co-creation in a multi-stakeholder ecosystem: A managerial perspective. *Journal of Business Research*, 69(10), pp. 4033–4041.

Perkmann, M., Tartari, V., McKelvey, M., Autio, E., Broström, A., D'Este, P., & Sobrero, M. (2013). Academic engagement and commercialisation: A review of the literature on university–industry relations. *Research Policy*, 42(2), pp. 423–442.

Perkmann, M. & Walsh, K. (2007). University–industry relationships and open innovation: Towards a research agenda. *International Journal of Management Reviews*, 9(4), pp. 259–280.

Pertuzé, J.A., Calder, E.S., Greitzer, E.M., & Lucas, W.A. (2010). Best practices for industry–university collaboration. *MIT Sloan Management Review*, 51(4), pp. 83–90.

Pettigrew, A.M. (2003). Co-producing knowledge and the challenges of international collaborative research. In Pettigrew, A.M., Whittington, R., Melin, L., Sánchez-Runde, C., van den Bosch, F.A.J., Ruigrok, W., & Numagami, T. (Eds.), *Innovative Forms of Organizing: International Perspectives* (pp. 352–374). Thousand Oaks, CA: Sage Publications.

Pettigrew, A. & Starkey, K. (2016). The legitimacy and impact of business schools: Key issues and research agenda. *Academy of Management Learning & Education*, 15(4), pp. 649–664.

Plewa, C., Quester, P., & Baaken, T. (2005). Relationship marketing and university-industry linkages: A conceptual framework. *Marketing Theory*, 5(4), pp. 433–456.

Pollitt, C. (2006). Academic advice to practitioners: What is its nature, place and value within academia? *Public Money & Management*, 26(4), pp. 257–264.

Raelin, J. (2018). What are you afraid of: Collective leadership and its learning implications. *Management Learning*, 49(1), pp. 59–66.

Rynes, S.L., Bartunek, J.M., & Daft, R.L. (2001). Across the great divide: Knowledge creation and transfer between practitioners and academics. *Academy of Management Journal*, 44(2), pp. 340–355.

Santini, C., Marinelli, E., Boden, M., Cavicchi, A., & Haegeman, K. (2016). Reducing the distance between thinkers and doers in the entrepreneurial discovery process: An exploratory study. *Journal of Business Research*, 69(5), pp. 1840–1844.

Shapiro, D.L., Kirkman, B.L., & Courtney, H.G. (2007). Perceived causes and solutions of the translation problem in management research. *Academy of Management Journal*, 50(2), pp. 249–266.

Shaw, S. & Allen, J.B. (2006). It basically is a fairly loose arrangement and it works out fine really. *Sport Management Review*, 9(3), pp. 203–228.

Skippari, M., Laukkanen, M., & Salo, J. (2017). Cognitive barriers to collaborative innovation generation in supply chain relationships. *Industrial Marketing Management*, 62(3), pp. 108–117.

Smith, S. (2018). In pursuit of rapid impact: Research with a difference. *Journal of Organizational Studies & Innovation*, 5(1), pp. 1–7.

Spekkink, W.A.H. & Boons, A.A. (2016). The emergence of collaborations. *Journal of Public Administration Research & Theory*, 26(4), pp. 613–630.

Van de Ven, A.H. (2007). *Engaged Scholarship: A Guide for Organizational and Social Research*. New York: Oxford University Press.

Vangen, S. & Huxham, C. (2003). Nurturing collaborative relations: Building trust in interorganizational collaboration. *The Journal of Applied Behavioral Science*, 39(1), pp. 5–31.

Vicari, S. (2013). Is the problem only ours? A question of relevance in management research. *European Management Review*, 10(4), pp. 173–181.

Walker, D. (2010). Debate: Do academics know better or merely different? *Public Money & Management*, 30(4), pp. 204–206.

Winkelbach, A. & Walter, A. (2015). Complex technological knowledge and value creation in science-to-industry technology transfer projects: The moderating effect of absorptive capacity. *Industrial Marketing Management*, 47(4), pp. 98–108.

Wu, J. (2014). Cooperation with competitors and product innovation: Moderating effects of technological capability and alliances with universities. *Industrial Marketing Management*, 43(2), pp. 199–209.

Yassi, A., Dharamsi, S., Spiegel, J., Rojas, A., Dean, E., & Woollard, R. (2010). The good, the bad, and the ugly of partnered research: Revisiting the sequestration thesis and the role of universities in promoting social justice. *International Journal of Health Service*, 40(3), pp. 485–505.

Ylijoki, O.-H. (2003). Entangled in academic capitalism? A case-study on changing ideals and practices of university research. *Higher Education*, 45(3), pp. 307–335.

Zhou, Y., Zhang, X., Zhuang, G., & Zhou, N. (2015). Relational norms and collaborative activities: Roles in reducing opportunism in marketing channels. *Industrial Marketing Management*, 46(3), pp. 147–159.

PART 3

Working with students

8. Guiding Ph.D. students

C. Anthony Di Benedetto, Adam Lindgreen, and Torsten Ringberg
In collaboration with Audhesh Paswan, Laura Peracchio, David Luna, Peter Naudé, Rod Brodie, John Nicholson, Markus Reihlen, Matthew Robson, Ken Peattie, and Hans Baumgartner

1. INTRODUCTION

As business academics, one of our tasks is to train the next generation of educators. We ourselves entered our Ph.D. programs years ago, full of enthusiasm about an academic career, but still in need of training and experience in research and lacking in teaching skills. Many of us think back to our time in the Ph.D. program, recalling the incredible amount of work that was required, and the guidance provided by our supervisors. In the succeeding years, we have paid it forward, and have attempted to emulate our supervisors and provide the same kind of support to our own students. In this chapter, we explore the challenges of Ph.D. student supervision. We have turned to several of our colleagues, who have collectively supervised many Ph.D. students who have gone on to successful academic careers, and have asked them to contribute their thoughts on the Ph.D. supervision process.

To focus our presentation, we asked contributors to reflect on the following series of questions:

- Will you share your Ph.D. guidelines with us?
- Is there anything unique about your school/university, or country, regarding the Ph.D. programs?
- What are your expectations of Ph.D. students? Have your expectations changed over the last 5–10 years—and how?

- What kind of challenges/difficulties do Ph.D. students face, and what is your role as supervisor? What are the typical 'mistakes' that Ph.D. students make?
- What are Ph.D. students' expectations of you (academics in general, as well as the school/university)? Have their expectations changed over the last 5–10 years?
- Will you share a brief positive story of a Ph.D. student you supervised in terms of what contributed to his/her success?
- Will you share a brief 'negative' story of a student you supervised, and how/why the relationship/collaboration deteriorated, and how you handled this situation?

We stated that a few lines for each piece of advice would be sufficient; but also that it would be wonderful if the contributors could share a short story or two to illustrate their points for each of the topics.

This chapter presents the collective thoughts of our colleagues. The remaining parts of this chapter are structured as follows. We first discuss the tasks of supervision, including how these may need to be adapted depending on student characteristics such as number of years of managerial experience. Next, we explore the challenges faced by Ph.D. students, and discuss how the capabilities of both student and supervisor can be employed to address these challenges. A later section discusses the role of the supervisor in helping build student capabilities in publishing and teaching. We then turn to a reflection on how one can measure the contribution of a Ph.D. thesis, and a discussion of the benefits of taking on supervisory responsibility. In the conclusion, the co-authors of this chapter each provide a personal retrospective on their own experiences as Ph.D. supervisors.

2. SUPERVISION AND MANAGING THE CAREER TRANSITION

Anyone who has supervised Ph.D. students knows that this is time-consuming work, which requires much flexibility and adaptation to different student capabilities and work styles. Conventional students, entering a Ph.D. program early in their professional careers, have different expectations, expertise, and weaknesses relative to mid-career executives seeking a career change. To supervise effectively, one must be ready to adapt to these differences and anticipate the issues that may arise. In any case, a major responsibility of the supervisor is to oversee the student's transition to a career academic. This section explores the challenges in effective supervision.

2.1   Meetings and Supervision

Supervision and guidance of a Ph.D. student is a major time commitment for both the Ph.D. student and the supervisor. Business schools will vary on the number or duration of meetings or other requirements, but there is general agreement that close supervision throughout the program is required to get students on track early so that they can reach their thesis goals, and keep them on track.

Matthew Robson notes that some flexibility often is built into the supervisory task, which is designed to keep the student moving forward incrementally and not lose research momentum:

> In terms of guidelines for supervisory arrangements, this is quite loose. In my previous School, Leeds University, students were meant to upload meetings records every month. This was checked by administrators. At Cardiff Business School, the meetings logs are uploaded to feed into a six-monthly progress review. This system is not so prescriptive in terms of how often supervisors would see their student and for how long. It can flex to suit the circumstances, for example, the evolving nature of the student–supervisor partnership and stage of the work. However, the Leeds system had the advantage of creating record logs that the next meeting can launch off, which gives those involved the sense of incremental forward momentum. (Robson)

The requirements at Copenhagen Business School are quite detailed, with several progress milestones along the way. The process requires the Ph.D. student to develop a research proposal very early and receive feedback from Ph.D. supervisors. Updates are required every six months to ensure the student maintains momentum:

> At CBS, the requirements of the Ph.D. students and the Ph.D. supervisors' roles are outlined and continuously monitored in great detail. Within the first three months, the student has to present and have approved a research plan for the entire Ph.D. study with tentative courses listed (30 ECTS in all), when to fulfill teaching/advising obligations, and a research plan (in addition, when/where a three–six months stay abroad takes place. Apart from having a primary supervisor from within CBS (minimum associate professor level), a secondary supervisor is required and can be from CBS or from outside of CBS. The research proposal has to be presented at a faculty meeting within the first six months of enrollment. Every six months, the student enters a progress report online, which is signed off by the primary adviser, the Ph.D. School's department representative, the head of department, and the head of the Ph.D. School in sequential order. Any of aforementioned individuals can request additional information and/or question the entered attained course ECTS, as well as the overall progress of the student's plan. The supervisors meet regularly with the students, who, by the way, are referred to as Ph.D. candidates because they are considered research colleagues and also salaried with a significant pay as a research assistant. There are no requirements in terms of physical meetings,

but each six months, the students allocate up to 30 hours to their adviser based on their ongoing engagement (at CBS, all activities are measured in hours). The Ph.D. can be terminated if not sufficient progress is evidenced. That is, if the primary supervisor cannot document sufficient academic and/or administrative progress, the six-month progress report is left unsigned. That signals a potential for termination of the enrollment if the student does not rectify the situation within an additional three months. (Ringberg)

2.2 Transitioning to a Career in Research and Teaching

An important characteristic of any Ph.D. program is transition: from graduate student to career academic with research and teaching responsibilities. Ph.D. supervisors not only guide Ph.D. students in writing and defending their thesis research; they also ensure that students leave the program with a wide range of research skills that they can access in the future. Many research skills and capabilities cross disciplinary boundaries, so multidisciplinary classes can efficiently be offered. Often, students also will have teaching opportunities, which allows them to develop teaching skills and also claim teaching experience on their resumes. Audhesh Paswan describes this aspect of supervision, as it is handled at University of North Texas, which is typical of many Ph.D. programs in North America:

> At University of North Texas, we have a single Ph.D. program with seven concentrations. This allows us to combine some of the common skills and knowledge across different concentrations and enhance our efficiency in terms of faculty resources, especially in the domain of research tools and techniques. This is based on an assumption that areas such as marketing, management, IT and decision science, and behavioral accounting and finance need a combination of psychometric and econometric skills and capabilities, whereas others like accounting and finance and some from decision science that use more archival data would need more of econometric modeling skills. These integrations, I hope, also help Ph.D. students see some commonality across different concentration areas. I also hope that it helps break down functional silos and barriers, and develop a cross disciplinary approach to business research. I am sure that a lot of schools follow this structure and philosophy. We also try to emphasize the teaching aspect of an academician's life by getting our students to participate in a teaching seminar and actual teaching activities through teaching assistantship and fellowship assignments. (Paswan)

This transition process is handled differently at Copenhagen Business School, where students become accustomed to life as a career researcher at the outset of their program. While details may vary across departments, the objective is to get Ph.D. students involved early in all faculty activities:

> At CBS, Ph.D. students are regarded as research colleagues, which means they participate in academic activities, meetings, outings, and discussions. They also form a Ph.D. union across CBS in which they discuss their general work conditions, their

interaction with and support from supervisors, and they take initiatives to useful activities that might advance their academic careers (e.g., invited guest speakers, access to a psychologist, work/life balance, and general course requirements). The Ph.D. life can be stressful, in spite of being well salaried, due to the short duration of the program (i.e., three years) during which the students have to fulfill a number of teaching and course requirements in addition to show research progress and submit the final thesis (typically three publishable academic manuscripts). Each department sets its own requirements in terms of which courses the students need to take. In some departments, there are cohorts that go through a very structured program while in other departments the students can take courses not only at CBS but across European institutions. Similarly, it varies considerably how many students are enrolled within each department, which also determines their work environment and inter-personal dynamics. (Ringberg)

2.3 Supervision of Conventional Ph.D. Students

Most Ph.D. students fall into one of two categories: the conventional student, with strong academic capabilities and possibly some relevant work experience, seeking a career in research and teaching; and the mid-career professional, with years of middle- or senior-level supervisory and managerial experience, who perceives research problems from a practical, decision-making perspective. This section discusses providing guidance for conventional students; the next explores the challenges when supervising experienced professionals.

Ken Peattie provides an interesting starting point, recognizing that conventional students differ in significant ways, and recommending that the supervisor's role can be tailored according to the apparent requirements of the individual student:

> My experience in the role of Ph.D. supervisor could be summarized using the 2x2 matrix beloved of marketers, with 'confidence' and 'capability' (relatively speaking, they are all bright) providing the two axes. For the low confidence/high capability student, your primary role is that of cheerleader to stop insecurity preventing progress. For the high confidence/low capability candidate, you act more as guardrail to counter thoughts like "Of course, CEOs of FTSE companies will want to be interviewed by me!" or "I'm assuming a 50 percent response rate for my survey." For those in the high/high quadrant, you are mostly a sounding board helping them to articulate their ideas and providing a little guidance, whereas in the low/low quadrant you more play the Jedi Master, contributing motivation, direction, philosophy, (sometimes harsh) lessons, hopefully a good example to follow, and even the odd mind-trick! Working out early on which quadrant a student leans towards can be very helpful in getting your supervision style right. (Peattie)

Echoing these sentiments, Peter Naudé stresses the importance of understanding conventional students as individuals, recognizing when to apply pressure and when to back off and allow for student creativity:

> As far as I am concerned, it is largely about getting two things right. The first is the selection process, identifying bright, curious, hard-working students (and I have not always got that right!). And then, once they are on board, it is to walk the middle road of not sitting on their shoulders telling them what to do, but also not leaving them feeling so lost that they do not know which way to turn. It is an important balancing act: providing guidance, while allowing and encouraging, autonomy, creativity, and personal investigation. (Naudé)

2.4 Supervision of Experienced Professionals

The professional who decides on a mid-career change carries a different set of tools. Unlike the conventional student, the experienced professional has first-hand knowledge of business decisions developed over many years. To best manage these students, John Nicholson advises to focus on theories that have pragmatic applications, allowing the students' wealth of experience to be channeled effectively into their research process. The supervisor should therefore remain open and pragmatic in the selection of research paradigm and method:

> Supervision of experienced professionals should differ from that of more conventional Ph.D. students. I believe that the ambition of Ph.D. programs for experienced professionals should be to produce theories that are performative in practice, that is, that drive practices to converge with the theory derived during the period of study (Kelly, Nicholson, Johnston, Duty, & Brennan, 2020). Accordingly, supervisors should respect the experience of such students and find ways to inculcate that experience into the research process, rather than seeing this as an unhelpful encumbrance to be erased in order to achieve a value-neutral approach to a subject matter that the student may know much better than the supervisor.
>
> Supervisors should not dominate experienced professionals for rigor, but allow them to bring in their vision of relevance as of at least equal importance to rigor. A key element is to allow research questions to emerge from a practical problem rather than from a traditional gap-spotting method grounded in academic literature. Who is to say that academic incrementalism is in step with practice and that taking inspiration from a practical trajectory could be anything but rewarding for our discipline? Is there not the opportunity here for a democratic co-creation of knowledge between the supervisor and the experienced professional in this arrangement?
>
> Experienced professionals should not be inculcated into a paradigm, potentially that of the supervisor, and then working down from that ontological fixed position to the problem. An alternative is to follow a methodological pluralism (Midgley, Nicholson, & Brennan, 2017) that allows for a more pragmatic approach to the choice of methods and methodologies, which nonetheless maintains a strong ontological position. (Nicholson)

Another alternative is for the experienced professionals to maintain their position with their company, where company management and academic supervisor may share supervisory duties, an arrangement that presents challenges, but which may benefit both student and company. This is an option offered at the Copenhagen Business School:

> At CBS, the industrial Ph.D. students spent half their time at CBS and the other half at their company that contributes financially to their salary (often in a 50/50 arrangement). Supervision of industrial Ph.D. students typically is done by a representative from the company and a CBS researcher (who is the primary supervisor). The academic requirements to the academic rigor of the thesis is the same as for normal Ph.D. students, but the industrial students do not have to teach. The focus is to match the academic rigor with an applied and relevant issue that might also benefit the company. At times, the coordination and especially the integration of these students into the daily department environment and activities can be logistically challenging and difficult. (Ringberg)

3. CAPABILITIES

The Ph.D. program is challenging for both student and supervisor. This section explores the major challenges faced by Ph.D. students, including unclear expectations and lack of research focus. We discuss how some students handle these challenges, and why others seem to have difficulty overcoming the roadblocks. We also reflect on the characteristics of the Ph.D. supervisor that are most appreciated by students in guiding them through the difficult moments.

3.1 Challenges that Ph.D. Students Face

Regardless of their academic background or work experience, all Ph.D. students face challenges and enter the Ph.D. program with uncertainties. Ph.D. supervisors should anticipate these issues and be prepared to handle them. Perhaps more now than ever before, supervisors take a more active role (both in guiding students and helping them achieve work–life balance) as the expectations of Ph.D. students have intensified over the years. Markus Reihlen notes that:

> Ph.D. students generally expect to receive insightful and timely feedback on their work. Have the expectations changed over the last decades? I think on average yes, they have. Students increasingly ask for how to balance a demanding research project with private life arrangement. They also demand more guidance, as well as feedback through which they hope to reduce uncertainty of their research venture. Highly independent research of students increasingly is replaced by close collaboration and feedback. They also demand more services and support of their Ph.D. research by the universities. (Reihlen)

Reihlen identifies some of the most common challenges confronting Ph.D. students, as they progress through their program:

- *Unrealistic scope of the research project*: This could be the case because there is a lack of focus, a lack of a clear academic conversation the Ph.D. research would like to contribute to, or a lack of methodological skills that would not allow a rigorous mixed method approach.
- *Unaware how to make a real contribution*: Students sometimes envision to make a study, but do not ask themselves under what conditions this study is truly interesting, engaging, and novel.
- *Unrealistic expectations of what it means to work on Ph.D. research*: Students should be prepared to go on a rollercoaster ride and not a merry-go-round.
- *Bad project management*: In some instances, students do not plan their research well. For instance, they may start to generate data for a cross-sectional study and then change their mind and jump on the process organization studies bandwagon. Yet, they did not adjust their research design towards a process study design. (Reihlen)

Some students will enter the Ph.D. program with a good idea of what they want to study, but this is not the case for other students. They may possess a general thought, but have difficulty developing it into a meaningful research question. The supervisor can play a supporting role in the creation of a worthy research study. Audhesh Paswan often recommends to Ph.D. students to think about their own realities and find inspiration there: he calls it a 'slice of life' approach:

In my mind, the most daunting challenge confronting Ph.D. students is how to imagine, create, and tell a story. In our seminars, we expose our students to a lot of tools and techniques and 'so and so said this' from the literature. However, we often do not teach them or have a platform that teaches them how to imagine, create, and tell a story. As a result, most of the students turn into technicians and develop a research question based on 'slice of literature', that is, read the literature till the cows come home, and then try to fill a gap in the literature. There is nothing wrong with this approach, except that it often results in a research that may not have much to do with real life. I like to tell my students to develop a research idea based on 'slice of life': look at what is going in our lives, society, and focal business context, and then develop a research question that tries to solve a life problem. Personally, I have had fun with this approach, and my students who take to it love it. I also look at this as the exploitation versus exploration approach. While I agree that we need both, I feel that we more of exploration mindset in our students. (Paswan)

All Ph.D. students know that they will be facing publish-or-perish pressures in their careers, and some may enter the review process for the first time fearfully. Audhesh Paswan reminds the Ph.D. supervisor of the importance of supporting their Ph.D. students through this challenging task and help them learn the ropes for future success:

> I believe the second biggest challenge for Ph.D. students is to overcome their fear of failure and the nightmarish review process. In our seminars, we expose our students to all the literature, which are the results of several failed attempts and trial and errors. We do not put the students in a situation where they can fail without paying a heavy price. As a Ph.D. supervisor, I see my role as getting my students to take that first step, that is, put their manuscript in the review process, and be supportive when it comes back rejected or gets a revise and resubmit. Most of my students who work with me get their first manuscript through this process. (Paswan)

Like many other schools, Copenhagen Business School places high publishing expectations on their Ph.D. students, whose thesis chapters may be three publishable manuscripts tied together with overall implications. Close supervision is required to guide students through this challenging process for the first time, and to ensure that they are on the right path for producing future research on their own:

> At CBS, the challenge is to reframe the Ph.D. students' way of thinking toward producing new research, and not merely consuming, and in addition finding something that contributes significantly to what experienced researchers already are producing in well-regarded journal outlets. That is a task that requires close and continuous interaction between the Ph.D. students and their supervisors. The Danish system is quite demanding on students, as they only get three years to submit their thesis. During this time, they need to take courses (30 ECTS), teach courses (624 working hours), ideally do a research stay abroad, and develop, write, present, and preferably submit three publishable manuscripts for medium- to high-level journals, which are included as part of their thesis, in addition to overarching chapters that ties it all together. It is quite a challenging task given that international Ph.D. students often have four–five years at their disposal. (Ringberg)

Markus Reihlen summarizes many types of challenges faced by Ph.D. students, and outlines the kind of support that can be provided by the Ph.D. supervisors to help students to cope. While some of these challenges pertain specifically to the German university system, many are familiar to academics in Ph.D. programs worldwide. He lists the following categories of challenges and how he personally has dealt with them:

- *Committing Ph.D. students to the ethics of science*: While in general this is not necessarily an issue, I put clear emphasis on ethical principles as laid out by the German Research Foundation. Among them are clear rules concerning co-authorship, methodological, and citation practices, etc. These are important prevention measures.
- *Aligning Ph.D. students' motivation with an interesting topic*: Not every hot topic is a good topic for an individual student. Therefore, a key task for me is to

find out and guide students in their venture, especially negotiating the right topic that fits for them and their deeper interests.
- *Dealing with a lack of scientific skills*: This is an issue, but usually less problematic because either I try to skill them by myself—starting with a reading list, meeting to explore interesting topics, etc.—and/or sending them to good Ph.D. courses, conferences, and summer schools.
- *Dealing with personal challenging situations*: Finishing a Ph.D. thesis can become a rollercoaster ride for students. Going on this ride means that students have to learn how to deal with the lows, rejections, and critical feedback, while enjoying the acceptance and positive feedbacks of their work. However, sometimes stress is unrelated to the Ph.D. research, but rather located in particular contextual conditions such as private relational issues or that the students have decided to found their own start-up venture. Conducting these talks as counselor goes beyond the normal supervision.
- *Dealing with a lack of ambition*: A lack of ambition is critical, and this is not always clear from the start. One way of dealing with this is a clear signaling strategy in the beginning and intensive talks before the person is accepted as a Ph.D. student. In the German system, you are not 'simply' accepted into a program, but you have to be accepted by a specific supervisor before you can enter the program. In addition, a lack of ambition will trigger intensive face-to-face talks and more formal feedbacks that document the lack of engagement.
- *Dealing with non-collaborating practice partners*: Especially students who work in close collaboration with companies, or are financed by their companies, sometimes face challenges. For instance, the company was supposed to be the subject of the empirical study, but in the process is unwilling to do so. As a supervisor, I try to save the topic by arranging talks with the company gatekeeper, which sometimes works, but sometimes, we have to invent a new topic, which does not require company data in order to save the Ph.D. research. (Reihlen)

3.2 Characteristics of Capable Ph.D. Students

Experienced Ph.D. supervisors can reflect on their Ph.D. students over the years, and recognize which ones stood out. What do they look for in a student? Perhaps not surprisingly, many contributors favored ambitious students with positive attitudes who successfully made the transition from graduate student to research colleague. Here are some of the thoughts on this topic:

My expectation of the Ph.D. students are usually threefold:
- *Individual attitudes and skills*: I expect my Ph.D. students to show a great commitment, curious for their field of research, and a high intrinsic motivation. Do they really have the taste of science? In addition, the CV should indicate a high level of commitment to research.
- *Ambitious research*: I expect the students to work with my help on research that is truly ambitious and can make a real impact to the field. The metaphor 'try to reach out for the stars' has been commonly used, although we know that it will not always happen. Yet, this should be the level of ambition.

- *Realistic contextual conditions*: It is important that the Ph.D. research operates under realistic contextual conditions. For instance, I have had a number of students who worked in the industry. Having clear arrangements with the employer that gives students enough time to explore their research topic independently and with the necessary depths is critical. (Reihlen)

I try to accept Ph.D. students with the aspiration to want to be an academic at a good place, which ultimately means to publish well. After a couple of years in the process, these students should 'kick on' and want to work on manuscripts. My style is not to haul them in and force this, but rather is to leave the door ajar. Students should take ownership of matters and the opportunity to use a co-author who has the experience to guide the crafting of one or more manuscripts. Probably, if a student is not kicking on in this way it is a bad sign ...

The best students are the ones who can manage the transition seamlessly into being staff members. Good students know their literature, are strong methodologically, and can write. But because they wanted to be academics throughout their Ph.D. journey, they have learnt broadly about the profession. As such, there is no hiatus in their research when they take their first job. This said, sometimes such students get a first job that involves too much teaching emphasis. They should know how to protect their margins if this is the case. In sum, positive stories tend to involve students who mature quickly as professionals. (Robson)

I expect Ph.D. students learn to become independent scholars/researchers. My best students will have at least two manuscripts accepted while doing their Ph.D. research. (Brodie)

Also, many collaborators reflected positively on students who showed an ability to work independently, and to take an idea and run with it:

My Ph.D. students, the ones who opt to work for me, happen to be more independent and do not like too much of hand holding. In turn, I like to treat them as adults and not mollycoddle them. I respect their crazy ideas and help them develop their own ideas. Some of my students still come back after several years and ask me to work with them. I can think of three students in the last five years who asked if I would work with them, and would I give them a topic that they can work on. I turned around and said that is a bad idea. I asked them what they were interested in. When they started talking, I could see that they were not sure to start with but became very excited. I asked them to tell me a story. In turn, I just doodle and give back drawings of crazy models. They took those crazy drawings and ran with it. We went back and forth, and eventually they all ended up getting a publication in *Industrial Marketing Management*. (Paswan)

My first Ph.D. student had some negative experiences with other faculty and ended up with me, as last resort. I took the student reluctantly, but he ended up being great, out of sheer determination. The student was not the best trained initially, but in the end was able to learn by doing and became fairly successful. (Luna)

My latest Ph.D. student is a very positive and also unusual example. She worked for five years in the industry, in the end as a senior product manager for a large multinational company. She started her Ph.D. program with a scholarship, which paid only a fraction of her former salary. By blending her curiosity in science with her industry background, she became a great and very valuable person of my research team. She finished her Ph.D. with a *Journal of Management Studies* publication (as first author), won the best Ph.D. paper award from the Research Methods Division of the Academy of Management and is now shortlisted for the EGOS best Ph.D. thesis award in 2020. She will now continue her academic career at Leuphana. (Reihlen)

3.3 Characteristics of Less Capable Ph.D. Students

What, then, about the cases where the Ph.D. student's experience was not as positive? Are there signs that can be recognized early, and is there anything that can be done by the Ph.D. supervisor? Typical problem areas include lack of effective collaboration, difficulties with English as a second language, or an inability to maintain focus after a promising start, sometimes because of personal reasons:

> It is not so much the case that the collaboration deteriorates. It is more likely that the collaboration never really fired on all cylinders in the first instance—it did not kick on. A Ph.D. student needs to be good at each step of the way. I am not familiar with a case where the literature review, conceptualization, and fieldwork were accomplished with aplomb, and then the work deteriorated. Usually, the signs are there. This said, sometimes you get a student who is absolutely brilliant at specific aspects of a study. Probably, such a student has real value as a member of a high-quality publishing team that includes complementary colleagues, although not in terms of producing sole-authored work. (Robson)

> We have international Ph.D. students who have English as a second language. Learning to write well for these students is challenging. (Brodie)

> The main challenge is that Ph.D. students may lose focus throughout their years as students. Five years is a long time for an adult person, and life has a way of derailing initial plans. Divorces, abusive relationships, deaths, all kinds of things can happen. The result is that the investment we put into a student may not pay off with a good placement in the end. That is totally outside of our control, though. (Luna)

> One of my Ph.D. students started on an externally funded research project. He was very ambitious, skilled, and well socially embedded in our research team. A first manuscript was successfully published, and it looked like that things would continue that way. Yet, in his private life things radically changed (I keep it here in abstract terms), and this disrupted his Ph.D. program. For three years, we met regularly, yet more for counseling than research guidance meetings. Unfortunately, the research has not advanced and is likely to be terminated soon. It started out as a very promising research program with a highly talented person, and then life took a wrong turn, and we could not set the program on the right track again. (Reihlen)

> A Ph.D. student who had a lot of promise ended up dropping the ball and would disappear for long periods of time. He did not accept suggestions very well, and ended up not publishing any of his thesis work. He claims he ended up hating his thesis topic, which probably had something to do with his lack of follow through. (Luna)

> I have had a Ph.D. student who did all right while in the program. However, after graduation and getting his first job, he fell into the trap of "I will do research because I have to." This led to that person getting into a tight spot in his three-year evaluation. Thankfully, he woke up, reached out to me, and we were able to salvage the situation. That particular student will probably not be a stellar researcher, but he will probably be fine. Such people are adults and must find their own place in life that they are comfortable with. My role is to help them find that place in life. (Paswan)

Procrastination, perfectionism, occasional inability to deal with life's pressures, and other human failures can also inflict damage on a Ph.D. student's progress. If the Ph.D. supervisor can recognize such issues early and take action, perhaps the student can get back on track:

> A common mistake is to wait too long to start a research program. These days, it seems like most of the Ph.D. students see the need to hit the floor running and get started on research during their first year, but it is hard to get the students up to speed on the literature and methods fast enough, unless they come to us with some research background. As a result, we really try to admit new students only if they have previous research backgrounds. (Luna)

> Serving both in the capacity of the department's Ph.D. representative and as Ph.D. supervisor for numerous Ph.D. students, I have experienced many types of students. The procrastinator, the blame others, the perfectionist, and the realist types. At times, you come across a Ph.D. student who possesses several of these types (excluding the realist type), which makes it next to impossible for the interaction, as well as the Ph.D. research to end on a positive note. Each type requires very different strategies from the supervisor. Yet, in spite of extensive efforts by supervisors, I have yet to see any successful outcomes from the 'blame others' type. The next in line are the procrastinator, the perfectionist, and the realist in terms of being successful. I have experienced successful outcomes in all of these cases, but with an inclining likelihood toward the realist students (who realistically assesses their chances for fulfilling the requirements and finishing up). I have personally experienced all four types, and it does feel uphill when one recognizes too late in the process what one is up against as supervisor requiring having to make an assessment of whether to proceed or consider it sunk costs. In addition, there are some students who, when under pressure, experience sudden mental blackouts, depression, borderline personality, etc. and require professional psychological intervention to get back on track. (Ringberg)

3.4   Characteristics of Good Ph.D. Supervisors

So what is a good Ph.D. supervisor? Certainly, it is not a one-size-fits-all position, as some Ph.D. students may thrive under one supervisor and be a very poor match for another. Audhesh Paswan addresses this point, noting that some students will require more guidance, while others will be fine with a lighter touch. He implies that it is up to us to recognize and adapt to these differences:

> In the last 5–10 years, I do not think the expectations of our Ph.D. students have changed. I still feel that they expect us to mentor them in both research and teaching. The level and type of mentoring desired may differ from person to person. Some may expect a lot of hand holding, while others like to be gently guided and nudged, and not taken by hand through every corner. (Paswan)

Peter Naudé provides details on the kind of guidance the Ph.D. supervisor needs to provide, including academic guidance, network building, and emotional support, noting that this work can be a major time commitment. He also stresses the need to challenge the Ph.D. student to keep the on the right path and make progress:

> A good Ph.D. supervisor should provide conceptual and methodological guidance and advisement; offer guidance in terms of the process (e.g., where to start, what to focus on, how to move on to the empirical sections of the Ph.D. research, literature review, and conceptual grounding); open up for networking opportunities (putting the student in touch with experts in terms of the topic, as well as methodologies); open up for networking and relationship-building opportunities with other students; respond to the students' questions; and, finally, directing the students to the appropriate resources … It is a time-consuming exercise. Do not think you can do it on a half-time basis. You have to be committed to the process. You have to offer regular contact and availability, as well as emotional support … A supervisor should not be afraid to challenge students, for example in terms of their rate of progress. (Naudé)

Peter Naudé shared some of the feedback he has received over the years from Ph.D. students he supervised. The comments showed that he had provided value in many different ways, for which students were very appreciative. These include:

- *Being a mentor*: providing support and help beyond expectation.
- *Knowledge of the subject*: asking challenging questions and giving direction.
- *Networking*: introducing academic colleagues, encouraging presentation at conferences, which provided experience and aided in further development of research ideas.
- *Getting published*: helping in the preparation of manuscripts for submission and throughout the review process.
- *Attention*: Always giving full attention, being available for in-person or Skype meetings, traveling for face-to-face meetings with students who were studying abroad; quick turnaround time for feedback.
- *Creativity*: Always encouraging of student creativity, avoiding judgmental comments, letting the student decide on research direction.
- *Encouragement*: Providing positive commentary, but being ready to correct when necessary.

- *Gatekeeping*: Helping the student through administrative issues, such as arranging for a work-abroad opportunity, cutting red tape on behalf of the student.
- *Collaboration*: Being more of a collaborator than manager; developing ideas jointly and encouraging research direction.
- *Reliability*: Showing total commitment to the student, providing timely feedback and reliable advice.
- *Innovativeness*: Ready to identify innovative frameworks or theories that the students might be able to integrate into their work, while not diminishing the students' own creative contribution.
- *The right amount of guidance*: An experienced researcher might be too passionate about their chosen subject and oversteer the student's research; this temptation is avoided and guidance is offered which is sensitive to the student's interests and passions.
- *Coaching*: Sound advice on the selection of external examiners, and suggestions on how to prepare for the thesis defense and not be intimidated.

4. PUBLISHING AND TEACHING

During their program, Ph.D. students develop essential skills in conducting research, academic writing and publishing, and effective teaching. In this section, our contributors offer their thoughts on the role of the Ph.D. supervisor in developing publication skills, while ensuring that the Ph.D. program provides opportunity to grow as an effective communicator in the classroom.

4.1 Monograph vs. Publishable Articles

Once the Ph.D. thesis is defended successfully (and sometimes even before that), the Ph.D. student has to convert the research into one or more publishable manuscripts. Ph.D. supervisors can play a major role in helping their students get their work published in the best possible (journal) outlets. As Matthew Robson explains, this supervisory task may be particularly challenging in a more traditional setting, where the student is expected to produce one large piece of research (as opposed to the newer trend of requiring three chapters, which are meant to be distinct research manuscripts):

> Cardiff Business School seems to be a typical UK place in how it treats its Ph.D. students and program. Students ultimately are tasked with producing one large document, rather than a set of individual manuscripts. This has pros and cons. The pro is that such a magnum opus type Ph.D. can really advance the state of the art—it is amazing what a student can learn and achieve with the time and a liberal word count. The downside is that it is difficult to then turn such a piece of work into publications. Students are not developing skills to write in the most succinct and efficient way possible, and they are not focusing on how to craft publishable manuscripts. Going from 80,000 words down to 6,000 words is a tall order even for experienced academics. I like the three-/four-manuscript Ph.D. model that some other academic

systems follow. Still, this can raise issues with a lack of thematic focus. The storyline that is meant to unite the manuscripts commonly does not hold up. (Robson)

In today's academic work environment, the expectations of graduating Ph.D. students are higher than ever. The supervisors' role is even more critical in this environment: they need to set up realistic expectations, and also help the student establish a strong track record upon graduation that leaves the student poised for future publishing success:

> Modern Ph.D. students face the depressing realization that (1) they must publish to get a good job that gives them the academic freedom to continue as active researchers, and (2) scholarly journal space is at a premium, as review funnels have become clogged with increasing submissions from all parts of the world. To get a job, a student now needs an early publication, coupled with medium-term work that shows a quality trajectory. For early career-researchers, the learning never really stops. It is no longer the case that you can do good Ph.D. research and be set for the next five years. (Robson)

> Expectations keep increasing. The timeline has accelerated because of the need to start projects early on. We expect Ph.D. students to have two–three essays (three is the normal expectation). We also hope they will have at least a publication or a manuscript in advanced review at a top journal. (Luna)

Article publication and job placement, ultimately, are intertwined. The Ph.D. students are under time constraints to complete their thesis and publish articles, develop teaching skills, and meet their responsibilities in their personal lives. Ph.D. supervisors can only do so much, but they can provide opportunities for their students to develop their skills, and eventually create and communicate knowledge themselves. Hans Baumgartner and Audhesh Paswan offer their thoughts on this point:

> I think the main challenge these days is to find a good job in academia. This means that you have to start working on publications as soon as you join a Ph.D. program, so you have publications by the time you go on the market. I do not think that necessarily is a good thing because Ph.D. students do not have the time to take courses and read widely. (Baumgartner)

> We would like our Ph.D. students to become future change agents through knowledge creation and transfer, and, even more important, capability developers. Accordingly, we expect our students, at least in the area of marketing to have (a) at least one journal article and (b) taught a couple of classes by the time they go into the job market. (Paswan)

4.2 Building Teaching Skills

While much of the supervisor's time is taken up in providing research and writing guidance, many universities provide opportunities for Ph.D. students not only to teach, but also to develop their teaching skills through seminars or courses in pedagogy. Initiatives of this type ensure that the students have built up the required capabilities and are ready to take on teaching duties.

> The teaching capability enhancement part is taken care of through our teaching seminars and the Teaching Assistantship/Fellowship assignments. The research expectation is taken care of in our research tools seminars, as well as seminars that focus on major and/or minor areas. For example, in my business-to-business seminar, one assignment is to have Ph.D. students develop a publishable quality manuscript, and most students do eventually end up with either a conference or a journal article with a focus on business-to-business marketing. Several of my students have published in *Industrial Marketing Management* because of this initiative. This also boosts a student's confidence. I also encourage the students in my seminar to volunteer for reviewing for a journal and/or a conference. (Paswan)

> At CBS, we require that full-time employed Ph.D. students (who are paid as research assistants) contribute with 624 hours of teaching, advising (e.g., of master's theses), and/or co-examiner (oral/written). The students are not (as of yet) required to take a course in pedagogics and thus often have to do 'the best they can'. Most often, it goes quite well, although at times the students end up dreading the experience, which can be quite intimidating when standing in front of 100+ undergraduate students in a big auditorium. Teaching academic material is demanding, as it requires the ability to go beyond the textbook material to make the material come alive with other examples while providing additional academic depth. It is a sink or swim experience, but surprisingly many students survive the process and do quite well (based on teaching ratings). It is not an ideal situation, but with so many other chores at hand, as well as serving their dues (financially to CBS), it is probably the best set-up. I had similar experiences when I was a Ph.D. student at Penn State where I taught undergraduate courses. (Ringberg)

5. REFLECTIONS ON THE SUPERVISION

In this section, we gather some of our contributors' overall reflections on the supervision process. How can we assess the contribution to knowledge made by our Ph.D. students? How should one handle the student who is not planning a traditional academic career? And what are the long-term benefits of taking on supervisory responsibility?

5.1 Contributions of a Ph.D. Thesis

Once the Ph.D. thesis has been defended, how can its contribution to knowledge be measured? John Nicholson suggests a novel way for the Ph.D. student to assess the type(s) of radical or incremental contribution that has been made. This technique can be used to enumerate the expected contributions in the introductory section, then to close the circle in the concluding section to show how these contributions have been achieved.

> One of the key measures of whether a thesis is awarded is the affirmation that a contribution to knowledge has been made. (For a comprehensive framework for writing contribution sections in journals, see Nicholson, LaPlaca, Al-Abdin, Breese, & Khan, 2018.) However, I believe we should number contribution claims in the same way that we number objectives and questions. Why do we leave contributions vague when these are the essential measures of a Ph.D. thesis' quality? For example, a grid could be placed in introduction sections relative to the two main contribution types, that is, incremental (gap-spotting) and revelatory (assumption challenging). In an introduction, and in a simple table, the Ph.D. student could number each contribution, stating in which section of the literature review the gap is exposed or the assumption identified; then where the thesis' material fills that gap, or challenges that assumption; and, finally, that this table is returned to in the conclusions to complete the loop. This leaves an examiner few places to go in terms of the communication of the thesis' contribution, leaving only its substance to be challenged. (Nicholson)

John Nicholson also reminds Ph.D. supervisors that one should not discount publications in non-traditional targets, such as trade journals, especially when working with experienced professionals. For this category of Ph.D. students, a publication that is widely read by practitioners in their field may be viewed as just as impactful (if not more so) than a publication in an A-journal. In fact, the experienced professional's objective in entering the Ph.D. program may be to return to industry with newfound understanding and knowledge. A good supervisor is receptive to these different goals and will be willing to adapt to them:

> Ph.D. supervisors should accept that the ambitions of experienced professionals may not be the same as those of a career academic. An engaged supervisor should accept that impact in such student's community of practice may be a greater drive than publishing in highly ranked journals and building citations. Engaged supervisors should not see publications in trade journals as 'wasting' good material. Equally, engaged supervisors should not see their role as assimilating a practitioner into academia where the student may wish to return to practice as a better practitioner. (Nicholson)

5.2   To Supervise or Not to Supervise

As a final topic, our contributors weighed in on the responsibilities of the Ph.D. supervisor, and what one is 'getting into' when agreeing to serve as a Ph.D. thesis committee chairperson or member. The job is time-consuming and is perhaps not for everybody. However, it can be very rewarding for those who want to see their graduates make a real difference in the academic community.

A further benefit is that some will become co-authors, possibly for years to come:

> I expect my students to go on to become research active scholars. Simply, I expect 'to bump into them on the conference circuit'. This is my base expectation, and I have not changed it over the years. Our responsibility is to leave something behind. This can be taken as advancing knowledge through publishing, but also it involves building the academy. Hence, I have supervised 17 students to completion thus far, which is a high number for someone with just over two decades of academic experience. There are professors who do very little supervision, viewing this as a distraction from their core business of publishing few, good manuscripts with other senior academics and professing generally. I won't criticize that approach too much. Each to their own. (Robson)

> Although I have served on the committees of many Ph.D. students over the years, I have only been the main adviser for a relatively small number. Over the last 20 years or so, I have increasingly become interested in methodological issues related to survey research, and we do not have a lot of students who are interested in this topic and it is probably not a good topic for students if they want to find a tenure-track position. Almost all the students that I have worked with have exceeded my expectations, and I have worked with most of them long after they left Penn State. (Baumgartner)

Those who undertake Ph.D. supervision need to be aware of the time commitment and level of bureaucracy, which can vary by university or host country. They should be aware of the bureaucratic requirements, which can be quite strict:

> Ph.D. advising at CBS represents less of supervision and more of a collegial process during which the supervisors are rewarded with hours (max. 30 per semester) by the Ph.D. students based on their active contribution to the Ph.D. process. Obviously, supervisors do not take on students due to the additional hours (which count toward their own 840 hours of yearly obligations), but the opportunity to develop a productive collaboration that benefits both the student's and the supervisor's publication records. The students have the upper hand in terms of deciding whether they will change adviser during the process, whether they will change topic of the Ph.D. thesis, etc. In fact, I have seen students whose salary has been financed by a grant attainted by a faculty, request and get another faculty person and keep the salary part of the grant, to the great frustration of the grant holder. That is part of Danish law. We have had several students who have changed supervisor mid-stream, but we try to amend the situation such that any manuscripts the supervisor has contributed to will include the supervisor as one of the authors. This is not an ideal situation for the supervisor. On the other hand, the student could end up with a supervisor (who might have been recommended by the department when accepted into the program) who is a bad fit, in which case the department's Ph.D. representative and head of department will try to find another person. The collaboration between the supervisors and the Ph.D. students is both based on a legal arrangement (Danish law) and a moral arrangement, which involves a fair give-and-take by all parties involved.

Most times, it goes quite well, but at times, a resolution might require quite some work and involve multiple administrative processes and time. (Ringberg)

6. CONCLUSIONS

After having considered the comments of our contributors, this chapter's co-authors took the time to reflect on their own experiences as Ph.D. supervisors, and our role in guiding our students and responding to their requirements.

> As a Ph.D. supervisor, I expect that Ph.D. students are critical thinkers who also are interested, curious, and willing to put in the time it takes to produce academic work, and last, but not least, willing to entertain advice I provide to their research path going forward. It is quite discouraging to spend time and effort guiding students with very relevant advice, only to realize that they either did not grasp the depth of the advice, or that they still want to go ahead with their idea without structure or hope of any contribution to the literature. That said, I expect students to engage critically with what I say, and, of course, appreciate if they constructively revise and further improve such advice.
>
> It can be discouraging when students 'think they know best' and continue down the path against advice without being able to substantiate any academic support for their plan. It has only happened once with a colleague who decided that he/she was not able or willing to provide the necessary support this student apparently needed. It turned out that the next supervisor had the same problem and also ended up opting out, still without the student recognizing this being his/her issue. I have very much enjoyed the collaboration and back-and-forth discussions with students about their research, which often turned into a shared publication of articles and even books.
>
> I do expect to be a co-author of my student's manuscript when submitted to a journal provided, of course, that I have contributed to the overall content at a level similar to when I engage in collaborative research projects with other colleagues.
>
> In one case, I entered as supervisor after the previous supervisor left. Here, I only helped change the format and structure from a three-manuscript submission to a monograph. In this case, I did not contribute to the content, only to the structural changes, and did not co-author later work based on the thesis.
>
> On a more foundational level, I expect the students to have sufficient maturity to be in charge of their Ph.D. process, so I do not have to be the controlling (i.e., supervising) force that requests ongoing meetings and deliveries beyond the semi-annual requirements although in some cases it has been necessary. More broadly, I try to be compassionate when needed, as well as have patience. I would rather err on this side than being too authoritarian or rigid, as I think, ultimately speaking, part of the Ph.D. process requires the students to be responsible for reaching the end goal. This is probably very different from the German model!
>
> That said, it is not easy to determine how good a student is from the onset, and it can lead to a situation where neither I, as the supervisor, nor the student benefits much from the entire Ph.D. process. Thus, it might be useful with more rigorous admission processes to save everyone from only later finding out that achievement of a Ph.D. is not realistic for the student. In the US many universities rely extensively on graduate admission tests (e.g., GRE, SAT, or GMAT), which I believe have been shown to correlate the best among a range of other predictive variables

(e.g., GPA, motivation letter, research proposal, etc.) with the potential for successful completion.

More generally, I find it intriguing and inspiring to interact with the vast majority of my students with whom I often engage in quite close academic collaborations. In some cases, it has led to long-lasting academic collaborations and friendships.

What students expect from me varies depending on their particular training, personality, and research topics. Most of the students I have worked with appreciated my active engagement in helping them refine and develop their research topics, and also me being part of two of their three thesis manuscripts (the third has to be single authored). They typically have cherished our ongoing and more informal interaction, in contrast to more strictly 'planned ahead' interactions (although some personality types and perhaps younger students might benefit from more structure). The students also appreciate to be shown compassion/sensitivity during stressful times. We have all been there, and it is only human to feel out of sorts during a Ph.D. process, and they may request some personal advice on how to handle such situations. (Ringberg)

I believe that Ph.D. students need to be curious, critical, and creative (Lindgreen, Vallaster, & Vanhamme, 2001). Although Ph.D. supervisors have gone through a Ph.D. program themselves and subsequently published in academic journals, students soon should know more about the intricacies of their chosen topic than do their supervisors. In contrast, the supervisors should be able to provide guidance that is more general in nature, for example, suggestions on how to identify original and courageous ideas; how to collaborate with practitioners; and how to undertake cross-disciplinary research. If the students need to apply for research funding, the supervisors also can provide sound advice from their own research-funding experience. Similarly, because the supervisors have a past record of publishing in academic journals, they are able to guide the student on how to develop a conceptual framework, to write up the methodology, to present and discuss research findings, and, generally, to frame a manuscript.

In addition to these three personality characteristics, students should demonstrate independence, energy, and determination. Equally important is that the students have self-discipline, persistency, and organizational skills. Put it on the rocker, the supervisors already have a Ph.D. degree whereas the students do not. Thus, students need to mobilize all their energy and determination, make the best of all their intelligence, knowledge, and skills, and, ultimately, find their wow factor that will enable them to go through three to five years of incredible hard work.

When supervisors find a student (or vice versa) with the above personality characteristics, building blocks are in place for a fruitful research collaboration because experience (in research and supervision) has been paired up with creativity, energy, and determination. What could be better than to have highly motivated students who write up, for example, their thoughts on an original and courageous idea and outline possible avenues for future research on that idea? Such shared documents between supervisors and their students allow them to meet as equals early on in the Ph.D. program. Oftentimes, the research collaboration between a supervisor and a student continues long after the student has graduated! And in some cases, a former supervision turns into a friendship. (Lindgreen)

The Ph.D. student enters the program as a graduate student, and is familiar with graduate-student activities (attending classes, writing manuscripts, and taking exams). The first couple of semesters in the Ph.D. program will be familiar ground. By the time of the thesis defense, however, students have transitioned into a junior researcher, capable of identifying a research topic, conducting the research, and publishing the results. The graduate student skills may get the student to the ABD (all-but-dissertation) stage, and no further. One of the roles of the supervisor, and indeed the entire Ph.D. program, is to manage this transition so that the student acquires the skills to succeed as a career academic. Different schools do this differently, but at Temple's Fox School and many others, the student will be assigned to a mentor when entering the Ph.D. program. This assignment is based on general student areas of interest, and as the student progresses, it may become clear that another mentor's research interests are a closer match, in which case the student can change. (Often, the student will not switch, and the mentor becomes the thesis supervisor. But from Day 1, the students will have someone they can work and share ideas with.) Working with the mentor, the student begins roughing out a research progress report in the first year, gradually getting this into the form of a required research proposal. This process eases the transition from term-paper-writing graduate student to independent-thinking researcher.

As my colleagues pointed out earlier, Ph.D. programs attract both conventional students and experienced professionals, and these two groups are in many ways mirror images of each other. Conventional students are knowledgeable and excited about conceptual models and analytical techniques, but lack much business experience; experienced professionals can formulate a realistic practical problem easily based on their years of experience, but may have difficulty creating a satisfactory conceptual model. The supervisor needs to recognize the individual strengths, be aware of where the weaknesses will appear, and be prepared to help the student overcome weaknesses. In working with students with 20 years of senior management experience, I start almost immediately with helping them build a sound conceptual model. Often, they will build a model that is really more like a 10-year research agenda, and the challenge is to get them to focus on the part that will make a good academic contribution and will become the basis of the thesis. The rest can come later!

Finally, one needs to be very sensitive to individual differences in work style. Our collaborators spoke of the need to find a balance between too much and not enough supervision, and that has been my experience. Some students thrive when left alone, with a rough idea of what research to look up, and will do most of the work on time with the occasional check-in with the supervisor. Others will make no progress in this environment. The supervisor may need to give some students explicit, monthly deadlines for every step of the Ph.D. research, and hold the student to those deadlines. The constant pressure, which is unnecessary and even distracting for some, might be a requirement for others to meet deadlines and ultimately pass. (Di Benedetto)

REFERENCES

Kelly, S., Nicholson, J.D., Johnston, P., Duty, D., & Brennan, R. (2020). Experienced professionals and doctoral study: A performative agenda. *Industrial Marketing Management*. https://doi.org/10.1016/j.indmarman.2020.02.018.

Lindgreen, A., Vallaster, C., & Vanhamme, J. (2001). Reflections on the PhD process: The experiences of three survivors. *The Marketing Review*, 1(4), 505–529.

Midgley, G., Nicholson, J.D., & Brennan, R. (2017). Dealing with challenges to methodological pluralism: The paradigm problem, psychological resistance and cultural barriers. *Industrial Marketing Management*, 62, 150–159.

Nicholson, J.D., LaPlaca, P., Al-Abdin, A., Breese, R., & Khan, Z. (2018). What do introduction sections tell us about the intent of scholarly work: A contribution on contributions. *Industrial Marketing Management*, 73, 206–219.

9. Translating research into teaching
Adam Lindgreen, C. Anthony Di Benedetto, Roderick J. Brodie, and Peter Naudé

1. INTRODUCTION

At any business school worth its salt, one of the most important goals is to foster an environment of successful academic research. This is especially true at research-intensive business schools where a core of solid, productive researchers leads to recognition and ranking among the top business schools. The Financial Times' Business School Rankings and Bloomberg Business Week's Best B-Schools Ranking are among the most well-known. A select number of business schools, about 1 percent in total, are triple accredited (with accreditations from AACSB, AMBA, and EQUIS). This scholarly recognition attracts not only undergraduate and postgraduate students who want to achieve their full potential by acquiring the necessary capabilities and skills to manage and accelerate their career in business, but also Ph.D. students eager to establish careers in a strong research environment.

Business schools have long had their research quality assessed. For example, in the UK, the impact assessment evaluation of higher education institutions' research is the Research Excellence Framework (REF), which is the successor to the Research Assessment Exercise (RAE). These impact assessment evaluations provide benchmarking information according to which UK business schools (and other higher education institutions) are ranked (see, for example, *The Guardian* and *Times Higher Education*). Highly ranked business schools (i.e., schools that are conducting world-leading research in terms of originality, significance, and rigor) use this information unashamedly when seeking to attract the best talent, be it researchers or students.

With the RAEs/REFs putting much emphasis on higher education institutions' research, there has been an increasing realization that it also is important to evaluate institutions' teaching. The UK government introduced a Teaching Excellence and Student Outcomes Framework (TEF) in 2017. Although participation in the exercise is voluntary, most UK colleges and universities have chosen to participate. An institution with gold status delivers consistently outstanding teaching, learning, and outcomes for its students. At research-intensive business schools, the aim of the research strategy therefore should be to conduct demonstrably impactful research that influences society; can be deployed usefully in developing education; and can be communicated to and used by practitioners. Fulfilling this aim starts with publishing research with a high impact.

Business school leaders would like to attract and keep the top research talent in order to stay competitive, attract high-potential students, and recruit the most promising young faculty. To accomplish these objectives, a successful research environment for its business academic researchers needs to be established so that these researchers can produce a sustainable research stream. In another chapter, we examined important antecedents including business school research strategy, leadership, and governance, and from these we developed a set of conditions that are related to long-term success of research programs in academic business institutions. As detailed illustrations, we elaborated the experiences of two active research institutions—the Industrial Marketing and Purchasing (IMP) Group and the Contemporary Marketing Practices (CMP) Group—and discussed how each of these groups has implemented the conditions for success. We concluded that chapter with general observations on the environmental conditions most conducive to sustainable business school research, and presented implications regarding the role of the journal editor as a gatekeeper.

Building on the above chapter, we now examine how business schools contribute to education by translating their great research into great teaching for graduate business-to-business marketing classes (including MBA programs with such classes). To achieve this goal, the remaining parts of the chapter are organized as follows. First, we present some of the most recent findings on teaching excellence, which pertains to business instructors, as well as to academics in general. Next, we explore the specific opportunities and responsibilities facing the business-to-business marketing academic. We then discuss the process by which business-to-business marketing academics can transform our research in meaningful ways and deliver value to our practitioner audience in the classroom.

2. WHAT DOES GREAT TEACHING MEAN?

While it may be impossible to pin down the details, one can argue that great teachers facilitate the co-creation of learning with their students and thereby provide value. To understand this concept, one can apply the principles of service dominant (S-D) logic (Vargo & Lusch, 2004), with the instructor playing the role of the 'supplier' and the student as the 'customer.' According to S-D logic premises, the student is a co-creator of value, and the instructor does not deliver value, but can offer value propositions (for a detailed discussion of this topic, see Chalcraft & Lynch, 2011). The S-D viewpoint stresses the nature of the exchange between supplier and customer—or, in this case, instructor–student and even student–student interaction. The student is not a passive receiver of value from the instructor, since the instructor does not deliver value unidirectionally. Rather, the instructor's value proposition potentially can be converted to value, which is co-created by both instructor and student (Ballantyne, Williams, & Aitkin, 2011; Vargo & Lusch, 2008). Suppliers know this and willingly invite customers to participate in the development of the value proposition (Vargo & Lusch, 2008). To ensure a long-term relationship between supplier and customer, each must offer satisfactory value to the other, sometimes referred to as reciprocal value propositions (Ballantyne & Varey, 2006). Working jointly, the supplier and customer can integrate their resources to co-create value, which can then be used by the customer to generate value in specific applications, or 'value-in-use' (Vargo & Lusch, 2004).

The parallel to the business-to-business marketing education scenario is clear. As service providers, instructors who provide the greatest value to students provide the requisite resources to students, who bring with them their own skills, capabilities, and initiative, such that together instructors and students can co-create value. This value can then be exploited to co-create value-in-use, which allows students to achieve their potential (Chalcraft & Lynch, 2011). Once their resources have been developed, students will then be able to enact the value-in-use through time and in different applications into the future. To achieve this co-creation of learning, the traditional unidirectional, instructor-to-student learning process will not be enough. Great teaching ideally facilitates learning processes in three different directions to encourage co-creation of learning: instructor-to-student, student-to-instructor, and student-to-student (as actors all participate in the creation of value and all benefit from reciprocal value propositions).

Several actions can be undertaken to facilitate these three learning processes. First and perhaps most traditionally, instructors guide students, drawing on their academic and practical knowledge. This, of course, can be done well, or not well; and a later section will discuss the translation process from great research and practical experience into great teaching. Students can also interact with the instructor, applying and developing new ideas based on their own practical experience, under the guidance of the instructor, translating the lesson learned in the specific context to a resource that provides value-in-use in the future. A later section will explore how instructors can effectively use cases and other classroom tools to accomplish this translation process. Finally, students can interact with each other, sharing and developing their new ideas drawn from experience. While synergy and reciprocal value creation can be produced from all of these processes, it is this last one that might be the most fruitful if managed well. As will be discussed later, a typical graduate business-to-business marketing class will include students of all different backgrounds and levels of experience. This, of course, can be viewed as a challenge by the instructor, but is really an opportunity for students with differing backgrounds to apply their knowledge in possibly unexpected ways.

Great teaching also recognizes the power of the available technology, and uses it to advantage. Both instructor and student have access to a wealth of knowledge about business-to-business practices and management, as well as strategy applications of all types. The challenge is to develop processes so that these resources can be used sensibly and efficiently to create value. Most business schools have moved to a platform such as Canvas, Brightspace, or the like, which offer diverse ways for instructors and students to interact: discussion boards, video lectures, access to media, in-class polling, breakout groups, online quizzes, and so on. Needless to say, many business schools are offering online versions of their classes, as well as conventional on-site classes, and these platforms are critical to the effective functioning of online programs. All of these tools can be used profitably to improve the classroom experience, and indeed to facilitate all three directions of learning processes discussed above.

Whether teaching online or on-site, the instructor can benefit from the flipped classroom format (Green, 2015; Jarvis, Halvorson, Sadeque, & Johnston, 2014). Using this format, the traditional 'lecture in class/assignments outside of class' structure is flipped; video lectures and discussion boards are assigned as class work, to stimulate student-to-student and student-to-instructor interaction. Class time then is used for intensive discussions, case analyses, group work, and so on. That is, the flipped classroom can be used effectively to facilitate learning processes in all three directions, and encourage the co-creation of value, which is central to S-D logic, as applied in the classroom (Jarvis et al., 2014). The instructors then can further personalize the course to bring their own perspective or even personality into the course. This can be done in many ways, limited only by the imagination of the instructors: constantly scanning for and posting current articles illustrative of course material and encouraging students to do the same (for example, by adding to discussion boards), adding weekly announcements including thought-provoking websites, humorous but relevant videos or YouTube clips, and so on. There are many relevant articles in publications such as *Business Horizons*, *California Management Review*, *Harvard Business Review*, and *Sloan Management Journal* that can be added to the weekly readings, or online reports about recent company successes or failures. Adding these, and periodically updating them, provides a wealth of information to the students that shows the relevance of course material in real situations and helps to further the co-creation of value.

In addition to facilitating student–instructor and student–student interaction, the online class platform permits online group project work. Especially in an online class where students are recruited from miles away or even from different countries, the virtual meeting room facilitated by the online platform may be the only realistic way to meet. Students therefore have to get used to using technology as a substitute for travel when doing their group projects, which is a skill they will put to good use when they are working for multinational corporations that want to reduce their CO_2 footprint or are under price pressure to cut back on international travel and therefore turn to virtual meetings.

The above discussion, of course, assumes an ideal context for instruction. It should also be noted that, at times, some adjustments will need to be made, as conditions may not permit easy transmission of information in all directions. A very large class (100 or more students) poses major challenges. Whether on-site or online, it is unrealistic to expect a free-flowing class discussion, which includes all students. Even if class discussions go well, there will be dozens of students who did not participate and/or may feel left out. There are a few adjustments that may overcome some of the challenges: hiring several course assistants, or organizing small discussion breakout groups to encourage student–student communication. The assistants will need to be well-trained and dependable, though, as otherwise the classroom experience will be compromised. Also, for anyone who has taught globally, or has had a class with a high percentage of international students, the challenges of effective student-to-instructor or student-to-student information flow are well known. In China and some other East Asian cultures, students are often very reluctant to participate in class, in spite of good English skills in many cases. When teaching in Japan, one of the authors used mandatory short presentations by individuals or student pairs, just to ensure that everyone does speak at least a couple of times during the semester! (This works especially well if there is support staff who can help students with accurate translations in good business English for their PowerPoint slides.) Even teaching a mixed group of European students reveals national differences regarding willingness to participate enthusiastically in class discussions.

3. WHAT DOES GREAT TEACHING IN BUSINESS-TO-BUSINESS MARKETING MEAN?

The previous section explored teaching in general from the perspective of value creation; here we examine the issues and challenges when applying these concepts specifically to the effective teaching of business-to-business marketing.

An obvious starting point is to know the students: their level and their level of experience and preparedness. Usually, basic marketing is a prerequisite for business-to-business marketing, and students at graduate level will have taken at least one marketing principles course. Therefore, the instructor can focus the business-to-business marketing course on how it adds to existing knowledge. A relevant question may be: how do basic marketing principles, such as research, customer behavior, segmentation, or integrated marketing communications, apply in business-to-business marketing? A classroom group assignment might be to take a business-to-business market, segment it, select a target and a positioning strategy, and make marketing mix recommendations for the targeted customer groups. The instructor may also ask whether the basic principles do indeed apply, or whether we need new principles adapted to the business-to-business context.

Depending on student level, there is the possibility of prior relevant work experience, and the amounts of work experience can vary greatly. In a traditional MSc program, students typically come directly from their undergraduate program. In an executive MBA program, in contrast, students often have 10 or more years of managerial experience, and some may be senior marketing executives at business-to-business companies. Others may come with a medical or engineering background and will have little or any interaction with marketing people on the job. The disparity therefore poses a real challenge for the instructor, but also presents an opportunity for student–student interaction. By focusing classroom time on cases, relevant online media reports, or hands-on projects, and requiring group project work and discussion board participation outside of class for project work, students can be put into interactive situations. Ideally, the ones with the strongest marketing backgrounds can take a lead role and mentor those for whom the material is quite new. Real-world examples that the instructor or the students themselves find are an ideal basis for teaching should be stressed in discussion board posts.

The instructor can insist on hands-on projects based on real issues faced by real companies, and, in a graduate class, can require that students work on current projects (sometimes within their own companies). This may not always work out, and the instructor may need to provide a plan-B project, such as to report on a major company of their own choosing and search online for relevant background material. But, on project presentation day, it is always enjoyable for senior managers from the companies to come and listen to the presentations, ask questions, and give feedback.

The instructor must always keep in mind what students will expect of a business-to-business marketing course. Business-to-business marketing is usually taken by marketing majors, some of whom have significant experience. They will not want to hear about segmentation or the 4Ps yet again, unless the instructor can show successfully how the familiar concepts apply in a business-to-business setting. The students will find the content much more relevant if the instructor uses a business-to-business context with which they are familiar: a focus on the buyer–seller interaction, customer relationships and external network partners. Recent cases of good or not-so-good practice can be very effective here. In addition, students are unlikely to be interested in elegant academic theories, so the instructor needs to think carefully about translation of current research for relevance; we will take up this discussion below. Most importantly, students will want take-aways that they can apply right away—first and foremost to their class projects, perhaps, but especially out in the workplace.

One useful technique to achieve relevant take-aways is to make term papers as applied as possible. The term paper could be based around a business-to-business marketing principle, as in: "Using the business-to-business segmentation concept as described in class, discuss how you might effectively segment the market served by your company," or, for executives, "Consider the organizational buying models discussed in your text and describe the buying process within your buying center, outlining how you resolved conflicts in a recent purchase situation." To make the assignment even more realistic, one can use a 'boss test' grading structure: the instructor, playing the role of work supervisor, provides grades on a three-point scale:

- This is brilliant. I did not realize how much value you could add to our company. I am promoting you immediately. I am really glad you are doing this program. The program is clearly adding value to you and to our company (high pass/distinction).
- This is OK, but all you have done is to describe what we already know/do. I need to know what we need to do differently and why (low pass).
- You have not fully appreciated just what we do and why. I fear we are wasting our time and money sending you on this program (fail).

Taken together, the last two sections illustrate that there is no one clear answer to the question of what makes a great teacher. Rather, it is better to accept the principle of equifinality in teaching: there are many different routes to becoming a great teacher. Much of this will depend on the audience and their level of academic knowledge and practical experience. However, it will also depend on the individual instructors: to recognize their own strengths and to develop a style that works, rather than trying to copy anyone else.

The next section addresses the issue of translating the best research into great teaching: the challenge of making relevant the work that we do as academic researchers.

4. TRANSLATING GREAT RESEARCH INTO GREAT TEACHING

At the outset, we recognize that great research must be presented in ways that add value to students. According to the S-D logic, we as instructors can only make value propositions, not create value ourselves. As is the case for any service provider, we need to understand customer needs such that we can develop the best value proposition for our customers (i.e., students) so that we can co-create value. The exoteric theories in and of themselves are not of interest to students. Instructors need to be able to pick the ones that potentially add the most value, and find a way to demonstrate their relevance to students so they will see the value in use.

A gifted teacher knows how to bridge the gap between academic research and practice. If our research is motivated by real, practical, managerial problems, the translation process is facilitated, since the academic contributions are at the same time relevant solutions for decision-makers. Luckily for us, much of our work in business-to-business marketing is like this. We study practically relevant problems, and our findings can substantially improve managerial decision-making. As business-to-business marketing researchers, we are also fortunate in that our target journals (*Industrial Marketing Management* and other top marketing journals) require statements of managerial implications. These publications ensure that the published articles have some managerial relevance.

Having said this, one must still note that the value-adding process is by no means easy in all cases. Much of the great academic marketing articles, published in the highest-ranked marketing journals (*Journal of Marketing, Journal of Consumer Psychology, Journal of Marketing Research, Journal of Retailing, Journal of Service Research, Journal of the Academy of Marketing Science, Marketing Science*) and also in *Industrial Marketing Management* (the top business-to-business marketing management journal) require substantial analytical skills on the part of the reader. It is safe to assume that the majority of MSc/MBA students do not have these skills. The answer is not necessarily to cut out all of the math. To simply present the results without justifying how the conclusions were reached trivializes the issue, probably oversimplifies the results, and ultimately frustrates the students. This translation process therefore is hard work.

Keeping in mind that students want answers, the instructor can use the available tools to demonstrate the relevance of academic research to practical decision problems. Many business-to-business marketing classes are designed around the use of large Harvard-style cases, which allow for in-depth discussion of complicated situations without a single clear answer. The instructor can stimulate deep group discussion, encouraging the use of conceptual models brought into class and/or application of textbook principles. One way this can be done is by using the set of questions that accompany most cases in the corresponding teaching note: break the class into groups (this works on-site, as well as with online virtual groups) and allow each group some class time to address one of the questions and then present their findings to the class. After a healthy discussion and student-generated recommendations to the company, the instructor can reveal what the company actually did (the epilogue is frequently included in the teaching note). The class can conclude with a discussion of whether the students agree with the company's actions and what the long-term consequences of the actions taken were.

Especially when teaching postgraduate students or mid-career executives, there is always the question of relevance of cases. One might use, for example, a case about LEGO to illustrate the changing role of innovation of a company in transformation, or discuss Fitbit to develop strategies for sustaining a significant competitive advantage in a maturing market. It is important to remind students that the cases are chosen to illustrate specific concepts, and that the settings (in this case, the toy industry and the wearable technology industry) are just the context. This is an effective strategy to avoid the occasional question of relevance, such as "Why am I studying a toy company? I work in pharmaceutical management." To go a step further, the instructor can ask students to submit a report of at least one or two take-aways from the case that is directly relevant to their own company or can be implemented immediately.

The contemporary marketing practices (CMP)-based case study approach can be used effectively to ensure the relevance of academic research. A characteristic of CMP is the emphasis on active discussion with executive students, through research-led teaching and teaching-informed research. CMP researchers are typically experienced teachers of executive programs. CMP research efforts are designed to be integrated with teaching activities, to achieve a continuous cycle that connects research and learning. The CMP-based approach is characterized by using case studies drawing on the students' work environments and action research, as well as ongoing feedback both to and from the classroom. This leads to what Little, Brookes, and Palmer (2008) refer to as a "zone of mutuality" between research and teaching. They state (p. 126):

> While purpose and form of cases for research or teaching are very distinct, this does not necessarily imply these two endeavors are mutually exclusive. Rather, they can be seen as complementary activities and may even draw from the same source material. Both require a purposive and systematic approach. Both require the application of creativity in arriving at conclusions and in developing new knowledge or testing and exercising current knowledge about management practice or management theory. Whilst academic capability is required in both forms of case development, they differ fundamentally in their purpose and approach to theory: either a methodology to build or test theory in a rigorous manner, or a pedagogical technique that illustrates theory by adopting a narrative approach intrinsic to which is student engagement and participation. In addition, different quality criteria apply: case research is required to be rigorous and valid, whilst a teaching case must deliver against the teaching objectives. Internal consistency, face validity, acceptability and comprehensibility for students are of primary importance.

Central to the idea of living case studies is the notion of 'theories-in-use', a term used by Cornelissen (2002), which draws from Schön's (1983) notion of reflective practitioners and the work on the interface of theory and practice by Argyris and Schön (1974) and Zaltman, LeMasters, and Heffring (1982). The living case study technique recognizes that practitioners and practical knowledge can play an important role in the theorizing process and the way managers use theory. The practices and experiences of previous actions of executive students can lead to expertise that offers important insight for theory development. Nevertheless, the process by which practitioners absorb understandings means that theory development may have subtle differences and that therefore indirect and formal processes are required to theorize with practitioners (Nenonen, Brodie, Storbacka, & Peters, 2017). While the living case study approach was developed when teaching part-time executive students, the approach has been adapted to other types of student settings; graduate students may have work experience and hence can reflect on theories-in-use.

The evolution of CMP research has lessons for all academics wishing to make their own personal research meaningful to practitioners. At this point, however, action research-based articles are relatively poorly represented in the academic journals, so there is much room for growth and improvement. As discussed by Nenonen et al. (2017) and Brodie and colleagues (Brodie, Nenonen, Peters, & Storbacka, 2017), abductive reasoning plays a central role in the collaborative processes when theorizing with practitioners. This is because most accounts of theorizing with practitioners use—explicitly or implicitly—abduction as the main mode of inference. For example Nenenon et al. (2017) explore the use of abductive reasoning when theorizing with practitioners. They articulate a theorizing process that integrates general theoretic perspectives and contextual research to develop midrange theory. The process is based on the principles of pragmatism and abductive reasoning, which have their origins in the 1950s when the management sciences were being established. This provides philosophical foundations of the living case study research.

Another important consideration when using living case studies is to develop a research design, which leads to knowledge that is meaningful to practitioners. As outlined by Little, Motion, and Brodie (2006), attention needs to be given to understanding the differences between academics and practitioners. These differences, summarized in Table 9.1, are profound and must be understood and addressed to alleviate problems in communication between the two groups. As shown in the table, academics and practitioners differ greatly in terms of their overall career goals (publication versus personal and organizational performance), how to achieve these goals (conceptual breakthrough versus proprietary solutions), kind of knowledge sought (why versus how), even the kind of language used in communication (scientific versus business-oriented). The differences between the two groups are noticeable in

Table 9.1   Differences between academics and practitioners

Issue	Academics	Practitioners
Goal	Publication	Personal performance, organizational performance
Means of achieving goals	Conceptual breakthrough	Proprietary problem solutions
Most valuable resources	Data, idea, insights	Time, energy
Time horizon	Medium to long term	Short to medium term
Key sources of frustration	Data not delivered or available	Time-consuming tasks
Knowledge sought	Why?	How?
Language	Academic/scientific	Organizational/business
Confidentiality	Not an issue	An important issue
Most common mode	Reflection	Action

Source: Adapted from Little et al. (2006, Table 2).

a classroom of senior management graduate students with years of experience in writing business reports, but who are new to academic writing. One of the authors of this article teaches in a DBA program whose students average 15 years of management or entrepreneurial experience. An anecdote from this program reveals much about the gap between the two groups. One student commented at the end of a semester that he thought his DBA class was going to be easy: he only had to write two papers that semester, and he was used to writing a paper every week at work! He admitted that he had no idea how much more difficult it would be to write a scholarly paper (such as a progress report on his academic research), as compared to writing a weekly report for his boss. As shown in Table 9.1, practitioners are in 'action mode,' seeking solutions to their organization's problems and used to writing business reports; it is a major change in direction to adopt an academic's 'reflection mode' and to write research papers in academic style.

Also important is an understanding of the way practitioners use theory. Of particular importance is the research by Cornelissen and Lock (2005) and Åge (2014) who examined how and why practitioners use conceptual devices in business-to-business research. The research shows that practitioners, through translating research into their specific context, can find a new spectrum of research usage in their organization, but can also contribute to research in an interactive and creative way. A distinction is made between three ways in which practitioners use theory. The first is instrumental use, implying that practitioners use research to directly solve a problem. Much of the discussion in marketing regarding the use of research is based on this perspective on direct and instrumental use (e.g., Deshpande & Zaltman, 1982). In contrast to instrumental use, there is conceptual use where concepts and theories are used to influence practitioners' thinking, but are not applied directly. Here "ideas, problem definitions, and interpretive schemes [are viewed] as a set of intellectual tools available to the practitioner in understanding and anticipating real-world phenomena" (Cornelissen, 2000, p. 319). Conceptual devices also offer practitioners considerable scope and flexibility and play a key role in learning from work experience. Finally, Åge (2014) discusses symbolic use. This is where the use of concept and scientific research is deliberately taken out of context and used by practitioners, and is used for its symbolic value to legitimate the actions of the practitioner. Brownlie and Saren (1997, p. 150) elaborated upon this more 'partisan' method of science, arguing that "Marketing managers are typically very adept at using this conceptual vocabulary to provide interviewers with persuasive accounts of their activities as marketing managers. In that sense they are authors too."

Åge's research suggests that, "[c]ontrary to what extant literature suggests ... research that is abstract in nature has inherently greater possibilities for managerial relevance compared to other research, due to its potential for flexible and dynamic interpretations. The present study also suggests that researchers are not simply the producers of research for managers to passively consume or reject. Instead, B2B research can benefit from encountering the messiness and chaos of the managers' worlds" (Åge, 2014, p. 440). This stream of research suggests that conceptual and symbolic, as well as instrumental use of research, can all be used by the business-to-business marketing academic to translate business research into effective teaching, though it is probably fair to say that we still rely greatly on instrumental use. Case studies derived from research can be adapted into teaching cases as a way to incorporate learning from work experience into the classroom. Especially in a class of senior executives with varying backgrounds, 'messy' (to use Åge's term) teaching cases will take students out of their comfort zones and encourage student-to-student learning, stimulate communication, and add more value to the classroom experience.

In conclusion, the CMP experience shows that case studies developed for teaching purposes and case studies developed for research purposes are not mutually exclusive. The needs of both students and researchers can be met contemporaneously if the research and learning projects are designed and implemented effectively. The value to students is created through the provision of an engaging 'living' learning experience, enabling engagement in and application of theory, thereby creating enhanced understanding and greater perceived value. Using the living case study method, managers' tacit knowledge and experience can be accessed and used inductively. As committed teachers, we always should look for alternative ways to create and construct knowledge. The CMP approach has provided this group of instructors with a means of creating "requisite variety" (Weick, 2007), that is, has provided a rich basis of knowledge on which to construct theoretical frameworks that acknowledge the complexity and multidimensional nature of CMP. The living case approach provides a rich "zone of mutuality," whereby the needs of both learners and researchers can be met.

5. CONCLUSIONS

Business-to-business marketing academics can learn much from current trends in higher education to increase the value proposition to their students. As educators, we are service providers; the literature on service-dominant logic has been applied to the academic context, yielding insights on how we can encourage the co-creation of value. Since many of us teach in environments with their own peculiarities (MBA/MSc students, mid-career or senior professional students, occasionally large class sizes, online classes, and international classes, among others), we often must make adjustments or workarounds to adapt the ideal academic service encounter to fit the setting.

Furthermore, as business-to-business marketing academics, we potentially have an advantage in the classroom. Like many of our colleagues in the business school, our own academic research is very much driven by real-world problems faced by decision-makers. Our research is inherently practical; many times, our next research project is stimulated by a discussion with senior managers about the challenges they are currently facing. Ideally, we should be able to take our academic research, make some positioning adjustments to it, and deliver a presentation to a group of senior executives who will find value in it.

Despite these advantages, it is still not necessarily smooth sailing ahead, and we need to understand the nature of the gap between academics and practitioners so that we can recognize the slipping points and overcome them. Our goals do not match those of the practitioner community. In our publish-or-perish world, publications are the currency; this is quite foreign to most practitioners. We write in an academic style designed to please reviewers and editors, and to demonstrate our theoretical contribution to the extant literature; these are issues that are not of concern to a practitioner writing a report for senior management or for stakeholders. Even our definitions of what a 'report' is can differ wildly. Furthermore, no matter how relevant the findings may be to practitioners, we must demonstrate analytical rigor and may use statistical jargon that will bog down any decision manager looking for a quick and practical answer. For all of these reasons, we need to be aware of the translation process between our research and potential classroom application. While not prescribing it as a one-size-fits-all strategy, we note the success that the CMP has had with their 'living' learning experience, in which practitioners' knowledge and experience are used inductively. Using such a case study method, students can apply and engage in theory, increasing their understanding and the co-creation of value. This technique helps us to incorporate more conceptual and symbolic use of our research, as well as to complement instrumental use of research, which is more prevalent in business schools.

REFERENCES

Åge, L.-J. (2014). How and why managers use conceptual devices in B2B research. *Journal of Business and Industrial Marketing*, 29(7/8), pp. 633–641.
Argyris, C. & Schön, D.A. (1974). *Theory in Practice: Increasing Professional Effectiveness*. San Francisco, CA: Jossey-Bass.
Ballantyne, D. and Varey, R.J. (2006). Creating value-in-use through marketing interaction: The exchange logic of relating communicating and knowing. *Marketing Theory*, 6(3), pp. 335–348.
Ballantyne, D., Williams, J., & Aitkin, R. (2011). Introduction to service-dominant logic: From propositions to practice. *Industrial Marketing Management*, 40(2), pp. 179–180.
Brodie, R.J., Nenonen, S., Peters, L.D., & Storbacka, K. (2017). Theorizing with managers to bridge the theory-praxis gap: Foundations for a research tradition. *European Journal of Marketing*, 51(7/8), pp. 1173–1177.
Brownlie, D. & Saren, M. (1997). Beyond the one-dimensional marketing manager: The discourse of theory, practice and relevance. *International Journal of Research in Marketing*, 14(2), pp. 147–161.
Chalcraft, D. & Lynch, J. (2011). Value propositions in higher education: An S-D logic view. *Proceedings of the 44th Academy of Marketing Conference*. Liverpool, UK.
Cornelissen, J.P. (2000). Toward an understanding of the use of academic theories in public relations practice. *Public Relations Review*, 26(3), pp. 315–326.
Cornelissen, J.P. (2002). Academic and practitioner theories of marketing. *Marketing Theory*, 2(1), pp. 133–143.
Cornelissen, J.P. & Lock, A.R. (2005). The use of marketing theory: Constructs, research propositions, and managerial implications. *Marketing Theory*, 5(2), pp. 165–184.
Deshpande, R. & Zaltman, G. (1982). Factors affecting the use of marketing research information: A path analysis. *Journal of Marketing Research*, 19(1), pp. 14–31.
Green, T. (2015). Flipped classrooms: An agenda for innovative marketing education in the digital era. *Marketing Education Review*, 25(3), pp. 179–191.
Jarvis, W., Halvorson, W., Sadeque, S., & Johnston, S. (2014). A large class engagement (LCE) model based on service-dominant logic (SDL) and flipped classrooms. *Education Research and Perspectives*, 41(1), pp. 1–24.
Little, V., Brookes, R., & Palmer, R. (2008). Research-informed teaching and teaching-informed research: The Contemporary Marketing Practices (CMP) living case study approach to understanding marketing practice. *Journal of Business & Industrial Marketing*, 23(2), pp. 124–134.
Little, V., Motion, J., & Brodie, R.J. (2006). Advancing understanding: The contribution of multi-method action research-based approaches to knowledge creation. *International Journal of Learning and Change*, 1(2), pp. 217–228.
Nenonen, S., Brodie, R.J., Storbacka, K., & Peters, L.D. (2017). Theorizing with managers: Increasing academic knowledge as well as practical relevance. *European Journal of Marketing*, 51(7/8), pp. 1130–1152.
Schön, D.A. (1983). *The Reflective Practitioner: How Professionals Think in Action*. New York: Basic Books.

Vargo, S. & Lusch, R. (2004). Evolving to a new dominant logic for marketing. *Journal of Marketing*, 68(1), pp. 1–17.

Vargo, S. & Lusch, R. (2008). Service-dominant logic: Continuing the evolution. *Journal of the Academy of Marketing Science*, 36(1), pp. 1–10.

Weick, K. (2007). The generative properties of richness. *Academy of Management Journal*, 50(1), pp. 14–19.

Zaltman, G., LeMasters, K., & Heffring, M. (1982). *Theory Construction In Marketing: Some Thoughts on Thinking*. New York: John Wiley & Sons.

PART 4

Getting published

10. Framing a manuscript

Adam Lindgreen and C. Anthony Di Benedetto
In collaboration with Ad de Jong, Luigi De Luca, Heiner Evanschitzky, Michael Mol, Robert Morgan, John Nicholson, and Tobias Schäfers

1. INTRODUCTION

In a recent editorial (Lindgreen and Di Benedetto, 2020), we invited several colleagues to reflect on the reviewing process, and to discuss what they looked for when judging manuscripts under review. Our collaborators provided enlightening comments on the importance of writing style, presentation, avoiding mistakes, and responding to reviewer comments thoroughly. For this chapter, we invited a different team of experienced academic researchers to address a related, but different question: what specific advice would they give to authors in order to best frame their manuscript, that is, put the manuscript into the best possible light and increase its chance of acceptance?

To prepare this chapter, we asked colleagues who are experienced authors to provide some thoughts and insights on how authors should frame manuscripts for top academic journals. We asked for three to five pieces of advice for young scholars on this topic. Our goal with this chapter is to provide some non-obvious recommendations to young scholars. Accordingly, we encouraged our contributors to think beyond the familiar, such as "write a really strong research question," and to provide insights gained from experience that would substantially improve the manuscript from the reviewers' viewpoint. For example, contributors could submit a few comments on what an author could do to nail the literature review, to write a convincing methodology section, to present coherent findings, to express a clear theoretical or conceptual contribution, or to write managerial implications or avenues for future research that do not sound like a superficial afterthought. Although a few lines for each piece of advice would be sufficient, we did ask that contributors share a short story or two to illustrate their points.

The remaining parts of this chapter are organized as follows. We first present our contributors' insights on the sections of a standard research manuscript, from introduction to conclusion and managerial implications. We then present some overall comments regarding manuscript length, use of visualizations, and management of the revision process. We conclude with a summary statement and overall thoughts on manuscript framing.

2. INTRODUCTION, RESEARCH FOCUS, AND CONTRIBUTION

2.1 Issues of Scope or Focus

John Nicholson reminds us of the importance of good fit with the target journal's aims and scope. This is important when a manuscript has been rejected from Journal A and the author seeks to submit it to Journal B. We have discussed the risks of submitting a recently rejected manuscript without taking thoughtful reviewer comments into account (LaPlaca, Lindgreen, & Vanhamme, 2018; LaPlaca, Lindgreen, Vanhamme, & Di Benedetto, 2018). Nicholson notes another danger: the aims and scope of Journal B may not line up with those of Journal A, and the author fails to take advantage of an opportunity to show how the article is potentially a good contribution:

> Too often, I see a manuscript that has clearly been round the houses of other journals and resubmitted to *Industrial Marketing Management* without modification. For instance, I have seen several manuscripts that clearly have been written for international business journals and then come [next] to *Industrial Marketing Management* for default. An author must build on a criticism and not just resubmit a manuscript. Many good, indeed classic manuscripts have been rejected multiple times before acceptance, but the key is to make the manuscript fit for the audience, that is, the readership of the journal. Accordingly, there must be reference to articles in the journal, or at least a strong case must be made why a previously unrecognized topic should be of interest to the readers of the journal. Using the same argument as used in previously rejected submissions is insufficient. (Nicholson)

Incidentally, an important takeaway from Nicholson is the reminder that many good articles may have been rejected more than once before eventual acceptance (and every top author has been rejected multiple times!). One must keep in mind that there is no shame in rejection, stay positive, and be sure to refocus the manuscript correctly to Journal B (its aims and scope are most certainly on the journal's webpage).

To properly frame the introduction section, a succinct statement of the research objective is just as important as a clear focus. Too often, editors see manuscripts with an unfocused statement of research objective/question, or no research objective/question at all. Rob Morgan reminds us of the importance of a clear, short research objective statement. If one cannot summarize it briefly, it is possible that it is not sufficiently well thought out yet!

> As Nietzsche famously claimed: "It is my ambition to say in ten sentences what others say in a whole book." Equally, Felelon asserted that "the more you say, the less people remember. The fewer the words, the greater the profit." Rehearse your manuscript in elevator pitch. A measure for this is: can you summarize your manuscript in 35 words? If you cannot, you should! Practice this, reduce and identify the core of your work. You can then dress the manuscript. When you *find the focus*, the reader *gets in focus*. (Morgan)

Additionally, we have previously discussed the need to avoid the 'so-what' reaction by reviewers (Lindgreen & Di Benedetto, 2020). But how can the author frame the introduction to create the opposite reaction—to get the reviewer (and reader) not just to keep reading, but to find it impossible to put the manuscript down? Luigi De Luca details a successful illustrative example that accomplishes just this, and provides inspiration for how to write a riveting introduction:

> Editors and reviewers constantly remind us about the importance of the introduction. Within this advice, I believe the very first page of your manuscript is particularly important. A stunning example of this is Harari's (2014) *Sapiens'* first page:
>
>> About 13.5 billion years ago, matter, energy, time and space came into being in what is known as the Big Bang. The story of these fundamental features of our universe is called physics.
>> About 300,000 years after their appearance, matter and energy started to coalesce into complex structures, called atoms, which then combined into molecules. The story of atoms, molecules and their interactions is called chemistry.
>> About 3.8 billion years ago, on a planet called Earth, certain molecules combined to form particularly large and intricate structures called organisms. The story of organisms is called biology.
>> About 70,000 years ago, organisms belonging to the species *Homo sapiens* started to form even more elaborate structures and cultures. The subsequent development of these human cultures is called history.
>> Three important revolutions shaped the course of history: the Cognitive Revolution kick-started history about 70,000 years ago. The Agricultural Revolution sped it up about 12,000 years ago. The Scientific Revolution, which got under way only 500 years ago, may well end history and start something completely different. This book tells the story of how these three revolutions have affected humans and their fellow organisms.

When I first read this page, I had a 'wow moment' only one minute into a book that at first looked a bit heavy and uninviting. I re-read this first page a few times. Out of curiosity, I typed it in Word, Times New Roman 12, doubled spaced, and it came out just over half a page. In under 200 words, this introduction brings the history of the universe into the text, and positions the text into the history of the universe. It summarizes and connects vast scientific domains (physics, chemistry, biology, history), using a simple language and consistent style. It goes straight to the point of what the book is about and is able to engage both the subject expert and the layperson. Finally, it is self-contained within the first page, which makes the overall effect even more powerful.

When crafting an introduction, I look out for examples like this. By the end of the first page, I try to achieve the following objectives: to introduce the research problem from a real-world perspective, using examples and quotes; to summarize what we know already from previous research; to state clearly what the manuscript is about, and why this is relevant. I try to keep the language simple and non-technical, using short sentences, and 3–4 well-balanced paragraphs. The aim is to make the reader/reviewer keen to turn the page and read on. I try to end the first page with a full-stop, making it self-contained. This is very important; a single line spilling over to the next page will dilute the effect. On page two, I introduce key concepts and describe the research design. Then, page three of the introduction is for describing the manuscript's contributions and why they matter. When possible, I try to keep the introduction to three pages, following the structure described above. (De Luca)

2.2 Judicious Use of Prolepsis

The author has other considerations when writing the introduction. Rob Morgan suggests the use of a writing style that reminds us of news style or journalistic style: the lead paragraph has the most important news, and subsequent paragraphs present additional news in declining importance. Morgan stresses the need to use prolepsis (start with the ending, then describe how you got there) to create interest early, for a very practical reason: readers of academic articles are not likely to read linearly:

> A manuscript needs to create a drumbeat immediately. It should tee up an expectation early, and to build anticipation and eagerness for the reader to read on. Script writers often refer to this as prolepsis, which is a framed story where the narrative begins with a flash forward to the ending and then continues with a flashback. In this way, the manuscript gives away its conclusions, but the article is read so as to allow the reader to navigate the entire story. This creates a lock-in effect for the reader, which also allows a line of sight or critical path through the argumentation, method, and discussion such that the reader is able to understand the destination. Some commentators might consider this a spoiler that takes away the surprise for the reader, but this makes one erroneous assumption: that all readers make it to the end of the article. This is frequently not how an article is initially consumed by the reader. (Morgan)

Morgan also presents a useful checklist for authors to help their readers navigate their article. Some of these points pertain directly to good writing style in the introduction, while others will be fulfilled in later sections of the manuscript:

> Does the manuscript satisfy the five Cs of 'first-pass' reading? For further consideration of how the readers consume an article, read the approach established by Keshav (2007) in an unpublished commentary on "How to Read a Paper." In the first pass, the reader is seeking five issues that need to be addressed by you. Does the manuscript describe: (i) "category—what type of paper is this?; (ii) context—e.g., which other papers is it related to? which theoretical bases were used to analyze the problem?; (iii) correctness—e.g., do the assumptions appear to be valid?; (iv) contributions—what are the paper's main contributions?; and, (v) clarity—is the paper well written?" (Morgan)

2.3 Scientific Contributions

A good introduction must present the intended theoretical contribution to the reader succinctly. As John Nicholson and Ad de Jong point out, the common author's claim to fill some gap in the academic literature may not be nearly enough to confirm a substantial contribution to theory. Both contributors suggest that a strong contribution may be in the application to practice, which too often is relegated to a couple of sentences in the concluding section:

> The author(s) must convince the editor and reviewers that there is a scientific contribution by the end of their introduction section. Without such a stated contribution, the chances—in my view—are prejudiced in terms of having a manuscript desk rejected or returned as a reject or a major correction. Many authors under claim their contribution(s), predicating their contribution(s) on a single gap, where often there is more in the manuscript. Also, by reducing the contribution(s) simply to gap-spotting (neglect or confusion), authors miss the chance to claim that they are making much bigger challenges to underlying assumptions in a whole body of work. Equally, from a quantitative perspective, that the possibility of replications of existing studies is shied away from and instead of celebrating this it is played down in favor of a claim for a much smaller contribution based on an insignificant area of neglect or confusion. Equally, there seems to be great reticence to predicate a contribution on a practical problem area. Instead, the contribution is in most cases led from a theoretical weakness. Therefore, how can authors claim impact in what we do without stronger reference to practice? Instead, these contributions tend to be afterthoughts tagged on the end of the manuscript. (Nicholson)

> Developing a manuscript for a top journal takes time. To deliver a substantive contribution to the extant marketing literature, it is essential to describe carefully the status quo and the research gap. However, this is not enough for a publication in a top journal in marketing. Especially in the field of marketing, the simple fact that the topic is a new concept, or a new framework that fills a gap in the existing body of literature, is in itself not sufficient as a contribution. Rather, this new concept or

new framework should also pinpoint an urgent problem that marketing practitioners struggle with, or help understanding a novel phenomenon that is trending in marketing practice. In addition, as an author you should be able to make a strong case and validate this problem or phenomenon by giving some clear and convincing examples from marketing practice. (de Jong)

Rob Morgan suggests a strategy for avoiding the too-familiar "seek to close this gap" type research objective, which has to do with where the research gap comes from in the first place:

> You do not find a gap, you 'create' it: Lack of conceptual or empirical precedent does not constitute a gap. Finding a research gap is elusive. Authors should construct arguments around the: (i) importance of the topic for research, policy, and practitioner audiences for example; (ii) deficits in prevailing insights and explanations; (iii) contributions that will be derived; (iv) novelty of the approach of your work; and (v) consequences of potential findings. (Morgan)

It is also a good idea to show how the contribution builds on the existing literature stream. Ad de Jong notes the importance of doing this constructively, and to avoid being overly critical of previous research. There are two good reasons for this: few authors are not standing on the shoulders of previous researchers, and their contribution to the existing stream should thus be clear; and those previous researchers may be the reviewers assigned to the manuscript and may be less open to new ideas that are harshly critical of the work most familiar to them!

> Do not step on reviewers' toes! One nice way to deliver a top contribution is to enthusiastically introduce a new concept or method to the marketing literature. The key challenge then is how to present this new concept or method such that you as an author do not break down existing concepts and methods in the field. This is critical because the reviewers of your manuscript and who are knowledgeable about the topic probably are adepts of these existing concepts and methods. That means that these reviewers often have more difficulty in digesting your critical view on 'their' existing concepts and methods and will be less open to accepting new ones. It is therefore of importance to carefully introduce the new concept or method by using compelling arguments and presenting a constructive view on the current ones. (de Jong)

In sum, the introduction should clearly show the importance of the manuscript to the reader, which is sometimes challenging. The manuscript may be important to its author; the author cannot forget to communicate this enthusiasm to the reader. Tobias Schäfers makes several good suggestions to ensure this task is done right.

> Authors should use the manuscript's introduction to demonstrate clearly why what they are investigating is relevant to both academia and managerial practice. For the former, a good way is to refer to existing literature reviews or quote the Limitations and Further Research sections of published articles. For the latter, using industry figures, such as those published by government agencies or by market research companies, can be useful. That way, authors can prevent that after reading the Introduction, the readers ask themselves the question: "why exactly are the authors investigating this topic?" Essentially, a good manuscript convinces the reader right at the beginning that the topic is important. (Schäfers)

3. LITERATURE REVIEW AND RESEARCH DESIGN

As we have noted (Lindgreen & Di Benedetto, 2020), a strong literature review accomplishes several objectives: shows the author's familiarity with the literature, supports the author's conceptual model, and shows what is missing or under researched in the literature. Once the conceptual model is set up and the hypotheses are defined, the author can choose the most appropriate research design.

3.1 Literature Review

Heiner Evanschitzky provides some valuable guidance on how to frame a solid literature review, which would accomplish all the objectives stated above:

> My main concern with literature reviews is that most of the time the manuscripts selected to form part of such a review seem arbitrary. In my opinion, an ideal literature review on empirical manuscripts would be a simple effect-size meta-analysis for the main relationship(s) under study. Such an analysis would convincingly show the current empirical knowledge of a certain relationship and as such demonstrate where further research might be needed. For both empirical and non-empirical manuscripts, another good option to craft a perfect literature review would be to do a bibliometric analysis to visualize trends and patterns in the relevant literature. In particular, such an analysis will uncover critical points in the development of and seminal contributions to a particular field of research. (Evanschitzky)

3.2 Research Design

Michael Mol notes that research design problems emerge in all kinds of research studies, both qualitative and quantitative, and can cause bigger problems at later stages of the manuscript. He identifies five important research design problems that frequently crop up:

> I have increasingly found that problematic aspects of my own empirical research manuscripts, as well as of the manuscripts I get to review for a range of journals, or be an action editor on, suffer from what I would call problems in research design. I broadly understand research design as any empirical setup that is proposed in response to a theoretically inspired question. Research design is not the choice of theory as such or the strength of the theoretical logic. Neither is research design concerned with the (technical) quality of the empirical analysis. Thus, not all problems in research manuscripts are to do with research design. Nonetheless, in my experience probably a large number of serious problems are research design problems. Research design problems pop up in quantitative and qualitative work, and whether authors collect their own data or rely on secondary sources.
>
> In decreasing order of importance, the top five research design problems are as follows: (1) *post hoc* theorizing, where hypotheses and the accompanying theory actually follow the results, but supposedly lead them; (2) endogeneity, with many manuscripts suffering from omitted variable bias or the possibility of reverse causality; (3) common method bias or variance, when data collection from a single source artificially inflates correlations; (4) relevance, when authors happen to have data that is employed to address an insignificant or even non-existent problem; and (5) overly descriptive work, which is most commonly found in qualitative manuscripts. (Mol)

Mol comments on the origins of research design problems, and why they are prevalent:

> These are not new problems, of course, and articles and even entire books have been written to address each of them. There are also some good research methods books that address sets of research design problems. However, research design problems tend to perpetuate. Without wanting to dwell on the reasons in any great detail, they relate to the behaviors of teams of researchers themselves, but equally to pressures exerted by employers, funding bodies, journal editors, and respondents. Perhaps more interestingly, what can (junior) scholars do to try and overcome problems in research design? (Mol)

Mol also makes several recommendations on how one can frame the research design section to improve presentation. He urges care in the selection of research design to suit the specified research question, anticipation of possible problems associated with the selected research design, undertaking robustness checks to justify the choice of research design, and to present research design methodology with full disclosure:

> A first step, taken at the beginning of projects, is to try and to answer the question: "what would a good study design look like for this research question?" While this may sound obvious, in reality, many research projects do not have a clear beginning and are developed on the fly. Projects can, for instance, start when a junior scholar

with previously collected data contacts a senior scholar, who might have some theoretical notion he wishes to put to the test. There is no telling whether the data and theory can be fitted. Another issue is that most (teams of) authors do not sufficiently discuss their initial research design with colleagues. And internal agreement over a research design often simply does not equate to external agreement.

I would urge (junior) scholars to develop a checklist of potential research-design problems. Then, before the study takes place and prior to submitting an empirical manuscript, they should run through this list to check whether these problems have been tackled sufficiently. The exact items are to an extent context dependent because business marketing differs from consumer marketing or strategic management, and certainly are method dependent. Common method variance problems, for instance, typically do not arise when secondary data are used.

I find that as an author it is of paramount importance to try to continuously justify the steps that were taken in the research. This includes an answer to the question why the research was conducted in a certain way. However, it also involves thinking through and then reporting the answer to the question: "are there any reasonable alternatives for the choices that have been made?" Too often, I find that authors still present their research design and the empirical results it produces as "the only possible answer." In reality, there are always alternatives, and robustness checks can for instance bring those out.

It is really important to write up the research design in such a way that the reader can work out what was done. Some research methods sections feel more like an attempt at promoting the work than a description of what was actually done. Authors should never try to obfuscate problems that are there; in fact, good scientific practice is to share with the reader what problems exist, and how these have been tackled.

... I would argue that some of the key qualities (junior) scholars can put into their work is to be conscious (about what they are doing), conscientious (in terms of how they go about doing their research), and transparent (by sharing with their audience the good and the bad of their work). (Mol)

4. METHODOLOGY AND METHODS

The choice of methodology and methods can also help frame the manuscript, in that a correct choice will support not only the theoretical contribution, but will also increase managerial relevance of the results. John Nicholson suggests that much is to be gained by reviewing articles in the extant literature, which have appeared in the target journal, to get an idea of how the phenomenon previously has been studied in the journal and to make a stronger case for how the manuscript will contribute to the dialogue. It is fine to import a new methodology, but one must not sacrifice managerial relevance in doing so. He positions this argument in terms of a trade-off between rigor and relevance:

> Methodologically, I often see references to core ideas outside of the journal, which I believe is absolutely fine, but then many authors do not look inside the journal to see who else has applied this methodology within the subject area. Accordingly, for each seminal methodological principle, add a few references to who has used it in the target journal, and how that has been adapted, changed, etc. With quantitative

articles, there tends to be a focus on methods over methodology. Put another way, discussion starts with statistical rigor, and the relevance can be overlooked. This requires more methodological discussion and an argument why such rigor is relevant to practice. Authors must address the disjoint between practitioners who largely are skeptical about what we do. (Nicholson)

Tobias Schäfers expands on this idea. He reminds us that, regardless of the methodology that is chosen, there must still be meaningful managerial implications. He suggests careful selection of mediators and moderators, particularly stressing that moderators are most valuable in a model if they are managerially controllable and therefore actionable. Lacking this quality may raise 'so-what' concerns:

> In empirical studies, I very much appreciate when authors not only describe a phenomenon and the main effects causing it, but also dig deeper. This means looking at underlying processes that explain an effect (i.e., mediators), as well as boundary conditions that explain whether an effect occurs (i.e., moderators). With regards to moderators, I prefer authors investigating variables that are within managerial control, as this increases the likelihood of generating actionable insights. For example, while it may be interesting to show that certain personality characteristics of a purchasing manager influence an outcome variable, such as sales success, it would be difficult to use these insights in managerial decision-making (send every purchasing manager a personality questionnaire before negotiations? Probably not a good idea). In contrast, if a study showed that the success of two sales tactics differs depending on the situation in which they are employed, companies could use these findings to change their own way of doing business. (Schäfers)

5. CONCLUSIONS AND MANAGERIAL IMPLICATIONS

We arrive at the concluding section, and even here the author has an opportunity to frame correctly and improve the overall impression made by the manuscript. Earlier sections stressed the importance of the managerial contribution. Heiner Evanschitzky suggests that a strong conclusion, including theoretical contributions and managerial implications, might win over a reviewer and encourage a revise-and-resubmit decision. To boost managerial relevance, he also recommends reporting a simulation based on the quantitative results, showing the practitioner reader what outcomes would be expected due to changes in the independent variables:

> To be honest, manuscripts are hardly ever rejected for a weak managerial implication section. However, I think having written a very strong case for the practical importance of the research might be a way to get a manuscript past the first round of reviews. Despite some weaknesses in other sections, if I as a reviewer can see how relevant findings are for practice, I am inclined to not reject a manuscript because

my strong belief is that our research must be relevant outside of academia. The reason for that is that manuscripts typically are rejected for lack of contribution, and if I can see at least a strong implication for management practice, I am willing to work with the authors to re-focus and tease out the overall contribution.

If you write a quantitative, empirical manuscript, a nice way to demonstrate the managerial relevance of the findings would be to do a simulation. What would happen if your independent variable(s) change(s) by one unit? What would be the consequence(s) for down-stream outcome variables? How important or relevant would those changes be? (Evanschitzky)

Tobias Schäfers expands on this idea, noting that the author more generally can discuss how the methods presented in the study can improve accuracy of results or minimize unforeseen outcomes:

When reading a manuscript, whether it is empirical or conceptual, I always ask myself what the impact of the findings could be. Ideally, a study should result in suggestions for how companies or researchers should go about addressing a current challenge. For instance, a study may provide evidence that using a different analytical method provides more accurate results, that a common marketing practice leads to unintended negative consequences, or that addressing customers differently will change their behavior. (Schäfers)

The final word on this topic goes to Luigi De Luca, who offers actionable advice on how to frame the discussion of managerial implications:

Managerial implications should not be an afterthought. They are a great opportunity to elevate your manuscript. A strategy I have used in recent manuscripts is to write managerial implications in 3–5 action-oriented paragraphs, each opened by a direct and normative statement for managers such as "Create a data-driven culture" or "Sync your data strategy with your industry digitalization." When possible, I try to engage managers, as I am writing the manuscript, to generate and/or validate these statements, for example by presenting my findings at a company workshop or executive education session. Also, I try to make the managerial implications section reference-free, and to keep them within a single self-contained page. (De Luca)

Another part of the conclusion section that sometimes receives insufficient attention is the discussion of limitations. Editors occasionally see manuscripts that do not even acknowledge limitations of the study. Certainly, even the best designed and implemented study has some limitations that can be addressed in future studies! Michael Mol notes that the author can improve the framing of the conclusions by proactively offering a realistic statement of limitations, rather than waiting for reviewers to suggest limitations. Of course, if the manuscript is invited for resubmission, the reviewers will no doubt have added their concerns, and some of these will be added to the statement of limitations for the revised version:

> I would advise authors to always include the limitations of their study and use those limitations wisely. There are still a significant number of manuscripts submitted for review to journals that do not contain a limitations section. Perhaps the thinking behind this is that the reviewers are supposed to bring out the limitations, and only then will the authors include a limitations section. That is neither reasonable, because authors know their study far better than reviewers, nor realistic, because it creates a pretense that a study does not suffer from limitations. (Mol)

6. ADDITIONAL ISSUES TO CONSIDER

In this section, we note several other topics mentioned by the contributors that did not fall neatly into one of the previous sections.

6.1 Manuscript Length

Manuscript length is always an issue. Some journals have maximum numbers of words or pages, and editors will insist on authors revising to meet length standards. Reviewers will most likely comment on the contribution-to-length ratio of an unusually long manuscript, especially if it is about a rather minor, incremental topic. Rob Morgan suggests that authors might question whether all those pages are really necessary, and reframe the presentation to be more compact and efficient. In fact, business academics can take a lesson from the leading natural science journals, which highly value concise and succinct writing style:

> Less is more (as alpha faculties, let us learn from science and the beta and gamma faculties): One of the leading global scholarly publications is *Science*, published by the American Association for the Advancement of Science. Their research articles are typically half of that in most marketing and management journals at a maximum of 4,500 words including references and figures etc. The length-to-contribution ratio is therefore exceptional in *Science*. Equally, *Nature*, published by Springer Nature, has a similar length-to-contribution ratio and, as is often argued, they extol the virtues of concise, accurate, and succinct text as the key means to communicate complex scientific information. (Morgan)

As anyone who has edited a manuscript for length will attest, trimming 2,000 or 3,000 words from a manuscript is easier said than done. It is painstaking work. Entire sections cannot simply be cut out; rather, each word and sentence may need to be rethought. Luigi De Luca presents a very thoughtful guide on editing for length, and the realistic problems encountered:

> Whether the length of a manuscript is limited by word count, or by the number of pages, I try to make the best use of each line of text. Once I have a full draft, I carefully edit any line of text taken by only one or few words, at the end of a paragraph. Often, replacing a long word (e.g., therefore) with a shorter one with the same meaning (e.g., so) works well; often though, this process leads to identifying and cutting redundant words or entire chunks of text. More generally, every word should deserve its space in the manuscript. (It is always easier to apply this logic to someone else's writing than to one's own, so be ready for occasional 'disagreement' with your co-authors on whether adding or removing a word will change the destiny of the world!) Some words or sentences may not seem wrong or harmful per se, yet they are redundant. They do not add anything to the text, yet they may annoy reviewers as every word is a little 'tax' on their time. The aim is to say what you need to say with the least number of words. This is a forensic exercise, but can also be enjoyable.
>
> Related to the previous point, I try to keep the text (excluding references) between 30 and 36 pages, and to divide it into three symmetrical sections of 10–12 pages: introduction, conceptual framework, and hypotheses; methods and results; and discussion, implications, and future research. This establishes a rhythm in the manuscript and keeps it to an acceptable length. Also, it is ideal to place each of the main subheadings (particularly conceptual framework, methods, and discussion) at the beginning of the page. (De Luca)

6.2 Visualizations

An important part of any manuscript is correct choice and design of tables and figures. While a picture may say a thousand words, too many tables and figures can be overwhelming, and poorly-designed ones become a barrier to effective communication. Thus, another opportunity for the author to improve framing is to carefully design tables and figures, which effectively convey meaning to the reader. Both Tobias Schäfers and Luigi De Luca offered insights on this topic:

> Obviously, any visual cues are processed much more quickly than text. Therefore, figures and tables contribute to the readers' first impression and also set their expectations. Authors should therefore include meaningful visualizations such as a research model or graphs of the results, and also make sure that tables are self-explanatory and well-arranged. (Schäfers)
>
> Figures, diagrams, and tables are very helpful to succinctly visualize the positioning of the manuscript, and to summarize the contributions compared to existing research. For example, Venn diagrams are often used to identify the intersections among different streams of literature and to evidence research gaps. Tables help summarizing the key literature by identifying important 'dimensions' to dissect existing contributions (each dimension would be a column in a table). Examples of

these dimensions are key theories, methods, findings, the presence of mediators and moderators, the geographical context, main limitations, and what your study adds in these respects. Very often, reviewers ask authors to develop such figures and tables in the review process, so why not include them in the first submission? Even when figures and tables do not appear in the manuscript, they are very helpful to guide the writing of the introduction and discussion narratives. (De Luca)

6.3 Revising as a Project Management Skill

Finally, there is the revision process itself. Once the revise-and-resubmit decision has been made, the author needs to work hard to keep the editor, and the reviewers, positive towards the manuscript (this topic has been discussed in depth in LaPlaca et al., 2018). Ad de Jong suggests applying project management skills to the review process. As with any other kind of project team, the challenge should be well understood by all participants, the team's capabilities to tackle the project should be assessed, and others with complementary capabilities may be invited to be ad hoc or full team members. In a revise-and-resubmit situation, that means seeking out a colleague who may have the needed expertise to address the reviewers' comments, and possibly inviting this colleague on as a co-author (assuming this is allowed by the journal):

> When preparing a manuscript for a top-marketing journal, the first aim is to get a revision. However, once you are lucky to get such a revision, it is not yet a done deal. You should realize that doing a proper job on the revision concerns an essential follow-up task, which is at least as tough as the preparation of the manuscript itself for the first submission. It takes two to tango! Once having obtained a revision, please ensure that your review team is strong enough to properly handle the revision process. It often is a matter of good project management. In some situations, the members of the author team lack the right inspiration and motivation and are tied up with too many other things. Then, the revision is no one's priority and doomed to fail. Hence, being driven and prioritizing the revision is the most important success factor. In addition, good management of revision processes also means ensuring that the author team contains enough knowledge to do a decent job on the revision. For instance, if you as an author think that you, or your co-authors lack certain expertise to adequately tackle some tough reviewer comments, you should not hesitate to contact and ask another scholar who has expertise to help out. It sometimes may even make sense to add this person as an additional co-author (note: remember to check with the editor that is allowed), assuming that his/her contribution is indispensable for increasing the likelihood of successfully completing the revision. (de Jong)

7. CONCLUSIONS

This chapter addresses the issue of framing the manuscript. Just as an artist will painstakingly choose a frame to best display a work of art, authors need to consider how to best display their research contribution. As we have seen, each section of the manuscript can be framed for maximum impact, and the authors can undertake minor or even major improvements to each section before submitting the manuscript for review. Also, just as the frame sets off the painting, making it more attractive for the art gallery patrons, proper framing of the manuscript will increase its appeal to reviewers and editors, maybe in a subtle way. A concise statement of research objective that pulls the reader in, or a statement of managerial implications that shows the practical applications of the findings, might just be enough to win over the reviewers and result in an opportunity to revise and resubmit.

In the recent editorial mentioned earlier (Lindgreen & Di Benedetto, 2020), a team of collaborators provided their insights on what they specifically look for when reviewing a manuscript. That editorial showed that reviewers may approach a manuscript from different directions, and prioritize different parts of a manuscript, but there is certainly agreement on what constitutes a good contribution to the literature stream. This chapter turned again to a team of collaborators, who responded to a similar question, but from the author's point of view. That is, when preparing the manuscript for submission, what kind of frame should be put on it? Based on the perspectives of the collaborators presented here, it is clear that reviewers do very much care about the choice of frame, it can make at least a minor difference in the reviewers' overall impression, and authors should not overlook this important task. It is hoped that the contributors' comments encourage prospective authors to consider the importance of framing their research to maximum effect.

REFERENCES

Harari, Y.N. (2014). *Sapiens: A Brief History of Humankind*. London: Random House.

Keshav, S. (2007). How to read a paper. *ACM SIGCOMM Computer Communication Review*, 37(3). https://doi.org/10.1145/1273445.1273458.

LaPlaca, P., Lindgreen, A., & Vanhamme, J. (2018). How to write really good articles for premier academic journals. *Industrial Marketing Management*, 68(1), 202–209.

LaPlaca, P., Lindgreen, A., Vanhamme, J., & Di Benedetto, C.A. (2018). How to revise, and revise really well, for premier academic journals. *Industrial Marketing Management*, 72(5), 174–180.

Lindgreen, A. & Di Benedetto, C.A. (2020). Editorial: How reviewers really judge manuscripts. *Industrial Marketing Management*, 91, pp. A1A–10.

11. Developing conceptual frameworks for business-to-business marketing
Adam Lindgreen, C. Anthony Di Benedetto, Roderick J. Brodie, and Elina Jaakkola

1. INTRODUCTION

Robust conceptual frameworks play a critical role in advancing academic and practical knowledge. Development of theory requires high-quality, novel conceptualizations and advancements that integrate existing theories, link research across disciplines, and provide multi-level insights to move the field forward with substantial leaps rather than incremental steps. For academic researchers in business-to-business marketing, it is essential for emerging theory to be a source of practical insight to support decision-makers. Despite the importance and contribution of insightful conceptual frameworks, existing methods, books, and articles have seldom elaborated on how to develop these frameworks. The issue of developing conceptual frameworks is relevant for different research approaches, both purely conceptual and those based on empirical data. As far as business-to-business marketing research is concerned, *Industrial Marketing Management*, as the leading business-to-business marketing journal, needs to take a leadership position by prioritizing the development of conceptual work, which meaningfully advances theory.

Conceptual frameworks can offer a substantive contribution to warrant publication on their own, without empirical data; or such frameworks can be motivated, illustrated, and fleshed out with empirical data. Articles of this type are typically labelled as conceptual or theoretical articles, as they use existing literature as their primary source for developing novel frameworks (Jaakkola, 2020) (see Figure 11.1). Conceptual frameworks also can be developed through an abductive process where researchers move between theory and empirical data to develop a framework. The theorizing process is guided, but not determined, by existing theory, as is typical for many qualitative studies (e.g., Dubois & Gadde, 2002; Nenonen, Brodie, Storbacka, & Peters, 2017). In contrast, the role of empirical data is substantial when the focus is on testing conceptual frameworks. This is also the case when the framework is devel-

Developing conceptual frameworks for business-to-business marketing 205

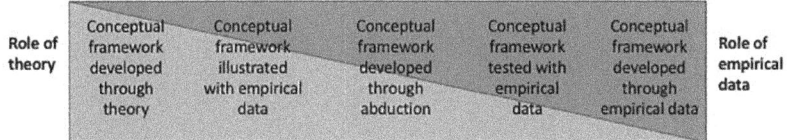

Figure 11.1   Role of theory vs. empirical data in developing conceptual frameworks

oped solely on the basis of empirical data (as in the development of grounded theory).

The purpose of this chapter is to consider explicitly various pathways to developing conceptual frameworks and how these pathways can be used to create new conceptual frameworks to support research, with a particular focus on business-to-business marketing. This chapter focuses on theorizing processes where existing theory plays a pivotal role (as shown in Figure 11.1). Following Brodie and Peters (2020), we see conceptual frameworks emerging from interfaces between (i) general theoretic perspectives and midrange theories; (ii) multiple midrange theories; and (iii) applied theories and midrange theories. Less attention is given to the more data-driven approaches such as grounded theory (e.g., Glaser & Strauss, 1967; Strauss & Corbin, 1990) because there are robust guidelines and established conventions to guide the theorizing.

To shed light on some of the challenges involved in developing, and writing about, conceptual frameworks, we frame our discussion around three specific styles of conceptual writing introduced by Cornelissen (2017) in his review of conceptual articles published in the *Academy of Management Review*. His examination identified three conceptual styles: (i) articles that are centred on a set of propositions (propositional style), (ii) articles that develop a process model (narrative style), and (iii) articles that build or elaborate on a theoretical typology (typological style). We outline practical research design considerations (see Jaakkola, 2020) for each style and present an illustrative example of each style.

Insightful conceptual frameworks are essential to integrating existing knowledge and setting the agendas for future business-to-business marketing research. A significant weakness of many conceptual frameworks is that the theory used is too narrow in scope; and that the resulting conceptual development lacks strong theoretical foundations and fails to bridge theory and practice. We contribute value by providing researchers with templates and guidance in developing conceptual frameworks in a more explicit and systematic manner.

2. HOW THEORY INFORMS THE DEVELOPMENT OF CONCEPTUAL FRAMEWORKS

Weick (1995), in his essay "What Theory is Not, Theorizing Is," laments that in organizational studies, there are few attempts to develop and use what he refers to as strong theory. In particular, he criticizes researchers of "lazy theorizing in which researchers try to graft theory onto stark sets of data" (p. 385). This occurs because there is confusion between theory as the outcome and theorizing as a process. Theory often is presented in the form of references, data, lists of diagrams, and hypotheses, which, while they are essential parts of the theorizing process, are not theory per se. Thus, when considering how theory informs the development of conceptual manuscripts, it is important to place emphasis on the theorizing processes.

While the question "what is theory?" has been debated extensively, for the purpose of this chapter we use a simple general definition that "theory is a statement of concepts and their interrelationships that shows how and/or why a phenomenon occurs" (Corley & Gioia, 2011, p. 12). In a previous editorial, we drew on Brodie and Peters (2020) to distinguish between three levels of theoretical abstraction (Lindgreen, Di Benedetto, Brodie, & van der Borgh, 2020b).

General theories: These theories are conceptions and perspectives utilizing theory that is framed at the highest conceptual level and provides a perspective or logic of explanation for a domain. The theories are broad in scope, integrative, and context-free, and thus the theories do not directly lead to empirical investigation. The theories provide the foundations for understanding and explanation and are informed by a paradigmatic perspective.

Midrange theories: Midrange theories are context-specific, which relates to specific phenomena. Hence, midrange theories provide conceptual frameworks to undertake empirical observation and models to guide managerial practices. Most of the theories currently used in business-to-business marketing research have these characteristics, so midrange theories characterize most conceptual frameworks.

Applied theories: Applied theories are embedded in the domain of empirical research and the research context. While the focus of applied theories traditionally has been with empirical research, 'theories-in-use' can play an important role (Argyris & Schön, 1974). 'Theories-in-use' (TIU) recognize that practising managers, customers, and other stakeholders in a service system use theory.

Zeithaml et al. (2020) argue that the TIU approach should be used to create theory that is developed from the mental models used by marketing stakeholders and thereby specific to the marketing issue being studied. The TIU approach builds on constructs, which are guided by marketing practitioners and grounded in marketing-specific contexts. Accordingly, this approach produces conceptual frameworks that are not only meaningful to marketing stakeholders, but can be communicated to them in language they use. Zeithaml et al. (2020) point out that this approach contrasts with the more commonly used approach of basing marketing theory on established academic theories developed in related disciplines. The authors note that this traditional approach limits the researcher's ability to find new, interesting marketing phenomena, ultimately widening the disconnect between academics and practitioners of marketing (Reibstein, Day, & Wind, 2009).

It has further been argued that neither traditional academic theory building, nor the TIU approach, optimally guides academics and practitioners in co-producing knowledge that is mutually beneficial (Crespin-Mazet & Ingemansson-Havenvid, 2020). Academics and practitioners inherently have different interests and contexts and require different kinds of knowledge (Di Benedetto, Lindgreen, Storgaard, & Clarke, 2019). To bridge this divide, the solution is to co-produce knowledge that is useful to both groups; this issue is known as the knowledge production problem (van de Ven & Johnson, 2006). To solve this problem, the interaction between academics and practitioners should produce context-specific knowledge; this knowledge will be useful to the extent that it can be combined with other contextual resources (Håkansson & Waluszewski, 2007). That is, both academics and practitioners should bring their own knowledge, competences, and partner networks to their collaboration so that knowledge is not just co-produced, but also can be used and further produced in other contexts over time (Crespin-Mazet & Ingemansson-Havenvid, 2020).

In Figure 11.2, we outline the domains of knowledge at three levels of theoretical abstraction. Midrange theory can be seen as the intermediary (bridging) body of theory that interfaces between the empirical and theoretical domains and hence are the foundation for conceptual frameworks. Within the theoretical and empirical domains, it is recognized that the boundaries between marketing and other management disciplines overlap. Thus, the theorizing processes in business-to-business marketing research can draw on these different disciplines.

The theorizing process for developing conceptual frameworks typically results in advancement of midrange theories and consists of the interplay between general theories and applied theories. However, prior to this theorizing process, it is essential to recognize the paradigmatic perspective that informs the theorizing process. As discussed by Lindgreen et al. (2020b), con-

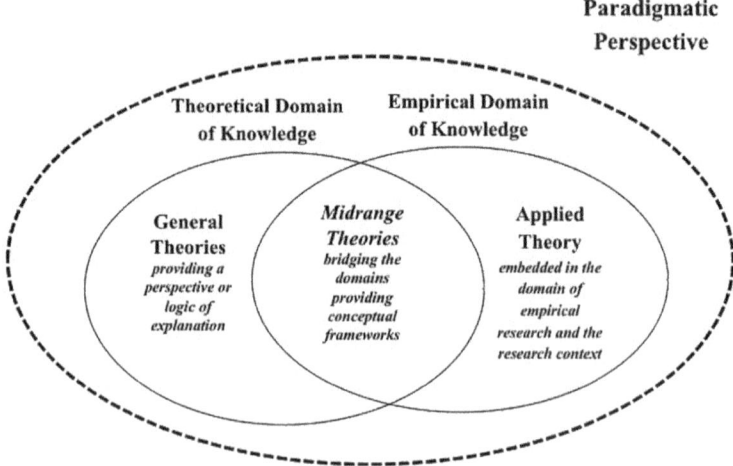

Source: Lindgreen et al. (2020b, p. 2).

Figure 11.2 Domains of knowledge and levels of theory

temporary business-to-business marketing research mostly adopts a network or systems paradigmatic perspective leading to general theories that are inherently cross-disciplinary and drawing on sociological and institutional foundations. While a focal general theoretic perspective can interface directly with midrange theory to develop a conceptual framework, the theorizing process also can be informed from other general theoretic perspectives and other midrange theories.

Recently, Jaakkola (2020) has elaborated on the process of theorizing for developing conceptual frameworks. She distinguishes between two starting points. One way to start is with a focal phenomenon that is observable, but not adequately addressed in the existing research. The researcher inductively develops a conceptual framework (midrange theory) in terms of particular concepts that reflect the phenomena. Nenonen et al. (2017) recognize that insight about the focal phenomena can come not only from researchers' observations but can also be initiated with researchers interfacing with managers and other actors involved with practice. An alternative starting point for developing conceptual manuscripts begins with a focal (midrange) theory and extends and refines this theory to reflect the phenomena of interest better. The process can be enhanced by taking into account the meta-level conceptual system provided by the general theory. As discussed by Lindgreen et al. (2020b) and Brodie and

Peters (2020), the process of theorizing for developing conceptual frameworks should not be considered linear, but should be seen as iterative, drawing on pathways.

3. STYLES FOR DEVELOPING CONCEPTUAL FRAMEWORKS

To identify the different ways for developing conceptual frameworks, Cornelissen (2017) examined articles published in the *Academy of Management Review*. While he did not find one straightforward formula, he does identify three styles:

1. *Proposition-based style*: The statement of theoretical propositions that introduces new constructs and cause–effect relationships.
2. *Narrative-based style*: The specification of a process model that lays out a set of mechanisms explaining events and outcomes.
3. *Typology-based style*: The specification of a typology that interrelates different dimensions to flesh out new constructs and causal interactions.

To develop guidelines for these styles, Cornelissen (2017) went through the reviewer reports and editorial letters for all of the *Academy of Management Review* articles he had handled as the editor for this journal. These styles and associated guidelines apply to advance the craft of developing conceptual frameworks. We also draw on four alternative templates for conceptual research design identified by Jaakkola (2020): *Theory Synthesis*, *Theory Adaptation*, *Typology*, and *Model* that can guide the theorizing process for developing conceptual frameworks. Next, we will discuss the three styles identified by Cornelissen (2017).

The *propositional style* refers to a theoretical framework that outlines a set of formally stated theoretical propositions (Cornelissen, 2017). These propositions can introduce new constructs and cause–effect relationships. This type of article develops a conceptual framework that takes the form of a research model detailing the antecedents, outcomes, and contingencies related to the focal construct (MacInnis, 2011). The propositional style suggests making claims about causal relationships and specifying testable relationships. However, Cornelissen (2017) suggests that insightful conceptual frameworks should make propositions that cover novel theoretical ground rather than merely summarize prior literature. The creative scope of such arguments is wider in articles that present the conceptual framework as their primary outcome, drawing on a theoretical or empirical domain of knowledge to model emerging phenomena instead of testing well-charted constructs (Yadav, 2010). The researcher should carefully justify the choice and role of different sources of knowledge in building the propositions: typically, the literature that addresses key elements of the phenomenon/concept to be explained is informed by another theory that enables the explanation of relationships between the studied variables (Jaakkola, 2020).

The narrative-based style of developing conceptual frameworks focuses on specifying a process model that lays out a set of mechanisms explaining events and outcomes (Cornelissen, 2017). This style represents a form of theorizing that emphasizes narrative reasoning that seeks to unveil 'big picture' patterns, connections, and mechanisms rather than specific causal relationships (Cornelissen, 2017; Delbridge & Fiss, 2013). This type of conceptual framework is often a process model involving the dynamics of constructs and critical events or turning points for the phenomenon. The framework contributes to extant knowledge by not only describing what is known, but making novel arguments about how a concept changes, the processes by which it operates, or why and how elements of a process lead to a particular outcome (Cornelissen, 2017; MacInnis, 2011). This type of framework can develop by synthesizing existing literature across multiple theoretical perspectives to form novel, higher-order understanding. It can also come from problematizing an existing theory and resolving the identified shortcomings by introducing a new theoretical lens that enables organizing the elements of the studied process in a better way (Jaakkola, 2020).

The typology-based style aims to logically and causally combine different constructs into a coherent and explanatory set of types (Cornelissen, 2017). A typology provides a more precise and nuanced understanding of a phenomenon or concept, as the typology dimensionalizes or categorizes existing knowledge of a phenomenon or construct (Jaakkola, 2020; MacInnis, 2011). As a theoretical framework, a typology delineates how variants of an entity differ and may help to recognize the entity's differing antecedents, manifestations, or effects (MacInnis, 2011) and causal relationships (Fiss, 2011). When building a typology, the researcher should carefully justify the logic of identifying dimensions of types. The dimensions of a typology can be identified by applying some general theory, or other midrange theories that are equipped to explain logically the differences between variants of the concept (Jaakkola, 2020). Another option is to tease out relevant dimensions through iterations between theories and knowledge in the empirical domain.

The three styles presented by Cornelissen (2017) ultimately aim at explaining relationships between concepts to answer questions *why*, *how*, and *when* something happens. The propositional style results in a research model depicting cause–effect relationships; the typology outlines variants of a concept that have different drivers, outcomes, or contingencies; and the narrative style lays out sequences of events (Figure 11.3). According to Jaakkola (2020), conceptual research also can be designed to increase understanding, thus answering

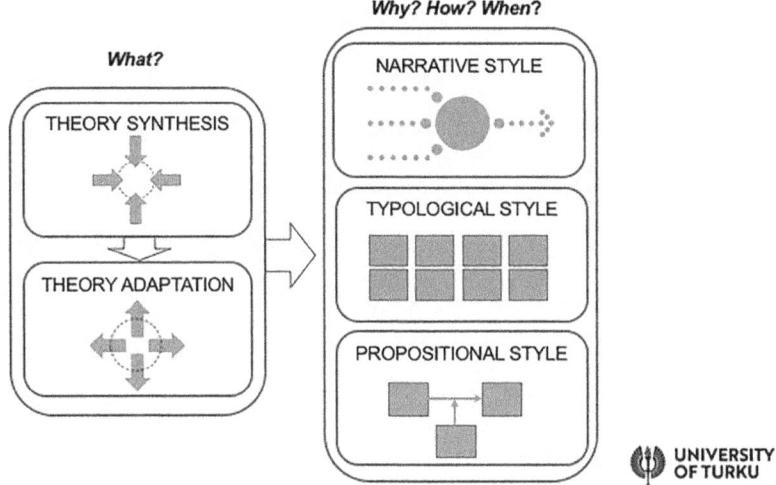

Figure 11.3   Styles of theorizing for building conceptual frameworks

the '*what*' question. A *theory synthesis* framework seeks to achieve conceptual integration across multiple theories or fragmented literature streams, to offer and enhance the view of a concept or phenomenon by linking previously unconnected elements in a novel way (Jaakkola, 2020). Theory synthesis frameworks summarize and integrate existing knowledge into a manageable whole and produce a new higher-order understanding of the concept under study (MacInnis, 2011). Another approach is to broaden, extend, or amend an existing theory by using other theories. *Theory adaptation* aims at revising extant conceptualizations by introducing alternative frames of reference to propose a novel, enhanced perspective (Jaakkola, 2020; MacInnis, 2011). For example, the researcher might draw from practical insights, that is, TIU, or other midrange theories to argue that an existing conceptualization is insufficient or conflicted, and suggest that broadening of perspective or scope is needed to align better the concept to its purpose (Jaakkola, 2020; Nenonen et al., 2017). Research aiming at theory synthesis or adaptation often serves as a stepping stone towards building frameworks that can explain (Figure 11.3).

4.   EXAMPLES

In this section, we discuss three business-to-business marketing studies, each of which is illustrative of one of the styles of developing conceptual frameworks (Cornelissen, 2017).

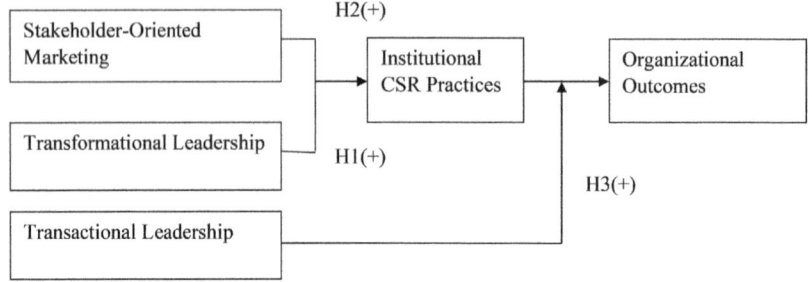

Source: Adapted from Du et al. (2013, p. 160).

Figure 11.4   Conceptual framework of Du et al. (2013)

4.1   Proposition-Based Style

The first study, by Du, Swaen, Lindgreen, and Sen (2013), examines the interrelationship between leadership styles and institutional corporate social responsibility (CSR) practices. The authors noted the critical role of organizational leadership style in developing organizational strategy, yet the shortage of research of how leadership style affects the practice of CSR. In particular, the authors investigated the relationship between transformational and transactional leadership styles and organizational CSR outcomes.

Du et al. (2013) developed a theoretical framework (Figure 11.4) based on their review of the literature on transformational leadership. They proposed three testable hypotheses, which can be summarized as follows:

First, transformational leaders are most likely to recognize the interrelationships and interdependencies between the organization's stakeholders, including the local community and the natural environment. Therefore:

H1: Transformational (not transactional) leadership is positively associated with an organization's institutional CSR practices.

Second, stakeholder-oriented marketing provides a wider environmental view, which provides deeper knowledge of the organization's stakeholders and their concerns. Therefore, transformational leaders can form even stronger relationships with stakeholders, and can work with stakeholders to provide CSR practices that better suit the needs of the stakeholders. Du et al. (2013) hypothesized a moderation effect:

H2: Stakeholder-oriented marketing positively moderates the relationship between transformational leadership and institutional CSR practices (that is, the relationship is more positive for organizations effectively practicing stakeholder-oriented marketing).

Finally, the value provided to secondary stakeholders is a societal impact allowing institutional CSR to generate positive organizational outcomes. If the organization uses its core competences appropriately, the organization will be able to effectively implement its corporate CSR initiatives. This is also modelled as a moderation effect:

H3: Transactional (not transformational) leadership positively moderates the relationship between institutional CSR practices and organizational outcomes (that is, the relationship is more favorable for organizations with higher transactional leadership).

Based on a survey of managers in 440 US organizations, Du et al. (2013) found support for their new conceptual model. Transformational leadership was positively related to institutional CSR practices, and stakeholder-oriented marketing did moderate this positive relationship. By contrast, transactional leadership positively moderated the relationship between institutional CSR practices and organizational outcomes. Thus, all hypotheses were supported, and the authors concluded that transformational and transactional leadership styles affect institutional CSR practices differently.

Du et al. (2013) also identified several important managerial implications derived from their conceptual model. Transformational leadership is most appropriate for initiating CSR practices, while transactional leadership may have an advantage in deriving the organizational benefits from these practices. The authors noted that both types of leadership are needed in order for the organization to achieve the 'circle of virtue' (the organization investing in CSR achieves its business objectives and therefore can ensure sustained CSR investment). The authors recommended that managers should consider how both transformational and transactional leadership can be implemented. Also, stakeholder-oriented marketing has significant implications in that organizational members must keep the welfare of all stakeholders in mind and create an organizational climate that fosters CSR practices. Stakeholder-oriented marketing supports transformational leadership and increases its effectiveness in promoting CSR practices. This finding suggests that transformational leaders should consider developing complementary capabilities that help them attain their institutional CSR objectives.

The Du et al. (2013) study is a clear illustration of Cornelissen's (2017) proposition-based style. The authors identified a significant gap in the literature: the organizational leadership literature had not investigated the effects of leadership on organizational CSR policy despite the growing importance of the latter. They proposed a new conceptual framework, built on organizational leadership theory, which included new cause-and-effect relationships among constructs from leadership theory to organizational CSR practices and outcomes. It is also notable that the authors employed the remedies recommended by Cornelissen (2017) for the proposition-based style. They develop and empirically test their conceptual model. They also use a broad theoretical perspective that required cross-disciplinary inputs from different business disciplines (organizational behaviour, marketing, and corporate strategy).

4.2 Narrative-Based Style

To illustrate the narrative-based style, consider Vallaster and colleagues' multiple-case qualitative study of for-profit hybrid organizations (Vallaster, Maon, Lindgreen, & Vanhamme, 2020). Due to their hybrid nature, sustainability-driven hybrids design organizational activities in line with social and environmental objectives and economic objectives simultaneously, which lead to tensions. The most successful hybrids will need to manage these tensions, yet the process by which they accomplish this has been under-researched in the literature. A much greater understanding of this process is warranted, from the viewpoints of both individual actions and collective organizational practices. To gain the required depth of understanding, Vallaster et al. (2020) conducted a qualitative study of for-profit hybrids.

Based on a review of the literature, the authors developed an initial conceptual framework. The existing literature discussed the tensions found within for-profit organizations attempting to transform their industrial and social environments, identifying four categories: learning, belonging, organizing, and performing tensions. To handle these tensions, organizations need to develop the ability to deal with specific issues that arise from each of these four categories; the literature provided some discussion of dynamic capabilities required for the organization to integrate, build, and transform internal and external resources in response to changing environmental conditions. Specifically, the literature mentioned sensing, seizing, and transforming dynamic capabilities. Nevertheless, little research on how these dynamic capabilities are developed and applied by for-profit hybrids was found.

To assess empirically how actors at the individual and collective levels develop these capabilities in a for-profit hybrid setting, they used practice-based theory to conceptualize the practices (individual and collective behaviours, activities, and processes) undertaken by actors to address each of the specific tensions and, ultimately, to create economic, social, and environmental value.

Next, Vallaster et al. (2020) applied a theory-generative approach, carrying out a qualitative study comprising several stages over a 15-month period. Each stage comprised several workshops. Stage A was designed to understand industry context, and experience in handling multiple goals. During Stage B, middle managers were interviewed about the activities, processes, and capabilities involved in developing a for-profit hybrid orientation. Stage C was devoted to identifying challenges, which had arisen from the initiatives undertaken. Post-workshop interviews, personal reflections, and diaries were used to take notes and to drive discussion at upcoming workshops. Finally, in Stage D, supplementary interviews with managers from other for-profit hybrids were conducted.

The theory-generative approach involved several phases. First, initial first-order codes were identified by the authors from the interview findings. Second, related concepts across case organizations were identified and linked by the authors, creating second-order concepts. These concepts primarily involved how the respondents addressed the tensions arising from their organization's hybrid orientation. Third, the authors conducted a cross-case analysis to identify consistent patterns. Finally, the authors completed the theoretical framework by refocusing on the hybrid-related tensions identified in the existing literature, and determining how dynamic capabilities and micro-foundations addressed these tensions.

The result of the analysis was a new conceptual framework of the micro-foundations of the dynamic capabilities of for-profit hybrids: the four dynamic capabilities of for-profit hybrids (sensing, seizing, transforming, and liaising; extant literature had not previously discussed the dynamic capability of liaising) and how these dynamic capabilities are supported by micro-foundations. Table 11.1 indicates the micro-foundations that were identified and how they aligned with specific for-profit hybrid tensions. The authors also draw several managerial implications. For-profit hybrid managers should recognize the need to constantly nurture both the individual and collective practices that support the micro-foundations. It is also important to monitor hybridity-related tensions since not all practices will be suitable for all business decisions. The organization should be able to capitalize on economic opportunities and also identify sustainability-oriented solutions.

In sum, Vallaster et al. (2020) provide a good illustration of the narrative-based style of conceptual model. The authors started with a 'theory adaptation' approach (Jaakkola, 2020), as they combined the dynamic capabilities theory with practice theory to conceptualize how actors develop capabilities, and then informed this theory-based understanding with knowledge from the empirical domain (cf. Nenonen et al., 2017). As a result, the authors developed a useful managerial framework that presents the underlying micro-foundations leading to dynamic capabilities. Managers of for-profit hybrids can make use of the

Table 11.1 *Micro-foundations of dynamic capabilities of for-profit hybrids*

Micro-foundations	Individual or collective
Sensing opportunities: Creating a sense of opportunity	
Experiential /grounded scouting	*Individual*
Attention to functional core	*Individual*
Paradoxical framing	*Individual & collective*
Seizing opportunities: Constructing possibilities	
Systems thinking	*Individual & collective*
***Bending institutional norms**	*Individual & collective*
Integrative learning	*Individual & collective*
Building resilience	*Individual & collective*
Continuous transforming	
Cross-vergence orchestration	*Individual & collective*
Flexible linking structures	*Collective*
Organizational entrenchment	*Individual & collective*
Liaising within and across organizational boundaries	
Enabling (inter) organizational spaces	*Collective*
Stakeholder-inclusive governance	*Collective*

Note: Cells marked '*' relate to practices and micro-foundations that do not contribute to addressing hybridity-related tensions.
Source: After Vallaster et al. (2020, in print).

framework to improve current practices, identify which practices are lacking, and ultimately support sustainable value creation. While some components of the model were available in the existing literature, the process by which for-profit hybrids could best manage ongoing tensions was not yet well understood. This conceptual framework helps managers understand the individual actions and collective practices that best support environmental and social objectives.

4.3 Typology-Based Style

In the study of purchasing practices by Lindgreen, Vanhamme, Raaij, and Johnston (2013), the authors develop a new framework and a measurement instrument. The purchasing literature usually assumes two categories of purchasing practices (transactional and relational), though, in practice, purchasing often involves both types. The issue of how and why organizations choose one type or the other, or to combine types, and how these choices affect organizational performance is not well understood. To remedy this situation, Lindgreen et al. (2013) needed to develop a new framework, based on the existing literature, which includes a broader range of purchasing practices, as well as a new measurement instrument to measure organizational purchase practice with greater precision.

The existing literature described two purchasing management practices. Transaction purchasing emphasizes the aggressive and continuous search for new suppliers to achieve the best terms. In contrast, network purchasing refers to the organization relying on a more extensive organizational system for purchasing from suppliers. Lindgreen et al. (2013) suggested adding two practices. Electronic purchasing refers to the use of the internet or other one-to-one or one-to-many technologies to support the supplier relationship, and interactive purchasing refers to interpersonal interaction between organizational employees and suppliers. Further, Lindgreen et al. (2013) identified eight formative indicators, which together describe the four different kinds of purchasing practices. These formative indicators are: purpose of exchange, managerial intent, nature of communication, type of contact, duration of exchange relationship, formality of exchange, managerial focus, and managerial investment. The authors also identified a general indicator that provides an overall view of each purchasing practice. Table 11.2 shows the four purchasing practices and how they are characterized by the formative indicators.

The authors surveyed 202 purchasing managers in the US. Each organization was scored on each of the eight indicators, for all four purchasing practices. By summing the eight indicators for each purchasing practice, an index was created, which indicates the extent to which each organization practices transaction, electronic, interactive, and network purchasing. The purchasing practice types are not mutually exclusive, so, as a result, each organization will have its characteristic mix of indices.

Lindgreen et al. (2013) used cluster analysis to group organizations into configurations of purchasing practice, based on these indices. This procedure resulted in a new conceptual framework of purchasing practices, consisting of four identifiable clusters or patterns:

1. *Transactional configuration*: High on transaction purchasing index and low on the other three indices.
2. *Integrative relational configuration*: Low on transaction purchasing index and high on the other three indices.
3. *Interpersonal dyadic configuration*: Medium on transaction purchasing index, high on interactive purchasing index, and low on the other indices.
4. *Interpersonal network configuration*: Medium on transaction purchasing index, high on interactive purchasing and network purchasing indices, and low on electronic purchasing index.

Table 11.2 Indicators pertaining to purchasing practices

Aspects	Transactional perspective	Relational perspective		
	Transaction Purchasing	Electronic Purchasing	Interactive Purchasing	Network Purchasing
Purpose of exchange: When dealing with our direct suppliers, our purpose is to:	achieve cost savings or other 'financial' measure(s) of performance (monetary transactions)	create information-generating dialogue with many identified suppliers	build a long-term relationship with specific supplier(s)	form relationships with a number of organizations in our supply market(s) or wider purchasing system
Nature of communication: Our communication with direct suppliers can be characterized as:	our organization using undifferentiated communications with all suppliers	our organization using technology to communicate with and possibly among many individual suppliers	individuals at various levels in our organization personally interacting with individual suppliers	senior managers networking with other managers from a variety of organizations in our supply market(s) or wider purchasing system
Type of contact: Our organization's contact with our direct suppliers is:	arm's-length, impersonal with no individualized or personal contact	interactive via technology such as the internet	interpersonal (e.g., involving one-to-one interaction between people)	across firms in the broader network (from impersonal to interpersonal contact)
Duration of exchange: The type of contact with our direct suppliers is characterized as:	transactions that are discrete or one-off (i.e. not ongoing)	technology-based interactivity that is ongoing and real-time	interpersonal interaction that is ongoing	contact with people in our organization and wider purchasing system that is ongoing
Formality of exchange: When people from our organization meet with our direct suppliers, it is:	mainly at a formal business level	mainly at a formal level, yet customized and/or personalized via interactive technologies	at both a formal business level and informal social level on a one-to-one basis	at both a formal business level and informal social level in a wider organizational system / network

Developing conceptual frameworks for business-to-business marketing 219

Aspects	Transactional perspective	Relational perspective		
	Transaction Purchasing	Electronic Purchasing	Interactive Purchasing	Network Purchasing
Managerial intent: Our purchasing exchanges are intended to:	continuously search for new suppliers to find the best deal (i.e., low prices)	create two-way, technology-enabled data exchanges with our suppliers	develop cooperative relationships with our suppliers	coordinate activities between ourselves, suppliers, and other parties in our wider purchasing and supply system (e.g., second-tier suppliers, key customers, service providers, and other organizations with which we interact through our purchasing activities)
Managerial focus: Our purchasing strategy is focused on issues related to:	the purchase item and its price	managing IT-enabled relationships with many individual suppliers	one-to-one relationships with suppliers, or individuals in supplier organizations we deal with	the network of relationships between individuals and organizations in our wider supply system
Managerial investment: Our purchasing resources (i.e., people, time, and money) are invested in:	specifying products, negotiations, ordering, and expediting activities	operational assets (IT, website, logistics) and functional systems integration (e.g., purchasing with IT)	establishing and building personal relationships with individual suppliers	developing our organization's network relationships within our supply market(s) or wider purchasing system
General indicator: Overall, our organization's general approach to our direct suppliers (of product-related items) involves:	using aggressive sourcing (continuously search for new suppliers) to obtain purchase items at the most favourable conditions	using the internet and other interactive technologies to create and mediate data exchanges between our organization and our suppliers	developing personal interactions between employees and individual suppliers	positioning organization within a wider organizational system or network

Source: Lindgreen et al. (2013, p. 76).

The authors also gathered marketing performance outcomes (customer attraction, retention, and satisfaction, sales growth, and market share), as well as a financial performance outcome (profitability). Therefore, once the framework was in place, the authors were able to link purchasing practices to performance outcomes in a very detailed manner. For example:

- Electronic purchasing practices needed to be combined with the interactive purchasing and network purchasing practices in order to achieve high levels of performance.
- Many organizations are pluralistic; that is, they utilize two or more purchasing practices.
- The organizations that use the integrative relational configuration outperform other organizations on all the marketing and financial performance outcome measures.
- The organizations that use the integrative relational configuration outperform all or most other organizations on some of the specific formative indicators as well, such as supplier quality and delivery reliability. However, in the case of supplier lead time, there were no noticeable differences among the configurations.
- Organizations tend to use interactive and network purchasing more with direct suppliers, and transactional purchasing more with indirect suppliers.

Lindgreen et al. (2013) were able to draw several critical managerial implications from their conceptual framework. A manager can, for example, set targets for each type of purchasing practice to use per cluster, and evaluate performance outcomes. Gaps between actual and target achievement levels can be identified, and ways to bridge the gaps can be discussed. Organizations can also use this information to specify (and, when necessary, adjust and re-specify) their strategies on how to achieve purchasing practice and performance outcomes.

In sum, this study effectively illustrates the typology-based style of Cornelissen (2017). The previous literature tended to view only two types of purchasing practices (transactional and relational), without delving into how the organization chooses one or the other, or whether to mix types. Lindgreen et al. (2013) built on this literature stream and extended it in meaningful directions. First, the relational purchasing practices type was defined too broadly, so they essentially split this type into three new purchasing categories (electronic, interactive, and network purchasing) each with different characteristics. The authors identified a set of specific formative indicators, developed a new measurement instrument, and empirically developed a typology of purchasing patterns based on cluster analysis. Finally, they identified relationships between the purchasing patterns and performance outcomes. Overall, the new cluster-based typology resulted in a more precise view of purchasing practices and key performance metrics, making an important conceptual contribution and offering actionable managerial implications as well.

5. GUIDELINES FOR DEVELOPING STRONG CONCEPTUAL FRAMEWORKS

In another editorial, Lindgreen, Di Benedetto, Brodie, and van der Borgh (2020a) discussed which types of articles typically get cited. One type of article that tends to get highly cited is the article that introduces a new conceptual framework. Di Benedetto et al. (2019) consider the necessary conditions that determine the success of authors' conceptual and theoretical development. In a summary of these conditions, the authors highlight the following points:

- Develop a clear and convincing logic to their theory so that researchers can see how the theory fits in the field.
- Define concepts clearly and concisely so that other researchers can use them in their own research.
- Ensure that there is a clear rationale for the conceptual development so that other researchers can understand why they should use the concepts, methods, or theories.
- Ensure that propositions and hypotheses are specific, well-argued, grounded in theory, and not tautological.

For any type of conceptual framework, it is elementary that the authors explicate and justify the choice of theories and concepts, as well as the role those different domains of knowledge play in the analysis (Jaakkola, 2020). There is no single best template for building a conceptual framework. Still, authors can use general theories, midrange theories, and theories-in-use in many different ways, as long as they make their approach clear for the reader. For example, the article should communicate if empirical data was used to illustrate a theoretical framework developed through conceptual analysis, or if the elements of the framework are derived from empirical data.

In an examination of how to undertake cross-disciplinary research, Lindgreen et al. (2020b) recognize that there are multiple pathways to develop midrange theory and hence undertake empirical research. First, the focal general theoretic perspective can interface directly with midrange theory. The second option is that other general theoretic perspectives provide pathways that can lead to other midrange theories, which then leads to a focal midrange theory that can be used in business-to-business research (Lindgreen et al., 2020b, p. 1).

Table 11.3 Three styles of developing theoretical frameworks and associated guidelines

Attributes of each style	Proposition-based style	Narrative-based style	Typology-based style
Definition	The statement of theoretical propositions that introduces new constructs and cause–effect relationships	The specification of a process model that lays out a set of mechanisms explaining events and outcomes	The specification of a typology that interrelates different dimensions to flesh out new constructs and causal interactions
Basic form	Identify cause–effect relationships that act as broad signposts and implications for further research	Provide generalized causal mechanism, as the underlying storyline of a process model	Explains the fuzzy nature of many subjects by combining different constructs into a coherent and explanatory set of types
Common problems	• Propositions are too narrow in scope and merely summarize the prior literature • Propositions include multiple clauses • Propositions lack detail on the causal agent	• Narrative and process model are too descriptive • Narrative and process model lack explanatory detail • Narrative features stylized arguments and claims (lacking nuance and contingent variation) • Narrative features complex compounds and phrases as constructs	• Typology is descriptive and does not offer multidimensional ideal types • Typology only systematizes and summarizes existing research but lacks explanation • Typology features various degrees of causal entanglement (including circularity and tautology)
Remedies	• Broaden the scope of the propositions and develop an original line of argument, with a novel set of assumptions as theorized grounds • Develop the arguments first, before formalizing them into propositions	• Elaborate the underlying conceptual linkages of a process model, foregrounding a clear mechanism or set of mechanisms • Add details and more contingent variation to the overall narrative, strengthening its explanatory potential	• Identify whether the proposed typology has a review or theory contribution, or both • Develop the typology from a theoretical angle, incorporating multiple theoretical dimensions • Draw out patterns of causality (using fuzzy set reasoning) and explicate the basic line of argument

Source: Adapted from Cornelissen (2017).

One pathway to develop midrange theory is by having managerial practices inform research processes. For a more in-depth discussion of this pathway, we refer to the editorial by Lindgreen et al. (2020b). However, little is known about university–business collaborations. Thus, Di Benedetto et al. (2019) discuss this type of collaboration including, for example, offering advice to business managers about how to collaborate with university academics.

In addition to these more general guidelines, Table 11.3 outlines more specific guidelines related to the three styles discussed in this chapter.

As outlined in Table 11.3, the common problem with these theorizing styles for developing conceptual manuscripts was that the theory used is too narrow in scope. Thus, the resulting conceptual development lacks strong theoretical foundations. Cornelissen's (2017) remedies for all three theorizing styles are to introduce a stronger theorizing process that facilitates the interface between general theory and applied theory and to explicitly recognize the social causal mechanisms that underpin midrange theory (Mason, Easton, & Lenny, 2013).

6. CONCLUSIONS

The purpose of this chapter is to draw attention to the important but demanding craft of developing insightful theoretical frameworks. We urge authors to consider the role of different domains of knowledge in building their frameworks, and explain their approach clearly in the article. Too often, reviewers face manuscripts that have conceptual frameworks based on descriptive literature reviews, but are devoid of more in-depth conceptual analysis or integration. Hopefully, business-to-business marketing scholars will be inspired by the different styles for building theoretical frameworks discussed in this chapter and make use of the guidelines and research design considerations we have outlined.

REFERENCES

Argyris, C. & Schön, D. (1974). *Theory in Practice: Increasing Professional Effectiveness.* San Francisco: Jossey-Bass.

Brodie, R.J. & Peters, L.D. (2020). New directions for service research: Refreshing the process of theorizing to increase contribution. *Journal of Services Marketing*, 34(3), pp. 415–428.

Corley, K.G. & Gioia, D.A. (2011). Building theory about theory building: What constitutes a theoretical contribution? *Academy of Management Review*, 36(1), 12–32.

Cornelissen, J. (2017). Editor's comments: Developing propositions, a process model, or a typology? Addressing the challenges of writing theory without a boilerplate. *Academy of Management Review*, 42(1), 1–9.

Crespin-Mazet, F. & Ingemansson-Havenvid, M. (2020). Rethinking the theory-practice divide: How academia-industry collaboration contributes to theorizing. *Industrial Marketing Management*. https://doi.org/10.1016/j.indmarman.2020.01.003.

Delbridge, R. & Fiss, P.C. (2013). Editors' comments: Styles of theorizing and the social organization of knowledge. *Academy of Management Review*, 38(3), 325–331.

Di Benedetto, C.A., Lindgreen, A., Storgaard, M., & Clarke, A.H. (2019). Editorial: How to collaborate really well with practitioners. *Industrial Marketing Management*, 82, 1–8.

Du, S., Swaen, V., Lindgreen, A., & Sen, S. (2013). The roles of leadership styles in corporate social responsibility. *Journal of Business Ethics*, 114(1), 155–169.

Dubois, A. & Gadde, L.-E. (2002). Systematic combining: An abductive approach to case research. *Journal of Business Research*, 55(7), 553–560.

Fiss, P.C. (2011). Building better causal theories: A fuzzy set approach to typologies in organization research. *Academy of Management Journal*, 54(2), 393–420.

Glaser, B.G. & Strauss, A.L. (1967). *The Discovery of Grounded Theory: Strategies for Qualitative Research*. Chicago, IL: Aldine Publishers.

Håkansson, H. & Waluszewski, A. (Eds.) (2007). *Knowledge and Innovation in Business and Industry: The Importance of Using Others*. London: Routledge.

Jaakkola, E. (2020). Designing conceptual articles: Four approaches. *AMS Review*. doi.org/10.1007/s13162-020-00161-0.

Lindgreen, A., Di Benedetto, C.A., Brodie, R.J., & van der Borgh, M. (2020a). Editorial: How to get great research cited. *Industrial Marketing Management*, 89. https://doi.org/10.1016/j.indmarman.2020.03.023.

Lindgreen, A., Di Benedetto, C.A., Brodie, R.J., & van der Borgh, M. (2020b). Editorial: How to undertake great cross-disciplinary research. *Industrial Marketing Management*, 90. https://doi.org/10.1016/j.indmarman.2020.03.025.

Lindgreen, A., Vanhamme, J., Raaij, E. van, & Johnston, W.J. (2013). Go configure: The mix of purchasing practices to choose for your supply base. *California Management Review*, 55(2), 72–96.

MacInnis, D.J. (2011). A framework for conceptual contributions in marketing. *Journal of Marketing*, 75(4), 136–154.

Mason, K., Easton, G., & Lenny, P. (2013). Causal social mechanisms: From the what to the why. *Industrial Marketing Management*, 42(3), 347–355.

Nenonen, S., Brodie, R.J., Storbacka, K., & Peters, L.D. (2017). Theorizing with managers: How to achieve both academic rigor and practical relevance? *European Journal of Marketing*, 51(7/8), 1130–1152.

Reibstein, D.J., Day, G., & Wind, J. (2009). Guest editorial: Is marketing academia losing its way? *Journal of Marketing*, 73(4), 1–3.

Strauss, A.L. & Corbin, J. (1990). *Basics of Qualitative Research: Grounded Theory Procedures and Techniques*. Newbury Park, CA: Sage Publications.

Vallaster, C., Maon, F., Lindgreen, A., & Vanhamme, J. (2020). Serving multiple masters: The role of micro-foundations of dynamic capabilities in addressing tensions in for-profit hybrid organizations. *Organization Studies*. doi.org/10.1177/0170840619856034.

van de Ven, A.H. & Johnson, P.E. (2006). Knowledge for theory and practice. *Academy of Management Review*, 31(4), 802–821.

Weick, K.E. (1995). What theory is not, theorizing is. *Administrative Science Quarterly*, 40(3), 385–390.

Yadav, M.S. (2010). The decline of conceptual articles and implications for knowledge development. *Journal of Marketing*, 74(1), 1–19.

Zeithaml, V.A., Jaworski, B.J., Kohli, A.K., Tuli, K.R., Ulaga, W., & Zaltman, G. (2020). A theories-in-use approach to building marketing theory. *Journal of Marketing*, 84(1), 32–51.

12. Writing a case-study methodology section
Adam Lindgreen, C. Anthony Di Benedetto, and Michael B. Beverland

1. INTRODUCTION

Business-to-business marketing academics study complex phenomena, aiming to describe these phenomena through theoretical frameworks, explaining the relationships among the framework's constructs, and provide guidance and insight to decision-makers (Hunt, 1994). Like all academics, business-to-business marketing academics work within a scientific paradigm, that is, they share assumptions about the phenomena they study so as to orient their research and define their lines of inquiry (Deshpandé, 1983).

The ontology used by a large proportion of business-to-business marketing researchers publishing in *Industrial Marketing Management* is that of relativism. That is, there is no assumption of an objective reality; rather, the researcher investigates individual actors' knowledge and perspectives in order to understand perceived reality in context (Carson, Gilmore, Perry, & Grønhaug, 2001). These business-to-business researchers also operate within the realistic paradigm: they interpret the processes of social actors within situations and seek to understand socially constructed meanings. By reconstructing these meanings with scientific language, the researchers generate theory about the phenomenon under study (Blaikie, 1993). In a relativistic setting, multiple realities and the perspective of multiple actors are taken into account by the researcher so as to understand the phenomenon in its proper context (Carson et al., 2001).

In order to fully adhere to a realistic paradigm and comprehend marketing phenomena, these business-to-business marketing researchers participate in real-world situations. The researchers recognize that actors and experiences are intertwined with marketing phenomena, and subject to causal influences (Bhaskar, 1978; Robson, 1993). Further, they recognize that marketing phenomena must be considered as part of the real world, which may only be imperfectly understood (Lincoln & Guba, 1985). Accordingly, these researchers take the perspective that marketing phenomena are not hard and fast rules, but rather reflect tendencies. Therefore, research findings should be thought of not as the reality of the world, but a window to reality, and that further insight can be gained through triangulation with results of other studies (Perry, 1998).

Given the above background, it is clear why a large proportion of business-to-business researchers have made use of qualitative case studies (Beverland & Lindgreen, 2010). The qualitative case study is a desirable research approach for realists whose goal is to describe and explain phenomena, capturing the appropriate level of complexity (Bhaskar, 1979). Case studies are useful when the actors' behaviors cannot be controlled (Yin, 1994) and when the research wants to investigate 'how' and 'why' questions, which might require gathering data over an extended period of time (Miles & Huberman, 1994). By using a case-study method, researchers can take a holistic view and explore social processes in rich and complex detail. In this process, contextual variables that affect actors' behavior will be observed and identified.

In the following, we will discuss what we believe should be reported in the write-up of a case-study methodology section. We organize our discussion around some of the steps in Eisenhardt's (1989) framework.

2. WHAT TO INCLUDE IN THE WRITE-UP OF A CASE-STUDY METHODOLOGY SECTION

2.1 Selecting Case(s)

Researchers using the case-study method must first decide on the research setting for their cases (industry, region or locality, and so on). They should be able to justify this setting as appropriate for studying the phenomenon of interest. Therefore, researchers should be able to specify how the case study will contribute to theory: through replication of earlier findings, extension of current theory, identifying theoretical categories, or showing examples of positive and negative cases so one can diagnose how they differ. Furthermore, the researchers should stress how they will be able to make theoretical contributions given their chosen research setting, and whether these contributions can be generalized through replication.

For example, just because, say, corporate social responsibility (CSR) has not been studied in country X is not in itself a strong reason for undertaking a study. If, however, there are reasons to believe that there are different underlying factors of influence (to those compared to countries A, B, and C where CSR already has been studied) on CSR that pertain to, say, how managers can question, identify, and prioritize relevant elements of CSR, then there is a good reason to undertake the proposed study.

Once the research setting has been chosen, the researcher has to consider which companies to include, and which respondents to choose within each company. These decisions should be justified by the researcher. Continuing with the CSR research theme, then, the researcher would need to specify the criteria used to select companies. For example, have the companies set a goal of adjusting their supplier relationships to conform to CSR objectives? Did an industry expert help in the selection process? Companies may have been selected because they recently have made changes to their supplier relationships, in which case the study would be a *post hoc* assessment of CSR compliance. An issue with this kind of assessment is that it depends on the memories (and records) of the participants, which might not be perfect. How did the researcher address this issue? Alternatively, a company in the midst of making such changes could be studied, which allows the researcher to assess the compliance process as it unfolds, avoiding the issue of forgetting past details. In any event, the researcher must also consider which individual respondents to contact. If only CEOs are interviewed, would they have enough detailed information about specific CSR policies and activities? Should both C-level executives and middle managers responsible for CSR implementation be interviewed?

While there are no specific rules on how many companies to include or individuals to be sampled, one should be able to generalize from the data and generate meaningful theoretical propositions (Coffey & Atkinson, 1996). The case-study researcher should be able to determine that theoretical saturation was reached, and justify that determination. In their Voice of the Customer research, Griffin and Hauser (1993) provide an example of the metrics that can be used to assess theoretical saturation. In their work, it was found that deep interviews of 20 or 30 customers yielded 90 to 95 percent of customer needs, suggesting that this was a good target number of interviews for this kind of research.

The case-study methodology section appropriately should include a table(s) summarizing the qualitative case studies using column headings including, for example, 'study and number of case(s) + time of study', 'research topic(s) examined', 'type of industry and geographical scope of activities', 'revenue and number of employees', 'source(s) of information', 'individual respondent's position and years in company', and 'length of interview'. Another appropriate column heading would be 'background of company' that could explain in a nutshell what the company was about, and why it was relevant for the research (e.g., how the company has worked with CSR principles).

2.2 Crafting Instruments and Protocols and Entering the Field

Case-study researchers rely on in-depth, face-to-face interviews as the most effective means of gathering data. Just as the quantitative researcher develops, validates, and pre-tests the survey instrument carefully before entering the field, the qualitative researcher must develop an interview protocol to ensure that the questions will cover the relevant range of topics, and the interviews stay focused. The case-study methodology section must discuss this interview protocol. For example, which themes, identified in literature and business press or noted by industry experts, were covered during the interview? How were the interview questions standardized around the topics that covered these themes? Which specific prompts were interspersed to gain greater insight into the specific lines of inquiry? Finally, were the individual respondents provided with the opportunity of giving feedback on the findings? Did this feedback result in a reinterpretation of the findings? Incidentally, the case-study method sometimes has been criticized for yielding superficial insights (Dyer & Wilkins, 1991); other data may also be used to identify deeper insights and/or ensure generalizability of findings to other contexts (Eisenhardt, 1991).

The case-study methodology section could include a table or an appendix with the interview protocol including 'themes', 'topics', 'interview questions', and 'specific prompts'. Sometimes, however, a description of what was done is more useful, especially when doing theoretical sampling where the questions may shift. If included, the table could also list, in bullet points, the 'key findings' next to (in a second column) each theme, topic, interview question, or specific prompt. These key findings again could be supplemented with (in a third column) 'illustrative interview quotes', as well as 'other primary or secondary evidence' from, among others, business press articles, published reports, annual reports, and observations in the companies. If such primary and secondary evidence are presented and discussed in the article, then this third column could be omitted.

Not all the illustrative interview quotes and other primary or secondary evidence would (need to) be discussed in the manuscript. However, the abundance of rich quotes and evidence help to demonstrate that the findings discussed in the manuscript are grounded in actual facts; and that researchers have not used quotes selectively that are in support of their contentions. One way to overcome criticism that quotes are used selectively is to report on as many cases as possible. Without presentation of 'raw data', readers have to trust that the researchers have interpreted the data correctly (Beverland & Lindgreen, 2010). One could contemplate offering a supportive table, perhaps in an online appendix, that provides more data examples. Following that route should ensure readable articles with acceptable contribution-to-length ratios.

Finally, the case-study methodology section could at a minimum mention the number of pages (e.g., single spaced, Times New Roman 12) of the combined text with the information from the in-depth, face-to-face interviews and the other primary or secondary evidence. When researchers include, for example, images and recorded information, they need to consider other options (e.g., total file size) that capture the total sample of data.

2.3 Analyzing the Data

Case-data analysis techniques must be presented carefully to fully understand and explain the marketing phenomenon being studied and to show evidence of generalizability of results to either a population or to theory. This can be done in two steps, the first of which is the within-case analysis. Here, the researcher documents how the data from individual respondents within each company were handled, with respect to how specific research topics were addressed. This is generally accomplished by coding, in which the raw data are converted or coded to understandable components, which can be then more easily compared across respondents (Eisenhardt, 1989). A figure can be presented, which shows how the coding was done, and how themes and patterns within the data were identified using a coding scheme. The coding scheme itself should be included. A table can be included that shows how the data were interpreted and grounded-theory coding was developed (Spiggle, 1994). This coding and identification process could be supported with, for example, Atlas.ti software for qualitative research. However, this additional support may not be necessary in simpler cases involving single case studies.

If there are multiple companies, the coding scheme may be developed using data from interviews of one company's informants, and then can be used for the other companies; this process should be described. Additionally, if multiple researchers were involved in coding, the process by which they compared their coding results and resolved disagreements should be clarified as well. This could be expressed through, for example, inter-rater reliability.

Other decisions also should be disclosed in the methodology section regarding how the data were selected, analyzed, interpreted, and presented. Since the case-study methodology is discursive, full disclosure of all the evidence and findings may be prohibitive in length. The researcher will need to decide what should be included, and the presentation should convey the richness of the data to the reader. As noted above, the use of figures and tables may simplify presentation. Here and elsewhere, researchers should support their methodological choices with well-known references.

The second step is across-case analysis, which identifies differences and similarities on key dimensions across sets of cases. This step is important when the study includes multiple cases, and the step is used to determine if

Table 12.1 Case-study tactics to secure the design tests of validity and reliability

Design test	Theoretical explanation	Case-study tactics	Operationalized in this study by ….
Construct validity	To ensure correct operational measures have been established for the concepts being studied.	• Triangulation • Chain of evidence	• Multiple methods (interviews with different internal and external respondents; content analysis of data collected; case feedback from respondents; time in the field); multiple data sources (primary and secondary); multiple case studies and research settings; collaboration with knowledgeable colleagues; rich case descriptions • Providing a chain of evidence throughout the study
Internal validity	To establish a causal relationship. Internal validity is a concern for explanatory or causal case studies but not for exploratory or descriptive case studies that do not attempt to make causal statements.	• Pattern matching and rival explanation as pattern • Explanation building • Time-series analysis • Type of data • Triangulation	• Carrying out a cross-case analysis • Drawing on multiple perspectives and searching out negative cases • Building timelines for each case to form the basis of an initial coding scheme for the cross-case analysis • Collecting rich data; grounding phenomena in data • Allowing respondents to review the draft of a case and give feedback; discussing the findings with colleagues

Writing a case-study methodology section

Design test	Theoretical explanation	Case-study tactics	Operationalized in this study by ….
External validity	To demonstrate that the domain to which a case study's findings belong can be generalized.	• Specification of population of interest • Replication logic in multiple case studies • Research methods • Type of data collected	• Selecting data on the basis of population statistics • Providing a detailed description of the historical context of the study and locating each case within that context; using different research settings • Using a standardized interview protocol, clear procedures for data analysis, and a database • Collecting rich data
Reliability	To demonstrate that a case study's findings can be replicated if the case-study procedures are followed.	• Interview protocol • Clearly conceptualized concepts • Multiple indicators • Execution of pilot tests • Case-study database • Triangulation	• Developing a standardized interview guide • Using concepts from extant literature • Addressing multiple concepts • Developing an interview guide from pilot cases, as well as previous studies • Building a case-study database (perhaps using QSR NUD*IST or a similar program) • Using secondary data

Source: Lindgreen (2008, p. 49).

there are common patterns across the cases (Eisenhardt, 1989). For example, researchers will need to explicate how they moved back and forth between the established literature and the case data to develop theoretical categories and developed contextualized insights on the phenomenon under study. Figures or tables again can be used to facilitate communication of this process.

2.4 Validity and Reliability Concerns

The qualitative case-study researcher also must address validity and reliability concerns. According to the relativist view, research is the result of interaction between researcher and phenomenon (Alvesson & Skjöldberg, 2000; Seale, 1999), making it difficult to assess research quality since researchers each possess their own perspective or lens on how they see the world. Nevertheless, it has been argued that judgments about research quality can be made, even under the relativist view.

We argue that the validity and reliability of qualitative case-study research can be assessed using four design tests: construct validity, internal validity, external validity, and reliability. Beverland and Lindgreen (2010) note that the "lack of description of procedures makes replication difficult, thus undermining claims of reliability or dependability" (p. 58). For each of the four design tests, one can provide a brief theoretical explanation, a list of tactics that can be used to establish validity/reliability of case studies, and methods by which each of the tactics could be operationalized in a case-study context. Table 12.1 presents a general, non-exhaustive format that describes how each of the design tests could be operationalized; this can be used as a starting point by case-study researchers for establishing research quality (Flint, Woodruff, & Gardial, 2002; Lindgreen, 2008). To reduce the page space of the case-study methodology section, researchers could consider discussing validity and reliability in an appendix.

3. CONCLUSIONS

We have pointed out good guidelines for case-based research, as well as some examples of what generally would not be thought of as an interesting case study (a simple replication in a new country, where there is no theoretical reason why that country would be different for some cultural or business environment reason). Accordingly, we will end this chapter by discussing some case studies, which have been published in *Industrial Marketing Management*, that have the hallmarks of good case studies.

Choosing an exemplar multiple-case study within *Industrial Marketing Management* is difficult, given the high standard of research published in the journal. However, Flint and Woodruff's (2001) multi-site analysis of customer-desired value change is one standout example of a textbook case study. The authors provide a level of detail on their methods that for the time was unusual, and that meets the standards of this chapter. Readers understand each step of sample selection, data collection and subsequent analysis, and validity and reliability checks. The authors report their findings drawing on a range of compelling passages across the nine cases selected, and they summarize their data throughout as they build a theory of customer-desired value change. As the authors propose, value change is complex, and they fully capture this richness while never losing site of the need to order their material into a useful midrange theory that can further research.

Multiple-case studies often rely on single informants. However, theoretical insights can be gained when drawing upon multiple informants within cases. Ylimäki's (2014) examination of co-created product development between suppliers and users is one such example. The value of multiple inputs has long been demonstrated within new product development; however, this almost always gives rise to tension and the potential for conflict and poor outcomes. Understanding how actors from different disciplines come together to make team-based innovation work is critical. Ylimäki outlines his approach carefully, captures the ebb and flow of interaction between suppliers and customers, and brings to life the reality of joint product development, while also making use of figures, quotes, tables, and secondary data to ground his analysis.

Case studies are particularly suited to addressing issues of process and change. However, longitudinal work is difficult to undertake, given issues of access, time commitment, and the sheer amount of data one generates. It is heartening to see more longitudinal work being published in *Industrial Marketing Management*. One exemplar is Roehrich and Caldwell's (2012) examination of public–private procurement in the UK health sector. As well as providing all the details on method suggested in this chapter, the authors adopt a novel approach to presenting their data. They start with comparing the traditional model of public sector procurement with a possible novel model of thinking about public–private procurement. This device enables the authors to explore their rich data. They draw on as much interview, observation, and secondary material as they can within an article length, cleverly integrating data tables and figures into a classical qualitative narrative before discussing their adjusted model of public–private procurement. Seeing authors develop theory within an article always helps convince readers of the quality of the authors' approach.

REFERENCES

Alvesson, M. & Skjöldberg, K. (2000). *Reflexive Methodology*. London: Sage Publications.
Beverland, M.M. & Lindgreen, A. (2010). What makes a good case study? A positivist review of qualitative case research published in *Industrial Marketing Management*, 1971–2006. *Industrial Marketing Management*, 39(1), 56–63.
Bhaskar, R. (1978). *A Realist Theory of Science*. Brighton: Harvester-Wheatsheaf.
Bhaskar, R. (1979). *The Possibility of Naturalism: A Philosophical Critique of the Contemporary Human Sciences*. Brighton: Harvester.
Blaikie, N. (1993). *Approaches to Social Enquiry*. Cambridge: Polity Press.
Carson, D., Gilmore, A., Perry, C., & Grønhaug, K. (2001). *Qualitative Marketing Research*. Thousand Oaks, CA: Sage Publications.
Coffey, A. & Atkinson, P. (1996). *Making Sense of Qualitative Data*. Thousand Oaks, CA: Sage Publications.
Deshpandé, R. (1983). Paradigms lost: On theory and method in research in marketing. *Journal of Marketing*, 47(4), 101–110.
Dyer, W.G. & Wilkins, A.L. (1991). Better stories, not better constructs, to generate better theory: A rejoinder to Eisenhardt. *Academy of Management Review*, 16(3), 613–619.
Eisenhardt, K.M. (1989). Building theories from case study research. *Academy of Management Review*, 14(4), 532–550.
Eisenhardt, K.M. (1991). Better stories and better constructs: The case for rigor and comparative logic. *Academy of Management Review*, 16(3), 620–627.
Flint, D.J. & Woodruff, R.B. (2001). The initiators of changes in customers' desired value: Results from a theory building study. *Industrial Marketing Management*, 30(4), 321–337.
Flint, D.J., Woodruff, R.B., & Gardial, S.F. (2002). Exploring the phenomenon of customers' desired value change in a business-to-business context. *Journal of Marketing*, 66(4), 102–117.
Griffin, A. & Hauser, J.R. (1993). The voice of the customer. *Marketing Science*, 12(1), 1–27.
Hunt, S.D. (1994). On rethinking marketing: Our discipline, our practice, our methods. *European Journal of Marketing*, 28(3), 13–25.
Lincoln, Y.S. & Guba, E. (1985). *Naturalistic Inquiry*. Beverly Hills, CA: Sage Publications.
Lindgreen, A. (2008). *Managing Market Relationships: Methodological and Empirical Insights*. Aldershot: Gower Publishing.
Miles, M.B. & Huberman, A.M. (1994). *Qualitative Data Analysis*, 2nd ed. Thousand Oaks, CA: Sage Publications.
Perry, C. (1998). Processes of a case study methodology for postgraduate research in marketing. *European Journal of Marketing*, 32(9/10), 785–802.
Robson, C. (1993). *Real World Research: A Resource for Social Scientists and Practitioner-Researchers*. Oxford: Basil Blackwell.
Roehrich, J.K. & Caldwell, N.D. (2012). Delivering integrated solutions in the public sector: The unbundling paradox. *Industrial Marketing Management*, 41(6), 995–1007.
Seale, C. (1999). *The Quality of Qualitative Research*. London: Sage Publications.

Spiggle, S. (1994). Analysis and interpretation of qualitative data in consumer research. *Journal of Consumer Research*, 21(3), 491–503.
Yin, R.K. (1994). *Case Study Research: Design and Methods*, 2nd ed. Thousand Oaks, CA: Sage Publications.
Ylimäki, J. (2014). A dynamic model of supplier–customer product development collaboration strategies. *Industrial Marketing Management*, 43(6), 996–1004.

13. Writing articles for premier academic journals

Peter LaPlaca, Adam Lindgreen, and Joëlle Vanhamme

1. INTRODUCTION

Since its inaugural issue, *Industrial Marketing Management* has grown substantially in both qualitative and quantitative metrics. With the introduction of the Google Scholar search engine, new citation counts offer an alternative measure of journal impact and thus additional insights to those offered by the Thomson ISI Impact Factor. In 2009 and again in 2010, articles ranking marketing journals according to Google Scholar citations placed *Industrial Marketing Management* fifth out of 69 journals (Soutar & Murphy, 2009; Touzani & Moussa, 2010); its Google Scholar ranking was third among all marketing journals in 2015. Leonidou, Barnes, Spyropoulou and Katsikeas (2010) show *Industrial Marketing Management* as making the largest contribution of leading mainstream marketing journals to the international marketing discipline.

Three reasons for the continued increase in quality and influence of *Industrial Marketing Management* have been proposed (Touzani & Moussa, 2010):

1. *Industrial Marketing Management* is read by, and is of interest to, academics in related fields.
2. The quality of articles published in *Industrial Marketing Management* has increased.
3. Research topics covered by *Industrial Marketing Management* have grown in importance.

In this chapter, we discuss how to improve one's success rate when submitting manuscripts to major journals. (A later chapter will discuss the review and revision process that submitted manuscripts go through.) These helpful hints can make the journey to becoming a successful author easier with more acceptances and fewer rejections, albeit there are no guarantees. Clearly, the most critical factor in having one's research results published is the contribution(s) to the field. However, most of the leading journals in all fields routinely have rejection rates of 80 percent, 95 percent, or higher. All journals prefer articles that make significant contributions to the field. Seminal articles are highly cited thereby increasing a journal's impact factor. Many manuscripts routinely are sent to journal after journal after being rejected. Many potentially good manuscripts are rejected simply due to poor presentation. It is to combat this problem that we have put together this chapter highlighting the dos and don'ts for preparing better manuscripts thereby significantly increasing the likelihood of manuscript acceptance.

Before beginning any research project, it is therefore wise to do a small bit of research about the proposed topic. Ask a dozen or so people about the topic and the likelihood of citation should a manuscript eventually be published. Also look at various calls for manuscripts from journals; these calls for papers state specifically what types of papers journals are interested in publishing. Likewise, talk with companies to find out what their most important marketing problems and top priorities are. Occasionally, research centers such as the Marketing Science Institute or the Institute for the Study of Business Markets will issue statements on research needs. There are numerous videos available on the internet discussing methods to find research topics; simply Google "Finding research topics" and articles, publishers' hints, and YouTube videos will be easily identified. Conducting timely and interesting research topics will increase the chances of a manuscript being accepted for publication because, with potential for citation being a top factor in manuscript acceptance, editors are increasingly checking manuscripts on their originality and relevance. Before beginning any research project, ask yourself the following questions: 1. Is the proposed research new and interesting? 2. Is it challenging? 3. Is the work directly related to a current hot topic? And 4. Will it provide solutions to any difficult problems? Researchers clearly must delineate the type of contribution being claimed in the article.

Following the general format of typical academic journal articles, we structure the remainder of this chapter in the following six sections. First, we consider an article's title, abstract, and keywords. Second, we focus on the introduction and literature review of an article. Following that, while not all manuscripts deal with hypothesis testing such as exploratory research or descriptive case studies, manuscripts that do include hypothesis testing are frequently rejected due to the poor quality of the hypotheses themselves. We therefore discuss an article's hypotheses. The fourth section deals with the research methodology behind an article and the subsequent analysis. Finally, we discuss an article's findings and conclusions in the fifth and sixth sections.

2. AN ARTICLE'S TITLE

A published manuscript usually begins with a general introduction and proceeds through literature review, then hypotheses, research propositions, or research objective, then research methodology and analysis, then findings, and, finally, discussion and conclusions. However, when writing the actual manuscript, we usually start with the body of the manuscript, that is, conceptual framework and data (quantitative or qualitative) that serve as the foundation of the manuscript. Once this is complete, we can move forward to the introduction and backward to the conclusions. In fact, the last thing we should settle on is the title. In doing this, the research topic should not be confused with the title of the manuscript. The purpose of the title is to get the reader excited about the manuscript, and to invite the reader into the manuscript. The title provides an opportunity for the author to research their manuscript (as opposed to research for their manuscript, which they already have completed at this time).

We suggest that authors send their proposed title (nothing more) to six people who have not been involved with the research and ask them the following two questions:

1. If you saw this title, what would you expect in the manuscript?
2. Does this title make you excited to read the manuscript?

The first question is important because if authors get multiple responses then their title is poor because it is too ambiguous; if authors get six similar responses but these responses are not what the authors intended, then the title is poor because it is misleading. The answers to the second question will tell the authors if the published manuscript will stand out in the increasingly congested world of academic research. Once authors have received the responses from the six people, they can call the people to discuss why they responded so. The title of a manuscript creates the first impression with the reader and sets expectations of what will be in the manuscript. One should always write for the reader and remember that the very first reader is the reviewer. Unless one makes a good impression with this first reader, there is no second reader.

We suggest that a good title should contain the fewest possible words that adequately describe the contents of the manuscript and captures the reader's attention. As a general rule, effective titles identify the *main issue* of the manuscript; distinguish the subject of the manuscript; are accurate, unambiguous, specific, avoid unnecessary details, and complete; and do not contain infrequently used abbreviations. A good title attracts readers.

3. AN ARTICLE'S ABSTRACT

The abstract serves as an advertisement for the article. Although on many journal websites only subscribers to the journal (either individually or through their university or company) can access the entire article without charge, anyone can access the article's abstract. Therefore, the abstract must create sufficient interest in the article to justify its purchase, for example, the research question, the framework of the research, the research methodology, and/or the findings. Prices for individual article downloads can range from $25 to $75 depending on the journal and its policies. It is therefore a good idea to do some research on the abstract before submitting a manuscript to a journal because, just as the abstract can interest a reader to purchase the article, the abstract can influence a reviewer to develop a favorable bias toward the manuscript.

There are three main types of abstracts. The indicative (descriptive) abstract outlines the topics covered in a manuscript so that the reader can decide whether or not to read the entire manuscript. The informative abstract summarizes the manuscript based on the so-called IMRaD structure (i.e., introduction, methods, results, and discussion) but without these words explicitly presented in the abstract. Finally, the structured abstract follows headings required by the journal. For example, Emerald Publishing requires an abstract to be divided up into the following headings: purpose, design/methodology/approach, findings, research limitations/implications (if applicable), practical implications (if applicable), social implications (if applicable), and originality/value. One should check carefully which type of abstract fits the journal where one wants to submit.

We suggest that you again identify six people who are not involved with the research (and are not at your own institution) and send them just the abstract asking them the following questions:

1. Is the abstract written clearly, and is it jargon free?
2. Does the research described in this abstract interest you?
3. Does the research make a significant contribution to the field of study?
4. Would you pay $50 or €50 to download the article described in this abstract?

To create favorable answers to these questions, the abstract must emphasize the research's findings and its contributions to conceptual perspectives, methodological considerations, and/or managerial practices, amongst others. The abstract is the only place where authors can summarize their research, but they typically only are allocated 150–200 words to accomplish this. So what should be contained in this short space? We believe that, first and foremost, authors should state the research question or the focus of the research: what did they set out to accomplish? and why the research is relevant, interesting, and/or important. Then the abstract should give a one- or two-sentence summary of the research methodology (case study, survey, and/or experiment) and the research setting (industry). The rest of the abstract should focus on the research findings. After all, this is why the authors did the research, and this is why people read journal articles. Authors need to be very specific in telling people what they found out and why it is important. We frequently receive manuscripts where no findings are included in the abstract; it is as though the authors do not want people to know until they have read the article. However, unless people know what is coming in the manuscript, they will not bother to download, read, or cite the article.

The abstract should be written only when the manuscript has been finished to ensure that the abstract adequately summarizes the writing and also entices the reader to venture into the manuscript itself. Technical jargon should not be used; and no references should be cited. Statements that lack specifics must be excluded. One should never over promise in the abstract. It may take a week or more to write an excellent abstract, and it is one area where rushing can cause irreparable damage to an author's success. Thus, time is not of the essence; careful wording and clear thought are critical.

4. AN ARTICLE'S KEYWORDS

Keywords are used for indexing. Appropriate keywords will influence strongly whether or not readers will be able to locate the article and thus ultimately determine whether or not the article has a chance for being referenced. Keywords also help the editor select appropriate reviewers for the manuscripts. Words and phrases selected should reflect the essential topics of the manuscript, but words with a broad meaning should be avoided. Here, as elsewhere, we recommend that only abbreviations firmly and unambiguously established in the field should be used.

5. AN ARTICLE'S INTRODUCTION AND LITERATURE REVIEW

There are three main objectives for a good introduction to a manuscript: focus the reader on the research question or purpose of the manuscript; establish the proper frame of reference for the reader; identify the manuscript's contribution to the field; and convince the reader that there is justification for undertaking the research.

For a manuscript to be accepted it is critical that the reviewers and authors have a consistent frame of reference. The introductory section of the manuscript must present a complete framework for the research including historical development, current state of knowledge, and theoretical orientation. If the writing in the introduction is not sufficiently clear to bring the reviewer into the mind of the authors, there is ample opportunity to see things in a light different from what was intended by the authors with the reviewers reaching a sometimes conflicting basis for evaluating the manuscript. Many times, we receive responses from authors stating that "this is not what we meant" when they respond to reviewer comments. That this happens, however, is the authors' fault, as their manuscript did not establish the intended frame of reference in the reviewers' minds.

The literature review and theoretical development also are introductory aspects of a well-written manuscript. These aspects may be labeled as separate sections, or they may be embedded into a general introduction. While it is necessary to discuss adequately the knowledge base upon which the research is based so that readers can evaluate the work, it is not necessary to cite every possible reference or to go back in times to prehistoric eras. We regularly receive 30- to 40-page manuscripts, which have 10 or more pages of references. Only the most relevant prior published works need to be cited. It is a good idea to be respectful to other researchers' theoretical frameworks and research findings before one starts to criticize.

As part of the introduction the authors frequently demonstrate a gap or shortcoming in the existing literature or a conflict in previous studies and discuss how their research will help cover the gap or explain possible conflicts in previous studies. Authors also need to argue why this gap in knowledge or shortcoming about previous studies is important (e.g., how this gap may hinder progress in the field, how the gap may lead to companies making wrong decisions or having a biased view of a phenomenon). The introduction therefore answers a series of questions: What is the problem? Are there existing solutions? Which solution is the best? What is the main limitation in existing theory? How are these limitations problematic? And what do you hope to achieve? In answering these questions, the thematic scope of a manuscript usually progresses from general over particular to general. Words or phrases like "however," "remain unclear," "novel" and "first time" help convincing readers that the research is necessary although such words should not be overused.

A manuscript may for example present new, original results or methods or rationalize published results. A manuscript may also present a review of a particular field or summarize a particular topic. Literature reviews survey critical points in current literature relevant to a particular topic. By describing, summarizing, and evaluating critically previous work relating to a topic, such reviews should make a significant contribution to our understanding of a topic by providing integrative framework(s) and/or paths for further research.

However, just because some research has not been carried out before, this is no justification for undertaking that research now. Authors also should not publish reports of no academic interest; work that is out of date; exact duplications/replications of previously published work; or research with incorrect, unacceptable, or unjustifiable conclusions. Research that is purely descriptive or lacks theoretical implications is not interesting enough. We sometimes see research that although it is very well executed, it does not make a sufficiently large contribution to literature because, for example, the research is purely descriptive, is of no practical use, or it merely replicates exactly past research. Authors also should be aware of so-called 'salami' manuscripts, which are manuscripts based upon datasets too small to be meaningful. It should be noted that some journals, including *Industrial Marketing Management*, do accept case studies, but please do not extrapolate results from a single case study to an entire market! In short, manuscripts should present something new, interesting, and challenging that (often) relates directly to a current hot topic, and manuscripts should provide solutions to difficult problems. The introduction needs to answer the 'so what?' question.

As with the title and abstract, it is a good idea to conduct some research on the introduction. Authors could send just the introduction to six people not connected with the research and ask them to describe:

1. The research question or the manuscript's contribution.
2. The underlying framework of the research.
3. The gap that the research will fill and the importance of doing so.

If the responses to the above three questions vary among the people, the writing is not clear and needs improvement. If the responses are not what the authors intended, the writing needs clarification; and if the people respond that the gap is of little importance, authors have to demonstrate that the gap is indeed important (or submit the manuscript to another journal).

6. AN ARTICLE'S HYPOTHESES

Let us look at a typical research manuscript dealing with the testing of hypotheses. Researchers have identified a contribution earlier in the introduction and then detailed a theoretical framework that predicts how this contribution can be substantiated. This conceptual framework, which forms the basis for the research, has been well developed; and conceptual definitions of constructs are precise. To determine if predictions are valid, specific hypotheses are developed and then tested. But what constitutes good hypotheses? Perhaps this question best can be answered by looking at reviewer comments concerning poorly developed hypotheses.

Reviewers frequently complain about hypotheses that are obvious, results that are so expected that for the hypothesis not to be supported would be earth-shaking news. The fact that there may be no prior published research on the specific hypotheses is not justification for proposing it and testing something that is common knowledge.

Another common reviewer complaint concerns compound hypotheses, that is, single hypotheses comprising multiple components. Rejection of these hypotheses, therefore, has multiple possible explanations, and support (non-rejection) is difficult to interpret due to the same factor.

Reviewers—and editors—sometimes are amused by manuscripts that have so many hypotheses that they wonder why the researcher cannot be more focused. Sometimes, authors try to diminish the number of hypotheses by grouping them with many sub-hypotheses (1a, 1b, 1c, 1d, 1e; 2a, 2b, 2c, …). This, however, rarely fools reviewers.

Hypotheses must be derived from the theoretical development, but often reviewers note in their rejection comments that the hypotheses are not linked to the theory, but simply are stated in a vacuum. One wonders what the authors were thinking when they conducted the research and when they wrote the manuscript. When reviewers are left to wonder, manuscripts get rejected. Sometimes, authors write hypotheses that predict null effects. A null effect hypothesis is the default position that there is no effect, no difference (i.e., equal effects), no association between variables, and so on. In classical statistics, null hypotheses cannot be tested, however. To advance knowledge (and thus correctly test hypotheses in classical statistics), authors need to show that there is an effect, an association, a difference, and so on (this effect is the 'alternative hypothesis') meaning that they need to reject (i.e., disprove) the null hypothesis thereby showing that the alternative hypothesis is true (i.e., there is a difference, a relationship, an effect, and so on).

If authors cannot reject the null hypothesis, their results simply are inconclusive. Null results are not advancing knowledge because very different reasons could explain why the results are not significant. For example, it could be that the sample size is too small to detect the effect (power issue), but it also could mean that the theory is wrong (in fact, many null results are *type 2 errors*). Another common caveat is hypotheses that are stated in a non-directional matter (e.g., variable A and variable B have a different effect), but the interpretation of rejection depends on whether the inequality is positive or negative (e.g., the effect of A is larger or smaller than the effect of B). This may occur in research about relationships. While there may be one relationship between two actors, there may be two perceptions of that relationship by the actors (i.e., the perceptions of actor A and actor B differ). Which perception is more positive and which perception is more negative is often relevant to know, but is frequently not discussed. A good hypothesis should include a specific prediction so that it is very clear what pattern of results the authors expect.

Finally, when developing hypotheses, authors mostly focus on *type 1 error*, rejecting the null hypothesis H_0 when H_0 is true (e.g., saying that variable A has a larger positive impact on the dependent variable than has variable B when this is not true) and neglect to consider *type 2 error*, failing to reject the null hypothesis H_0 when the alternative hypothesis H_A is true (e.g., reporting non-significant results when, in reality, the effect of A is larger than is the effect of B). To avoid *type 2 errors*, authors need to pay careful attention that their study has enough power (i.e., ability to detect statistically significant relationships when these truly exist). This includes using reliable measures and avoiding sloppy coding of data, using standardized procedures if authors carry out experiments, and using larger sample sizes. Consideration of both types of errors will result in better crafting of hypotheses and, therefore, better theoretical development (Mitchell & Jolley, 2006).

So what are some guidelines for preparing excellent hypotheses?

1. Avoid obvious hypotheses; avoid hypotheses that are truisms; avoid hypotheses that are common knowledge.
2. Make sure each hypothesis focuses on a single testable item.
3. Limit the number of hypotheses in a single manuscript.
4. Link hypotheses to the theoretical development in your manuscript.
5. When writing hypotheses, make sure to avoid null hypotheses and to specify directional effects and clear patterns of expected results.
6. Do not forget about *type 2 error* when writing hypotheses.

7. AN ARTICLE'S RESEARCH METHODOLOGY

A well-written methodology section of a research manuscript serves two primary purposes: to demonstrate that you have followed acceptable scientific standards in conducting your research and to enable another researcher to replicate your study so that their results can be compared to your results. Empirically focused manuscripts in industrial marketing management research can employ either a case research methodology or quantitative methods. In the remaining parts of this section we present methodological and analysis considerations. We subsequently focus specifically on case research methods.

7.1 Methodological Considerations

While researchers have a very broad field of methodologies from which to select, chosen methods need to be justified and linked back to research objectives (why and how does the chosen method address the objectives in an appropriate manner?). One needs to ask: Is the methodology used in the research clear? Is the methodology appropriate for the research question?

Methods have limitations; one needs to be cognizant about these limitations (e.g., discuss possible rectifications in the limitations section of the manuscript's closing discussion). One should not assume that limitations are infinitely flexible; at some point, the methodology becomes inappropriate. Limitations also point to possible avenues for future research.

Methods also have assumptions. For example, one analytical method may require continuous and/or normally distributed data, while another method requires skewed data or is to be used for ordinal or nominal variables. Failure to recognize and satisfy the requirements for a specific analytical technique is a fatal flaw and will result in rejection of a manuscript.

Research methods often seem to follow a fashion cycle with one or more methods suddenly being in vogue. Researchers see what recently has been published and try to apply currently fashionable methodologies to their specific research project. One always should link the methodology to the needs of the research and not the research to the needs of the methodology. Too often we see manuscripts employing a certain 'hammer' to inappropriate problems. Sometimes, a screwdriver is necessary; leave the hammer in your toolbox for a future project.

One should not always 'play safe' with one's method choice; new methods can provide new insights and stimulate new discussions (see for example the current developments around fuzzy set qualitative comparative analysis, variance and covariance based structural equation modeling/partial least squares, Bayesian modeling, multi-level modeling, and event structure analysis, as well as computational models such as agent-based modeling, simulations and their applications in business-to-business marketing and supply chain management).

One should not be afraid of borrowing a research methodology from different fields to investigate a research problem. Established methodologies in other disciplines often can be used successfully to explore marketing issues, frequently providing unique and enlightening perspectives.

Methodology that uses multiple methods in a step-wise progression normally delivers added value. Each step complements the preceding one(s), builds on them, and adds a specific contribution. This can include mixed methods (e.g., a qualitative study to define concepts and overall model, followed by a quantitative survey using structural equation modeling), or the use of the same method in different steps (e.g., multiple experiments, where outputs/results of one experiment provide the input for the subsequent follow-up experiments).

However, good methodological considerations usually include a discussion (and often also a pictorial representation) of the overall research process or model. In quantitative studies, this could include the underlying logic of a causal model (i.e., a nomological model) for use in structural equation modeling (this can be done also in the context of the hypotheses development), or, for qualitative studies, it can outline a research framework (e.g., a dimensional model of concepts of interest), which is juxtaposed with data. If no preconceived model or framework is integral to the chosen study (e.g., for grounded theory approaches), a clear process overview of the research progression and reasoning steps can be provided.

As with the other sections of your manuscript, you need to substantiate your evaluation of this section by obtaining the opinion of others. Send the methodology section to a half dozen other people and ask if the methodology used in this research is clear and is it appropriate for the research question? If there are any "Nos," you need to fix the methodology section or redo the research.

7.2   Analysis Considerations

Quantitative analyses: When it comes to the analysis, one needs to ask the following questions: Is the analysis used in this research clear? Is the analysis appropriate for the research questions? Most quantitative studies submitted to *Industrial Marketing Management* use survey instruments for data collection. When a single informant design is used for answering the questionnaire, common method bias is a concern that has to be cleared, particularly when both the antecedent and the dependent variables are perceptual measures derived from the same source. Common method bias refers to deviations in observed relationships from 'true' relationships caused by the similarity in methods used to obtain the data. It can bias the estimates of reliability and validity of latent constructs, as well as the estimates of empirical relationships between constructs (inflate or deflate). One should avoid or minimize common method bias in the *ex ante* research design stage by using different sources of information for dependent and independent constructs (e.g., multiple informants, objective data, or time intervals), or by considering remedies in designing and administrating the survey (e.g., use different methods—interview, paper/pencil questionnaire, and so on—and response formats for gathering data for the dependent and independent constructs; include a measure of response style, impression management, or social desirability; use an ideal marker variable, which is a variable with no expected theoretical relationship with variables of interest in the study). It always is preferable, as said, to obtain information from both sides of a dyad (buyer–seller) than to only question one side and then ask the same respondent to estimate the other side's perspective. *Ex post* approaches also should be used to verify and, if necessary, reduce common method bias through a variety of statistical procedures. Using more complicated models (e.g., introducing non-linear interaction effects) makes it more difficult for the respondents to second-guess the aim of the survey and hence it reduces common method bias. Harman's one factor test is insensitive and therefore insufficient to prove that common method bias is not a concern. Instead, one should try to use more sophisticated tests such as common latent factor or common marker variable methods. The recommendation here is to use a combination of multiple *ex ante* research design and *ex post* statistical analysis remedies.

For quantitative studies, construct operationalizations (e.g., item wordings) and validity and reliability tests should be shown clearly. Often, reviewers want to see certain things that may not make it into the published version of the manuscript (e.g., a confirmatory factor analysis for all constructs); thus, this information should be provided in an appendix.

Robustness tests of one's analyses should be done. For example, one should not just run the model for the whole sample; rather, one should test for heterogeneity in the sample (through latent class analysis, split-half comparisons, or multi-group analysis, especially if there are hypotheses about the causes of heterogeneity).

Researchers need to be cognizant that the overwhelming number of quantitative methods normally used in business marketing and supply chain management does not corroborate causality (this is only stipulated by the nomological model). Thus, most studies are open to the question of the issue of 'reversed causality' (i.e., is it, in fact, not the dependent construct, which drives the independent one?). This needs to be discussed and possibly even tested as part of the analysis (e.g., Granger-causality tests), or recursive models may need to be considered.

Qualitative analyses: For qualitative studies a clear narrative and logic about how the researcher reaches a certain result or interpretation needs to be provided. Too often, manuscripts laconically state that a "content analysis was done" ... without providing any further details.

Case studies and interviews in particular both constitute a relevant minority of research studies published during the years 2014–2016 (Di Benedetto & Lindgreen, 2017). Thus, of the 412 articles published in this period, these two categories accounted for 17 percent and 20 percent, respectively, of all articles published. In addition, we find evidence that the research quality of the qualitative case analyses published in *Industrial Marketing Management* steadily has increased over the years (Beverland & Lindgreen, 2010), and therefore we would like to encourage high-quality submissions using case studies and interviews.

Case method research is an in-depth investigation (description) of a specific situation or phenomenon. The research may focus on a company, an agreement, a sale, a dyad, or a network. As such, a case analysis cannot be extrapolated beyond the specific focus of the case; the case is illustrative only.

Researchers should argue why the situations they study are somehow interesting for revealing new aspects of a focal phenomenon or a group of phenomena.

However, this single focus limitation of case studies does not mean they are without value. Indeed, due to the extended buying process involved with many industrial buying decisions, as well as the time required to develop buyer–seller relationships in business-to-business settings, an extended case study may be the only way to gain an understanding of the underlying processes involved in industrial marketing. Indeed, *Industrial Marketing Management* always has welcomed well-researched case studies. But what constitutes good case research?

One of the characteristics of case method research is the ability of the researcher to dig into the specific situation and provide many details that would be lost in a broad quantitative study (Yin, 1994). A case focuses on a point, not on the average or typical results. Yet, case method researchers, maybe in an effort to emulate quantitative researchers, attempt to generalize the case to the broader market. In doing so, they tend to move away from the very details that are so enriching of case method research and instead focus their analysis on broader theoretical constructs. But how can one generalize based on a sample of one? Quantitative research, primarily as used in consumer markets, looks to uncover underlying antecedents and mediators of activities and results to develop theoretical linkages among components to the buying decision process. Increasingly, reviewers focus on the question "where is the theory?" Authors respond by generalizing and removing discussion of details, which would be quite interesting and informative to the readers.

However, case method researchers should not avoid a discussion of theory, particularly in setting the case framework. What aspect of extant theory is relevant to the case description? By launching directly into the case with little attention to theory, many case method researchers reinvent the wheel. Situation 'A' demonstrating a trait or process already described in situation 'B' does not constitute new theory. Another weakness of case method researchers is trying to create a large case rather than developing a series of comparative cases (looking for differences rather than similarities and discussing why they may occur) or focusing on a longitudinal series of cases looking at one situation over an extended period of time. We are in need of more theory-based comparative and longitudinal case method research.

Case method research presents an opportunity to fully explore complex phenomena, but case method researchers tend to rush the process. They only interview one half of a dyad, asking that party how the other party might perceive the situation under study. It would be far better to expand the case investigation to interview parties from both sides of the dyad. Further, a single interview in a company or organization does not explain, nor fully describe how that company or organization thinks; multiple interviews at multiple levels are needed to fully explore the nuances and different perspectives involved in the case. In a similar vein, case method researchers should go beyond the sales or marketing department and include interviews with customers and their customers. After all, by its very nature, industrial marketing includes a series of buyer–seller dyads. This is particularly evident in network-based cases. If selling organizations are reluctant to divulge customer names, perhaps the case method researcher should start with buyers and ask them for contacts in their supplier organizations. This would be working up the supply chain rather than down the demand chain.

Wherever possible, case method researchers should include quantitative data to complement qualitative data developed as part of the case method research process. Actual sales data would reinforce managerial perceptions (or show managerial biases.) Even if, in a case study, the empirical material does not warrant generalization, and the focus is on complex, detailed, and underlying processes, reporting the outcomes, and documenting the activities-to-outcomes link is very valuable and helps increase our understanding of the situation and the ramification of decisions made. (Note: Likewise, quantitative researchers would do well to add illustrative qualitative data to increase understanding of the quantitative results by providing a fuller context from which the results are derived. This is actually an opportunity for cooperative research undertakings.)

Useful protocols for conducting and reporting on case studies have been developed (see, for example, Eisenhardt, 1989, 1991). For example, an article needs to consider the study's sampling procedure and sampled cases. How and why were the particular cases selected? Another important issue relates to how data were collected to build the cases. Which kind of data was used (primary and/or secondary data)? If an interview protocol guided in-depth interviews, then this protocol should be reported in the article. Especially important for qualitative case studies is how the case method researcher analyzed the case(s) to understand, for example, the processes behind the phenomenon of interest. Data can be analyzed within and across cases; and tools such as SQR: NUD*IST often can be useful. Open, axial, and selective doing procedures for elaboration on theoretical categories should be considered (cf. Strauss & Corbin, 1998). The article's methodology section should discuss such issues. The final issue mentioned here concerns methods to improve the quality of a case study research. For example, did the case method researchers apply criteria of credibility, transferability, dependability, confirmability, integrity, fit, understanding generality, and control in order to improve the trustworthiness of their findings?

As a final note, one needs to be aware that there are sophisticated qualitative methods available that provide a rigorous frame for the systematic comparison and interpretation of case studies.

Methodological pluralism: For both qualitative and quantitative analyses the issue of time effects is crucially important, but often neglected in research: the independent construct may affect the dependent one, but not immediately. Thus, it is important to model such time issues in the analysis (which has implications for the data capture) to test for time-lags. Qualitative studies, for example process analyses such as event structure analysis, can provide a granular understanding of such phenomena, but are used only rarely in business marketing and supply chain management studies.

Overall, we would advocate a call for methodological pluralism. Structural equation modeling (for quantitative researchers) and, to a lesser extent, case studies based on content analysis (for qualitative researchers) may dominate the field, but there is much more methodological richness out there. Cross-fertilization from other disciplines is a good thing in boosting methodological and analytical rigor, and in developing study contributions based around method usages.

As with the other sections of your manuscript, you need to substantiate your evaluation of this section by obtaining the opinion of others. Send the analysis section to a half dozen other people and ask if the analysis used in this research is clear and is it appropriate for the research question? If there are any "Nos," you need to fix the analysis section or redo the research.

8. AN ARTICLE'S FINDINGS

As the name implies, this section is a descriptive presentation of what was found out in the research. Differences between the findings in the research and what was known from previous publications can be highlighted. The section can include the results of a survey, results of hypotheses testing, a regression model, structural equation modeling/partial least squares, or other type analysis, as well as a summary of the key aspects of a qualitative study. That is, the research findings section must be associated with qualitative and quantitative research reported on earlier in the manuscript. One would not usually include a findings section in a review article or a theoretical article, as there really are no findings per se.

One of the most common problems when authors prepare this section of their manuscript is combining findings with interpretation or discussion. In fact, many manuscripts have a section called "Findings and Discussion" or "Results and Discussion." The section is then a jumble of what was found with how it fits in with the authors' theoretical development or research question(s). In fact, it is, unfortunately, not that uncommon to find no findings in the entire section, merely a discussion purportedly supporting the authors' original perception of the phenomena being investigated. While a few authors can present findings and then discuss them in a "Findings and Discussion" section, it is usually far better to separate these two critical components of the manuscript so as to clearly delineate them. A true "Findings" section should not have any interpretations or conclusions.

Let us look at presentation of quantitative data first. When writing the findings section, one should follow the same sequence used in the development of the research framework in the manuscript. If one has a series of hypotheses, one should present the findings for each hypothesis in the same order. Similarly with a regression or other model, present the findings in a way parallel to the theory or model developed earlier in the manuscript. It is difficult for readers and reviewers to understand the findings when these findings are presented differently than how the authors first explained what they set out to discover. When presenting quantitative results in this section, one can show descriptive information such as means, modes, medians, and measures of variance. Correlations, significance statistics, ranges, and confidence levels also are given, as are key statistics from other analytical techniques. However, authors often forget to show beta error or any power statistics; these statistics would help convince the reader of the conclusiveness of the analysis. Indeed, when only considering alpha error, researchers can end up with incorrect conclusions!

Care must be taken when presenting the findings of qualitative data. Sandelowski and Leeman (2012) define these findings as the "informational content or thematic syntheses, grounded theories, phenomenological descriptions, ethnographic or narrative/discourse descriptions or explanations, or other integrated or coherent interpretations" derived from interviews, observations, and documents of the organizational component being investigated. These findings must be presented in a manner that clearly describes them to the readers so they fully understand what happened. This is not the place where authors interpret what it all means or why it happened.

To guide the reader one can consider including figures and tables, as these often are the most efficient way to present findings. However, a lengthy table, which can be summarized easily in the text, should not be included. It is imperative that the captions of figures and tables contain clear and sufficient information to make these self-explanatory; and tables should not be too crowded. Figures and tables should not duplicate the information described elsewhere in the manuscript. Well-selected scales and appropriate axis label sizes should be used, and symbols must be clear to see and datasets easy to discriminate.

As with the other sections of your manuscript, you need to substantiate your evaluation of this section by obtaining the opinion of others. Send the findings section to a half dozen other people and ask if the findings as described are clear and interpretations logically derived from them. Likewise send any figures and tables to them and ask if they are clear. Can they understand the purpose of each figure or graph without the supporting text? Is each figure or graph important? Is there anything missing? If there are any "Nos," you need to improve the tables and figures.

9. AN ARTICLE'S DISCUSSION

As stated previously, there are three main objectives for a good introduction to a manuscript: focus the reader on the research question or purpose of the manuscript; establish the proper frame of reference for the reader; and demonstrate the gap in knowledge that the manuscript will fill. The discussion section of the manuscript is where the authors demonstrate to the reader how they fulfilled these three objectives. Here is where the authors turn the descriptive material from the findings section into a meaningful discussion or answer to the research question(s), and how the contribution to knowledge described earlier is now substantiated. Findings now can be related to the frame of reference and theoretical development previously established in the manuscript.

While previous sections of the manuscript were based on existing knowledge (introduction and theory development, hypotheses, etc.), established protocols (case method, experimental design, survey methodology, and analytical methods), and observable facts (qualitative and quantitative research data), the discussion section permits the authors to explain their research results as they accomplish the following:

- Describe how the results relate to the original question or objectives outlined in the introduction section.
- Develop a logical linkage from the data and findings to the conclusions.
- Provide interpretation for each of the results presented.
- Show how the results are consistent with what other investigators have reported or explain how, and why there are any differences.
- Demonstrate the importance of the research and why it deserves publication.
- Mention any limitations of the research and why, despite these limitations, the research is important and adds to our knowledge base.
- Describe logical extensions of the research and provide direction for future research.

In doing this, authors should not make statements that go beyond what the results can support; nor should authors introduce new terms or ideas.

Non-quantitative words (e.g., low/high, extremely, enormous, rapidly, dramatic, massive, considerably, exceedingly, major/minor, etc.) should be avoided, as they often are qualified by very, quite, slightly, etc. Quantitative precision, in fact, always is preferred.

10. AN ARTICLE'S CONCLUSIONS

The conclusions section is the final place where authors can demonstrate that the manuscript deserves to be accepted and published. It is where they close the circle from the questions posed in the beginning to the answers they established. A clear conclusions section helps reviewers to judge the authors' work easily.

What should be included in the conclusions section? Authors should present global and specific conclusions in relation to the objectives of their research. The authors should show how they have fulfilled the research questions and have made a contribution to existing knowledge. With so much trivial research being conducted today, authors should demonstrate why the research is significant and important. Authors also can indicate uses, extensions, and limitations of their findings if appropriate, and suggest future research and point out that this is underway.

There are some things that one should not say in the conclusions section. One should not summarize the manuscript (the abstract is for that purpose) or make a list of trivial statements of one's results. Of course, one should not overstate the impact of the research but, on the other hand, one should not accidentally undermine one's work by the use of words implying uncertainty such as "might," "probably," or "maybe" when discussing the results.

If appropriate for the journal where one submits, the manuscript should include clear managerial implications of the research. Implications should not be extended beyond the ability of the data to justify.

Many authors, unfortunately, sabotage otherwise well-written manuscripts with poorly done conclusions. This is the final place where one can influence the reviewers' decisions to accept or reject one's manuscript. Just as the title is where one creates the first impression of the manuscript, the conclusions section is the last impression left with the reader.

11. OTHER CONSIDERATIONS

As there are over 250 marketing journals published in English around the world (plus many marketing journals published in other languages), with new journals being launched almost daily, authors need to choose the journal that is right for their particular research. Authors will need to investigate candidate journals to find out about their aims and scope, types of articles, readership, and current hot topics. We discuss these and other issues a bit more in the following.

Authors may get help from their colleagues when deciding on the right journal. Articles in their references also likely will lead authors to the right journal. In considering the journal's audience, is the goal to reach specialists, multidisciplinary researchers, and/or a general audience, and is the journal's readership worldwide or local? Depending on the answer(s), information and writing style will need to be adjusted accordingly. To find out about current hot topics, authors are advised regularly to go through recent abstracts of articles published in the journal under consideration, as well as to read statements that the journal's editor may have made.

Also, it is important to realize that journals, even in similar subjects, reach readers with different backgrounds, and that, because of this, journals have their own style. To get a feeling for the style, authors should read other articles from the journal they want to submit to, and they need to adhere strictly to the journal's Guide for Authors, as poorly prepared manuscripts are a sign of disrespect and likely to be desk rejected.

The content of a manuscript is essential, and the manuscript accordingly must contain a clear, useful, and exciting scientific message. Also, the presentation of a manuscript is critical. The manuscript must convey the author's thoughts in a logical manner such that the reader arrives at the same conclusions as the author. Therefore, a manuscript must be constructed in the format that best showcases the author's materials, and the manuscript must be written in a style that transmits clearly what the message is. For example, referenced materials should be kept consistent throughout the manuscript and follow the journal's preferred style. It probably is advisable to avoid citing personal communications, unpublished observations, manuscripts submitted but not yet accepted for publications, as well as articles published only in the local language, which are difficult for international readers to consult. Authors should avoid excessive self-citation and journal self-citation. Spelling needs to adhere to Standard English; alternative spellings lead to confusion and must therefore be avoided; and the terminology should be consistent. Abbreviations—unless they are established firmly in the field—should be avoided. If an abbreviation is used then this should be defined on the first use in both the abstract and the main text.

An ideal manuscript typically consists of 25–40 pages that include essential data only. The abstract is of 100–150 words. The introduction is up to two pages long, the literature review and hypothesis section between four and six pages, the methods section about two to five pages, the results and discussion between 10 and 15 pages, and the conclusions about one to three pages. The number of references could be anywhere between 20 and 50. The number of figures and tables could each be about four to six.

Given the limited space available in journals (and time available for reviewers to evaluate submitted manuscripts), it is important that authors convince editors and reviewers that the manuscript deserves to be published. Therefore we recommend that at the end of every page, the authors ask themselves:

"What did I do on this page to convince the reader that the manuscript is worth publishing?" This simple step can greatly advance a manuscript's probability of acceptance.

Authors could consider including an acknowledgment section to thank people who have helped with (note: ask them if they can be named), for example, technical expertise, funding organizations, and (in the final accepted manuscript) reviewers and editor(s). The acknowledgment also states one's affiliation to research projects and programs, as well as grant number or reference.

12. CONCLUSIONS

This chapter summarizes our thoughts on how to improve one's publishing success. A manuscript begins with a question or objective, and then a framework is presented within which the authors want the reader to evaluate their research. Existing knowledge is surveyed, and a theoretical framework is outlined, and, oftentimes, hypotheses are developed. A manuscript describes the research methodology, the findings, and what all this means. Importantly, the manuscript along the way demonstrates that it makes an impact on what we know about business-to-business markets.

Specifically, we discussed the appropriateness of the title of a manuscript, as well as the role of the abstract and how a properly written abstract can improve the likelihood of the article being accepted, read, and cited. Following that, we discussed the introduction of a manuscript. We then considered methodology issues. For quantitative methodologies, we discussed hypotheses, and we stressed that a well-written methodology section of a research article serves two primary purposes: to demonstrate that one has followed acceptable scientific standards in conducting the research and to enable other researchers to replicate one's study so that their results can be compared to one's results. For qualitative methodologies, we particularly focused on case method research. Then we moved on to discussing a manuscript's research findings section and the discussion of these findings.

We hope this series of comments will help prospective authors prepare manuscripts that fare well in the submission process in *Industrial Marketing Management* and other top journals.

REFERENCES

Beverland, M. & Lindgreen, A. (2010). What makes a good case study? A positivist review of qualitative case research published in *Industrial Marketing Management*, 1971–2006. *Industrial Marketing Management*, 39(1), pp. 56–63.

Di Benedetto, C.A. & Lindgreen, A. (2017). The emergence of *Industrial Marketing Management* as the leading academic journal in business-to-business marketing. *Industrial Marketing Management*, 69, pp. 5–12.

Eisenhardt, K.M. (1989). Building theories from case study research. *Academy of Management Review*, 14(4), pp. 532–550.

Eisenhardt, K.M. (1991). Better stories and better constructs: The case for rigor and comparative logic. *Academy of Management Review*, 16(3), pp. 620–627.

Leonidou, L.C., Barnes, B.R., Spyropoulou, S., & Katsikeas, C.S. (2010). Assessing the contribution of leading mainstream marketing journals to the international marketing discipline. *International Marketing Review*, 27(5), pp. 491–518.

Mitchell, M.L. & Jolley, J.M. (2006). *Research Design Explained*, 6th ed. Andover: Wadsworth Publishing.

Sandelowski, M. & Leeman, J. (2012). Writing usable qualitative health research findings. *Qualitative Health Research*, 22(10), pp. 1401–1413.

Soutar, G.N. & Murphy, J. (2009). Journal quality: A Google Scholar analysis. *Australasian Marketing Journal*, 17(3), pp. 150–153.

Strauss, A. & Corbin, J. (1998). *Basics of Qualitative Research*, 2nd ed. Newbury Park, CA: Sage Publications.

Touzani, M. & Moussa, S. (2010). Ranking marketing journals using the search engine Google Scholar. *Marketing Education Review*, 20(3), pp. 229–247.

Yin, R.K. (1994). *Case Study Research: Design and Methods*, 2nd ed. Thousand Oaks, CA: Sage Publications.

14. Revising for premier academic journals

Peter LaPlaca, Adam Lindgreen, Joëlle Vanhamme, and C. Anthony Di Benedetto

1. INTRODUCTION

To young scholars, the review process seems to be a confusing black box. In goes the manuscript, something happens over the course of a couple of months, and out comes a response—the editor's decision. To all of us in academia, the process is familiar. The author carefully writes and proofreads, then sends his or her best effort to the editor of the targeted journal. Then the wait begins. Even if the website clearly states a typical turnaround time of two months, the delay seems unbearable. The author may turn to online tracking every so often, if available from that journal. The manuscript is with the reviewers. Then eventually the manuscript is in the hands of the editor, and a decision e-mail will be coming soon. The good news is that the author has been invited to revise and resubmit the manuscript for further consideration! Then the bad news sinks in. Three reviewers, six single-spaced pages of critiques and recommendations from each reviewer, some comments are mutually inconsistent, a couple of the comments seem impossible, and Reviewer 3 particularly seems to dislike the manuscript for some reason. After the initial emotional shock, and maybe a couple of days to sleep on it, the author reads the reviews again, dedicated to improving the manuscript and getting that acceptance on the next round.

What happens inside that black box can seem mysterious and a little intimidating. The objective of this chapter is to provide guidance on the revision process. We lay out some of the beginners' mistakes that can lead to desk rejection. We provide a look inside the review process at *Industrial Marketing Management*. We also provide strategies on how to respond to reviews, whether they are an invitation to revise and resubmit or an outright rejection. We hope that the guidance provided here helps prospective authors avoid the desk-reject decision, and develop revised manuscripts and replies to reviewers that ensure the reviewers keep liking the manuscript and the editor keeps moving the manuscript toward acceptance.

We structure the remainder of this chapter in the following sections. First, we explore the review process and make suggestions on how the manuscript does not get rejected by the editor even before the manuscript has a chance to reach the reviewers. Second, we go further into the editor's desk-reject decision, specifically at *Industrial Marketing Management*, noting how and why this decision has become a bigger factor in recent years. Third, we examine the reviewers' rejection decision, and the author's next best steps in this case. Fourth, we lay out suggestions and recommendations to authors on how to respond to the invitation to revise and resubmit their manuscript. Fifth, we present briefly the publication process. Finally, we conclude with a summary of recommendations, particularly suited to the young academic researcher.

2. THE REVIEW AND REVISION PROCESS

Before authors submit their manuscript, they should avoid an early rejection due to the fact that their manuscript does not fit the journal's mission. Thus, we advise strongly that authors read carefully the description of what the mission of the journal is (i.e., the journal that the authors want to submit to), as well as the editorials published by the current editor(s). These editorials are available on the journal's website. Editorials often highlight what editors find important to consider before submitting a manuscript. Reading the editorials might seem to be self-evident, but manuscripts frequently are desk-rejected by the editor (more on this below) because there is simply no fit to the journal's mission. A careless author might send a consumer-psychology article to *Industrial Marketing Management* after having done a quick search through a list of academic journals with "marketing" in the name, without noticing that the manuscript does not fit *Industrial Marketing Management*'s mission of publishing manuscripts pertaining to business-to-business marketing. Obviously, a mistake like this easily is avoided: check out the targeted journal, read the statement of mission or journal scope, download a couple of recent articles, and assess the fit with the journal's scope.

Other reasons for an early rejection are that the manuscript is of limited interest, or that it covers local issues only (e.g., sample type, geography, specific product, etc.). It needs to be stated explicitly at the outset what the manuscript's importance and implications are; and the manuscript needs to be interesting and relevant. Authors need to engage in the journal's conversation, for example, by citing relevant articles from the journal. Manuscripts also should not be a routine application of well-known methods, present a minor incremental advance in literature, or be limited in scope. Even in the case where manuscripts make novel and significant advances in literature, authors may not have explained these advances in an evident manner or justified these advances sufficiently well. There thus could be a note to the editor as to which people have commented on the manuscript prior to official submission because this shows seriousness and that at least these people found merit in the manuscript.

Reasons for an early rejection may also stem from the way that manuscripts are prepared. Does the manuscript meet submission requirements? Does the manuscript provide an appropriate coverage of relevant literature? On the journal webpage, there will be author guidelines on how to organize and present the manuscript. Some journals require Roman or Arabic numerals for section and sub-section headings; some journals do not. Many journals prefer reference callouts in the text in the form of (Smith et al., 2012), while others prefer a number in brackets like [1]. Some journals require a discussion of managerial implications, while others do not. All journals have a desired style for the reference list; most (but not all!) will insist that the references are in alphabetical order. In all cases, authors must adhere closely to the guidelines. It is worth spending an hour or two changing reference style to agree with journal requirements because it shows that the author took the time to do the 'little things' right, and this always makes a good impression on the editor.

Another frequent question is about writing quality and style. Is the level of English in the manuscript of unacceptable standards? If necessary, we recommend that authors send their manuscript for professional copy editing. (All major journals provide language assistance; just look at their websites.) A couple of small style errors will not sink a promising article, but if the English style is so poor that it becomes a distraction, or even makes it difficult to understand the point actually being made by the authors, it will result in a rejection. Have the manuscript checked by a professional to minimize the chance of a desk rejection. We refer the readers to our other chapter in this book that discusses how to write really good articles for premier academic journals (Chapter 13). That chapter discusses good practices to increase the chances of getting published.

The review and revision process for *Industrial Marketing Management* is depicted in Figure 14.1. When editors receive a manuscript, they acknowledge having received the manuscript before they identify three appropriate and available reviewers. Different ways are used to do that (often a combination of these ways). For example, editors may invite authors mentioned in the reference list, find reviewers using keywords from the journal's database, or consult experts in the field they know already or find through a Google search. A blind copy of the manuscript is sent to each reviewer, and the reviewers are asked to confirm that they are willing to review the manuscript. (If a reviewer for whatever reason is not willing to review, an invitation is sent to another reviewer.) Reminders, if necessary, are sent to reviewers after 60 days, 90 days, and 120

260 How to fast-track your academic career

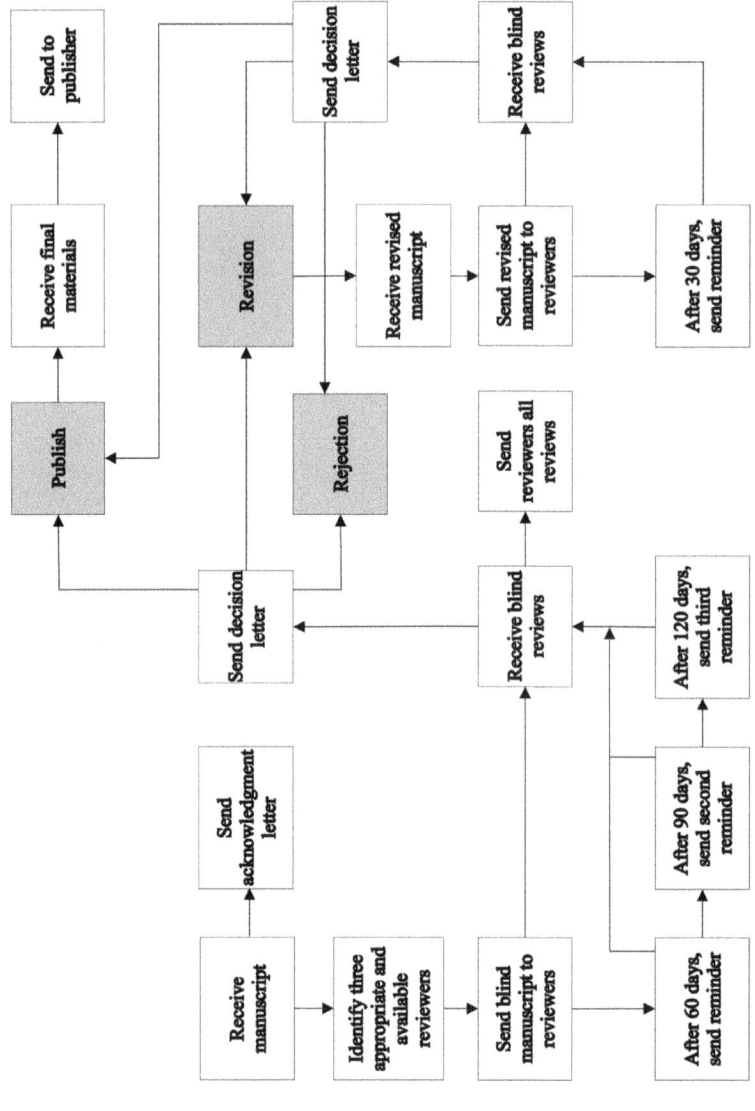

Figure 14.1 The review and revision process

days so that eventually the editors have received three reviews of the manuscript. Reviewers are expected to evaluate the manuscript constructively and then suggest a decision to the editor (this is, however, only a suggestion, as the editor is the one who makes the final decision).

The editors then read all reviews, make their decision, and send a letter to the author(s) including all three reviews. A copy of this letter and the three reviews also are sent to each of the reviewers. (Doing this ensures that more inexperienced reviewers learn how other reviewers evaluate the same manuscript.)

While authors all want to receive acceptance letters when submitting their manuscripts to journals, it is quite rare that this happens on the initial submission. When a manuscript is not desk-rejected, what usually happens is that the reviewers recommend that the manuscript be either rejected or invited for a (major) revision. (Reviewers, in fact, can recommend one of five decisions: (a) publish as is, (b) minor revision and publish, (c) minor revision and re-review, (d) major revision and re-review, and (e) reject. In this chapter, we have grouped (b), (c), and (d) together under the heading "Reviewers' Manuscript (Major) Revision." Let us next consider the first scenario.

2.1 Editor's Manuscript Desk Rejection

The editor carries out an initial evaluation of the submitted manuscript. In doing so, the editor identifies whether the manuscript sufficiently satisfies editorial guidelines of *Industrial Marketing Management*, provides implications for the domain of industrial marketing management, and has some likelihood to be evaluated favorably by the reviewers.

When a submitted manuscript fails to satisfy one or more of the above criteria, a decision is made to reject the manuscript instead of sending it to reviewers as a part of the journal's double-blind review process. The reason for a desk rejection mostly is associated with the uncertain theoretical contribution(s) that the manuscript may provide to current understanding of industrial marketing management. The contributions would be considered as relatively limited and do not exist to the degree that would be expected for a manuscript to be considered for publication in *Industrial Marketing Management*. In this respect, authors need a much better justification for why they examine the given research issue(s). What new conceptual insights will be derived from their examination, and how do these insights move research on industrial marketing management? For example, just because limited research may have examined a chosen aspect of industrial marketing management in a particular country this is not necessarily a reason for undertaking further research. There must be a stronger reason for why to do so, as otherwise the manuscript falls short in providing a solid conceptual contribution to industrial marketing management literature. In this scenario, the editor desk-rejects the manuscript because he (or she) believes it would be a disservice to subject the manuscript to a lengthy review process when ultimate acceptance appears to be very unlikely.

Reviewers play an important role in the remaining two scenarios, which we consider next. Before doing that, however, we first want to spend some time on what it means to be a reviewer.

Industrial Marketing Management has grown in many ways over the last decade: more submissions each year, more rejections, more articles published, more pages each year, better quality articles being published, more citations, and an increasing impact factor and reputation. The great bulk of the effort to achieve this quality growth has come from the more than 400 people who donate their time and talent to serve as reviewers for the journal. But what does it mean to be a reviewer, especially for a premier academic journal?

Yes, reviewers do evaluate submitted manuscripts and recommend acceptance, rejection, or revision. Revised manuscripts are then re-reviewed at least once and often two, three, or four times. More important than recommendations, however, are the critical comments to the authors. Good reviewers take this responsibility very seriously. Despite their own teaching and research obligations, reviewers take significant time to provide authors with constructive critiques on their submissions, even for manuscripts they recommend be rejected. For *Industrial Marketing Management*, it is quite common that three reviewers each will send in three-to-five pages of comments, and when the editor puts this all together for the authors, the resulting letter can be eight-to-twelve pages of feedback. (Of course, this is accomplished through our web-based editorial system so there are no real 'pages.') Reviewers also provide suggestions for additional research that would improve the manuscript, or they provide additional references that the authors did not include in their manuscript. Reviewers suggest improvements to tables and figures to better convey information to readers, and reviewers even make recommendations to improve the manuscript's title. Often, we have received thank you e-mails from authors of rejected manuscripts who—although they had their manuscript rejected—still appreciate the quality of the reviews they received.

Another obligation of reviewers is to render their recommendations and constructive criticism in a timely fashion. At *Industrial Marketing Management*, we ask that all reviews be completed in four to six weeks from the time they are sent to the reviewers. Most, but not all, reviewers do meet this expectation. To keep authors waiting three or four months or more is quite unfair and disrespectful to the authors and to the editors. If reviewers cannot complete their assigned reviews by the requested deadline, whether due to workload or lack of qualifications for the specific manuscript, they should let the editor know immediately so that an alternative reviewer can be invited.

The general criteria that reviewers consider in their evaluation of a manuscript (both when they recommend the manuscript be rejected and when they recommend acceptance subject to [major] revisions) are the extent to which a manuscript:

- Is pertinent to industrial marketing management.
- Makes a significant contribution to theory.
- Has a good likelihood of being cited.
- Is founded on a sound theory.
- Presents new or existing material in a new light.
- Presents its contents in a logical flow.
- Presents its contents with clarity.
- Has interest as a case study.
- Addresses properly managerial implications.
- Includes an adequate review of previous literature.

For empirically based manuscripts, reviewers additionally consider the following:

- Which method has been used?
- Are hypotheses properly developed?
- Is the sample size appropriate?
- Is the sample representative?
- Is the analysis appropriate?
- Is the analysis presented clearly?
- Does the analysis truly support the conclusions?

2.2   Reviewers' Manuscript Rejection

Often, at least for *Industrial Marketing Management*, authors receive notification from the editor rejecting the submission based upon the reviewers' recommendations and comments. This notification provides reviewer and editor feedback as to why the manuscript was rejected. Again, the most common cause is lack of contribution. When selecting a topic to research, authors need to make sure the research question is one of wide interest to the field of industrial marketing management.

If authors believe a reviewer has misunderstood what they have tried to say in their manuscript (note: it is, of course, most of the time, if not all the time, the authors' own fault for allowing a misunderstanding; misunderstandings often come from unclear writing or explanations), they should contact the editor immediately and explain their perspective and why they believe (in light of what their intent was) the reviewers' comments are not valid. Before doing so though, it might be a wise idea to ask colleagues what they objectively think of the comments (without telling them that you disagree, as this, of course, would bias the colleagues' answer). The editor then will discuss this with the reviewers or may seek the opinion of an expert in that specific aspect (for example, a specific analytical method). If different reviewers provide conflicting comments (such as asking for mutually exclusive changes), authors should point this out to the editor who then may provide suggestions as how to resolve the conflict. Ultimately, however, it is for the authors to satisfy the reviewers. It should be noted, though, that sometimes reviewers merely suggest different possibilities to improve the manuscript or solve an issue in the manuscript. Furthermore, it could be that the suggestions made by the reviewers are equally good, but mutually exclusive. In that case it is up to the authors to select the appropriate avenue to improve the manuscript. Often, there are different possible ways to tackle the same issue, and the authors are the ones who best know which solution will be most appropriate. Authors should, of course, clearly explain in their revision note why the approach they chose is better than alternatives. In the extreme, when the reviewer comments are incompatible (one literally says the manuscript should be longer and another says it should be shorter), or the author feels the reviewer clearly has missed a point or made a recommendation that is infeasible, the author should contact the editor directly for clarification.

Although a rejection always is disappointing, it is not the end of the world. Authors should try to understand why their manuscript was rejected. The reviewers have taken the time necessary to provide important feedback that can be used when revising the manuscript so that it can be submitted somewhere else. Authors should re-evaluate their work, taking in the reviewers' feedback, and then decide whether it is appropriate to submit the manuscript—after revision—elsewhere. One possible strategy could be that the authors enclose a cover letter, declaring that the manuscript was rejected at another journal (mention which one), include the reviewer reports and a detailed letter of response, discussing how each comment has been addressed. Authors also should explain why they are resubmitting the manuscript to this new journal, for example, this journal is a more appropriate journal, the manuscript has been improved as a result of its previous reviews, among other things.

We mention the above strategy because it could be that the manuscript is sent to the same reviewer who previously rejected the manuscript for another journal. It might seem to be a case of extremely bad luck to get the same (negative) reviewer at two different journals, but the author should keep in mind that the editor will be sending the manuscript to experts in the subject area, and there may be only a limited number of reviewers available. Reviewers will remember reading a manuscript they previously had rejected and will not look fondly on the manuscript if they discover that none of their suggested improvements was attempted, and the manuscript contains the same flaws as before. Even if not all of the recommended changes are made, authors should recognize that because two or three of the top academics in the world, in his or her own research area, have reviewed the manuscript and made suggestions for improvement, some of these suggestions certainly should be followed to improve the manuscript before resubmitting elsewhere. One of the authors of this manuscript was Editor-in-Chief of two journals when a manuscript was rejected at Journal A and was quite surprised to see the same author submit the same manuscript (without any revisions or changes whatsoever) later that same day to Journal B! This is the behavior of an inexperienced author who failed to appreciate the opportunity to learn from the suggestions included in the negative reviews and improve the manuscript. (Needless to say that the manuscript immediately was desk-rejected.)

2.3   Reviewers' Manuscript (Major) Revision

When authors receive a revise and resubmit letter, they should take time to digest the letter before beginning the task of revising the manuscript. We suggest they put the letter aside for a few days before re-reading it. This re-reading is to absorb the overall tenor of the letter, as well as the main points of the editor and the reviewers. It is most likely that authors will find it difficult to accept that their manuscript is being critiqued and will therefore feel defensive, resentful, or even angry when they first receive the letter. It is good advice to put the letter away until the negative emotions have subsided, then start the revision process objectively and with an open mind to the comments and critiques.

Although authors may not feel that way when they receive the editor's decision with the reviewers' comments, reviewers and editors try to perform the process constructively. This means that authors should try to see the revision process as a way, or even as an opportunity, to improve their work. It really is a matter of mindset. Keep in mind that the letter is a "revise and resubmit" letter and not a "respond to reviewer comments" letter. While a revision (and improvement) will involve responses to reviewers' comments, merely responding to them is insufficient to really improve the manuscript.

It is much easier for authors to see comments in a constructive way when they believe that reviewers try to help out rather than when the authors are upset or disappointed because they feel reviewers are being unfair. Some comments may sound harsh at times, but authors always should try to understand where the comments come from. It could be, for example, that the manuscript was not written very clearly and that reviewers therefore had a hard time understanding what the authors tried to say. Thus, adopting the proper mindset is really key for revising a manuscript successfully. If authors are flexible in their attitude and willing to accept criticism in a positive light, revising a manuscript will become a much simpler task than if authors are unable to accept criticism and resist the thought that their manuscript needs improvement. If the editor's decision was a "revise and resubmit," authors always should attempt to revise irrespective of the work required, as there is fair chance that if the manuscript is revised competently it has a chance of being accepted eventually. Also, sometimes sections or new studies added to the manuscript in response to reviewers' comments eventually become the most interesting parts of the later accepted manuscript.

The next re-reading is to look at the manuscript with fresh eyes and look at the specific points raised by the reviewers. Authors should remember to revise the whole manuscript, not just the parts that the reviewers point out. Although a reviewer may mention specific issues only, when addressing these issues it could mean that the authors need to add new research, improve the flow of the entire manuscript, revise tables and figures elsewhere in the manuscript, among other things.

Authors should block out enough time in their agenda for their revision because a good revision is a demanding task, and authors should seek to carry out the revision earlier rather than later (right away, if possible). However, some improvements do require significant amounts of time, such as collecting additional data, redoing analyses, etc. Don't rush this or take shortcuts.

Then authors should plan on how they will address the issues raised in the letter. Authors should remember that a revision is an opportunity to improve the entire manuscript, not just to respond to specific points raised by the reviewers. More importantly, with reviewers having provided precise suggestions and comments, authors will know exactly what to address, but not immediately how to do so. Authors should start by asking: "now that we have received some reaction to our manuscript, how can we really make it as good as possible?" Maybe the original manuscript was too broad and tried to accomplish too much. How can the manuscript be better focused? What does the manuscript need to make a real contribution to industrial marketing management? In answering these questions, authors can define more precisely the research question and the knowledge gap that their manuscript attempts to solve. Notice that the words "question" and "gap" are singular; too many manuscripts try to incorporate multiple research questions and knowledge gaps and, in doing so, fall far short of developing a quality manuscript. To demonstrate what truly is required to revise a manuscript, let us outline a quality response letter sent to the editor with a revised manuscript (note: the letter the authors received was a "revise and resubmit" letter, not a "respond and resubmit" letter. Revision takes much more than merely responding to reviewer comments). (The reader will note that we make this point several times in this chapter. Why? Because it is very frequently overlooked by authors; they simply respond to reviewer comments rather than truly revise and improve their manuscript.) Authors should write their response letter in a way that the letter can be given to the reviewers without the editor having to rewrite the letter. Throughout the whole letter, authors should strike the right tone: polite and grateful, confident, and robust. We write this because sometimes a review can be harsh, but it is important that authors do not take reviews personally. (Remember that this is a double-blind process; reviewers do not know who the authors are; they simply are commenting on the manuscript as they received it.) Instead, successful authors engage with the comments and rewrite their work, they deliver their revisions in a timely manner, and they explain their work and engage with the reviewers.

The first paragraph should thank the editor and the reviewers for the opportunity to improve the manuscript and for their valuable feedback. Authors may take the opportunity to highlight particularly valuable comments.

The second paragraph should summarize the overall improvement made to the manuscript. This might include large-scale changes to the manuscript's structure, purpose, breadth, and/or development. This paragraph sets the framework for the improvement (also known as the revision) and demonstrates to the reviewers that the authors have made a significant effort to improve their manuscript. It also gives the authors a chance to show how the improved manuscript makes a contribution to the field, and why the manuscript should be accepted. This is also a good opportunity to show where the manuscript has been improved in places other than those addressed by the reviewers, or to show how the authors have incorporated new research that has appeared since their original submission to the journal.

Following this, the authors should show clearly how they have responded to specific suggestions and comments offered by the reviewers. Reviewers should not have to work to see how authors changed the original manuscript in response to their comments. One way to achieve this clarification for the reviewers is to devote sections of the response letter to each reviewer. (In fact, authors simply can copy the entire decision letter into their own letter and then insert their interpretations and responses where appropriate.) Each section should be labeled clearly (e.g., Response to Reviewer A) and show each comment made by the reviewer, the authors' interpretation of why the reviewer made this comment, how the authors approached the revision, and the exact change(s) made to the manuscript. Authors can use different color fonts or use normal, boldface, or italics to distinguish reviewer suggestions and comments, and specific changes. If multiple reviewers made the same comment, this will be repeated in the section dealing with responses to that reviewer's comments. The rule here is to respond to every single one of the reviewers' comments. One option is to start each reply with a comment like "Done" or "Thank you, this has been corrected" and be sure to mention the page number where the changes can be found in the revised manuscript.

Occasionally, a reviewer may be undertaking research quite similar to that described in the manuscript and which would integrate nicely with it. The reviewer may contact the editor to indicate this possibility and request the authors' identification after the process has ended. When this occurs, the editor will contact the authors mentioning this possibility and, only if the authors approve, will identify them to the reviewer.

The closing paragraph is another opportunity to explain the manuscript's overall improvement. Some journals have guidelines for replies to reviewers, which, needless to say, should be adhered to. For example, some journals require that the changes in the revised manuscript be highlighted in a different color so that the reviewers can find them easily. Other journals may impose a maximum number of pages to a reply to reviewers. (It hardly seems necessary to write a 70-page reply accompanying a 30-page revised manuscript, and no, the reviewers will not be impressed just by the length of the reply.) Of course, the author must follow any such guidelines when writing the reply to reviewers. Taking a disciplined approach to manuscript improvement easily can eliminate one or two rounds of revision and review for a manuscript.

In this step of the review process, the editor expects authors to address all the issues raised, but not necessarily to agree with all the reviewers' comments and suggestions. The reason for this is that academic research should encourage debate and the exchange of information; the academic review process should do the same. Authors therefore should provide a scientific response to the comments they accept; and a convincing, solid, and polite rebuttal to the points where they believe the reviewers' suggestion would not help improving the manuscript (that is, the authors may disagree with the reviewers or even if they do agree, they may feel that the suggestion does not improve the manuscript or takes it in a direction that the authors do not want to pursue).

If authors believe that a comment by a reviewer is based on a misunderstanding, it is best politely to suggest that the text's lack of clarity might be the source of the issue raised (and apologize for it) and then rewrite the text in such a way that there cannot be any confusion. A similar approach can be used for comments that may be based on insufficient knowledge on the part of the reviewer. Authors need to make sure that readers understand what has been done and what has been written; if reviewers do not understand, chances are that readers might not understand either! Thus, authors need to provide simple explanations in the text that all readers will be able to understand. It is the authors' own fault if their text is too technical and uses too much jargon.

As long as authors work to enhance the rigor and quality of their contributions, editors usually encourage such interactions. In this context, editors aim to be true 'editors' rather than 'review collectors' so that they will adjudicate as necessary any significant disagreements across reviews or between reviewers and authors; indeed, the final publication decision is that of the editor. Once authors think they have gone through all comments and revised their manuscript the best they could, they should put it aside for a day or two and then read the manuscript and notes a last time before sending it all to copy editing (if needed) and resubmit it to the journal. Before resubmitting, it is also advised to check whether new relevant articles have appeared in the literature since the time of the first submission. Adding these articles likely will enhance the manuscript by providing a more complete and up-to-date view of the topic.

In general, not all comments in a review are equally important from the reviewer's viewpoint. Some of the comments are merely suggestions for improvement, and the reviewer leaves it up to the authors to decide what to do. However, in some instances, the reviewer deems a response to one or two particular comments as extremely important and a necessary condition for publication of the manuscript. Authors should make sure that they find out which comments are really key and address those comments very convincingly (it may be that authors need to collect additional data, re-run all analyses, rewrite all the theory because another theory is more suitable, and so on; these are all fairly common requests for major and risky revisions).

Because reviewers' opinions sometimes vary, editors expect reviewers to offer clear, well-substantiated comments. However, those comments also should focus on the substance of the submission content and their review, rather than the reviewers' beliefs about the most appropriate publication decision. That decision rests solely with the editor and may, in some cases, differ from the reviewers' recommendations.

Finally, although not always possible, *Industrial Marketing Management* aims to reach a final acceptance decision in no more than two rounds of reviews. Of note, however, is that editors ultimately are interested in publishing the best possible articles; thus, authors should ask for additional time to do their revisions if they need this. It is important to ask for an extension on time and not wait until the deadline for resubmitting has passed. Also, if authors ask for an extension, they should make sure to complete the revision before the end of the extension and not ask for yet another extension as this shows bad planning or lack of professionalism on the authors' part.

After the editors have received the revised manuscript, they send it out to those reviewers who had asked for revisions to be made (see Figure 14.1). After 30 days, if necessary, the reviewers will receive a reminder that their review is due. When the reviews are in, a decision is made as to whether to publish the manuscript as is, ask for further revisions, or reject the manuscript. Eventually, the manuscript will be accepted or rejected. Throughout the whole revision process, authors should bear in mind that even a minor revision does not guarantee acceptance after revision. Thus, authors should proceed with an invitation for a minor revision with the same care as they approach an invitation for a major revision.

For *Industrial Marketing Management*, we adhere—not always stringently, however—to the 'rules' given in Table 14.1. Also, if we as editors are in doubt

Table 14.1   Editors' decision 'rules'

Reviewer A	Reviewer B	Reviewer C	Decision
Reject	Reject	Reject	**Reject**
Reject	Reject	Anything	**Reject**
Reject	Total rewrite and resubmit	Total rewrite and resubmit	**Reject**
Reject	Total rewrite and resubmit	Major rewrite and resubmit	**Reject**, if editors don't believe the authors can satisfy the reviewers' objections; otherwise **revise and resubmit**
Reject	Major rewrite and resubmit	Major rewrite and resubmit	**Reject**, if editors don't believe the authors can satisfy the reviewers' objections; otherwise **revise and resubmit**
Reject	Major rewrite and resubmit	Major revision and re-review	**Revise and resubmit**
Total rewrite and resubmit	Total rewrite and resubmit	Total rewrite and resubmit	**Reject**, if editors don't believe the authors can satisfy the reviewers' objections; otherwise **revise and resubmit**
Total rewrite and resubmit	Total rewrite and resubmit	Anything other than reject or total rewrite and resubmit	**Revise and resubmit**
Anything other than reject or total rewrite and resubmit	Anything other than reject or total rewrite and resubmit	Anything other than reject or total rewrite and resubmit	**Revise and resubmit**

about the quality of a manuscript, we will put it into the review process rather than rejecting the manuscript. At least then four people and not just one person will have considered the manuscript.

The typical results for the review and revision process, based on 2014 data, are that of 100 submitted manuscripts about 80 manuscripts pass through the initial evaluation process and are sent out for review. Thirty-six of those manuscripts are invited for revisions. Most authors (34 of those manuscripts) submit a revised version of their manuscript. Of those 34 manuscripts, 13 manuscripts eventually are accepted for publication (either in this revision round or in a subsequent round). The process is depicted in Figure 14.2.

Revising for premier academic journals 271

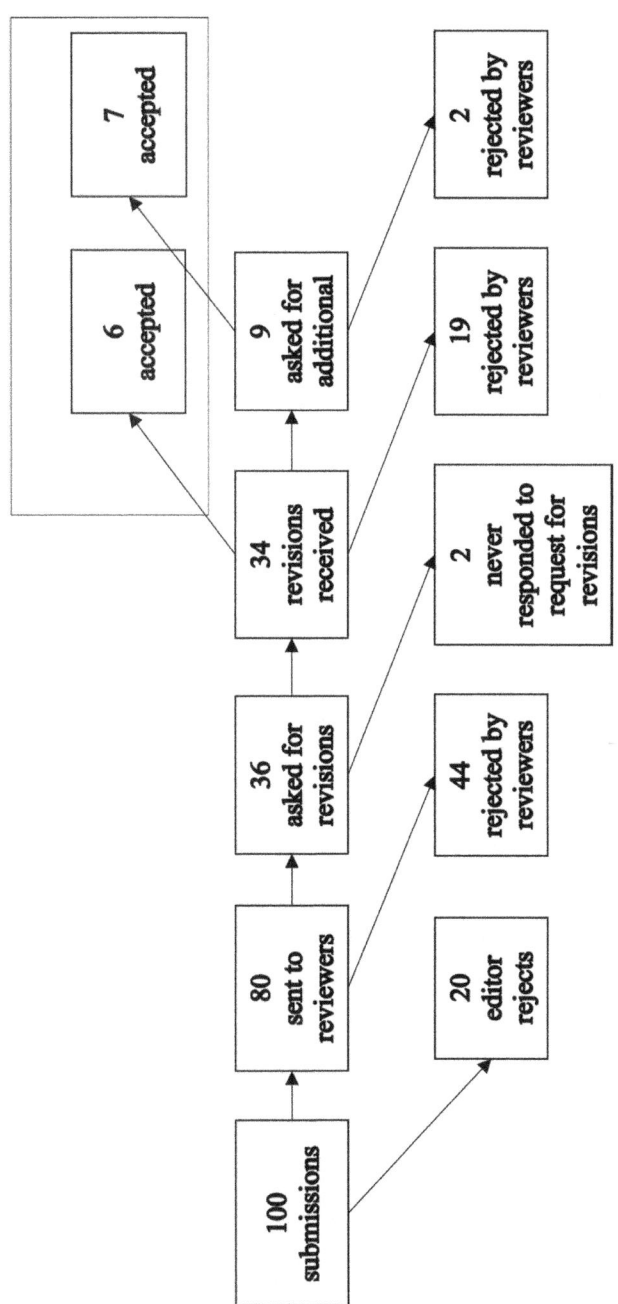

Figure 14.2 Typical results per 100 submissions (based on 2014 data)

3. THE PUBLICATION PROCESS

The finer details of the publication process probably are of less interest to authors. Important, however, is that an uncorrected proof of the manuscript is sent to the corresponding author who is asked to return a corrected proof of the manuscript. Before all of this happens, the publisher sends copyright transfer to the corresponding author who must sign this transfer. Both the uncorrected proof and the corrected proof of the manuscript are placed on the journal's homepage, but once the corrected proof appears here it usually no longer will be possible to request changes to the manuscript. If, for example, authors change their affiliation, it is still their old affiliation that will appear on their manuscript. But at this point, the authors should be breathing easy: the manuscript is in, it may be soon available online (if the journal pre-publishes accepted manuscripts), and soon enough the hard copy will be published.

4. CONCLUSIONS

This chapter summarizes our thoughts on the review and revision process. The process of responding to the editor's and reviewers' comments and substantially revising a manuscript to the point of acceptance can be challenging. This chapter has attempted to provide tips and examples of good practice to authors as they embark on this journey.

Collectively, the authors of this chapter have decades of experience as (section) editors. It is fair to say that many of the errors listed in this chapter are beginner mistakes, which probably will lead to a rejection in the review process, if not an outright desk rejection, and yet are preventable. A few of the obvious mistakes are the following ones: ensure there is a fit between the manuscript and the mission of the target journal; write in coherent English and enlist a professional style editor if necessary; follow all the style guidelines; respond to every single one of the reviewers' comments in the revision (seeking the help of the editor in case anything is unclear); and at least try to make the important changes suggested by the reviewers even in the case of a rejection. It is always a good idea to take advantage of the wisdom of two or three authorities in that research area who may sound harsh, but really just want to see a better quality manuscript with a more impactful contribution, and may have a good suggestion on how to do it!

We hope that this chapter will help authors in the process of getting their revised manuscript successfully go through the review process and hasten the road to publication. In addition, we hope this series of comments will help prospective authors prepare manuscripts that fare well in the review-and-revise process in *Industrial Marketing Management* and other top journals.

15. Reviewing manuscripts

Adam Lindgreen and C. Anthony Di Benedetto
In collaboration with Maja Arslanagić-Kalajdžić, Ad de Jong, Stephan Henneberg, Kristian Möller, John Nicholson, Mark Parry, Audhesh Paswan, Gerrit van Bruggen, Joëlle Vanhamme, and Chun Zhang

1. INTRODUCTION

In two previous chapters, we provided comments and guidance to young authors on writing and revising academic journals. The first of these chapters was on preparing a solid manuscript for submission to a good journal, and it presented our suggestions on how to construct each part of the manuscript (title, abstract, introduction, literature review, and so on), as well as some insights on what to avoid. The second chapter offered guidance on the revision process: how to respond to the reviewers, what to include in the reply document, what do to in the case of a rejection, and what to do if the author needs clarification. Together, these two chapters are meant to help authors, particularly researchers in the early stages of their careers, to avoid rookie mistakes in writing and revising, prevent desk rejection, and ultimately satisfy the editor and reviewers and get published.

We wanted to go further in depth, and to learn more about what reviewers really are looking for when reviewing a manuscript, from the reviewer's perspective. Accordingly, we asked several of our colleagues who are experienced reviewers to contribute some thoughts and insights on this topic and, specifically, asked for three to five pieces of advice for young scholars on this topic. We requested our contributors to think beyond the familiar such as "the introduction should position the manuscript clearly," and to provide insights gained from experience that would substantially improve the manuscript from the reviewer's viewpoint. Our contributors were encouraged to submit a few comments on what they look for in the abstract, introduction, literature review, methodology, results, discussion, and conclusions sections, and what might encourage them to read forward with interest. They could also write about which parts they read first and why, or what are fatal errors that young authors need to be aware of. Although a few lines for each piece of advice would be sufficient, we asked the contributors to share a short story or two to illustrate their points.

Before presenting our contributors' advice on the specific parts of a manuscript, a good place to start is with some general comments on the role of the reviewer. Gerrit van Bruggen offers a reminder that, while we need to be aware of satisfying reviewers and editors, the author's target is the readership. If the contribution is useful for the reader, there is a much better chance the reviewers will be supportive:

> This is an interesting question, and it seems that there is an increasing interest in it, as well as in how to deal with reviewers in general, given the number of workshops, conference sessions, and courses in Ph.D. programs. Mostly, these activities are targeted at Ph.D. students and junior faculty. Even though I recognize the relevance of the topic, I also feel somewhat uncomfortable with the (kind of) emphasis put on the role and value of reviewers. To me, it seems that we should not overvalue the role of strategizing during the review process. In some sense, this is just a tactical game, which at the best is just a minor part of a process. Authors should write for readers and, in some sense, reviewers are just gatekeepers. Their role is to secure that the research that is being presented meets methodological quality criteria and is sufficiently interesting to get published. So, what makes a manuscript relevant and useful for the reader will also help to get reviewers' support. Therefore, the question becomes, what makes a good readers' manuscript? (van Bruggen)

Audhesh Paswan would agree with this statement, reminding us of the gatekeeper role of the reviewer, allowing through only those manuscripts that make substantive contributions to the journal's research area:

> As academic researchers, our role is to create new knowledge that enhances our knowledge in a particular field and helps various stakeholders. As a reviewer, I see our primary role as someone who ensures that the knowledge in the manuscript to be published in the journal adds to the body of knowledge in the focal field, and that knowledge helps focal stakeholders behave differently, if not better. (Paswan)

2. THE MANUSCRIPT'S INTRODUCTION

Most of the contributors to this chapter agreed that the introduction needs to do two things: provide a positioning or 'hook', which encourages the reader (and reviewer) to keep on reading, and to clearly state the theoretical and managerial contributions. Attention to these issues should help prevent the dreaded 'so what' comments from the reviewers.

2.1 The Hook/Positioning

Stephan Henneberg, Audhesh Paswan, and Gerrit van Bruggen all noted the need to intrigue the reader, and to provide evidence that what he/she is going to read is indeed important, and time well spent:

> Set the hook quickly: I normally start reading the introduction and then immediately go to the nomological model (for empirical manuscripts, both qualitative and quantitative) or to a conceptual model/figure (for conceptual manuscripts). After reading this, I want to be excited: I need to have understood what the manuscript is all about, and I want to be intrigued (either because the topic is fascinating, or because I want to know the detailed argument or empirical evidence). Thus, in the introduction I want to know in the first paragraph what the manuscript is doing, and in the second paragraph why this is important. At this point, the manuscript (and for quantitative manuscripts, the model) must have passed the "I could have told you that before I had to read this manuscript" test. In other words, if there is something 'non-obvious' in the manuscript, this must be clearly visible/signposted early on. (Henneberg)

> What is the story? Why is this phenomenon, topic, or the story important? How will it affect our lives, and make focal stakeholders behave differently? What is the magnitude of the impact or change? This, to me, is the most important thing in a manuscript. Also, the purpose or the objective of the manuscript should be presented early and clearly enough, with proper lead in using data from industry and/or the context. I call this the 'slice of life' approach to identifying research questions. Although I understand that some research questions emerge out of the 'slice of literature' approach where the authors try to fill a gap in the literature, even these, in my view, should be anchored in 'life.' (Paswan)

> To me, the most important thing by far is that a manuscript deals with an issue that is highly interesting and relevant to the targeted readership. This relevance should be so obvious that the manuscript does not need a lot of words or selling to make this clear. Intuitively, readers should immediately feel curiosity and want to start or continue reading. I personally feel that the criterion, "will my students (non-Ph.D.) enjoy reading this manuscript?" is a really good one. If I can include the manuscript in my course readings (for undergraduate to executive courses), that is a big plus. In industrial marketing, this means that every industrial marketer should immediately understand why the documented research is important and relevant. An industrial marketer should be eager to read the manuscript. (van Bruggen)

Kristian Möller reminds us that getting the positioning right is harder than it looks, and why it is important to get it right:

> I probably regard the 'positioning part' trickier and give it more emphasis than many. Positioning is significant from several aspects. The positioning indicates the theoretical stream the author seeks to contribute. Claiming novelty/contribution is not possible without arguing relevant knowledge gaps, omissions, or need for a new perspective regarding the existing knowledge base. So positioning is instrumental in arguing for the relevance of the entire manuscript, that is, why the manuscript

should be read. The positioning sets the scene for the reader and provides the lenses through which the authors wish the reader to read and interpret their manuscript. In brief, positioning is essential in constructing and motivating the research purpose, and probably more narrow goals, and the way the author aims to research/fulfill these. Here, I want to emphasize the point that research goal/question/purpose should be constructed and not just plopped down to the reader.

A tricky issue in positioning the study is the relative theoretical narrowness or broadness issue. Paradigmatic research favors narrow focus within a chosen theory and research school. This, however, tends to offer only incremental and often rather dull results. Broader theoretical positioning involving utilizing more than one conceptual system (e.g., sales management research and control theory) offers better chances for more interesting contribution, as does challenging the taken-for-granted paradigmatic results or assumptions from a new theoretical perspective.

For me, this narrowness versus broadness issue is a bit of dilemma. As a reviewer, I would like to encourage highly relevant research, which, on the other hand, is more demanding to carry out. When facing very narrow positioning, and knowing that there is relevant research about the topic in a relating field, I recommend doing additional reading and trying to utilize it. Narrow readership is especially frustrating if the author makes strong, but unwarranted knowledge claims along the lines of "this aspect/issue has received very scant attention" when, in fact, there have been, say 15 articles, since late 1990s about the very topic, but seemingly outside the author's radar. (Möller)

2.2 Up-Front Statement of Theoretical and Managerial Contributions

A critical component of the introduction is the statement of theoretical and managerial contributions. As John Nicholson, Chun Zhang, and Mark Parry have pointed out, a manuscript without this statement, or lacking a convincing argument of the importance of the contribution, faces the prospect of a quick rejection:

> [The author must] convince the editor and reviewers that there is a scientific contribution by the end of the introduction section. If this is not done, the chances in my view are prejudiced in terms of having a manuscript desk-rejected or returned as a major revision. Many authors under-claim their contribution, predicating their contribution on a single gap where often there is more in the manuscript. Also, by reducing the contribution simply to gap-spotting (neglect or confusion), authors miss the chance to claim that they are making much bigger challenges to underlying assumptions in a whole body of work. Equally, from a quantitative perspective, the possibility of replications of existing studies is shied away from and instead of celebrating this, it is played down in favor of a claim for a much smaller contribution based on an insignificant area of neglect or confusion. (Nicholson)

Many manuscripts I reviewed can improve along the following two areas: (1) identify credible gaps and (2) frame counterintuitive hypotheses by presenting alternative arguments and perspectives. I consider identifying credible gaps fundamental to crafting a good manuscript. One way I see how some authors identify gaps is to provide a brief review of the literature in the introduction and then state that their chosen research topic has not been examined previously and thus should be examined. I think this type of gap identification raises many questions. For example, is it possible that the research questions are unimportant? If the research questions are important, why have they not been examined? Is it possible that the authors have not done a broad literature review to identify all relevant research streams? In any case, it would be helpful for authors to explain why their research topic is an under-researched area and provide convincing evidence for why the topic is important. For example, authors first could present their research questions by citing alternative viewpoints. Then they could explain the gap and why such a gap exists by citing relevant literature. I consider this way of identifying gaps more credible ... Regarding framing counterintuitive hypotheses, important relationships often have been debated from multiple perspectives. It would be interesting and credible if authors present alternative perspectives and then explain why they support a certain perspective. This can make the hypotheses more counterintuitive than authors presenting only supportive evidence for their proposed relationships. (Zhang)

The worst introductions briefly summarize a laundry list of articles related to the manuscript's topic. As written, the point of the laundry list serves no role other than to convince the reader that no prior article has done what the authors propose to do in their manuscript. The problem with this approach is the mere fact that something has not been done does not mean that it is worth doing. There may be good reasons why something has not been done. For example, the fact that an issue has not been studied in a particular country is not, in and of itself, justification for a study that simply replicates the methodology used in prior research in other countries. (Parry)

It is also important for authors to show how their theoretical contributions build on previous literature. This does not mean only the literature appearing in that journal, or even in that research stream, but wherever it may be available. What may be new and exciting to the author may not be too convincing to an experienced reviewer. Kristian Möller explains:

I often frustrate the authors by insisting that they should not 're-invent the wheel', but have a look at what was studied and reported in the 1980s, 1990s, and 2000s. The kind of repetitiveness we face in marketing studies would not be possible in sciences. I feel that we reviewers are part of the solution; we should not accept the 'theory-of-the-month club' phenomenon. My minimum requirement for the authors is that they should recognize the availability of other relevant research streams and provide reasons for their theory choice, as well as reasoning why not adopting any other relevant literature. For example, if a manuscript addressing some aspect of say 'managing strategic business relationships' only utilizes Industrial Marketing and Purchasing-driven studies I refer to the availability of the extensive literature within strategy and especially within the management of strategic alliances. I realize that this is tough, but 'one-eyed' seeing is getting narrower and narrower, and an old hand like myself would like to read new openings. (Möller)

Finally, John Nicholson reminds us that the introduction should be up front about the managerial importance, as well as the theoretical contributions, especially in a research area such as business-to-business marketing, which is so grounded in realistic, strategic managerial decision-making:

> There seems to be great reticence to predicate a contribution on a practical problem area. Instead, the contribution in most cases is led from a theoretical weakness. Thus, how can we claim impact in what we do without stronger reference to practice? Instead, this impact tends to be an afterthought tagged on the end. (Nicholson)

2.3 Structured Introduction

In order to achieve these objectives, it is a good idea to structure the introduction carefully. Many editors or reviewers simply will not keep reading if there is no clear statement of the "research question" or "research objective" right there in the introduction. Mark Parry, Ad de Jong, and Kristian Möller all provide perspectives on the importance of clear structure:

> In the introduction I am looking for the author(s) to briefly (1) identify a gap in the existing literature; (2) explain why that gap is important; (3) describe their approach to addressing that gap; (4) summarize their findings; and (5) outline the remainder of the manuscript. (Parry)

> As a reviewer, I always have a careful look at the introduction section and especially how this section has been organized. It is this section that strongly determines my opinion on the quality of the study. For instance, a well-organized introductory section contains the following four paragraphs: A first paragraph, which gives a brief overview of the status quo of the literature. Then, a second paragraph that establishes the gap and carefully defines it. By doing so, it is also of importance to compellingly argue why this gap is worthwhile examining. If the author does a proper job in these first two paragraphs, this paves the way to writing the third and fourth paragraph. The third paragraph tells the reader about the topic of the manuscript. Finally, the fourth paragraph discusses the contribution of the study to the literature. (de Jong)

> Although I am sure that all doctoral candidates and younger researchers have been instructed for umpteen times about the importance of the introduction, this section remains probably the weakest spot of most manuscripts. This is understandable, as the introduction should optimally contain the core aspects of the manuscript in a concise form making it very hard to write. Then what am I expecting to read in a 'perfect' introduction? First, I want to understand what the focal issue/theme/phenomenon the manuscript is addressing; that is, what the manuscript is all about. This is generally a broader view than the core problem or research goal of the manuscript. A closely related issue is writing about the research stream or theoretical perspective the author is using to address the core phenomenon. This discussion provides information on how the phenomenon and purpose of the manuscript is going to be addressed/solved. (Möller)

For the last word on introductions, we turn again to Kristian Möller, who reminds us to clearly state objectives and intended contributions in the introduction, while at the same time being modest and not overstating the contribution:

> The introduction should address and provide argued answers to the traditional questions of what the study is about (at a broader level/canvas and narrow level/the focal issue), why the question is important to study (relevance), which theoretical perspective(s) is utilized, and why and how the research is carried, and for whom the manuscript is relevant. These aspects are obviously interrelated and should form a logical section. The authors should recognize that these issues reflect their choices and should as such be argued for. Often, researchers deeply embracing a certain paradigm do not recognize their choices as choices, but take many of these core issues for granted. This and inflated knowledge claims really annoy many of the reviewers. (Möller)

3. THE MANUSCRIPT'S LITERATURE REVIEW

Literature reviews should describe, summarize, and critically evaluate previous work relating to the topic. These reviews must make a significant contribution to our understanding of the topic by providing integrative framework(s) and/or paths for further research.

3.1 Critical Literature Reviews

An important takeaway from our contributors is that a good literature review is not simply a list or report of what the previous literature states. A strong literature review demonstrates that the author is familiar with the literature and its ambiguities, clearly sets up the conceptual model and hypotheses, and provides a novel perspective that highlights what is missing in the current literature. The author should refrain from overstating the contribution of the research, and clearly show how the intended contribution builds on the extant literature stream:

> The best literature reviews change the way I think about the relevant literature. Often this is done by organizing the literature in a new way and/or introducing a new perspective from a different literature (either within or outside marketing) and explaining why this perspective suggests existing research has overlooked something important. (Parry)

> The literature review should demonstrate that the authors are not rediscovering the wheel, and there is ambiguity in the literature. It should also be presented in a manner which lets the reader logically and intuitively arrive at the proposed hypotheses. Authors should also avoid [a] "literature says this" [approach,] and use both inductive and deductive reasoning to arrive at their hypotheses. (Paswan)

As a reviewer, I put much emphasis on the conceptualization of key concepts in the manuscript. For instance, the introduction of a new concept requires an elaborate discussion on the nature of this concept, as well as a careful definition. In addition, authors should embed the new concept in the literature by reviewing how the concept differs from related, more established concepts. It should also be clear why the new construct is that relevant to be studied in the context of today's marketing practice. Ideally, the literature review nicely reflects a new phenomenon, trend, or problem in business-to-business marketing. The introduction of such a new concept should be careful without exaggerating the so-called benefits of this new concept and with keeping a constructive view on related, more established concepts in the field. (de Jong)

In the literature review, an essential aspect is not to just report about relevant research, but to analyze and 'discuss with the literature' using the perspective and goals of the current manuscript. It is more about constructing/refining/rewriting theory than just reporting it. The depth and tone of this discussion depends on the goals of the manuscript. The authors should pay attention to doing 'conscious' work, they should inform the reader about the choices made and provide justification for these. An additional aspect is the use of framework figures or tables. I appreciate illustrations when they depict the key aspects of the study, whether literature reviews, conceptual flow charts, or research designs. Based on my experience, figures and tables support the exposure and readership of the manuscript. (Möller)

4. THE MANUSCRIPT'S HYPOTHESES

4.1 Clearly Written and Well-Supported Hypotheses

A common theme among our contributors is lack of care in writing or defending hypotheses. As Ad de Jong notes, each hypothesis should be stated simply, and with sufficient argumentation to support it. There should also be a consistent theoretical underpinning supporting the conceptual model and the hypotheses derived from it:

I always carefully go over the hypothesis section. A good section contains a limited number of hypotheses. These hypotheses then should not just be new, but intriguing, relevant, and not too straightforward. In addition, I always love to see some moderating hypotheses, as this type of hypotheses helps to put things into context and usually allows for interesting managerial implications. Furthermore, the formulation of the hypotheses should not be too complex, but should be as simple as possible for the reader's understanding. In addition, the text leading up to the hypothesis should contain solid argumentation. It is not enough to simply cite and refer to findings from prior studies to motivate one's hypotheses. I insist on clarifying the causal mechanism underlying the hypothesized relationship. Authors really need to argue why A actually leads to B, or C strengthens the relationship between A and B, for instance. Finally, the arguments used to underpin the hypothesized relationship should be based on a similar kind of reasoning that stems from one theoretical approach. Authors who use arguments from different theoretical perspectives to motivate their hypotheses run the risk of encountering conflicting arguments, which is confusing. (de Jong)

Maja Arslanagić-Kalajdžić states that hypotheses should be clearly related to the initially stated research question, and that they should establish the links between constructs as would be predicted by the theory used by the researcher. Careful hypothesis development leads to correct operationalization of constructs and choice of research method in later sections of the manuscript:

> I assess rigor and relevance, as guiding principles of all top-notch research, throughout the manuscript. In terms of rigor, I inspect whether authors took care to clearly relate their focal research question to the existing theory (in the introduction section), whether they offer definitions of the concepts in line with the mentioned theory/theories (in the conceptual background section), whether the links between concepts have been established based on the mentioned theory/theories (in the hypothesis development section of quantitative manuscripts), whether the operationalization of those concepts to constructs fits the definitions (in the methodology section), whether an adequate research method is employed in order to provide robust findings (in the results section), and whether the contributions are explicitly discussed (in the conclusions section). (Arslanagić-Kalajdžić)

Mark Parry adds that one must also be consistent in developing the rationale for hypotheses. Inconsistency may cause some reviewer suspicion, and can lead the reviewer to question whether the author has fully thought out the hypotheses and how they relate with one another:

> If the authors develop multiple hypotheses, the rationale provided for each hypothesis needs to be consistent with the rationale provided for other hypotheses. As a reviewer, I try to ask myself whether the rationale explicated for one hypothesis has implications for any of the other hypotheses proposed by the authors. (Parry)

4.2 Construct Definitions and Dimensionality

Another trouble spot is construct definition. Authors need to be aware of competing definitions of a construct, or any evidence of construct dimensionality. Furthermore, authors need to be careful about how the constructs are linked conceptually, as this may lead to some real problems in terms of teasing out different effects. Careful hypothesis development should address this issue. Mark Parry explains:

> Authors need to define their key constructs. If multiple definitions exist, authors need to explain which definition they will use, and why that definition makes sense given the purpose of their research ... Authors need to be sensitive to the dimensionality of key constructs. I have seen many manuscripts in which the theoretical rationale provided by the authors indicates that the construct under discussion has

multiple dimensions, but the authors treat the construct as unidimensional in their hypotheses and in their measurement scales.

Authors need to be sensitive to the number of mechanisms linking two constructs. I have seen many manuscripts in which the theoretical rationale for a hypothesis describes more than one mechanism linking two constructs, but the proposed hypothesis involves a single path between the two constructs. Perhaps this is acceptable when the two mechanisms are perfectly correlated, but when they are not, the authors should develop separate hypotheses for each mechanism. If one lumps the two mechanisms together in a single hypothesis and then estimates a single path between the two constructs, it is impossible to make a statement about the relative importance of each mechanism. In general, if there are two mechanisms that are not highly correlated, the impact of each mechanism should be assessed individually. One way to do this is to identify conditions that increase the importance of one mechanism relative to another. (Parry)

4.3 Directional Hypotheses and Conflicting Predictions

A related issue is the theoretical direction of hypotheses. Sometimes the literature is equivocal about the direction, or even the significance, of a relationship. The author should resist taking the easy way out (ignoring this equivocality, or arguing that "most articles say it is a positive relationship, so we will hypothesize a positive relationship"). Indeed, it may be the case that the direction or magnitude is context-specific, so a better approach would be for the author to argue in favor of what would be expected for the context of that particular study:

> Sometimes authors describe conflicting theoretical predications about the sign (positive or negative) of a relationship between two constructs. When this happens, it is the authors' responsibility to identify the conditions under which each prediction should hold. For example, what is the relationship between product innovativeness and ease of use? The answer is that it depends on the nature of the product innovativeness. Some kinds of product innovativeness increase ease of use, while others reduce ease of use. When one finds a conflict between empirical tests of a hypothesis in prior research, it is not appropriate to resolve this conflict by comparing the number of previous studies that have found a positive relationship with the number that have found a negative relationship, and positing a single hypothesis based on the weight of this empirical evidence. Instead, authors should develop and test hypotheses about the conditions under which one mechanism is expected to dominate the other. (Parry)

Finally, in hypothesis development, it is important for the author to make it clear that testing these hypotheses will provide incremental research value. For example, finding support for a moderating variable might explain why previous results (that had ignored this moderating variable) were inconsistent:

that would be a contribution with some incremental value. Mark Parry explains this issue and provides illustrative examples:

> If the authors are proposing a new theoretical explanation (new to the relevant literature) for an observed phenomenon, they need to identify the ways in which the predictions of their proposed explanation differ from the predictions of existing phenomena. If the proposed explanation generates exactly the same predictions as existing explanations, the authors have failed to make the case for the incremental value of their contribution. Consider the case in which an author provides a new explanation for customer buying behavior and, based on this explanation, predicts that increasing price will reduce the quantity demanded. The problem with this prediction is that conventional pricing theory makes the same prediction. In this case, part of the job of the author is to identify and test predictions that differ from those of conventional pricing theory. It is not enough to observe that a proposed explanation is consistent with observed phenomena; authors need to identify the conditions under which their proposed explanation, relative to existing explanations, does a better job of explaining observed phenomena.
>
> Similar issues (i.e., if the proposed explanation generates exactly the same predictions as existing explanations, the authors have failed to make the case for the incremental value of their contribution) arise in the development of new approaches for making managerial decisions. For example, in case research targeting academic journals, it is not enough to show that a new process yielded satisfactory results in one or more practical applications. The real question is the magnitude of the incremental improvement in desired outcomes from the new process, relative to those obtained from existing processes. (Parry)

5. THE MANUSCRIPT'S METHODOLOGY

Regarding methodology, a recurring theme is the need to select the right methodology for the analysis. As Kristian Möller has pointed out, a proper choice of methodology will allow authors to support their claims for adding new knowledge and to achieve research objectives. There should be a clear justification for the selection of the methodology, and an appropriate acknowledgment of its weaknesses and limitations. It is also important to keep the importance of the methodology in context. As Stephan Henneberg reminds us, unless you are actually writing a manuscript about the methodology itself, your biggest contribution is your theoretical or conceptual contribution. While it is important to justify the selection of methodology, it is there to serve the manuscript's objective—it is the supporting actor, not the headliner:

> When examining the methodological approach, data, and methods I pay attention to how these are related to the goals and positioning of the manuscript. That is, do the selected approach, available data/empirical material, and methods used provide effective means for achieving the targeted results? What do they enable (and not enable) the authors to say about their topic ... When reviewing the empirical part of the study, I pay attention to the overall logic of the chosen research approach

and its methods, that is, to what extent this research approach and these methods enable the authors to meet the new knowledge claims they have set in constructing the goal(s) of the study. Especially, in case-based research the designs are often not effective, that is, the authors have not utilized the extant theoretical knowledge, but go for another single case study or 'deep description' in order to 'develop local theory'. Whatever research approach and methods the authors have chosen, they should make these selections transparent and argue for them. If there are problems or weaknesses/limitations—and there always are—these should be recognized and discussed. (Möller)

Methodologically, I often see references to core ideas outside of the journal, which is absolutely correct, but then many authors do not look inside the journal to see who else has applied this methodology within the subject area. Thus, for each seminal methodological principle, authors should add a few references to who has used this methodological principle in the target journal and how that has been adapted, changed, etc. (Nicholson)

Do not get excited by your method, or your context (e.g., industry or region). Both are usually not a meaningful contribution. Argue your concepts clearly (and outline your theoretical foundations). For me, the part in which most manuscripts fail is the concept discussion (not the empirical part). Here, you should provide very rigorous and dense arguments (if you run out of space, put some aspects of the method description or empirical analysis in an appendix; the reviewers will tell you if they want it in the main text). (Henneberg)

5.1   Issues in Using Quantitative Methodology

Many problems can arise from errors in applying quantitative methods. Reviewers are quick to focus on these, as they might undermine the arguments the author is making in support of the research findings. A non-representative sampling frame, or careless data collection, will be identified by reviewers as fatal flaws that invalidate the quantitative results:

Is the sample representative of the population being studied? I once reviewed a manuscript in which the authors said their research purpose was to understand perceptions of non-adopters, but analyzed data collected from adopters. Is it reasonable to think the survey respondents have the information that they are being asked to provide? For example, is it reasonable to think that employees in one part of the firm can provide information about the operations of another part of the firm? If respondents are asked to predict future behavior, is it reasonable to think that respondents can accurately make such predictions? (Parry)

As for the empirical material, the critical question is to how well they represent or cover the core research phenomenon. For example, I have seen arguments that a specific survey data describes radical innovation decisions, when a closer look at the data showed that the major part of the data concerned relatively small-scale incremental innovations. (Möller)

Another potential problem area: did the authors conduct all the required tests to support their quantitative conclusions? This means that the authors used appropriate, strong tests of reliability and all forms of validity, and checked for endogeneity and common-method bias. Reviewers will search for evidence that the author has accounted for all of these issues:

> Have the authors performed the appropriate tests for reliability and validity? I am always troubled when authors use confirmatory factor analysis to assess the validity and reliability of their measures, but then use a path model to estimate their structural model. Why did they not use structural equation modeling given that (1) structural equation modeling is a trivial extension of the confirmatory factor analysis model they have already estimated and (2) structural equation modeling controls for measurement error, while a path analysis model (in which items for each construct are averaged together) does not? My suspicion is always that they did not use structural equation modeling because the fit statistics were poor. (Parry)

> What I check in much detail is procedures used and analyses conducted in the manuscript. Today, there are plenty of tools to demonstrate the validity and reliability of the research conducted. Author(s) need to confidently show that they master different methodological aspects. For example, a quantitative study using latent variables needs to clearly demonstrate construct reliability, as well as nomological, convergent, and discriminant validity. Furthermore, the manuscript should address the common-method bias issue, as well as show considerations related to the statistical power. (Arslanagić-Kalajdžić)

> In many cases authors fail to account for the possibility of endogeneity. For example, this problem can arise when the direction of causality is unclear. Consider discussions of adoption and innovation attributes. What is the relationship between perceived ease of use and perceived risk? One can imagine situations in which perceived ease of use negatively influences perceived risk, but one can also imagine situations in which perceived risk negatively influences perceived ease of use. Endogeneity problems also can arise when an important variable is omitted from the analysis. For example, authors sometimes try to estimate the impact of A on B while ignoring the fact that unmeasured variable C influences both A and B. When C is omitted from the analysis, A and B will have correlated measurement errors, which leads to a biased and inconsistent estimator of the strength of the relationship between A and B. This is especially troublesome when the existing literature has established that C has a relationship with A and B. (Parry)

5.2   Issues in Using Qualitative Methodology

Qualitative methodology raises a different set of issues, which, if not handled well, can be red flags for reviewers. It must be clear that the chosen research is capable of adding new knowledge, so the choice of methodology must be strongly supported. As Kristian Möller points out, the author can make a much stronger argument for knowledge contribution if using multiple cases rather than a single-case study, so if the latter is chosen, the author must offer a convincing justification. It must also be clear that the questions included in the interview adequately cover the relevant domain and strongly support the results and propositions:

> Especially in reviewing case-based qualitative research, I have often met with very loose statements concerning the research method like "... case research approach was chosen because it allows deep description of the core phenomenon in its real life context. A single case was selected (over multiple cases) since we can get more detailed material ..." This kind of vague approach can only be justified when the focal phenomenon is truly novel and unstudied, or when the research perspective proposed is novel (for an already studied phenomenon). When this kind of methodological choice is provided for research, where the core phenomenon has been studied say for over 10 years, and there exists well-developed theories about the phenomenon, I tend to criticize that approach strongly. The research design is just inefficient in producing new knowledge compared to clearly theory-based comparative multi-case designs or doing longitudinal research over a single case. (Möller)

> A qualitative study using in-depth interviews should be able to clearly align the interview questions with the main research questions/domains to clearly address when and how saturation has been reached, and to use various methods such as meta-matrices and narratives in order to represent the results and support the resulting propositions. (Arslanagić-Kalajdžić)

5.3 Readability and Jargon

Our contributors also cautioned against a reliance on methodological jargon. While we do need to show methodological rigor, we must at the same time not sacrifice relevance and, ultimately, readability of our presentation.

> The method section should be written in a clear and legible manner. While most authors are methodologically proficient and good at the use of their tools, some get bogged down with research jargon. (Paswan)

> With quantitative articles, there tends to be a focus on methods over methodology. Put another way, discussion starts with statistical rigor, and the relevance can be overlooked. This requires more methodological discussion and an argument why such rigor is relevant to practice. We must address the disjoint between academics and practitioners who largely are skeptical about what we do. (Nicholson)

6. THE MANUSCRIPT'S ANALYSIS

6.1 Construct Measures and Definition Alignment

Our contributors had much to say about construct definition and measurement. There may be a mismatch between the constructs that the authors intend to study according to the research objectives, and what is actually being measured. A misalignment between construct definition and measure may be due to the use of secondary data that do not exactly fit, or the use of vague or carelessly worded definitions:

> If the manuscript is an empirical manuscript, I look to see whether the measures used by the authors to measure constructs are consistent with previously introduced construct definitions. This is often a problem with empirical analyses that use secondary data. The secondary variables available to authors often do not reflect the theoretical definitions previously provided by the authors. A further complication arises when a particular secondary variable has been used to measure different things in different articles. One example is the use of the R&D/Sales ratio to measure aspects of the innovation process. If the same variable can be used to measure multiple things, how can one be sure which of those things is actually driving significant relationships with dependent variables? (Parry)

> The 'definition alignment' problem also arises in manuscripts that analyze data collected by the authors. This is a particular problem when data is collected using existing measures before key constructs are defined. Consider the case of 'open innovation', which often is measured by the kinds of idea sources used by a firm. For me, a key question is whether the 'idea sources' measure aligns with the definition of open innovation provided by the authors earlier in the manuscript. (Parry)

> A related problem involves construct sub-dimensions. For example, studies of perceived risk often distinguish among sub-dimensions such as performance risk, financial risk, social risk, psychological risk, etc. I have seen manuscripts in which some of the measurement items used for one sub-dimension seem more appropriate for one of the other sub-dimensions analyzed in the manuscript. This also can be a problem in experiments. For example, I have seen authors theorize about customers in a particular situation, but the description of that situation does not align with the situation described to subjects participating in the experiment designed to test the authors' theory. (Parry)

Another problem that occasionally appears is a mismatch between research objective and measurement in terms of level. If the hypotheses are about individual employees, then individual-level and not firm-level measures should be obtained:

> Over the years, I have seen a number of manuscripts that develop hypotheses about individual employees, but test those hypotheses using firm-level variables. This is a problem when there is considerable heterogeneity across individuals within individual firms, and when the pattern of individual heterogeneity varies across firms. In this case, the reasoning that applies at the individual level will not necessarily apply at the firm level. (Parry)

6.2 Interaction Terms

According to Mark Parry, few authors do an adequate job in assessing the interactions when analyzing a model with moderating effects:

> A big problem I see in many manuscripts involves the reliability of the interaction term coefficients estimated by the authors. One issue is the small sample size used ... small sample sizes raise serious questions about whether the reported interaction effects are replicable. According to Murphy and Russell (2017), "500 observations are needed to test a single interaction variable ... [depending on the expected effect size] you might need samples of 500 ... to 3000." I often see manuscripts with fewer than 200 observations and three or more interaction terms. Given the lack of statistical power, it is reasonable to ask whether any reported effects could be reproduced in subsequent studies ... Another issue involves the range of variable values where interaction effects are significant ... To address this issue, Murphy and Russell (2017) recommend that researchers identify the region where a moderator does make a difference. I have never seen this done in any of the manuscripts I have been asked to review. (Parry)

7. THE MANUSCRIPT'S DISCUSSION AND CONCLUSIONS

Perhaps not surprisingly, reviewers expect a solid discussion and conclusion section, in which the author 'closes the circle', and shows how the research objectives stated in the introduction have been achieved. To achieve this successfully, be sure to stress how your study is not simply a confirmation of previous studies, but makes a theoretical contribution to knowledge in its own right. Also, summarize key takeaways effectively, presenting the relevance of the study to theoretical and managerial implications, and showing how the study contributes to the research stream as it has evolved in the targeted journal:

> As a reviewer, I am always keen on the discussion of results. One rule of thumb is to take the results related to the hypothesized relationships as a starting point. This ensures that the discussion in terms of structure and focus is in line with the preceding parts of the manuscript. Oftentimes, the discussion of findings resides too much on the level of individual findings. Therefore, I always recommend authors to discuss at a higher level of abstraction and focus on the most important takeaways of this study, for instance, by drawing some overarching conclusions based on the findings. Furthermore, the discussion of findings should go beyond just confirming findings in prior research. I therefore carefully consider whether authors take a contribution perspective and discuss how the findings of the study expand the extant body of research. (de Jong)

> In my experience, the discussion and conclusions do not contain game-stopper kind of problems. Generally, smaller issues are involved, which can be remedied with

editing. One of the most common and more problematic aspects is the underdeveloped nature of the theoretical conclusions. As educators, we should give more attention to encouraging theory construction, not only methodological skills. (Möller)

In terms of relevance, I ask three main relevance questions: (1) how relevant the study is for the theory it aligns with (in terms of its contribution potential); (2) how relevant the study is for the journal's readership (in terms of the manuscript–journal fit); and (3) how relevant the study is for practitioners (in terms of managerial implications). I believe that failing in any of the above-mentioned elements of rigor and relevance is a cause for major concern(s) and identification of fatal flaw(s) of the manuscript. (Arslanagić-Kalajdžić)

Good manuscripts are also holistic packages, that is, there is clear underlying logic linking all parts of the manuscript, from the Introduction to the Conclusions. This includes transparence; the author recognizes the choices made and provides arguments/rationale for them. (Möller)

Finally, bring the story together. What are the boundary conditions and limitations, and what are the key takeaways for focal stakeholders. In other words, explain who the hero and the villain are, and how the world is better because of this research. (Paswan)

8. GENERAL OBSERVATIONS ABOUT MANUSCRIPTS

In preceding sections of this chapter, our contributors have commented on their expectations in each section of a typical research manuscript. Here, we present, in no particular order, some of their thoughts and observations pertaining to overall presentation, and what factors tend to lead to a more positive reviewer opinion.

8.1 First Impression Matters

In academic writing, as in life, one does not get a second chance to make a first impression. There is no excuse for sending a poorly written manuscript out for review. It shows respect for the reviewers, and the journal, if the author carefully follows the journal's style guidelines, and does appropriate spell-checking and editing. There also is no excuse for not revising a manuscript after rejection from one journal, before submitting to another. The first journal's reviewers offered comments and criticisms, which, if even some of these are incorporated, will improve the reviewer's first impression and substantially strengthen the manuscript:

> First impression matters not only because in marketing we care about making an impression in principle, but because good manuscripts are by no exception distinguished from bad manuscripts by the ability to make a good first impression

(primarily on the editor who sends it out to review and then on reviewers). From my experience, there are several traits that first impression covers: (1) clarity: title clearly reflects the content of the manuscript (and is short); an abstract shows an unambiguous summary of what has been done in the manuscript; and the intended contributions of the manuscript to the theory are explicitly stated in the introduction; (2) representation: my mind works better if manuscripts offer graphical depiction of the authors' research framework; this is not a 'must', but definitely helps in forming the first impression and getting a grasp of what the study is all about; and (3) diligence: I get really upset when I see some obvious (even if pretty minor) mistakes when reading the front part of the manuscript. For instance, on several occasions, I have found spelling/wording errors in the opening paragraph. Then I ask myself, should I really invest my time and effort in this manuscript, when even the author(s) did not care enough to re-read what is written and did not turn the spell-check on. (Arslanagić-Kalajdžić)

Too often, we see a manuscript that clearly has been round the houses of other journals and resubmitted to *Industrial Marketing Management* without modification. For instance, I have seen several manuscripts that clearly have been written for international business journals and then come to *Industrial Marketing Management* by default. An author must build on a criticism and not just resubmit a manuscript. Many good, indeed classic manuscripts, have been rejected multiple times before acceptance, but the key is making the manuscript fit for the audience, that is, the readership of the journal. Thus, there must be reference to articles in the journal, or at least a strong case made why these previously unrecognized topics should be of interest to the readers of the journal. Using the same argument as used in previously rejected submissions is insufficient. (Nicholson)

8.2 Readability

Reviewers are not impressed by jargon. A good research manuscript communicates its content well. The author should consider the manuscript from the reader's, or reviewer's, point of view, and remember that the reader will be more receptive to a manuscript that is easy to understand and not weighed down by clunky writing style or too many references. The manuscript does not have to be unpleasant to read. Also, remember that a picture is worth a thousand words. Use figures and tables to illustrate points, and make sure they are easy for the reader to interpret! Finally, be sure to get informal reviews from academic colleagues (and even practitioners) before sending the manuscript out for review:

> I find it really important that a manuscript is readable by a broad readership. This ideally even includes family and friends. Use of excessive jargon, overly complicated technicalities, and extensive references do not make a manuscript enjoyable to read. Especially, if these elements are included just for the sake of impressing or convincing reviewers, authors may be doing the wrong thing. Only write up things which are needed to help readers get the message and learn and help them doing this in the most pleasant and effortless way. When a manuscript is fun to read for

readers, it will be fun for reviewers as well. This also means that figures and tables should be completely self-explanatory and easy to understand. Do not just dump all the details that are available, but present those results that are instrumental to getting the message across. Details that are critical to evaluating the quality of the study, and the evidence presented, should be available for readers and in the manuscript. However, (web) appendices may be the perfect location for this.

Many (industrial) marketing articles that are published nowadays have passed the hurdle of satisfying reviewers, but are not easy to read, let alone enjoyable. This means that creating impact will be difficult. Some of the most impactful articles address issues that make sense to a broad readership, but are also written in a way that make digesting the presented research easy and pleasant. Given the abundance of information that is available nowadays, all readers must make choices in what they will read and what not. A well-written text will increase the likelihood of being read. What will probably help authors a lot is reading broadly to get exposed to different writing styles and be able to discover the ones that really work. Finally, never submit a manuscript before having received peer feedback from both academics and non-academics (i.e., ideally practitioners), and always use a professional copyeditor. (van Bruggen)

> Use visualizations, which make the review easier, for example, by providing a bigger picture. This can be figures to show models or it can be tables. Even literature review tables can be made insightful, for example, by showing what has been done, how it has been done, and what is missing, why it is missing, and how your manuscript addresses this gap. However, visualizations never argue a point by themselves; this needs to be done in detail in the manuscript. (Henneberg)

> Is the story easy to read? I see so many manuscripts that become so unreadable because the authors get bogged down with academic and technical mumbo jumbo. I understand that there is limit to simplifications, but if the manuscript does not intuitively make sense, why should a member of a larger audience read it. (Paswan)

8.3 Work With the Reviewers

An earlier chapter provided much guidance on how to revise well for resubmission. Several of our contributors had specific ideas that offer additional insight for the revision process. First and foremost, accompany your resubmission with a detailed reply document that shows the reviewers what changes you made to the document. Remember that the reviewers are making time to re-read your article, so do not force the reviewers to work hard to find the changes. Also, be sure to address all of the reviewers' points. Reviewers are unlikely to be happy to see that their comments have been ignored in the rewrite. Finally, if there is some doubt about the review (you believe, for example, that the reviewer is mistaken on a point), do not hesitate to contact the editor and see what your options are:

> In case of 'revise and resubmit', work with the reviewers, not against them. As a reviewer, I want to see that you are making an effort (even if you argue against

my points). Reviewers and authors are there to make the manuscript better together to provide advancement to the field. Thus, when I get a reply-to-reviewers back, I want to clearly see what the authors have done, and how they have done it. I send manuscripts back which come with replies-to-reviewers that say: "Thank you for your comments, we have addressed them in the revised version." That is not enough for me to give up my weekends to do reviews. I want the authors to make my time worthwhile, which starts with making it easy for me to find out what they have done in detail without having to read the new version of the manuscript and compare it to the old. I am won over when I see that the authors have not just addressed and worked with my comments, but they may also have gone the extra mile, for example, collected more data/evidence, or introduced a new table or figure, even if not directly asked to do so by the reviewers. It shows the passion for excellence. By the way, I also read the other reviewers' comments (if the journal provides them) and have a look at how the manuscript addresses them. (Henneberg)

What I would recommend is to always try to see if you can accommodate (sometimes that may mean adding the extra analysis or request in the revision note to show that you have truly considered the reviewer's request) and then make it very easy for the reviewer to find out what exactly you did to accommodate/answer his request, both in the manuscript and in a letter to the reviewer. (Joëlle Vanhamme)

It is also important how the authors respond to criticism. Do they take critical comments into account or provide plausible explanations for the criticized material/decisions. The worst kind of response is avoidance or 'near avoidance', that is, just mentioning the issue, but not really addressing it. This is relatively common and can infuriate the reviewer who feels the time and effort invested to the review is not appreciated. I have found it highly useful to learn to 'read' not only the reviews, but also the reviewers. It is often helpful to group the reviewers' comments into three categories: highly crucial, relevant, but minor, and, finally, off-the mark or plainly misjudgments. Authors must take care of all of these comments, but they require different detail and justifications. In case a reviewer clearly does not accept a research approach, the authors need extra care to try to convince the reviewer. If this does not work, authors should contact the editor and discuss the dilemma. I have been in this position a couple of times, and contacting the editor has been helpful. (Möller)

9. CONCLUSIONS

This chapter sheds light on the review process, from the viewpoints of the reviewers themselves. We are grateful to all of our colleagues who graciously agreed to reflect on the review process, and what they prioritize when reading each section of a manuscript under review. The chapter complements earlier chapters about writing and revising manuscripts, as it provides insights on specifically what satisfies or frustrates these experienced reviewers when reviewing manuscripts.

When preparing this chapter, we were struck by how much agreement there was among contributors. Time and again, we found there were critical things to do, and to avoid, which were generally agreed upon among the reviewers. This is an encouraging finding for authors. Even though reviewers may disagree in their opinions, it seems that there are certain fundamentals, which serve as starting points for the review process. It is advantageous for the author to know what reviewers are likely to respond positively to, and to avoid what most reviewers would consider to be fatal flaws.

We have already written extensively about the writing and revising processes in previous chapters, so we will not add much here. But if we had one point to add to this chapter, it is: please read the webpage of the targeted journal! There are several benefits to be gained:

1. Most journals will have a clear statement of the journal's aims and scope, or research objectives, on their webpage. As editors-in-chief, we see many manuscripts that have little or nothing to do with business-to-business marketing, and have no choice but to desk-reject them for poor fit. A quick online search would indicate to the author that *Industrial Marketing Management* would not be a good fit for their article, though it may be just fine for a differently targeted journal.
2. The webpage provides detailed instructions to authors, including all required format guidelines. Failure to use the correct format sends a strong signal that little care was expended in preparing the manuscript for submission, so not following the guidelines is a red flag for editors and reviewers.
3. The webpage often has links to free sample recent issues or recent publications. If so, please download one or two of these, to see what kinds of articles the editors are seeking to publish in their journal, what format is typically used, how the manuscripts are organized, and the kind of methodologies that are popular in the journal. If there are no free sample articles, download one or two articles through your university's online library.
4. The webpage usually posts impact factor statistics, which are helpful in assessing the reach and impact of articles published in the journal.
5. Finally, the webpage will list the contact information of the Editor(s)-in-Chief. If you have a question about a recent review or a specific reviewer's request, do not just guess. Please feel free to contact the editor.

REFERENCES

Murphy, K. & Russell, C.J. (2017). Mend it or end it: Redirecting the search for interactions in the organizational sciences. *Organizational Research Methods*, 20(4), 549–573.

PART 5

Being relevant

16. Getting research cited

Adam Lindgreen, C. Anthony Di Benedetto, Roderick J. Brodie, Julia A. Fehrer, and Michel van der Borgh

1. INTRODUCTION

Academic success traditionally has been assessed by publications of articles in highly ranked journals. Hence, it is important to understand the different rankings when profiling research. Different groups of scholars and research groups that are committed to maintaining the very best research have developed different journal rankings. For example, in the UK, most business schools follow the Academic Journal Guide (AJG) from the Chartered Association of Business Schools, while business schools in Australasia adhere to the Australian Business Deans Council's (ABDC) journal quality list, business schools in France frequently rely on the Comité National de la Recherche Scientifique's (CNRS) categorization of journals in economics and management, and business schools in Germany follow the JOURQUAL list from Der Verband der Hochschullehrer für Betriebswirtschaft e.V. (VHB). And, of course, there are the *Financial Times*' list of the 50 journals (FT 50) used for ranking global business schools, as well as the UT Dallas' list of the 24 leading business journals. Other business schools, such as Rotterdam School of Management, have developed their own journal rankings. Thus, many different rankings exist, with different criteria for journal ranking.

In recent years, however, other research quality measures have become available, and these offer a wider perspective of academic contribution beyond simple article counting. Citations now are an important consideration when evaluating research impact and quality. Google Scholar, Scopus, Web of Science, and other data aggregators are readily available to provide citation counts. Other measures such as Hirsch's h-index, Egghe's g-index, and the hg-index, to name a few, have also been developed. Furthermore, there are measures that provide a finer view than citation counts. The Field Wright Citation Index, for instance, assesses the number of a researcher's citations relative to the average obtained by other similar publications as indexed by

Scopus. PlumX Metrics (focus on online interaction) and others can offer additional perspectives on research output and use. In this changing environment, citations are increasingly viewed as a measure of the impact of a researcher's work, and directly or indirectly impact the evaluation of that researcher by his/her institution. In this chapter, we discuss the issue of research citation, focusing on strategies that can be used to ensure that one's research output is read by the intended academic and practitioner audiences.

Before examining how to get great research cited, the topic of this chapter, it is important to revisit the conditions that lead to great research. In an editorial, Lindgreen, Di Benedetto, Brodie, and Naudé (2019) reflected on this, suggesting it is necessary to have research problems that lead to research opportunities that are of practical and academic interest, which lead to new research opportunities. It is also valuable to be embedded in a network of talented scholars with complementary abilities. The team needs to refine their research to obtain clarity in expression so that the contribution clearly can be understood. To make a significant original contribution, fresh thinking about the role of theory and theorizing plays a valuable role (Brodie & Peters, 2020). Finally, a crucial challenge is to have the persistence to get research accepted in highly ranked journals.

Once a manuscript is accepted for publication, the challenge is to build citations. This requires the publication to become visible and its original contribution understood. Use of the online environment and social media plays an important role here. Platforms for knowledge sharing and dissemination of academic research include ResearchGate, ResearcherID, mySCOPUS, ORCID, Publons, Google Scholar, LinkedIn, and others. Authors need to become active participants on these platforms.

In this chapter, we first examine why articles get cited. We then outline how to set up and present research. Third, we provide guidelines to create visibility and understanding of the article's contribution in the offline research community and beyond. Fourth, we examine the critical role of the online environment in creating visibility for an article. We conclude by cautioning about unethical practices to increase citations.

2. WHY ARTICLES GET CITED

2.1 Types of Articles

Different types of articles are cited for different reasons. For an overview of types of articles, we refer to Benoit, Scherschel, Ates, Nasr, and Kandampully (2017). In the following, we will discuss the types that typically get cited.

Articles that elaborate on methods generally get well cited, especially tutorials. For example, Diamantopoulos and Winklhofer's (2001) article is a highly cited tutorial on a methodological issue. The authors propose four critical steps for constructing indexes based on formative indicators. Following that, they suggest two methods for testing the validity of formative measures. As such, this article will be highly relevant to many researchers' work and therefore frequently cited.

It is also possible to pick a topic that is not well understood or used and write a primer on this. Articles reviewing the literature also generally get well cited. Consider, for example, *International Journal of Management Reviews*, a journal with an impact factor that has increased significantly over the years. Its current impact factor is 7.6, and in the ISI Journal Citation Reports Ranking, the journal ranks 8/147 in Business and 8/217 in Management. This journal's first ever special issue considered the topic of corporate social responsibility (cf. Lindgreen & Swaen, 2010). All articles in this special issue were literature reviews/overview articles and, including the guest editorial, were among the journal's 12 most accessed pieces in the year of their publication; and in each year since then, several of the pieces have been among the journal's most downloaded pieces. In fact, this special issue made a substantial contribution to the improved impact factor and the raised profile that *International Journal of Management Reviews* has enjoyed.

Many journals, in fact, publish compelling special issues that raise debate and attract widespread citations. Typically, a hot, high-potential topic is singled out, and with the permission of the special issue editor, guest editors solicit a collection of research articles on the topic, selecting the best of them for publication in the special issue. Thus, special issues serve two functions: alert the journal's readers to the growing importance of a topic while summarizing what is known so far about it, and present the newest research, often authored by a mix of senior academics and the best and brightest of the most recent generation of assistant professors. A special issue ideally becomes the go-to issue for researchers interested in that topic for many years to come. The result is that articles in these special issues have a good chance of becoming highly cited.

A variant of the literature review is the meta-analysis, or the summary of 'where we are' in a research stream, which might be part of a journal's special issue on the topic (and therefore probably stands a higher chance of being included in this special issue). In *Industrial Marketing Management*, some of the 'citation classics' articles (cf. Lindgreen & Di Benedetto, 2018) are of this special issue type. Another example is the special issue that *Journal of Product Innovation Management* published a few years ago (Biemans, Griffin, & Moenaert, 2010) where three of the five top articles were meta-analyses. These articles were judged by the journal's editorial board members in terms of impact, not strict analysis of citation counts.

Conceptual articles that introduce new core concepts to a field are one of the best ways to attract citations. Writing conceptual articles is challenging, however. One reason is that many editors and reviewers resist accepting new ideas, constructs, and theories. Editors and reviewers prefer more well-known ideas, constructs, and theories. One strategy for authors to mitigate this challenge is to emphasize how they are building on the 'shoulders of giants', as they say, even if their ideas, constructs, and theories are quite different. Rather than saying that "the Smith-Jones model from the 1970s is now outdated and obsolete, and here is a newer and better model," it might be good—if possible—to position one's work as an extension or alternative to Smith-Jones. Doing that means that researchers using the older and more popular model are more likely to find and cite your article. Another benefit is that Smith or Jones, or one of their students, is probably going to be one of the reviewers of your article. Thus, if you speak well of their model while showing your contribution (and avoid implying the Smith-Jones model is obsolete), they will be more receptive to your article.

2.2 Types of Citations

The nature of the scientific impact of the cited articles is an important consideration in understanding why articles get cited. Stremersch, Camachoa, Vanneste, and Verniers (2015) distinguish between five citation types:

- *Application citations* occur when authors cite an article because they use the article's concepts, methods, or findings.
- *Affirmation citations* occur when authors cite an article because their results confirm the findings of the cited study.
- *Negation citations* occur when authors cite an article because they critique, attack, or disconfirm the cited study.
- *Review citations* occur when authors cite an article to illustrate what prior literature has been studied.
- *Perfunctory mentions* occur when authors cite an article without really using it.

Application, affirmation, and negation citations indicate a higher level scientific influence of the cited article than review citations. More specifically, application citations reflect the scientific contribution through the direct usage of the concept, technique, or theory proposed by the cited article, while affirmation citations reflect contribution because the cited article confirms the correctness of the cited article. Negation citations contribute to an academic debate by highlighting theories or concepts that need revision or show some kind of contradiction. In contrast, review citations clarify the scope or contribution of the cited article or justify the cited article. Because of that, such cited articles are regarded as playing a less significant role for theory development. Finally, perfunctory citations, by definition, do not contribute to the development of a concept, and might even be wrong. Perfunctory citations are usually used to signal a reference to a certain research field, but this citation type does not refer to the specific concepts developed in the specific article that was cited.

Following their distinction of citation types, Stremersch et al. (2015) report the first large-scale study of the scientific impact of citation types in marketing journals. They examined the citation types of 659 articles in leading marketing journals (*International Journal of Research in Marketing, Journal of Consumer Research, Journal of Marketing, Journal of Marketing Research,* and *Marketing Science*) over the period 1990–2007. Their analysis showed that for the cited articles, there were 10 percent application citations, 5 percent affirmation citations, 53 percent review citations, and 32 percent perfunctory mentions. They conclude that only 15 percent of citing articles (i.e., application, affirmation, and negation types of citation) used the cited article in a way that made a substantial scientific contribution. Review citations were much more common if the cited article made a lesser contribution. Of note: almost a third of citations were perfunctory, thus indicating no scientific contribution, and hence the citations should not have been made in the first place.

Recent research by Li, Brodie, Fehrer, and Juric (2018) challenges the generalizability of Stremersch et al.'s (2015) findings. A similar approach that was used by Stremersch et al. (2015) examined the impact of two conceptual articles that have had a foundational influence on the development of a new research stream on customer engagement. The articles were "Customer Engagement: Conceptual Domain, Fundamental Propositions, and Implications for Research" (Brodie, Hollebeek, Juric, & Ilic, 2011) and "Consumer Engagement in a Virtual Brand Community: An Exploratory Analysis" (Brodie, Ilic, Juric, & Hollebeek, 2013). Li et al.'s (2018) analysis for these two seminal conceptual articles showed that over 35 percent of the citations were due to application and over 55 percent to review citations. Less than 5 percent were perfunctory citations. It can be argued that the reason for this somewhat different distribution of citations for these three articles relates to their role in developing a new field of research. The two articles are seminal for the development of engagement research and thus arguably represent a new category of citations, one that refers to original work in a field. On a more general level, the type of citations likely relates to the type of study conducted.

We suggest that when describing the contribution of potentially great articles, authors should clarify the scientific contribution, and hence the potential for citation. Are citations likely to occur because authors refer to an article that is seminal in an emerging field, illustrates what prior literature has studied, or the article's concepts, methods, or findings are central for specific research questions the researchers want to examine? Purely perfunctory citations are problematic, as they blur knowledge development in a field and send wrong signals. Authors, reviewers, and editors need to be aware of perfunctory citations and reduce their usage.

3. HOW TO SET UP AND PRESENT RESEARCH

All leading journals prefer articles that make significant contributions to the field. LaPlaca, Lindgreen, and Vanhamme (2018) discussed ways of how authors can improve their publishing success with such journals. We discuss some of these ways next.

3.1 Strong Contributions to the Field

Research will be judged, and published in top-rated journals, after consideration of its contribution to the literature stream. Before undertaking a research project, one should be sure that there is some potential for a valuable contribution. The researcher can ask academic colleagues their opinions on the research topic and their assessment of likely publication. It is also a good idea to consult associations such as the Marketing Science Institute and/or the Institute for the Study of Business Markets, who regularly publish research priorities. The highest-priority topics are likely to be both very publishable and also important to decision-makers in the practitioner community. By doing this homework up front, the researcher increases the likelihood of writing articles that have potential for citation, a consideration of great importance to journal editors.

In performing their gatekeeping duties, editors and reviewers insist on seeing clear research objectives. In the article's introduction, the researcher should clearly show a gap in the literature stream, and/or evidence of equivocal research findings. This is not enough, however; the researcher also has to clearly present why it is important to study this gap or this equivocality, and how the research will contribute theoretically or conceptually to the literature stream. Therefore, as a starting point to any research project, the author should try to answer the following questions:

- What is the research problem? Are there existing solutions?
- Is the proposed research new and interesting? What is the main limitation in existing theory?
- Is the proposed research challenging? Does the proposed research challenge the status quo?
- Is the proposed research directly related to the literature on a current hot topic? How does the proposed research add to this literature?

- Will the proposed research provide solutions to any difficult problems? What do you hope to achieve?

If yes to the above questions, then there might be the promise of a great manuscript. Thus, a manuscript may present new, original results or methods, or rationalize published results. A manuscript may also present a review of a particular field or summarize a particular topic. Literature reviews survey critical points in current literature relevant to a particular topic. By describing, synthesizing, and evaluating critically previous work relating to a topic, such reviews should make a significant contribution to our understanding of a topic by providing integrative framework(s) and/or paths for further research.

However, just because some research has not been carried out before, this is no justification for undertaking that research now. For example, research that is purely descriptive or lacks theoretical implications is not interesting. Ultimately, the chance of having a manuscript accepted for publication depends on whether the authors are able to build a convincing story and show 'something' that was not known before and that will change the way we think about this 'something'. To improve a manuscript's focus and clarity, the story line should be kept comparably simple (i.e., does the manuscript pass the 'grandma test'?). In a nutshell, manuscripts must answer the 'so what?' question.

3.2 Conceptual and Theoretical Development

Lindgreen et al. (2019) discuss five necessary initial conditions that determine the success of a research stream:

- *Research problems leading to research opportunities*, that is, the capability to identify an important research problem, which is of practical and academic interest that creates future research opportunities.
- *Initiation of a research stream*, that is, the capability to initiate the research stream by bringing together talented groups of scholars to realize research opportunities.
- *Clarity in expression*, that is, the capability to provide clarity in academic arguments that provide foundations for the emerging research stream.
- *Teamwork within a network of scholars*, that is, the capability to develop a network of talented scholars who continue to embrace research opportunities.
- *Platform to consolidate knowledge*, that is, the capability of the network of scholars to produce research that consolidates the knowledge in the area.

Additionally, there are five key conditions that build on these initial conditions and also impact the success of a research stream:

- *Role of theory and theorizing*, that is, greater emphasis needs to be given to the process of theorizing rather than to the focus on theory.
- *Sustained leadership and innovation*, that is, a process needs to be put in place to sustain leadership and innovation.
- *Acceptance of research*, that is, scholars within the research stream have the persistence to get research accepted in high-quality journals.
- *Recognition of research*, that is, the research stream needs to become visible and understood by other researchers.
- *Tenacity and resilience*, that is, the researchers must possess these two qualities.

Researchers have been successful in their conceptual and theoretical development when they have developed a clear and convincing logic to their theory so that researchers can see how the theory fits in the field; when they have defined concepts clearly and concisely so that other researchers can use them in their own research; have ensured there is a clear rationale for the conceptual development so that other researchers can understand why they should use the concepts, methods, or theories; and, finally, have ensured that propositions and hypotheses are specific, well argued, grounded in the theory, and not tautological.

3.3   Compelling Findings

In its discussion, a manuscript needs to refocus the reader on the research question(s) or purpose(s) of the manuscript; re-establish the frame of reference for the reader; and demonstrate the gap in knowledge that the manuscript has filled. That is, the authors need to ensure congruence with their original research motivations, objectives, and questions. Accordingly, authors turn their descriptive material from the manuscript's findings section into a meaningful discussion or answer to the research question(s), and how the contribution to knowledge described earlier is now substantiated. Findings can be related to the frame of reference and theoretical development previously established in the manuscript. The discussion section permits the authors to explain their research results as they accomplish the following:

- Describe how the results relate to the original research motivations, objectives, and questions.
- Provide interpretation for the results presented.
- Show how the results are consistent with what other investigators have reported or explain how and why the results are different.

- Demonstrate the importance of the research and why it deserves publication.

3.4 Clear Conclusions and Implications

As noted above, it is important to state clear research objectives in the introduction section. It is equally important to return to these in the conclusions, to show how these objectives were achieved. Again, playing the gatekeeper's role, the editor and reviewers will want to see evidence of the quality of contribution, and the researcher should seize this opportunity and write a strong conclusion that shows the research objectives were met. Needless to say, the conclusion should not be a mere repeat of the results section. The researcher should offer evidence that the presented research is important and relevant. A strong managerial implications section may be required by the target journal, increases relevance and visibility to the practitioner community, and is valued by business schools who increasingly prioritize relevance of academic research. While not overstating the importance of the research, the researcher should avoid phrases such as "may make an impact" or "might be useful to managers in the future," which cast doubt and uncertainty about the importance or usefulness of the findings.

Finally, the manuscript needs to discuss limitations of the research, as well as avenues for future research:

- Mention any limitations of the research and its design and why, despite these limitations, the research is important and adds to our knowledge base.
- Describe logical extensions of the research and provide directions for future research.

4. CREATING RECOGNITION OFFLINE: THE RESEARCH COMMUNITY AND BEYOND

We will now discuss different ways of creating recognition of the article offline, that is, in the research community and beyond.

Collaborating with top authors in a particular field may drive citations, as the article probably will be recognized easier. For example, the creation of value is key in marketing, as the role of business is to co-create value for its customers that is superior to competitors' offering. Many researchers, therefore, will include considerations of value in their research streams and, as a consequence, cite top authors in the field and see what they might have written since their first articles—and this is where your co-authored article with one of these top authors could be cited.

Publishing multiple articles on a particular topic to create a critical mass around a certain topic is another interesting idea. Researchers could contemplate running a conference session around a topic or idea that they write articles on; other researchers will then perhaps cite these articles. The same goes with having a special issue or a research volume where researchers could raise interest in their research.

Making sure to use the correct labels of concepts, methods, and theories and choosing outlets wisely is paramount to getting cited. Sometimes, a researcher introduces a concepts as the first one, but then is not cited because the labeling is not adopted or is incorrect, and/or the article is published in an outlet that is not read by the main target group. For example, Patrick Matthew, a gardener in Scotland, arrived (crudely, though) at the principles of natural selection in 1831 and published his thoughts in an appendix of the book *Naval Timber and Arboriculture*. When Charles Darwin and Alfred Russel Wallace presented their joint publication of natural selection many years later, in 1859, they did not cite Patrick Matthew who was infuriated. A very apologetic Charles Darwin explained, in his defense, that he had never come across the book! Maybe a little closer to home, the classic Utterback-Abernathy model of product and process innovation, depicting the development of the "dominant form," was first published in *Omega* (Utterback & Abernathy, 1975), *Technology Review* (Abernathy & Utterback, 1978), and in a book (Abernathy, 1978). While these two journals are well-respected, they might not have been the first places where an innovation researcher would have looked!

Send your articles out not only to top authors in the field, but also other authors who are working in the same area—and who might become the next top authors. Some authors include their recent published articles in their e-mail signature so that, with a click, one is taken to the journal where the article appears. It is interesting to know that if an article has been cited within its first year of publication, it is much more likely that the article will garner even more citations. This also means that authors should not wait sending out their articles or including their recent published articles in their e-mail signature. The reason why such articles accrue more citations probably relates to the fact that one should try and reference more recent articles.

Publish in high-impact journals as opposed to lower-ranked journals because articles in such journals generally are cited more. To some extent, a researcher can self-cite, but not excessively and really only when relevant. A researcher can also collaborate with co-authors who might also (again, not excessively and only when relevant) self-cite, and their combined network will be wider than just the researcher's own network, and so their contacts will add to the pool of those aware of the researcher's work who might cite the researcher! We caution, though, that both are walking a fine line! Thus, one could report Google Scholar, Scopus, and Web of Science citations without self-citations.

Attending relevant conferences to present research work is a way for researchers to raise their profile additionally. Increasingly, researchers set up a profile on sites such as ResearchGate, ResearcherID, mySCOPUS, ORCID, Mendeley, SSRN, Kudos, Publons, Google Scholar, and LinkedIn where interested people can follow their latest updates.

A focus on writing fewer but more impactful articles ensures that one's CV is not polluted. Lots of publications might not necessarily be considered a good thing, especially if they are not all in top-notch journals. With fewer articles, it is possible to write more comprehensive articles with more content and impact.

Write managerially oriented intepretations of your articles. This expands your readership outside the academic community, since practitioners probably will not read the academic journals publishing your work. With timely relevance and interest to practitioners, you might try developing a managerially oriented version with the technical part streamlined and the focus on implications for improving competitiveness. Journals such as *Business Horizons*, *Harvard Business Review*, *Journal of World Business*, and *Sloan Management Review*, among others, are possible targets.

And a few more ideas for creating recognition of the article offline: Researchers always should cite their work correctly. Increasingly, this means that researchers should use a Digital Object Identifier (DOI) to describe the location of their article. If possible, they should also publish their data because when other researchers can check (and trust) the data, they are more likely to cite the article. Researchers could also contemplate publishing other types of works in journals: for example, research notes sometimes are cited heavily, as they introduce something new for other researchers to take further.

5. CREATING RECOGNITION ONLINE: ACADEMIC SEARCH ENGINE OPTIMIZATION

5.1 Overview of Academic Search

Getting an academic manuscript published is often perceived as the final step, celebrating a successful finish of a multi-year journey of wrestling and engaging with reviewers, editors, and co-authors. The publication should, however, not be viewed as the final step. There is one more milestone to consider in today's networked age: Academic Search Engine Optimization (ASEO). Social media and the digital landscape request additional tasks from authors, some of which can be outsourced (e.g., social media content creation), and some that refer more directly to the design and structure of the article and therefore should be thought of when polishing the manuscript during the revision.

Authors need to ensure that their articles and research profiles are indexed correctly by academic search engines such as Google Scholar, Scopus, Web of Science, ResearchGate, and others. This greatly increases the visibility of their work in their academic community and beyond. Equally important is that the indexed articles rank high on Google Scholar and other databases, that is, ideally the articles should show on the first page of the search list for as many searches as possible (Beel, Gipp, & Wilde, 2010). While, as emphasized in the previous section, citations and the authors' reputation play an important role to rank high in academic search engines, there are several additional elements, which can be optimized and influenced, even by an early-career researcher with single digit h-index and no 'big name' author on the article.

Optimizing academic articles for search requires some knowledge of how search engines work, and how other researchers use them. We consider five elements of particular importance: (1) keywords, (2) design and structure, (3) graphics, (4) metadata and university research repositories, and (5) interactive social media content (for more practical advice, see a recently published blog by one of the authors in collaboration with the digital marketing agency Pure SEO, https://pureseo.com).[1]

5.2 Keywords

Keywords are the building blocks of any search engine optimization (SEO) strategy. Academic search engines, however, use specific ranking mechanisms to determine in which position an article is displayed. Common ranking factors include publication date, citation count, author, journal name, citations and reputation of authors, and, most importantly, the relevance of the article for specific search terms (Beel et al., 2010). The relevance is a function of how often and where search terms occur in the article.

Relevant search terms are particularly important in the title, abstract, and keywords of an academic article. For example, if the article contributes to understanding phenomena in the sharing economy, it is—from an ASEO perspective—recommended to have the phrase 'sharing economy' in the title, as a keyword, multiple times in the abstract, and frequently in the main body of the article. While arguably the word 'collaborative economy' describes many of the empirical phenomena in the field better than the phrase 'sharing economy', it is important to be aware of the fact that most researchers—and thus potential citation providers—would still search for the more established term 'sharing economy'. Thus, authors need to consider carefully whether they use the more accurate or the more common language when designing their manuscript and describing their concepts. If authors, in this case, decide for the term 'collaborative', it is crucial to still create the link to 'sharing economy', for example by mentioning this latter term in the keywords, abstract, and introduction of the article. This way, the article ranks for both searches on 'sharing economy' and 'collaborative economy'.

Another very important principle for ASEO is that an article should rank for as many searches as possible. This can be achieved through smart combinations of more general keywords[2] (e.g., engagement, if your article is on business-to-business engagement) and more specific, so called long-tail keywords (specific word phrases, for example, SME business-to-business engagement) (Conway, 2019). While it is unlikely that one will rank on the first page for the search 'engagement' a couple of months after publication, it is more likely to rank high for more specific searches. At the same time, it is important to make sure that keywords are not too specific because researchers might search for broader or similar terms such as, for example, 'small business engagement'.

The above examples illustrate that keywords should not be viewed as an afterthought, to be filled in carelessly when submitting a manuscript for review. Keywords are critical for navigating the readership and thus most central for reads and citations. Keywords require careful strategic consideration and planning. Indeed, early-career researchers sometimes have difficulties with keyword selection: they work with too many key terms, too few, or poorly worded ones that will rarely be searched for. Tools such as Keyword Planner can support to determine keywords (Conway, 2019). However, observations of academic colleagues' search practices might be even more effective for staying informed about relevant keywords. Different from websites where keywords can be changed at any time, academic articles remain. This makes the choice of the right keywords even more central.

5.3 Design and Structure

The title and abstract are central and not only from an academic, but also from an ASEO perspective. While an article might, for example, at its core explore "the design of business models in increasingly digital sociotechnical systems from a combinatorial evolution perspective," this might be something that only very few researchers would search for. This article might, however, more generally offer a "new design approach for digital business models." Thus, there is, again, a trade-off for authors to decide between a more general 'encrypted' and search-optimized or a more accurate title. From an ASEO perspective, a title like "A new design approach for digital business models" would work better because it relates to a broader academic readership.

The abstract should include the topic, argument, and conclusions of the article, while using central keywords, as mentioned previously, throughout. The abstract needs to be written concisely and communicate well. The abstract and the title are the elements of the article, which are always open access and available for all academic search engines. Thus, the abstract and the title need to be very convincing so that even researchers who do not have full access to the journal will make the effort to contact you in person or pay for the article to get access to your work.

Further, many journals now ask to provide the highlights of an article. These highlights should be written for practitioners and attract broader audiences than the immediate research community. Finally, the main body of an article should be keyword-optimized and—from an ASEO perspective—structured in a way that algorithms can 'make sense' of it. That is, clear hierarchical structures are recommended. For example, it needs to be clear where the literature review ends, and where the development of the new conceptual framework starts, where the findings are, and what refers to future research avenues. To sum up, many of the recommendations regarding the design and structure of an article for ASEO also hold in general and refer to good practice in academic writing, as mentioned previously.

5.4 Graphics

Search engines cannot read images, yet. Thus, image-based raster graphics (e.g., jpeg, .png, .pdf, and .gif) cannot be understood by search engines. Many publishers however, provide figures and tables as open access, even if the full article is not available open access. This makes graphics an important, but often missed, opportunity to reach a broader audience. Graphics have great potential for broader impact because, if produced in a smart way, they appear not only in academic search engines, but more broadly in Google image search. From an ASEO and SEO perspective, there are three important elements to consider:

- Graphics, independently of how they are created, need a good description. That is, a graphic only described as "Figure 1" does not do the trick. Ideally, graphics should include relevant keywords and describe precisely what they depict because this description is what the search engine can read (Conway, 2019).
- Graphics should communicate their essence in a stand-alone manner without its surrounded text. This is critical, as Google image search only presents the graphic.
- Vector graphics (e.g. .svg, .ai, .eps, and .emf), instead of raster graphics, should be used. Vector graphics can be linked, copied, and adjusted in scale without losing their readability. Furthermore, text in figures can only be indexed if embedded in a vector graphic (Beel et al., 2010).

5.5 Metadata and University Research Repositories

Search engines use bibliographical metadata to identify documents. While the publisher is usually responsible for including the complete meta-information to articles, there are two points to consider.

First, most editorial systems nowadays allow for linking the metadata of an article to the author's ORCID Identifier. This has the advantage that all work of the author is connected by one unique identifier, which then is used by the academic databases (e.g., Google Scholar, Scopus, or Web of Science) to create author profiles. These profiles—as previously discussed—are particularly important for early-career academics, as they give an indication about the potential impact of their academic work.

Second, while published articles, if set up correctly, are linked directly with a researcher's academic profile and usually also with the researcher's university website, it is—from an ASEO perspective—of central importance to deposit the accepted manuscript in university research repositories. Such repositories are indexed by Google, Google Scholar, and other academic databases. That is, having the metadata, abstract, and accepted manuscript stored in the university research repository increases visibility and discoverability of academic research. Depending on the agreements with publishers, which are usually checked carefully by university librarians, accepted manuscripts can be published via the university research repositories and thus create greater access to academic work. University research repositories are further a particularly relevant source for universities in emerging countries that cannot afford licensing of the established academic databases.

5.6 Interactive Social Media Content

Finally, for great impact, academic work needs to be in the social media buzz within and beyond the academic community. That is, it is important to market and shape markets for academic knowledge. This includes interactions with journalists, university communications, PR, and social media marketing. While it is somewhat controversially discussed if authors should invest time into their own social media marketing, we suggest at least to use and co-create with the resources that are available. For example, many publishers offer support for communicating research on social media. Most universities nowadays are very supportive when it comes to creating social media content, in particular related to research that is within their strategic directions. Further, there is an increasing number of online platforms that have expertise in translating research to business practice. Usually, online platforms offer such service for free to researchers. Finally, we recommend researchers to link their academic work to their personal and professional social media profiles. Social media activities, at least indirectly, influence ASEO. Research that is in the social media buzz gains traction and consequently increases in search. This positively influences the relevance of an article and hence its search rank in academic search engines in general, and Google Scholar in particular.

6. ETHICAL CONSIDERATIONS

Goodhart's Law famously states that "when a measure becomes a target, it ceases to be a good measure." Since citations are used as a measure of research quality and impact, and increasingly as a consideration in evaluation of an academic's research portfolio, there is the temptation to try to 'game' citations unethically. Researchers should view citations as a measure of the value of their research, not the so-called target in and of itself.

We have already addressed one ethical issue above: self-citation, which could be done in an unscrupulous manner. It is inevitable that a researcher's work will extend on, or borrow from, work they have done in past years, so some self-citation is inevitable, and acceptable. The generally accepted rule is that one should apply the same rules to self-citation as to any other citation. For example, consider Stremersch et al.'s (2015) citation categories and avoid perfunctory citations and, by all means, avoid overstuffing the reference list with one's own work just to boost citation numbers. But, there are other concerns as well, such as the unethical use of citation clubs (where everyone agrees to cite everyone else's work as much as possible), 'fake' citations (citing one's own unpublished and unreviewed manuscripts), citing both a conference paper and a journal article (that overlap greatly and say much the same thing), or even cherry-picking one's own articles to boost one's h-index. There are other unethical practices involving citations as well: some unscrupulous journal editors require authors of accepted manuscripts to include several articles from their journal to boost impact factors; reviewers insist on adding references to several of their own articles when recommending a revise and resubmit, and so on.

It is beyond the scope of this chapter to address these and related ethical issues in detail. However, it bears mentioning here that one must not lose sight of the objective. It should not be to get as many citations as possible, perhaps even acting unethically in the process. If one is writing impactful work, as we have outlined in this chapter, this work will be recognized by the academic community and the citations will follow.

7. CONCLUSIONS

The academic publishing landscape has changed in numerous ways, and it is up to us to keep up with these changes to ensure our work reaches the desired academic and practitioner audiences. As we have outlined in this chapter, the academic objective has not changed: we as always seek to make a strong theoretical or conceptual contribution to our chosen research area. However, citation counts are now readily accessible metrics, and we work in an environment that increasingly uses these metrics as a measure of research quality and, directly or not, as a consideration in academic contribution. We must therefore also be aware of the ways by which we can increase the visibility of our research, not only to our academic colleagues, but also to the practitioner community who can benefit from our work. To that end, we have examined ways by which the academic researcher can create online recognition, select keywords properly, and use social media effectively, among other considerations, without compromising ethics.

NOTES

1. Google Search Marketing for Academic Articles SERVSIG. Posted December 18, 2019. See: http://www.servsig.org/wordpress/2019/12/google-search-marketing-for-academic-articles/.
2. With keywords in this section we mean not only the specific keyword section of an article, but more general—as it is understood in SEO—important terms and phrases in an article.

REFERENCES

Abernathy, W.J. (1978). *The Productivity Dilemma*. Baltimore, MD: Johns Hopkins University Press.

Abernathy, W.J. & Utterback, J.M. (1978). Patterns of industrial innovation. *Technology Review*, 80(7), 40–47.

Beel, J., Gipp, B., & Wilde, E. (2010). Academic search engine optimization (ASEO): Optimizing scholarly literature for Google Scholar & Co. *Journal of Scholarly Publishing*, 41(2), 176–190.

Benoit, S., Scherschel, K., Ates, Z., Nasr, L., & Kandampully, J. (2017). Showcasing the diversity of service research: Theories, methods, and success of service articles. *Journal of Service Management*, 28(5), 810–836.

Biemans, W., Griffin, A., & Moenaert, R. (2010). In search of the classics: A study of the impact of *JPIM* papers from 1984 to 2003. *Journal of Product Innovation Management*, 27(4), 451–484.

Brodie, R.J., Hollebeek, L.D., Juric, B., & Ilic, A. (2011). Customer engagement: Conceptual domain, fundamental propositions, and implications for research. *Journal of Service Research*, 14(3), 252–271.

Brodie, R.J., Ilic, A., Juric, B., & Hollebeek, L.D. (2013). Consumer engagement in a virtual brand community: An exploratory analysis. *Journal of Business Research*, 66(1), 105–114.

Brodie, R.J. & Peters, L.D. (2020). New directions for service research: Refreshing the process of theorizing to increase contribution. *Journal of Services Marketing*, 34(3), pp. 415–428.

Conway, R. (2019). *How to Get to the Top of Google Search: A Practical SEO Guide*. Auckland: Penguin Random House New Zealand.

Diamantopoulos, A. & Winklhofer, H.M. (2001). Index construction with formative indicators: An alternative to scale development. *Journal of Marketing Research*, 38(2), 269–277.

LaPlaca, P., Lindgreen, A., & Vanhamme, J. (2018). How to write really good articles for premier academic journals. *Industrial Marketing Management*, 68(1), 202–209.

Lindgreen, A. & Di Benedetto, C.A. (2018). Editorial: Citation classics from *Industrial Marketing Management*: Celebrating forty-seven years of publications on business-to-business marketing management. *Industrial Marketing Management*, 73, 1–6.

Lindgreen, A., Di Benedetto, C.A., Brodie, R.J., & Naudé, P. (2019). Editorial: How to build great research groups. *Industrial Marketing Management*, 81, 1–13.

Lindgreen, A. & Swaen, V. (2010). Corporate social responsibility. *International Journal of Management Reviews*, 12(1), 1–7.

Li, L., Brodie, R.J., Fehrer, J.F., & Juric, B. (2018). Developing the customer engagement stream: Exploring the role of seminal papers. *Proceedings of ANMAC Conference*, Adelaide.

Stremersch, S., Camachoa, N., Vanneste, S., & Verniers, I. (2015). Unraveling scientific impact: Citation types in marketing journals. *International Journal of Research in Marketing*, 32(1), 64–77

Utterback, J.M. & Abernathy, W.J. (1975). A dynamic model of process and product innovation. *Omega*, 3(6), 639–656.

17. Defining, identifying, and measuring societal value

Adam Lindgreen, C. Anthony Di Benedetto, Ann Højbjerg Clarke, Majbritt Rostgaard Evald, Niels Bjørn-Andersen, and Douglas M. Lambert

1. INTRODUCTION

For universities, societal value represents an added demand, beyond academic capacities (Di Benedetto, Lindgreen, Storgaard, & Clarke, 2019; Lindgreen, Di Benedetto, Brodie, & van der Borgh, 2020a, 2020b). This societal value agenda is particularly demanded by a society that turns to universities for solutions to global issues; some national governments even have started to use societal value as a criterion to allocate funding (Lindgreen et al., 2019). When the value of business-school research to business practice itself is being questioned (Bennis & O'Toole, 2005; Glick, Tsui, & Davis, 2018), academics need to define and document how their research adds value to business and wider society.

We examine societal value in order to provide inspiration to academics such that they can provide helpful and productive contributions (Bornmann, 2013). To achieve this, we understand societal value as the product of two sub-components: societal relevance and societal impact. First, we define societal relevance and provide examples of how academics can integrate societal relevance to define their vision and contributions to business and the wider society. Second, we define societal impact and propose ways by which academics can measure the societal impact of their research. Accordingly, we hope that this chapter offers some clarity and ideas to the broad, sometimes messy societal value agenda.

The inclusion of societal value in *Industrial Marketing Management* is appropriate, considering one of the journal's principles, as detailed by the founding editor Derek Medford in the inaugural issue. Medford stated that it was not intended that the journal "should exclusively cater to either the highly numerate theoretician or the more practically motivated specialists. The aim is to provide information relevant to the whole spectrum of industrial marketing, which will be of interest to all" (1971, p. 2). That is, from its start, *Industrial Marketing Management* has sought to build on and contribute with research that offers societal value, not only to practitioners, but to society as a whole.

In more recent years, societal value has emerged in universities and beyond as part of an important process of measuring, benchmarking, and documenting that resources invested (in this case in university research) are not wasted. Accordingly, some journals now also ask for a discussion of the broader societal value of authors' submitted work, prompting academics to seek out research topics with relevance for society (Martin, 2011; Ozanne et al., 2017; Salter, Salandra, & Walker, 2017; Trencher et al., 2017).

Three main drivers seemingly have prompted this ongoing shift from solely academic impact to the inclusion of societal value. First, universities are being held more accountable for how they spend public funding. National governments seek appropriate measures of societal relevance and societal impact (we shall return to a discussion of these two constructs in the following section of this chapter) that they can use to determine funding allocations. Research that highlights its societal value invites public validation that the universities are spending the funding to benefit society (Olmos-Peñuela, Castro-Martinez, & Cukierman, 2014). For example, in the UK Research Excellence Framework (REF) 2021, 'impact cases' will count for 25 percent (up from 20 percent in REF 2014) of the score of a university's submission, while research output will count for 60 percent (down from 65 percent in REF 2014) (Research England, 2020). Accordingly, universities have begun to communicate, legitimize, and brand themselves according to a societal value agenda, designed to create societal relevance and societal impact for partners from other parts of society (Phillips, Moutinho, & Godinho, 2018). In cases where academics seek private funding, the corporate partner is usually most interested in business-performance improvement; but even here there may be indirect societal benefit: businesses provide employment to taxpaying individuals, business taxes can be used by governments for social programs, and so on.

Second, global challenges in society—big data, climate change, emigration/immigration, energy and environmental sustainability, human health, and national security, among others—demand input from experts and scholars who can take big-picture perspectives (Boon & Edler, 2018; Hughes et al., 2011; Martí, 2018; Purcell, Henriksen, & Spengler, 2019). In examinations of the consequences of a closer link between producers of research and users of research (Newig et al., 2019; Rau, Goggins, & Fahy, 2018; Sivertsen & Meijer, 2020), some academics (Bornmann, 2013; Hill, 2016) highlight a radical change in knowledge production, from "normal" (Mode 1) to "post-normal" (Mode 2) science. Mode 1 science is academic, disciplinary, homogeneous, autonomous, and subject to traditional quality controls; Mode 2 science instead is transdisciplinary, heterogeneous, socially accountable, reflexive, subject to novel forms of quality control, and generated in an application context. This distinction reflects the different foci (internal to the research community or external to the society) and accountabilities (to peer academics or a broader set of stakeholders) of the modes, though the distinctions are not necessarily mutually exclusive. Rather, academics can satisfy the requirements and norms of their peers, but also address societally valuable problems with partners from other parts of society (Gibbons et al., 1994; Hill, 2016).

Third, some critics complain that universities only produce knowledge for a small community of peer academics (Bennis & O'Toole, 2005; Butler, Delaney, & Spoelstra, 2015, Lambert, 2019; Narasimhan, 2018; Pfeffer, 2007; Stentoft & Freytag, 2018) and measure success solely by the number of publications in highly ranked journals. Yet, other measures of research quality are available, suggesting the need for a wider perspective on the meaning of academic contributions (Lindgreen et al., 2020b). Accordingly, some universities have come to acknowledge that publications in highly ranked journals may not always be the best and certainly not the only way to document the social, cultural, environmental, and economic returns of universities' publicly or privately funded research (Bornmann & Marx, 2014; Ozanne et al., 2017).

Instead of further arguing these points, we take a pragmatic approach that recognizes that the societal value of research depends on its contributions to, and effects over time in, complex, often indirect processes with multiple, multidirectional influences (Morton, 2015). For example, societal value may be fostered both by Mode 1 and Mode 2 knowledge-production processes. Regardless of the process, academics need to close the gap between academic research on the one hand and societal value on the other, both for accountability reasons and for moral/ethical reasons. How can we with good conscience as researchers use funds from taxpayers and students for research if our research does not contribute to societal value? Excellent research should improve business practice, should have societal relevance, and should result in measurable, documented societal value. In other words, hard-to-solve, real-world problems and societal challenges should drive academics to seek concrete, applicable solutions (Rau et al., 2018).

2. DEFINING SOCIETAL VALUE

Typically, research has been thought of in terms of its academic impact that implies "research, which breaks the dominant paradigm and influences future research investigations" (Reale et al., 2018, p. 299). Academic impact refers to an intellectual contribution to an academic's field of study (Wolf et al., 2013), often measured by proxies such as the number and rank of publications, number of citations, and/or h-index. Academic impact measures are easily available and quantifiable through databases such as Google Scholar, Scopus, and Web of Science, and are widely used to determine the quality of journals, research projects, academics, and research groups.

What about the societal value of research? Its first sub-component—societal relevance—can take on several meanings, including research with "third stream activities, societal benefits, societal quality, usefulness, public values, knowledge transfer" (Bornmann, 2013, p. 217). Its second sub-component—the societal impact—is the effect that such research has over time. However, the ambiguous definitions and related terminology of societal value create problems (Reale et al., 2018), so in an effort to detail how to identify research with societal value and how to measure and enhance the research's societal value, we seek to consistently distinguish between the two sub-components of societal value. We do this because societal value only can be achieved if the research has both societal relevance and societal impact. Accordingly, we argue that:

- Societal relevance entails "research activities providing results for use and benefit beyond science (e.g., [benefits to] practitioners and society)" (Wolf et al., 2013, p. 105), often conducted through productive interactions of researchers with society (Spaapen & Van Drooge, 2011), individual beneficiaries, organizations, or nations (ESRC, 2020). In short, societal relevance relates to whether the researcher is working with issues of interest to others. It is important to accept that the issues can cover issues from economy and health to environment and culture.
- Societal impact, on the other hand, is concerned with value measured in terms of monetary, quantitative, or qualitative measures. Societal impact can be defined as the demonstrable contribution that research "makes to society and the economy, and [in] its benefits to individuals, organizations, and/or nations" (ESRC, 2020). This could include, for example, who cares about the research, to what extent is the research noticed, and does the business community await the research results. The contribution can be measured directly or indirectly.

3. IDENTIFYING RELEVANT SOCIETAL VALUE

Most academics consider societal value as a complex, indirect process with multiple, multidirectional influences (Morton, 2015). Societal value is intrinsically domain specific and diverse, and may be difficult to capture in one indicator or a small set of indicators. For example, we often forget or suppress that highly used measures like publication counts and h-index are influenced strongly by research discipline. For instance, the number of co-authors per article is typically high in fields like medicine and astrophysics, and length and effort of writing and documenting research in articles in social science is on average much higher than in fields like medicine or physics. Equally, it is evident that the societal value of research is multi-factored, created in non-linear multi-interaction with many approaches, channels, and instruments (Van den Akker, Spaapen, & Maes, 2017). As a consequence, 'one-size-fits-all' assessments cannot account for all scientific disciplines or capture all types of long-term impacts in addition to all types of direct effects in society (Bornmann, 2013; GECES, 2014). In fact, in the latest REF (which took place in 2014), 150 different forms of impact were identified (Martin, 2011).

Despite societal value being multi-factored, there have been some recent attempts to develop meaningful assessments of societal value, and it is instructive to see how these have been constructed, and what factors are considered most relevant. Thus, some academics have taken it upon themselves to define and promote societally valuable research, having initiated a network (Responsible Research in Business and Management, or RRBM) and developed a set of principles to guide and reward research that is socially responsible. The principles include (RRBM website, quoted in Davison & Bjørn-Andersen, 2019):

- service to society (the knowledge benefits society broadly, not only business);
- stakeholder involvement (non-academics are involved, without compromising the objectivity of the research);
- effect on stakeholders (the knowledge impacts non-academics and helps to build a better world);
- values basic and applied contributions (the research should advance theory and also have applied implications that address societal issues);
- values multidisciplinary contribution (interdisciplinary collaboration is necessary to address complex societal issues);
- strong methodology (scientific methods are not compromised in terms of either theoretical or empirical contributions); and
- broad dissemination (knowledge is transmitted widely to academic and non-academic audiences).

In line with the varied ways in which societal value can be created, multiple approaches might be operationalized in different research areas, depending on the type of relevance the academic wishes to achieve. Among 3,428 Danish university academics who reported their engagement with practitioners, for example, the most common forms of engagement were attending conferences with business executive participants (71 percent), providing informal advice

Table 17.1 Societal value: activities and measures

Dimensions	Activities contributing to societally relevant and impactful research	Measures for societal value
Dissemination of knowledge (i.e., informing)	• Publish in academic journals • Produce books (college texts or guides for executives), reports, manuals, and guides • Publish in managerial journals, trade magazines, and social media • Present at academic conferences and practitioner events • Provide interviews with press and in news channels	• Number of publications or (paid) presentations to industry • Attention outside of academia (e.g., social media) • References in popular media • Number of citations in academia • Number of awards from academia and industry/society
Commercial activities (e.g., patents and licensing)	• File patents for a concept, procedure, method, measure, or tool for managers • License • Set up spin-offs	• Amount, effect, and monetary value • Number of companies implementing method/tool
Consulting (contract research)	• Provide consultancy services • Undertake contract research • Discuss research outcomes with managers	• Depends on type of consultancy
Education (university and executive training)	• Conduct executive training • Design undergraduate and graduate courses • Perform action research	• Evaluation of training/teaching activities • Use of method or model by the company

Defining, identifying, and measuring societal value 319

Dimensions	Activities contributing to societally relevant and impactful research	Measures for societal value
Contribution to public policy	• Publish policy papers • Interact with policy actors such as politicians or interest groups • Sit on committees and conduct commissioned research	• Change in policy • Number and type of committees joined • Effects of commissioned research • Citations in calls for research or in policy documents
Interaction and collaboration (e.g., co-creation, action research, and learning)	• Participate in workshops • To engage in intervention-based research • To conduct experiments • To theorize with managers	• Degree to which the practitioner problem is solved • Changes in firms' behaviors, strategy, or structure, including the extent to which the other entity adopts a concept, procedure, or measure that shapes legislation and improves practices • Change in stakeholders' experience, performance, relationships, and systems • Change in behavior among citizens (e.g., healthier living, rehabilitation, or less consumption) • Extent of dissemination

to public or private actors (69 percent), giving public lectures (60 percent), publishing in non-scientific outlets (56 percent), conducting joint research with public partners (52 percent), training employees (44 percent), contracting research with public partners (42 percent), working with private partners (42 percent), and television or radio appearances (28 percent) (Kongsted et al., 2017).

Building on these insights, we now consider six dimensions of societal valuable research activities, as listed in Table 17.1. Although measures for societal relevance and societal impact also are included in the table, we will discuss those issues in the following section.

We want to make the disclaimer that societal value may depend on time periods and durations (Alvesson, 2017). The effects of research happen over time and traditionally do not follow a linear process, but result from a wide range of interactions (Amo, 2007). Academics have to be aware of how to increase the likelihood that their projects and research can create societal value. If a research project integrates a series of activities over time, that effort ultimately might produce societal value. Therefore, across these dimensions, academics should consider ways to increase the relevance of their research over time and in an overall sense.

3.1 Dissemination of Knowledge

Dissemination of academic knowledge to a non-academic audience often relies on indirect channels such as books, reports, manuals, guides, managerial journals, trade magazines, practitioner events, and social media since direct contact among parties is rare (Olmos-Peñuela et al., 2014). This is not surprising. Practitioners rarely read academic journals, which they find largely incomprehensible; some research even finds that academic articles increasingly are becoming unreadable (Brown et al., 2005; Crosier, 2004). Accordingly, practitioners are more likely to obtain academic knowledge through indirect channels (Anderson, Ellwood, & Coleman, 2017; Hughes et al., 2011).

Few publication arenas, however, create a space for academics and practitioners to share and debate knowledge (Hughes et al., 2011), with the exception of some successful hybrid journals that explicitly aim to appeal to both practitioner and academic audiences such as *Harvard Business Review*, which we will explore later. Promoting societal value often involves external, third-party channels such as interviews with press and in news channels, as well as contributions to professional events and social media. Using these outlets, it is possible to summarize findings and spread awareness among the general population (Levin, 2004).

Promotion in the mass media or through social media can be a slippery slope, however, and the urge to 'game' the system must be avoided. 'Brownie points' should not necessarily be handed out every time there is a media mention. A small-scale study (possibly conducted among undergraduates) should not be presented to the media to get a quick publicity boost, as the caveats and limitations will not be mentioned by the media and, ultimately, there may be no (or even negative) societal value, if the results are unrepresentative of society as a whole.

We can present a successful example of dissemination of academic knowledge. One of the authors of this chapter published an article (Cooper, Lambert, & Pagh, 1997) on the definition and scope of supply chain management, which caught the attention of the Vice President of the Council of Logistics Management (CLM, now CSCMP). A short time later, CLM modified its definition of logistics to state that it was only part of supply chain management, making it clear that the two terms were not synonyms. The article has been very widely cited, but more importantly, it has had an impact on the academic study and has been contributing to the management practice of supply chain management.

3.2 Education (University and Executive Training)

Contributions to education span a broad range in that education can convey new understanding, knowledge, and questions (Amo, 2007). Unlike broad education, formalized courses are tailored to the specific needs of a business, government agency, or professional group (Olmos-Peñuela et al., 2014), with a short-term, targeted consideration of a limited range of issues. Anderson et al. (2017) propose relational management education as a societally valuable intervention that expands management education beyond an instrumental-solutions teaching approach to foster critical thinking.

Here is an example illustrating the effective use and application of executive training. In 1992, one of the chapter's authors started a research center consisting of a team of academics and executives, which later became the Global Supply Chain Forum. The mission of the forum was to provide the opportunity for leading practitioners and academics to pursue critical issues related to achieving excellence in supply chain management. The forum developed the cross-functional, cross-firm supply chain management framework, which uniquely focused on value co-creation to drive revenues and profit. The framework has since been delivered in week-long executive programs at leading companies and universities worldwide.

3.3 Consulting (Contract Research)

Consultancies and contract research require direct contacts. Olmos-Peñuela et al. (2014) designate consultancy as service work commissioned by non-academic actors that does not need to involve original, academic research. In contrast, contract research requires original research, conducted by academics at the behest of non-academic organizations. In Germany, 17 percent of academics serve as formally paid consultants, and 20 percent of academics have jointly published with industrial partners, according to one survey (Grimpe & Fier, 2010). Both academic consultancy and contract research can expand knowledge and training options, in interaction and discussion with clients (Hughes et al., 2011), so they can broaden clients' perspective, expertise, and knowledge and thereby potentially influence their non-academic practices. In parallel, the clients might help identify new research issues for the academic community (e.g., Ruiz & Holmlund, 2017). Researchers who have had an effect tend to have significant industry knowledge, as well as theoretical knowledge, and they also have an ability to apply their theory-based understanding to a business or industry context (Hughes et al., 2011).

Consider the following example of contract research. One of the authors of this chapter contacted a manager at Herman Miller, Inc. about funding a Ph.D. student's dissertation, after the student had successfully completed a project for the company that substantially lowered logistics costs. A research proposal to study marketing services that provide competitive advantage and improve profitability was funded for $70,000, which covered the Ph.D. student's stipend, the cost of research assistants, and all other costs. In addition, several publications came out of the research.

3.4 Commercial Activities (e.g., Patents and Licensing)

Commercial activities such as patents, licensing, and spin-offs are also a form of knowledge transfer (Olmos-Peñuela et al., 2014), though they tend to be more common in STEM disciplines than in the social sciences and humanities (Olmos-Peñuela et al., 2014). Broader forms of commercial activities also include tools, educational materials, programs, and games such as learning tools for education or games developed to encourage certain habits (Amo, 2007).

Let us consider three examples. First, for their research project, Nissen, Evald, and Clarke (2014) developed a set of tools for private firms and public actors to use in different phases of their public–private innovation projects. The tools were made available through a Danish national innovation cluster (www.welfaretech.dk/opiguide).

The second example concerns the development and validation of a multidimensional scale of knowledge brokering that BrainCompass uses to assess and profile how potential job candidates perform, and how they might improve, their current activities (www.braincompass.com; see also, for example, Van den Berg et al., 2014).

In the third example, the Global Supply Chain Forum, having studied 18 corporate relationships that were identified as successful by forum members, developed The Partnership Model, which has been used to structure more than 100 corporate relationships worldwide.

3.5 Contributions to Public Policy

Researchers can contribute to improved policy making, provide a foundation for policy decisions at different levels in society, stimulate new approaches to social issues, and inform public debates (Bornmann, 2013; Pettigrew, 2011). Societal value in relation to policy might be direct, but more often, it appears indirect and diffuse (Amo, 2007). For example, politicians and officials might learn about research findings from intermediaries such as lobbyists, interest organizations, or think tanks, then use those findings to advance or define their political agenda (Levin, 2004). End users also might seek to leverage research to influence policy, such as farmers or people diagnosed with diseases (or associations representing them) who need data to support their causes (Bornmann, 2013). Finally, societal value might arise if researchers participate in policy committees or commissioned research, then actively engage in research that is directly applicable to policy problems, such as defining parameters for new laws or evaluating the potential impacts of proposed legislation (Bandola-Gill, 2019).

For example, one of the authors of this chapter sits on the international scientific advisory panel that engages with New Zealand Food Safety Science & Research Centre. This center coordinates food safety research and provides a collective resource that enhances New Zealand's reputation as a source of safe food. Three Crown Research Institutes, three universities, and the Cawthron Institute form a partnership with the industry and the government. The international scientific advisory panel helps to provide a credible voice for food safety, as well as a strong science base for decision-making in public health and the food industry.

3.6 Interaction and Collaboration (e.g., Co-Creation, Action Research, and Learning)

Sharing knowledge across communities can be challenging (Brown & Duguid, 1998); in particular, academic approaches tend to be ineffective for bridging the knowledge gap between academia and practice (Tranfield, Denyer, & Smart, 2003). Increased collaboration between researchers and practitioners might aid this effort (Butler et al., 2015; Hughes et al., 2011; Möller & Parvinen, 2015), such that in a two-way co-production of knowledge, practitioners can participate in essential ways in problem formulation, design, explication, and knowledge creation (Hughes et al., 2011; Shapiro, Kirkman, & Courtney, 2007; Van de Ven & Johnson, 2006), beyond practical outcomes (Hatchuel, 2001). The aforementioned Global Supply Chain Forum is an illustrative example of successful collaboration.

In collaborative, intervention-based research projects, the goal is not solely to collect data, but also to offer some solution (Arnaboldi, 2013). Different approaches to establish partnerships of businesses with universities include action learning, action research (Gustavsen, 2003), theorizing with managers (Nenonen, Brodie, Storbacka, & Peters, 2017), and collaborating with practitioners (Shapiro et al., 2007) through facilitation and workshops (Storvang, Mortensen, & Clarke, 2018), tangible interviews (Buur, 2018), experiments (Haug, 2018), improvising (e.g., theater, role playing; Larsen & Friis, 2018), value co-creation, focus groups, and participant observation (Marroun & Young, 2018).

Evers, Marroun, and Young (2017) illustrate insights that can emerge from collaborations with firms for business development when researchers apply pluralistic data, obtained from a combination of participatory workshops and one-on-one interviews. Laursen and Andersen (2016), in a quasi-experimental study, also document how new product development task ambiguity affects buyer–supplier interactions over time. Using action research designs, Abrahamsen, Henneberg, Huemer, and Naudé (2016) worked with a group of managers over a three-year period to study how they use network pictures to make strategic decisions. Alternatively, Ozanne et al. (2017) propose a relational engagement approach, aimed at research co-creation with practitioners, and argue that persistent interactions are more likely to effect positive social change; and Di Benedetto et al. (2019) offer suggestions for how academics can collaborate with practitioners.

Consider, for example, that the Global Supply Chain Forum research on partnerships and supply chain management would not have occurred without the involvement of business executives, who identified the topics for research priority. Academic–practitioner collaboration on this forum has been very productive: since 1996, 36 publications have resulted from forum research (Lambert & Enz, 2017) including the most cited and downloaded paper in *Industrial Marketing Management* (Lambert & Cooper, 2000).

4. MEASURING SOCIETAL VALUE OF RESEARCH

Societal value increasingly is weighted as a measure of the value of research. It may be possible to use proxies to roughly measure the benefits accruing to businesses involved in academic research (financial performance, letters from business executives supporting a promotion and tenure decision, and so on). However, there are no generally accepted proxies (criteria and methods) for the calculation of bibliometric (quantitative) values for societal value that would be comparable to, for example, the h-index or journal impact factor (Galletta et al., 2019).

The above-mentioned difficulties highlight the need for being thoughtful when considering how to measure societal value (Lauronen, 2020), keeping in mind that societal value may need to be measured at different levels such as the level of institutions, research groups, programs, projects, or individuals, as well as over time, just to mention a few.

4.1   Frameworks for Understanding Societal Value

The question is whether it is possible to come up with an overall common framework for research assessment as generic as, for example, the h-index, which in spite of its many methodological flaws is used extensively. Such an alternative measure would be relevant to be used on the aggregate for comparison of institutions, departments, projects, and individuals. The further we drill down using the framework, the more detailed the criteria will have to be in order to adjust and modify for each research discipline.

In assessing research quality in UK higher education institutions, the REF system, among others, requires academics to demonstrate and document the effect of their societally valuable research: "effect on, change or benefit to the economy, society, culture, public policy or services, health, the environment or quality of life, beyond academia" (Research England, 2020).

In addition to the REF, several other initiatives exist, such as Social Impact Assessment Methods Productive Indicators (SIAMPI) which is a European Union-funded initiative including studies from various countries in Europe, and now is used as a metric for societal impact assessment in the Netherlands. Other programs include IMPACT-EV (developed by the European Union), STAR Metrics (from the US National Science Foundation), and the ERC Impact Framework (developed by the European Research Council). Further, the Hong Kong government has increased the importance of societal relevance when assessing research funding, and is developing a metric similar to the UK's REF (Davison & Bjørn-Andersen, 2019).

Another recent attempt to develop meaningful measures of societal value is the Academic Rigour and Relevance Index, which is a theoretical model for measuring the societal value of academic journal articles based on a variety of different dimensions thereby providing a more holistic assessment of societal value:

- significance of the contribution;
- academic scholarly intelligence;
- relevance to business system;

- perceived content by society and citizens;
- implications and recommendations; and
- citations and impact factor (Phillips et al., 2018).

Furthermore, there can be different approaches to a measurement analysis. The case study approach has been used frequently to capture the societal value of research and to assess and demonstrate the societal value of research on the advancement of knowledge, society, and/or the economy. The case study approach often is preferred when measuring societal value, as a multitude of methods can be used to collect and triangulate data (Bornmann & Marx, 2014; Lauronen, 2020; Samuel & Derrick, 2015). An example is the UK REF, which contains a variety of methods for documenting societal value, including case descriptions of knowledge collaboration, idea development, counseling, media presence, and other knowledge dissemination.

Popular metrics for measuring societal impact include the use of altmetrics. Altmetrics in scholarly and scientific publishing is defined by Wikipedia as "non-traditional bibliometrics, proposed as an alternative or complement to more traditional citation impact metrics, such as (academic) impact factor and h-index." The large publishing house Wiley argues that a "single research output may live online in multiple websites and can be talked about across dozens of different platforms. At Altmetric, we work behind the scenes, collecting and collating all of this disparate information to provide you with a single visually engaging and informative view of the online activity surrounding your scholarly content" (www.altmetric.com). Altmetrics is a fast growing field (see www.aesisnet.com), and a substantial part of the academic community is embracing analytic results primarily stemming from social media data since such results represent one measurement of the extent to which society notices an academic's research.

No matter what approach is taken to measure societal value, and whether the measurements are done *ex ante* or *ex post*, four problems often are cited (Martin, 2011; Sivertsen & Meijer, 2020):

- causality problem: the relationships between research and innovation inputs, activities, outputs, and the effects of societal value are often unclear or non-linear. It is not clear which societal impact can be attributed to which cause;
- attribution problem: it is difficult or even impossible to separate the societal value of research and innovation from other inputs and activities. It is not clear what should be attributed to research or other inputs;
- internationality problem: the effects of the societal value of research and innovation are international by nature. It is not possible to identify activities in specific relations; and

- evaluation timescale problem: the societal value in the science, as society relations are generally realized over a very long time and only extraordinarily over a short time. It is not possible to avoid premature measurement of societal value if research, which yields only short-term benefits, is emphasized.

Even though difficulties in assessing and measuring societal value exist, decision-makers and funding bodies still wish to stimulate and allocate funds based on the value for society of successful research (Martin, 2011; Salter et al., 2017), and researchers and universities still wish to justify and argue for their societal relevance, societal impact, and, accordingly, necessity.

We recognize the 'relevance versus elegance' criticism of academic research, and the implication that academic research does not have much relevance to business and the wider society. Despite the obvious challenges of measuring societal value, we acknowledge that the agenda of societal value is here to stay. Accordingly, we should support efforts in bringing forth meaningful frameworks for measuring societal value, and we propose that a full consideration of the societal value of academic research should be considered more broadly.

4.2   v-index

A meaningful example is the v-index (Davison & Bjørn-Andersen, 2019; Galletta et al., 2019), designed to be a complement to the h-index, but focused on societal research. So far, the v-index has not been used except in smaller isolated settings, although a larger test is proposed. The v-index measures societal value in terms of both relevance and impact. In the v-index framework, societal value can be assessed in terms of the potential contribution to at least one of five areas, which are similar to those included in the UK REF: economic or commercial benefit; health and welfare; public policy and service; culture and entertainment; and quality of life and work. To measure societal value, the v-index framework recommends a five-point self-assessment scale, measuring the extent to which:

- the academic uses public presentations, public media, and so on to disseminate research to non-academics;
- the results (methodologies, conclusions, etc.) have been implemented by non-academics;
- the academic is involved in non-academic networks, committees, and so on and actively offers research advice;
- the academic partners (through collaboration, consulting, action research, etc.) with non-academics to address societal issues; and

- the research is funded by non-academic stakeholders from industry or government.

In Table 17.2, we present an extended framework based on five dimensions of engagement and dissemination, suggested by the v-index measure. The horizontal axis for each dimension is a continuum, where "Low" represents a baseline of pure academic contribution, and "High" represents an extremely high level of business or societal contribution (maybe exceedingly high in most cases). So, for example, for the first dimension (where research results are published), "Low" is the "academics writing for other academics" case, while "High" represents the academic as a public figure who regularly makes presentations for politicians or multinational companies.

A criticism may arise because some academic contributions are not recognized by business or wider society. This could be because some academic business research rightfully has been criticized for lacking in relevance or value to the business community (Storbacka, 2014), but it could also signal that the accepted definition of what constitutes 'societal value' is too narrow. Table 17.2 is designed to provide specific recommended guidelines on how academics can approach their research and, especially, disseminate the results of their research in multiple ways, corresponding to the five dimensions, depending on the research domain and/or particular project.

While it may be not realistic for most academics to consistently aim for the "High" target with every research project, Table 17.2 does present some specific recommendations on how one can increase societal value, as shown in the "Intermediate" suggestions (appearing between the "Low" and "High" endpoints in Table 17.2). For example, through the research conducted by academics, universities contribute to the education of future generations, which is both societally relevant and impactful. This societal value can be measured, for example, by the extent to which the research is used in the classroom for degree programs or executive education seminars, at the researcher's university or elsewhere.

Table 17.2 presents the dimensions of the v-index as an expanded framework. At least three of the dimensions can arguably be evidence of the direct value of academic research for the non-academic community (1: research results ... published at industry and public events, in articles for newspapers, etc.; 2: the extent ... research results ... have been picked up by ... non-academic stakeholders; and 4: partnerships ... with non-academics ... to solve societal issues). A similar argument could be made for the other dimensions in this index.

The framework depicted in Table 17.2 can be used as a dynamic tool for individual academics scaling up the societal value of their research through time. Different societal value approaches may develop over time, as academics

Defining, identifying, and measuring societal value   329

Table 17.2 *Societal value: the societal relevance and societal impact of an individual's research*

Dimensions of engagement and dissemination	Low	Intermediate	High
	Examples of contributions to academia	⟷	Examples of contributions to business and wider society
1. Where research results are published	I am writing only for academics, and I am not likely to be giving public presentations outside academia	• I take part in industry and exhibition events, where I might enter into dialogue with practitioners to learn and to provide research-based comments • I give presentations at public conferences attended by practitioners, write on blogs, write articles for newspapers or other media, etc. • I am invited to provide presentations for private companies, governments, and/or international bodies and will often take part in public debates	I am a key public figure, and I am often called upon for comments by media, politicians, and/or international organizations
2. The extent to which my research results (theories, methodologies, tools, and conclusions) have been picked up by 'relevant' non-academic stakeholders	My research is pure or basic academic research where results exclusively are published for other academics	• It is possible to identify potential beneficiaries of my publications, but nobody outside the academic environment is likely to have read the publications, or have used the results • There will be individuals (e.g., former students) who are familiar with my research results, but recognition is limited and results not likely to have had direct effect • It will be fairly easy to identify organizations or sectors of society actually using my tools, theories, methodologies, and conclusions	There is widespread use of my published research in individual organizations and/or on societal level in global associations, regions, global NGOs, supra-national bodies, international courses, etc.

Dimensions of engagement and dissemination	Low	Intermediate	High
	Examples of contributions to academia	⟷	Examples of contributions to business and wider society
3. Offering oral research-based advice in networks, committees, etc. outside academia	I will typically not take part in any activities in industry or societal organizations	• I am a member of informal networks outside academia having practitioners as members • I am a member of formal practitioner networks attend seminars and conferences in order to offer advice to practitioners • I take an active role in advisory boards, board of companies, assessment committees, national/international policy committees, etc.	I am a member or director on advisory boards, governance boards, assessment committees, government committees, national or international committees, etc.
4. Partnership (interaction, collaboration, consulting, action research, engaged scholarship, etc.) with non-academics like industry or government in order to solve societal challenges	My basic research results are not directly applicable to current societal challenges; my focus is on issues of theoretical interest	• I will discuss with practitioners on an ad hoc basis, for example, at conferences or other events influencing but without any sustainable commitments for action • I develop research reports useful for social actors, typically responding to requests from practitioners, societal institutions, or government agencies • I collaborate with social actors or organizations on solving practical challenges, for example, through action research	I consult to industry and/or local, regional, or government agencies, taking time off for brief assignments outside research environments for solving societal problems, developing reports for societal actors
5. Obtaining research funds from relevant external stakeholders	I obtain research funds exclusively from academic sources for basic research	• I obtain funds from academic sources for research in industry • External stakeholders have taken part in formulating my research application from academic sources • I have joint applications with external stakeholders from non-academic funding bodies	I have major research grants from industry, government agencies, professional associations, etc., or have developed and manage a research center

become more familiar with different forms of societal value. The framework thus can be used to track the progress toward greater societal value, or to suggest alternative approaches to increase societal value. The Table 17.2 framework can be used as a template for how individuals in research groups or departments can improve societal value. The template provides the research group with an overview by which overall research patterns can be identified and, based on these patterns, research groups, departments, or universities can work actively in broadening the societal value approaches. We explore this issue further in the next section.

5. THE WAY FORWARD

At this point, we tie together the ideas presented above, and provide suggestions on how to increase the societal value of academic research.

5.1 How Can Individual Researchers be Supported When Undertaking Societally Relevant Research?

Academics benefit from fostering societal value. In particular, a societally relevant research objective can strengthen the research and its usefulness, which tends to improve the academic's research profile, increase funding opportunities, and produce more positive career review assessments.

Nevertheless, academics seeking to create societal value face notable challenges, especially in early stages of their career. They do not yet have a pool of research results, reputational resources, or network contacts. Efforts to collaborate often are time-consuming and offer uncertain, long-term payoffs, particularly if they require the academic to establish a strong network first. It takes time to build relationships with essential stakeholders and gain legitimacy as a contributor to a field, two features that increase access to good research data, as well as funding. At the same time, academics need to invest effort to gain expertise before they can determine what issues are socially relevant and might provide valuable insights to relevant stakeholders. In this sense, creating societal value cannot be the sole responsibility of individual academics; research organizations and systems must create career structures to support impactful research.

In their survey of academics in the social sciences and humanities, Olmos-Peñuela et al. (2014) found that a deliberate focus on societal value relates strongly to the active engagement of research groups in various knowledge transfer modes. Academics need to consider questions of relevance and impact upfront to ensure these goals are inherently included in the research design and its definition of the societally valuable activities, communications, and measures that the research will feature.

Because both research and societal value processes are dynamic, though, the plan also must be open to continuous change and revision. Academics should remain open-minded, but also selective when considering new opportunities. We recommend basing the research planning on the answers to three questions, which we define in the following subsections.

5.2 Who Might Benefit from Societally Relevant Research, and When Should Practitioners be Involved?

To incorporate collaboration with practitioners into the research process, academics need to identify several relevant details:

- which practitioner level is appropriate for engaging in the process, according to the underlying goal, such as to ensure political support, gain resources and ideas, influence organizations, or gather research data;
- at which stage in the research process will the practitioners be integrated (mutually decided by researcher and practitioner);
- which benefits the practitioners will receive from their collaboration in the research and when they will be available, to ensure practitioners' buy-in; and
- an updated map of practitioners who might be essential to the project and in which order to engage them to acquire necessary research data at the appropriate moment.

Different levels of engagement have implications for the societal value of the research, due to their distinct links with time, scale, and finances, as well as audiences. For example, business-to-business marketing research might be especially relevant for policy in areas such as industrial policy, employment, and regional development. Alternatively, an academic might actively seek to become an industry specialist, attend industry-related conferences, cultivate networks, and build a strong reputation. In this case, the research may align with industry priorities, offering societal value for the sector. Finally, academics also might seek collaborations with other academics who specialize in a specific research method. Case studies bring issues to light for practitioners and policy makers; quantitative studies usually identify measurable outcomes and effects. Both methods are pertinent.

5.3 What Societally Valuable Activities and Measurements Should be Applied in Research?

In Table 17.1, the different activities and measurements, which all potentially may contribute to the creation of societal value, are categorized. Applying this, an academic should determine:

- what societal value approach one might apply, and how this approach will be implemented;
- the desired relevance/impact dimension and outcome such as policy changes, new practices, innovation, or business development;
- how to ensure the achievement of the desired societal value;
- whether the societal value might be diffused through partners and stakeholders; and
- the time and method for communicating societal value, both during and after the research process (e.g., articles, social media, trade magazines, briefs, and reports).

A clear engagement strategy should include considerations of the diffusion process for wider audiences, which might cite social media, trade associations, press releases, or university channels. The communication strategy also should be included in grant applications, reports, and releases that highlight best practices. Wider awareness also might be achieved through links on social media sites or short 'so what?' videos.

5.4 How Can Societal Value be Demonstrated and Documented?

Demonstrating societal value requires a plan that addresses whether the effect is likely to be shorter or longer term, whether the impact is evident, and how it might be captured, using various methods. Therefore, the research, societal value, and funding strategies all should be developed in conjunction. To identify new or additional sources of funding for business-to-business marketing-related questions, researchers can consider working across disciplines. For example, relatively substantial resources are available to support business-to-business marketing efforts to address issues in healthcare, infrastructure, networks, manufacturing, and food and agriculture. Indeed, academics may need to modify their research interests and become more customer-focused (a concept that should not be new to marketing academics!). The days of deciding what research to conduct based exclusively on researcher interests may be over.

5.5 How Can Increased Societal Value be Supported through Knowledge Exchange?

Knowledge exchange, or the enabling of two-way exchange between academics and research users to share ideas, research evidence, experiences, and skills is fundamental to our understanding of what makes excellent research partnerships (Bullock & Hughes, 2016). In many ways, knowledge exchange thus is mutually dependent on a relationship between academic and non-academic stakeholders in order to guide societally valuable research. Moreover, knowledge exchange often is associated with activities that can be planned and costed; from seminars and workshops to placements and collaborative research. However, good knowledge exchange is equally about approach, mindset, personal qualities, and researcher mission. This means that the scope of actions included in the plan for societal value should be wider rather than narrower in nature and include ways of encouraging reflection, conceptual advancement, and adjustment among the research team as well as users.

Through evaluation and commissioned work on knowledge exchange, we have found that more co-productive forms of research (that is, research undertaken with rather than on people in a collaborative, iterative process of shared learning) offer a particularly high potential for academic impact and societal value. We encourage such applications, which can include working with people in community, public policy, and business settings. The Global Supply Chain Forum research stream is an example of successful research co-production. Additionally, anecdotal feedback from academics who have participated in such co-production have reported benefits for their networks, job satisfaction, and careers, as well as financial benefits, balancing out the challenges faced in undertaking collaborative research.

Academics are encouraged to include proven and innovative methods for undertaking high-quality collaborative research, for example:

- include people from user organizations as co-investigators;
- request funding to meet the practical costs that research partners incur when they partake in projects; and
- include activities that enable innovation, reflection, and negotiation at key points during the research (e.g., learning events with research partners).

Having funded hundreds of research projects in the UK, the Connected Communities Programme documented several key considerations when forming a successful collaborative research venture (Facer & Enright, 2016):

- Research partners should explore why they want to collaborate. In the case of academic–non-academic collaboration, the reasons might include

a shared personal interest in the research topic, a need to gain access to resources, or even to strengthen the university's relationship with the outside community. The executives usually enter the collaboration with a problem they want to solve, which provides a useful starting point. The motives for collaboration, and their implications, should be well understood.
- Accountabilities may compete and should therefore be established. Research partners have accountability to internal stakeholders (the partners themselves), as well as external (personal networks, the 'public good'). The executives will have to justify their expenditures inside the company based on achieved results. Some negotiation may be required if these accountabilities are not compatible.
- The collaborative approach and its implications should be considered. Partners should answer several questions that have implications for the design and implementation of the research. These questions include the potential contribution by the partners, whether the partners will have a relationship that extends past the duration of the research, and research topic choice, governance, and accountability.
- Financial resources and time commitments need to be discussed, as well as how these resources will be administered.
- Other considerations include tangible products, new relations and networks created, contribution to knowledge, effect on the partners' institutions, and groundwork for future collaborations.

As illustration, we will return to a research study previously presented in our How-to series. A recent research stream examined managerial assumptions about ecological sustainability, recommending transformational marketing strategies for firms with respect to both the business and the natural environments (Borland, Ambrosini, Lindgreen, & Vanhamme, 2016; Borland & Lindgreen, 2013). Consider Dimension 1 of Table 17.2 (where the results are published). The research is on a topic of great interest to firms seeking to establish more sustainable business practices, and potentially also to politicians and other involved decision-makers. Societal value can be increased to the intermediate range if the authors attend practitioner conferences, events, and exhibitions. The university's communications department may be able to generate publicity and do outreach to appropriate practitioner associations to facilitate these opportunities. Another strategy is to seek publication in one of the journals that are targeted to the business community (*Harvard Business Review*, *Sloan Management Review*, *California Management Review*, *Business Horizons*, *McKinsey Quarterly*, or *Journal of World Business*).

As a second example, Beverland, Lindgreen, and Vink (2008) studied how brands project authenticity through advertising message ambiguity. In addition to seeking out practitioner-oriented publications, the authors can apply some of the recommendations for Dimension 2, namely identify non-academics from business or government who might benefit from this knowledge, former students and other contacts who may be familiar with the authors' work and who can recommend it within their work organizations, or possibly identify some companies who are actually using the results and leverage that positive implementation.

As a third example, consider Maon, Lindgreen, and Vanhamme's (2009) study of disaster relief operations, and its effect on commercial supply chain and logistics management operations. According to Dimension 4 (partnership with non-academics to solve societal challenges), the authors can develop research reports showing the managerial implications of their theoretical model, which would be useful to societal institutions or government agencies, or may collaborate with social actors in future projects using an action-research approach.

Finally, Vallaster, Maon, Lindgreen, and Vanhamme (2020) applied a theory-generative approach to develop a conceptual framework of the micro-foundations of the dynamic capabilities of for-profit hybrids. To develop the framework, the authors engaged in a qualitative, multiple-case study over a 15-month period. After presentation of the framework to the for-profit hybrids, the research was written up as an academic journal article.

Similar examples could be constructed for the other dimensions in Table 17.2.

In all of the above examples, we are recommending activities that would increase the contribution to business or society to "Intermediate" levels. As noted earlier, the "High" level might be unachievable or unrealistic in most cases, but it is not impossible. Academics with a stellar track record, at the top of their game in terms of research funding and industry connections, and possibly part of a well-funded institute within their universities, may well attain "High" status (be viewed as a public figure, frequently seen in media as a topic expert, or invited to serve on or manage national or international committees; their work is used as a basis for national guidelines). This will not always happen, but that is not important. Keep in mind that the goal is to increase societal value without sacrificing academic rigor, and that moving from "Low" to "Intermediate" is respectable progress in the right direction.

5.6 How Can Business Schools Support Research with Societal Value?

Business schools must provide support and infrastructure that encourage researchers to get interested in and conduct societally valuable research, in varying forms and at different levels. The business school overall, as well as its individual departments and research groups, need to develop societal value strategies to define optimal approaches, important stakeholders, strategies for dissemination, measures, and documentation methods. In particular, the school should take responsibility to identify explicitly which local, regional, and national constituencies are critical.

In addition to establishing a general research norm that societal value is important (e.g., by posting small case examples on school webpages), the business school should offer incentives to encourage academics who aim to deliver findings with relevance to society. Ideally, research funding from the institution should be contingent on evidence of societal value; the research objective should not exclusively be a narrow, incremental contribution to established theory (Storbacka, 2014). Further, the promotion system should acknowledge societally valuable activities or even require them for career advancement. The criteria for bonuses also should include this standard. A creative approach might offer department-shared professorships. The University of Aalborg and Bang & Olufsen Electronics maintain a shared professorship in which the professor split his time between the two institutions to help transfer knowledge from one to the other. Encouraged collaborations also should focus on various departments within the school or outside it (e.g., STEM departments). Finally, a school could invest seed money in strategic societal challenges, then apply for external funding to support them further.

In terms of infrastructure and support, business schools should realize that it may feel transgressive for academics, with no prior experience in designing socially relevant research or extensive collaborations, to start engaging with practitioners. To help such academics build this capability, the school could provide training to early-stage academics in engagement, co-creation, project management, interpersonal and dialogue skills, and so forth. Furthermore, the school could establish programs in which academics devote some of their time to working in public or private organizations to gain relevant experience. Such efforts also encourage closer dialogue with businesses, public organizations, and industries, enabling involved partners to find common ground and closer relationships. Research engagement programs could connect younger with more experienced academics, likely at the research group or team level. Olmos-Peñuela et al. (2014) demonstrate the critical role of research group leaders in ensuring the group's engagement in knowledge transfer activities.

For communicating the results, business schools have a role as well. Some UK universities grant academics additional time to document the effects of their projects if these projects are used as REF impact cases. Another option is to launch business review magazines, positioned as an outlet for sharing relevant research by academics within the school. Furthermore, the school could develop overview reports of research trends of interest and list potential collaborators. A research support unit should have resources to help academics incorporate relevance and societal value considerations in their grant applications, including budgeting for expenses required to perform societal value-related activities.

Considering these incentive and support schemes, business schools should not limit their quality measures to journal rankings or citations counts; they must find a way to acknowledge academics who achieve additional broad societal value with their research. Doing so requires that each school clearly defines what it means when it calls for societally valuable research by its academics. These definitions also must integrate stakeholders' perspectives (i.e., the targets of these socially relevant efforts). Although the business school should set the directions and priorities for societal value in these various ways, the school also must take care not to restrict academic freedom. For example, a business school might encourage research on sustainability but must avoid micro-managing academics' activities.

Business school deans should articulate a vision and work to remove the barriers to faculty entrepreneurship. Faculty should be encouraged to look for research funding from industry. The benefits would be twofold: research that addresses real business problems and a faculty who are able to support executive education. It is reasonable to expect faculty members' research to be of sufficient practical value that businesses or organizations outside of the business school would view it as worthy of financial support (Lambert & Enz, 2015).

Rather than being rewarded solely for the number of 'A' journal articles written, faculty members also should be rewarded for the effect of their research on practice and the extent to which the research can be integrated into degree program curricula and executive education programs. Faculty who by the nature of their research do not interact with practitioners should be encouraged to engage in consulting activity in order to help them focus on solving business problems (Raju, quoted in Brown et al., 2005). The metrics used to judge the contributions of faculty members should be different, as they progress through career stages. For example, senior faculty might develop and/or serve as directors of research centers, write books, or obtain large research grants. The specific metrics chosen to evaluate faculty members should be aligned with the institution's mission (Lambert & Enz, 2015).

5.7 How Can Academic Journals Support Research with Societal Value?

An increased demand to undertake societally valuable research with high relevance and high impact puts pressure on academic journals and their editors. Practitioners are not likely to turn to academic journals and seek out research studies on management strategy or practice when making business decisions (Rynes, Bartunek, & Daft, 2001). Often, practitioners experience that collaborations turn out as unsuitable outputs that do not meet the needs of their businesses (Pertuzé, Calder, Greitzer, & Lucas, 2010; Marzo-Navarro, Pedraja-Iglesias, & Rivera-Torres, 2009). From the outset of a business–university collaboration project, most businesses expect the collaboration to show feasibility and practical usefulness of the businesses' innovative ideas. Characteristically, however, universities work at a slower pace, and businesses may not be able to influence the collaboration process (Lazzarotti, Manzini, Nosella, & Pellegrini, 2016). Businesses, therefore, sometimes find it almost painful to work with universities that focus on long-term academic endeavors (Darabi & Clark, 2012).

Most journals require authors to offer evidence that the presented research is relevant and important. A strong managerial implications section may be required by the target journal to increase relevance, visibility, and impact to the practitioner community, and it is valued by business schools who increasingly prioritize societal value of academic research. The managerial implications section should not be an afterthought, and unsupported phrases such as "may make an impact" or "might be useful to managers in the future," which cast doubt and uncertainty about the importance or usefulness of the findings, should be avoided. The writing of managerially oriented interpretations of one's research helps to expand one's readership outside the academic community, since practitioners probably will not read the academic journals.

Journal editors have a role here. They can prioritize research that is cross-functional, process oriented, and problem driven. Research that influences management practice should be favored over research that only make incremental advances in theory. According to Kerin (quoted in Brown et al., 2005, p. 13), "research, regardless of topic, should explore multifunctional, business-level issues; identify cause-and-effect relationships; and, focus on metrics that matter to CEOs and corporate boards." Business executives can be added to the editorial review board to ensure that an article potentially influences management practice. Including an epilogue to each article in which an executive or an editor speaks to the merit and quality of the research could be an excellent addition. If the research is conducted with a company, an estimate of the resulting company benefits should be included (Lambert & Enz, 2015). In fact, this is already a requirement at *INFORMS Journal on Applied Analytics* (formerly *Interfaces*). Articles submitted for review must be accompanied by a signed letter from a company representative, verifying that the research was used, and that the company benefited as a result. The letter is published along with the article. The benefit of providing support for the value of the research in financial terms will be twofold: first, it is a measure of the value of the research beyond the journal in which it is published and citations by other faculty members; second, the participating company will benefit because management behavior is influenced by the numbers (Enz & Lambert, 2015). In some cases, non-financial performance measures may be appropriate as well (e.g., improved performance of hospitals or disaster relief).

At *Industrial Marketing Management*, we have decided to serve our managerial constituency by fostering academic–practitioner collaboration and by encouraging research projects that design specific solutions to managerial challenges. With its new Academic-Practitioner section, *Industrial Marketing Management* invites manuscript submissions co-authored by academics and practitioners. This type of manuscript addresses current topics in the area of industrial and business-to-business markets. The objective of Academic-Practitioner research is to develop managerially relevant and actionable insights using rigorous scientific methods. Journals such as *Harvard Business Review* and similar managerially oriented journals are other outlets for authors to submit articles, which focus on managerial takeaways from their academic research such as improved strategic decision-making or competitiveness.

Suitable manuscripts should report how specific marketing actions, processes, or systems were designed, implemented, and evaluated with regards to achieving specific outcomes. Academic-Practitioner manuscripts thus build pragmatic knowledge developed by engaging with real-life problems, challenges, or opportunities in the realm of industrial and business-to-business marketing. The journal will evaluate manuscripts submitted to the section based on pragmatic validity and practical relevance.

6. CONCLUSIONS

We advocate that high-quality research is at the foundation of all undertakings of a business school. Quality research is, in a sense, the 'license to operate' as an academic business institution. Governments and institutions fund academic institutions, and their investments in academic research provide non-academic payoffs when the findings are valuable to the practitioner community, or more indirectly, when the academic's store of knowledge is applied to support managerial decision-making. In addition, teaching is an impactful outcome of the investment, as graduates become business leaders and entrepreneurs, as well as educators of future generations of business students.

While some of the above outcomes are measured using conventional metrics (number of articles or citations, h-index, or monetary value of grants received), some of the other outcomes, perhaps seen as more indirectly related to business school funding (collaboration or consulting partnerships), are not as clearly measured yet, but they should not be overlooked in assessing the results of the funding. Traditional metrics do not provide a totally accurate picture of the value of academic research. For example, the societal value of basic or pure research, particularly in non-business areas, may not be recognized immediately, and would remain underestimated using conventional metrics. The commercial value of pure scientific research in quantum mechanics or advanced mathematical theory may not be known for many years. As an ongoing example, neuromarketing research is an emerging branch of consumer behavior with its roots in neuroscience research in medical schools.

Other measures probably also underestimate the societal value derived from the governmental appropriation to fund universities. Pure 'outside' consulting to industry is generally considered a (possibly lucrative) side job rather than an outcome of business school funding. But what about academics who provide their insights and expertise in collaborating with a new business start-up, or support entrepreneurial student teams developing a real-life business plan as part of a course requirement? This activity might have a large effect on the local economy or community. In other cases, there may be broad measures that do not correlate clearly with governmental appropriations. For example, one measure of business school teaching is the number of graduates from bachelors' or masters' degrees, or the number of graduates who stay local and thereby contribute to the local economy, but better measures might more convincingly argue for the societal value of the business school (number of local jobs created by entrepreneurs, indirect economic impact of industry growth within a community, etc.). In short, the need for better measurement of some of the outcomes in Table 17.1 is an issue that remains to be addressed and further discussed, so that the true societal value of the governmental investment in academic research and teaching can be assessed accurately.

By adopting metrics such as we have presented (cf. Table 17.2), business school administration makes it clear to its faculty that aspects other than pure academic research (that is, societal value) are considered and valued when assessing research output. In fact, the 'relevance versus elegance' dichotomy is arguably a false one: it assumes that in order for academics to produce societally valuable research, they must sacrifice academic quality. Academic administration has a vested interest in motivating and rewarding faculty to attain the highest quality publishing standards; faculty will not want to spend valuable research time on projects with low publication potential. We hope that our discussion here (and summarized in Table 17.2) provides guidelines for how academics can approach their research so that they can ramp up the effect on business and on wider society.

6.1   *Industrial Marketing Management*

Academics in the business-to-business marketing discipline contribute to public value agendas, historically through publications in journals such as *Industrial Marketing Management*. However, mounting pressure to establish and demonstrate societal value coming from governments, research funds, business schools, and even academics themselves, implies an even stronger motivation for such efforts. We have sought to inspire academics with examples and suggestions for how to work to attain relevance, by defining their vision and approach to ensure public value. Specifically, academics should address three broad considerations when planning their future research to ensure their thoughtful, deliberate focus on societally relevant research and its impacts:

- Who benefits from the research, and when should practitioners be involved?
- Which societally valuable approaches and activities should be applied across research phases?
- How can the effect of the societal value be demonstrated?

This chapter, however, does not define what counts as sufficient societal value or how far academics should go to ensure their findings are useful and influential. These questions need to be addressed by each academic, research group, department, or business school; societal value is intrinsically domain specific and diverse, so it depends on the domain being investigated. There are no easy ways to measure relevance and impact, which together constitute societal value; no one-size-fits-all assessment could account for all scientific disciplines or capture all the long-term impacts across society. Accordingly, each academic or research group must decide whether to adopt existing approaches, activities, and measurements to achieve societal relevance and societal impact, or else to supplement them with new, innovative approaches, methods, and activities. Such efforts will be helpful in that we recognize the ongoing need for new, innovative approaches, methods, and activities to advance the still nascent theme of societal value.

We call for academics to explore how closer links between those who produce scientific knowledge and those who can use it might redefine traditional views on the relationship of science with society. The capacity to do so depends on the expertise and resources available for such research. However, for most academics, intellectual curiosity is a primary motive, suggesting that they are unlikely to settle for existing solutions. Business schools must encourage such endeavors, providing support and infrastructure that can help researchers achieve societal value in varying forms and at different levels, through closer dialogue with businesses, public organizations, and industries. Academic journals can also support this valuable dialogue, for example, the introduction of the Academic-Practitioner section at *Industrial Marketing Management*, designed to serve its managerial constituency and encourage academic–practitioner collaboration.

REFERENCES

Abrahamsen, M.H., Henneberg, S.C., Huemer, L., & Naudé, P. (2016). Network picturing: An action research study of strategizing in business networks. *Industrial Marketing Management*, 59, 107–119.

Alvesson, M. (2017). *Return to Meaning: A Social Science with Something to Say*. Oxford: Oxford University Press.

Amo, C. (2007). Conceptualizing research impact: The case of education research. *The Canadian Journal of Program Evaluation*, 22(1), 75–98.

Anderson, L., Ellwood, P., & Coleman, C. (2017). The impactful academic: Relational management education as an intervention for impact. *British Journal of Management*, 28(1), 14–28.

Arnaboldi, M. (2013). Consultant-researchers in public sector transformation: An evolving role. *Financial Accountability & Management*, 29(2), 140–160.

Bandola-Gill, J. (2019). Between relevance and excellence? Research impact agenda and the production of policy knowledge. *Science and Public Policy*, 46(6), 895–905.

Bennis, W.G. & O'Toole, J. (2005). How business schools lost their way. *Harvard Business Review*, 83(5), 96–104.

Beverland, M.B., Lindgreen, A., & Vink, M.W. (2008). Projecting authenticity through advertising: Consumer judgment of advertisers' claims. *Journal of Advertising*, 37(1), 5–15.

Boon, W. & Edler, J. (2018). Demand, challenges, and innovation: Making sense of new trends in innovation policy. *Science and Public Policy*, 45(4), 435–447.

Borland, H., Ambrosini, V., Lindgreen, A., & Vanhamme, J. (2016). Building theory at the intersection of ecological sustainability and strategic management. *Journal of Business Ethics*, 135(2), 293–307.

Borland, H. & Lindgreen, A. (2013). Sustainability, epistemology, ecocentric business and marketing strategy: Ideology, reality, and vision. *Journal of Business Ethics*, 117(1), 173–187.

Bornmann, L. (2013). What is societal impact of research and how can it be assessed? A literature survey. *Journal of the American Society of Information Science and Technology*, 64(2), 217–233.

Bornmann, L. & Marx, W. (2014). How should the societal impact of research be generated and measured? A proposal for a simple and practicable approach to allow interdisciplinary comparisons. *Scientometrics*, 98, 211–219.

Brown, J.S. & Duguid, P. (1998). Organizing knowledge. *California Management Review*, 40(3), 90–111.

Brown, S.W., Webster Jr., F.E., Steenkamp, J.E.M., Wilkie, W.L., Sheth, J.N., Sisodia, R.S., Kerin, R.A., MacInnis, D.J., McAlister, L., Raju, J.S., Bauerly, R.J., Johnson, D.T., Singh, M., & Staelin, R. (2005). Marketing renaissance: Opportunities and imperatives for improving marketing thought, practice, and infrastructure. *Journal of Marketing*, 69(4), 1–25.

Bullock, A. & Hughes, R. (2016). *Knowledge Exchange and the Social Sciences: A Report to ESRC from the Centre for Business Research*. Cambridge: University of Cambridge.

Butler, N., Delaney, H., & Spoelstra, S. (2015). Problematizing 'relevance' in the business school: The case of leadership studies. *British Journal of Management*, 26(4), 731–744.

Buur, J. (2018). Tangible business interviews. In Freytag, P.V. and Young, L. (Eds.), *Collaborative Research Design: Working with Business for Meaningful Findings* (pp. 175–195). New York: Springer.

Cooper, M.C., Lambert, D.M., & Pagh, J.D. (1997). Supply chain management: More than a new name for logistics. *The International Journal of Logistics Management*, 8(1), 1–14.

Crosier, K. (2004). How effectively do marketing journals transfer useful learning from scholars to practitioners? *Marketing Intelligence and Planning*, 2(5), 540–556.

Darabi, F. & Clark, M. (2012). Developing business school/SMEs collaboration: The role of trust. *International Journal of Entrepreneurial Behaviour & Research*, 18(4), 477–493.

Davison, R.M., & Bjørn-Andersen, N. (2019). Do we care about the societal impact of our research? The tyranny of the H-index and new value-oriented research directions. *Information Systems Journal*, 29(5), 989–993.

Di Benedetto, C.A., Lindgreen, A., Storgaard, M., & Clarke, A.H. (2019). Editorial: How to collaborate really well with practitioners. *Industrial Marketing Management*, 82, 1–8.

Enz, M.G. & Lambert, D.M. (2015). Measuring the financial benefits of cross-functional integration influences management's behavior. *Journal of Business Logistics*, 36(1), 25–48.

ESRC (2020). *What is Impact?* https://www.esrc.ukri.org/research/impact-toolkit/what-is-impact/.

Evers, W., Marroun, S., & Young, L. (2017). A pluralistic, longitudinal method: Using participatory workshops, interviews and lexicographic analysis to investigate relational evolution. *Industrial Marketing Management*, 67, 182–193.

Facer, K. & Enright, B. (2016). *Creating Living Knowledge*. Bristol: University of Bristol and AHRC Connected Communities Programme.

Galletta, D., Bjørn-Andersen, N., Markus, M.L., Straub, D., Leidner, D.E., McLean, E.R., & Wetherbe, J. (2019). If practice makes perfect, where do we stand? *Communications of the AIS*, 45(3). doi.org/10.17705/1CAIS.04503.

GECES (2014). *Proposed Approaches to Social Impact Measurement in European Commission Legislation and in Practice Relating to: EuSEFs and the EaSI*. Brussels: Publications Office of the European Union.

Gibbons, G., Limoges, C., Nowotny, H., Schwartzman, S., Scott, P., & Trow, M. (1994). *The New Production of Knowledge: The Dynamics of Science and Research in Contemporary Societies*. Thousand Oaks, CA: Sage Publications.

Glick, W.H., Tsui, A., & Davis, G.F. (2018). The moral dilemma of business research. *BizEd*, May/June, 32–37.

Grimpe, C. & Fier, H. (2010). Informal university technology transfer: A comparison between the United States and Germany. *Journal of Technology Transfer*, 35(6), 637–650.

Gustavsen, B. (2003). Action research and the problem of the single case. *Concepts & Transformation*, 8(1), 93–99.

Hatchuel, A. (2001). The two pillars of new management research. *British Journal of Management*, 12(Special Issue), 33–39.

Haug, A. (2018). The use of experiments in business development. In Freytag, P.V. and Young, L. (Eds.), *Collaborative Research Design: Working with Business for Meaningful Findings* (pp. 223–250). New York: Springer.

Hill, S. (2016). Assessing (for) impact: Future assessment of the societal impact of research. *Palgrave Communications*, 2, 1–7.

Hughes, T., Bence, D., Grisoni, L., O'Regan, N., & Wornham, D. (2011). Scholarship that matters: Academic-practitioner engagement in business and management. *Academy of Management Learning & Education*, 10(1), 40–57.

Kongsted, H.C., Tartari, V., Cannito, D., Norn, M.T., & Wohler, J. (2017). University researchers' engagement with industry, the public sector and society: Results from a 2017 survey of university researchers in Denmark. Copenhagen Business School (CBS) and the Think Tank DEA.

Lambert, D.M. (2019). Rediscovering relevance. *International Journal of Logistics Management*, 30(2), 382–394.

Lambert, D.M. & Cooper, M.C. (2000). Issues in supply chain management. *Industrial Marketing Management*, 29(1), 65–83.

Lambert, D.M. & Enz, M.G. (2015). We must find the courage to change. *Journal of Business Logistics*, 36(1), 9–17.

Lambert, D.M. & Enz, M.G. (2017). Issues in supply chain management: Progress and potential. *Industrial Marketing Management*, 62, 1–16.

Larsen, H. & Friis, P. (2018). Improvising in research: Drawing in theatre practices. In Freytag, P.V. & Young, L. (Eds.), *Collaborative Research Design: Working with Business for Meaningful Findings* (pp. 341–376). New York: Springer.

Lauronen, J.-P. (2020). The dilemmas and uncertainties in assessing the societal impact of research. *Science and Public Policy*. doi.org/10.1093/scipol/scz059.

Laursen, L.N. & Andersen, P.H. (2016). Supplier involvement in NPD: A quasi-experiment at Unilever. *Industrial Marketing Management*, 58, 162–171.

Lazzarotti, V., Manzini, R., Nosella, A., & Pellegrini, L. (2016). Collaborations with scientific partners: The mediating role of the social context in fostering innovation performance. *Creativity and Innovation Management*, 25(1), 142–156.

Levin, B. (2004). Making research matter more. *Educational Policy Analysis Archives*, 12(56), 1–20.

Lindgreen, A., Di Benedetto, C.A., Brodie, R.J., & van der Borgh, M. (2020a). Editorial: How to undertake great cross-disciplinary research. *Industrial Marketing Management*, 90, 1–5.

Lindgreen, A., Di Benedetto, C.A., Brodie, R.J., & van der Borgh, M. (2020b). Editorial: How to get great research cited. *Industrial Marketing Management*, 89, 1–7.

Lindgreen, A., Di Benedetto, C.A., Verdich, C., Vanhamme, J., Venkatraman, V., Pattinson, S., Clarke, A.H., & Khan, Z. (2019). How to write really good research funding applications. *Industrial Marketing Management*, 77, 232–239.

Maon, F., Lindgreen, A., & Vanhamme, J. (2009). Developing supply chains in disaster relief operations through cross-sector socially oriented collaborations: A theoretical model. *Supply Chain Management: An International Journal*, 14(2), 149–164.

Marroun, S. & Young, L. (2018). Multi-method systematic observation: Theory and practice. In Freytag, P.V. & Young, L. (Eds.), *Collaborative Research Design: Working with Business for Meaningful Findings* (pp. 195–221). New York: Springer.

Martí, I. (2018). Transformational business models, grand challenges, and social impact. *Journal of Business Ethics*, 152(4), 965–976.

Martin, B.R. (2011). The Research Excellence Framework and the 'impact agenda': Are we creating a Frankenstein monster? *Research Evaluation*, 20(3), 247–254.

Marzo-Navarro, M., Pedraja-Iglesias, M., & Rivera-Torres, P. (2009). The marketing approach in relationship between universities and firms. *Journal of Relationship Marketing*, 8(2), 127–147.

Medford, D. (1971). Introduction to industrial marketing management. *Industrial Marketing Management*, 1, 2.

Möller, K. & Parvinen, P. (2015). Editorial: An impact-oriented implementation approach in business marketing research. *Industrial Marketing Management*, 45, 3–11.

Morton, S. (2015). Progressing research impact assessment: A 'contributions' approach. *Research Evaluation*, 24(4), 405–419.

Narasimhan, R. (2018). The fallacy of impact without relevance: Reclaiming relevance and rigor. *European Business Review*, 30(2), 157–168.

Nenonen, S., Brodie, R.J., Storbacka, K., & Peters, L.D. (2017). Theorizing with managers: Increasing academic knowledge as well as practical relevance. *European Journal of Marketing*, 51(7/8), 1130–1152.

Newig, J., Jahn, S., Lang, D.J., Kahle, J., & Bergmann, M. (2019). Linking modes of research to their scientific and societal outcomes: Evidence from 81 sustainability-oriented research projects. *Environmental Science and Policy*, 101, 147–155.

Nissen, H., Evald, M.R., & Clarke, A.H. (2014). Knowledge sharing in heterogeneous teams through collaboration and cooperation: Exemplified through public–private-innovation partnerships. *Industrial Marketing Management*, 43(3), 473–482.

Olmos-Peñuela, J., Castro-Martinez, E., & Cukierman, P.D. (2014). Knowledge transfer activities in social sciences and humanities: Explaining the interactions of research groups with non-academic agents. *Research Policy*, 43(4), 696–706.

Ozanne, J.L., Davis, B., Murray, J.B., Grier, S., Benmecheddal, A., Downey, H., Ekpo, A.E., Garnier, M., Hietanen, J., Le Gall-Ely, M., Seregina, A., Thomas, K.D., & Veer, E. (2017). Assessing the societal impact of research: The relational engagement approach. *Journal of Public Policy & Marketing*, 36(1), 1–14.

Pertuzé, J.A., Calder, E.S., Greitzer, E.M., & Lucas, W.A. (2010). Best practices for industry–university collaboration. *MIT Sloan Management Review*, 51(4), 83–90.

Pettigrew, A.M. (2011). Scholarship with impact. *British Journal of Management*, 22(3), 347–354.

Pfeffer, J. (2007). A modest proposal: How we might change the process and product of managerial research, *Academy of Management Journal*, 50(6), 1334–1345.

Phillips, P., Moutinho, L., & Godinho, P. (2018). Developing and testing a method to measure academic societal impact. *Higher Education Quarterly*, 72(2), 121–140.

Purcell, W.M., Henriksen, H., & Spengler, J.D. (2019). Universities as the engine of transformational sustainability toward delivering the Sustainable Development Goals: "Living labs" for sustainability. *International Journal of Sustainability in Higher Education*, 20(8), 1343–1357.

Rau, H., Goggins, G., & Fahy, F. (2018). From invisibility to impact: Recognising the scientific and societal relevance of interdisciplinary sustainability research. *Research Policy*, 47(1), 266–276.

Reale, E., Avramov, D., Canhial, K., Donovan, C., Flecha, R., Holm, P., Larkin, C., Lepori, B., Mosoni-Fried, J., Oliver, E., Primeri, E., Puigvert, L., Scharnhorst, A., Schubert, A., Soler, M., Soòs, S., Sordé, T., Travis, C., & Van Horik, R. (2018). A review of literature on evaluating the scientific, social and political impact of social sciences and humanities research. *Research Evaluation*, 27(4), 298–308.

Research England (2020). *REF Impact*. https://re.ukri.org/research/ref-impact/.

Ruiz, C.D. & Holmlund, M. (2017). Actionable marketing knowledge: A close reading of representation, knowledge and action in market research. *Industrial Marketing Management*, 66, 172–180.

Rynes, S.L., Bartunek, J.M., & Daft, R.L. (2001). Across the great divide: Knowledge creation and transfer between practitioners and academics. *Academy of Management Journal*, 44(2), 340–355.

Salter, A., Salandra, R., & Walker, R. (2017). Exploring preferences for impact versus publications among UK business and management academics. *Research Policy*, 46(10), 1769–1782.

Samuel, G.N. & Derrick, G.E. (2015). Societal impact evaluation: Exploring evaluator perceptions of the characterization of impact under the REF2014. *Research Evaluation*, 24(3), 229–241.

Shapiro, D.L., Kirkman, B.L., & Courtney, H.G. (2007). Perceived causes and solutions of the translation problem in management research. *Academy of Management Journal*, 50(2), 249–266.

Sivertsen, G. & Meijer, I. (2020). Normal versus extraordinary societal impact: How to understand, evaluate, and improve research activities in their relations to society? *Research Evaluation*, 29(1), 66–70.

Spaapen, J. & Van Drooge, L. (2011). Introducing 'productive interactions' in social impact assessment. *Research Evaluation*, 20(3), 211–218.

Stentoft, J. & Freytag, P.V. (2018). Guest editorial: Journal rankings and the notion of 'relevance' within business research. *European Business Review*, 30(2), 94–100.

Storbacka, K. (2014). Does publish or perish lead to stylish rubbish? *Journal of Business Market Management*, 7(1), 289–295.

Storvang, P., Mortensen, B., & Clarke, A.H. (2018). Using workshops in business research: A framework to diagnose, plan, facilitate and analyze workshops. In Freytag, P.V. and Young, L. (Eds.), *Collaborative Research Design: Working with Business for Meaningful Findings* (pp. 155–174). New York: Springer.

Tranfield, D., Denyer, D., & Smart, P. (2003). Towards a methodology for developing evidence-informed management knowledge by means of systematic review. *British Journal of Management*, 14(3), 207–222.

Trencher, G., Nagao, M., Chen, C., Ichiki, K., Sadayoshi, K., Kinai, M., Kamitani, M., Nakamura, S., Yamauchi, A., & Yarime, M. (2017). Implementing sustainability co-creation between universities and society: A typology-based understanding. *Sustainability*, 9(4), 594–621.

Vallaster, C., Maon, F., Lindgreen, A., & Vanhamme, J. (2020). Serving multiple masters: The role of micro-foundations of dynamic capabilities in addressing tensions in for-profit hybrid organizations. *Organization Studies*. doi.org/10.1177/0170840619856034.

Van den Akker, W., Spaapen, J., & Maes, K. (2017). Productive interactions: Societal impact of academic research in the knowledge society. Position Paper. Leuven: LERU.

Van den Berg, W.E., Verbeke, W., Bagozzi, R.P., Worm, L., de Jong, A., & Nijssen, E. (2014). Salespersons as internal knowledge brokers and new products selling: Discovering the link to genetic makeup. *Journal of Product Innovation Management*, 31(4), 695–709.

Van de Ven, A.H. & Johnson, P.E. (2006). Knowledge for theory and practice. *Academy of Management Review*, 31(4), 802–821.

Wolf, B., Lindenthal, T., Szerencsits, M.J., Holbrook, B., & Heß, J. (2013). Evaluating research beyond scientific impact: How to include criteria for productive interactions and impact on practice and society. *GAIA – Ecological Perspectives on Science and Society*, 22(2), 104–114.

PART 6

Offering our final thoughts

18. Offering our final thoughts on *How to Fast-Track Your Academic Career*
Adam Lindgreen and C. Anthony Di Benedetto

Throughout this book, we have presented a wide range of responsibilities of the business academic: generating ideas, working with Ph.D. students, obtaining research funding, getting published, crossing boundaries and forming alliances with other functional areas and with industry, and making valid societal contributions—all while balancing personal and professional lives. We have attempted to present insights that will be helpful to early- and mid-career academics in order to fast-track their career. While we have specifically taken the perspective of the business-to-business marketing academic, we believe that many of the insights will be valuable to academics in any business school department.

We conclude with a few final thoughts on several of the key topics we have addressed in previous chapters.

ACHIEVING WORK–LIFE BALANCE

Business schools invest heavily in researching, recruiting, developing, and retaining academics. Newly hired academics should have clear direction of expectations and a realistic sense of support that will be offered by the hiring department, so they can feel fully vested in academic citizenship within their department and business school. Through the delegation of responsibility, decision power, and competence development, academics should experience an enhanced sense of ownership, and be engaged in delivering the school's vision and mission. Importantly, the performance measurement system should be clear and also flexible enough to allow for different competence profiles depending on seniority, research interests, and similar considerations. Having these clear guidelines in place will help academics understand how to achieve the requirements of a top scholar at their institution and ultimately allow them to achieve balance between the tasks of teaching, research, and service, and between work and personal life.

DEVELOPING COURAGEOUS IDEAS

Devising original, courageous ideas is difficult, but is critical in developing impactful research. One way to address this difficulty is to consider the three actions of the observe–bridge–challenge model presented in an earlier chapter. First, to be relevant, concepts and theories must be grounded in compelling, interesting, and real-world observations. The importance of a notion is proportional to the vividness and relevance of the phenomena it can explain. Accordingly, original, courageous research ideas might best be gathered from real life. Second, bridging joins two or more disciplines and can shed new light on one's own discipline (see later). This strategy can reveal original, courageous ideas, as well as produce new theory construction if theories are redesigned to fit the new, combined discipline. Third, one can push the boundaries by challenging the assumptions and theories on which prior studies rely. Thus, original, courageous ideas demand that academics step back from the obvious theoretical layer and identify questionable core assumptions. Additionally, it is possible to execute each of these strategies independently or in combination.

DEVELOPING STRONG RESEARCH GROUPS

To produce a sustainable research stream, it is essential to establish strong research groups embedded in a wider ecosystem. A core of talented academics must continue to embrace research opportunities, provide leadership, and facilitate an ecosystem consisting of national and international collaborators. The research group must produce research that consolidates the knowledge in an area. This will provide foundations for further innovative research. Further keep in mind that research groups will not be static. With the research stream developing, a research group and its wider ecosystem must embrace distributed leadership that will lead empowerment to propagate new initiatives and to keep the momentum in the research stream. Eventually, when research ambitions are achieved, the research group might embrace broader challenges in the field or, more drastically, reinvent itself by identifying a new important research problem and thus initiating a new research stream.

PURSUING 'GOOD' RESEARCH FUNDING

To pursue 'good' research funding (i.e., funding not given for consultancy), the business school or department must develop a strategy that identifies research funding opportunities and considers how to navigate the funding review process, and that supports and rewards research funding activity. At the departmental level, one could organize seminars on how to write research funding applications, or identify prestigious research foundations. A research funding committee should discuss and review research funding applications. Allocation of work hours and top-ups of individuals' research budget should reflect research funding activity and success, which also must be entry criteria for promotion consideration. At the business school level, initiatives that encourage cross-disciplinary strategic alliances with other institutions (see next section) can be implemented; aggregated, cross-disciplinary project initiatives are often preferred by government funding institutions.

UNDERTAKING CROSS-DISCIPLINARY RESEARCH

As an applied social science, business-to-business research is inherently cross-disciplinary in nature. This is because the general theories that provide insight into business relationships, systems, and markets have disciplinary foundations in many different disciplines. Importantly, cross-disciplinary research should not be the end in and of itself! Forcing some vaguely defined cross-disciplinary agenda on researchers can lead to wasted effort or, at best, projects that would be difficult to fund or publish. A better approach would be to start with the research problem, identify to which problem class it belongs, and if the research problem is big or complicated enough to warrant cross-disciplinary work, and questions arise that require input across multiple disciplines, then the contacts are made, and the joint research is initiated.

COLLABORATING WITH BUSINESS AND THE WIDER SOCIETY

To develop fruitful collaborations with business and the wider society that result in publishable research, academic researchers should engage in long-term relationships with practitioners. This perspective is necessary because researchers may realize publication opportunities only after a longer period of engagement. It is essential that both parties know the particularities of university–business research. Moreover, researchers must be prepared to open a project for new research problems and paths. Equally important is that researchers become familiar with the practitioners' knowledge and develop an appreciation for it.

TRANSLATING RESEARCH INTO TEACHING

Academic researchers who can bring their expertise into the classroom will create substantial value for the student. At the department level, it may be a good idea to encourage and reward academics who successfully translate research into great teaching. As we have noted earlier, one can apply the principles of service dominant (S-D) logic, with academics playing the role of the 'supplier' and the students the role of the 'customer'. According to S-D logic, the students are co-creators of value, with the academics offering value propositions. Academics who can bridge the gap between research and practice, and make their own research relevant to the student, impart the newest knowledge to their students, who themselves are current or future business decision-makers.

PUBLISHING IN HIGHLY RANKED JOURNALS

In addition to publishing relevant books, anthologies, textbooks, and in practitioner-oriented magazines, academics should publish in highly ranked journals, for example AJG 3/4/4* journals (increasingly becoming standard across business schools), not only in the academic's specific field, but also outside this field. FT 50-ranked journals would be of particular interest. A number of initiatives should accompany this strategy. First, academics should develop personal research plans to be discussed with their department head and/or research group leader. Second, academics should collaborate with others, thereby receiving mentoring. Third, globally or nationally known academics can be invited to present their own research and meet one-to-one with academics. Rewards such as work hour or research budget allocation should reflect publications in highly ranked journals, which also must be entry criteria for promotion consideration.

ACHIEVING SOCIETAL RELEVANCE

Increasingly, national research funding agencies are insisting on research projects, which provide societal value, and will deliver value to the academic community, as well as to the society at large. Universities worldwide are responding to this challenge. The important implication of this new 'contract' between universities and society is that universities still must produce excellent research (that is, articles in highly ranked academic journals), while simultaneously pursuing activities with societal value (that is, solving wicked problems or grand challenges).

Appendix 1: Example of charters for research groups: IMP and CMP

C. Anthony Di Benedetto and Adam Lindgreen

INTRODUCTION

In Chapter 4, we presented the Industrial Marketing and Purchasing (IMP) Group and the Contemporary Marketing Practices (CMP) Group as examples of research groups whose purpose is to support and stimulate high-impact research that is visible in the research community, provides value to practitioners, and influences society. Here, we take a closer look at the governance structure of both groups to identify how these goals can be achieved effectively.

As noted in the chapter, a business school can choose a governance structure that supports research and education, which again has implications for recruitment, personal development, and retention of faculty. Similarly, a research group is comprised of like-minded academics with a clear vision and research mission, which will impact choices for individual research topics, as well as teaching objectives. Agreement should be reached on numerous initiatives, including publication strategy, funding strategy, impact on university education (focus on research-based or teaching-based education, for example), services to be provided to the academic community, and interaction with society as a whole in terms of delivery of societal value.

INDUSTRIAL MARKETING AND PURCHASING GROUP (IMP)[1]

The IMP Group is a community of scholars from many research backgrounds (marketing, purchasing, innovation, management, and technology) with an interest in inter-organizational interactions and business exchange relationships. The group has three underlying features, which drive its activities: a dynamic approach to economic exchange, empirical research on inter-organizational interactions, and an international network of researchers with shared interests.

The research focus of IMP is on the interaction between business actors in business relationships through time. These relationships include economic, as well as social, informational, and technological exchange processes that impact the business actors through time. This focus ensures that IMP research recognizes the interconnectedness and direct and indirect impacts among business relationships, and considers inter-organizational interactions as organizational innovation processes. As a result, business actors are interdependent on the capabilities and activities of many other actors; individual decision-makers are dependent on other decision-makers in terms of how to develop and implement strategic practices. Due to this focus on business interactions and networks, IMP researchers often rely on specific analytical tools that are useful in these contexts: the Interaction Model, the Activity-Resource-Actor Model, and the Four Resources (4R) Model. This research approach is in sharp contrast to the 4Ps model and the analysis of the discrete purchasing decision, which were prevalent in the mid-1970s during the time of the founding of IMP.

Further, IMP research is grounded in empirical studies of real companies and their interactions. As a result, a characteristic of IMP research is that it is conducted within the context of specific business relationships, taking into account the interdependencies that exist in that specific relationship. The environment within which these business networks exist also is changing rapidly due to increased globalization and digitalization, calling for IMP researchers to study how business interactions diffuse globally, and how tensions that arise (between global and local interests, between economic and environmental goals, and so on) are managed. Due to these and related issues, new and advanced business models may need to be developed and employed in IMP-related research.

Finally, an important objective of the IMP Group is dissemination of research findings. There are annual IMP Conferences, starting with the first in 1984 in Manchester, and, more recently, the organization has sponsored journal seminars, doctoral consortia, and a biannual IMP Asia Conference. Thus, the IMP Group is invested in both the creation, and the dissemination, of knowledge, as it pertains to the long-term interrelationships between partners involved in business exchange.

THE CONTEMPORARY MARKETING PRACTICES GROUP (CMP)[2]

The CMP Group has a more limited agenda by comparison, but has been nonetheless influential in the relationship marketing literature. The stimulus for this group's development was Coviello's Ph.D. research on the internationalization of entrepreneurial technology-based ventures and the marketing approaches used by these ventures. Coviello found that managers were comfortable using a combination of traditional transactional (4Ps) practices and relationship marketing practices, which was at odds with the then-current academic debate about whether the transactional or relationship paradigm was the correct one. This academic–practitioner gap led to further study, which questioned how marketing is conceptualized and taught in the classroom, and how this compares to marketing practices in the real world. The CMP Group was thus founded, with the objective of profiling contemporary marketing practices, and to examine the relevance of relationship marketing practice in context. The core group of CMP researchers is international, but much smaller than IMP.

CMP Group research builds on the idea that the debate over transactional versus relational marketing paradigms overly simplifies reality. To challenge the emerging paradigms required theoretical and empirical research, employing multiple research perspectives and maintaining a balance between theoretical argument and managerial practice. The CMP Group also wanted to investigate the possibility of other marketing practices in addition to the accepted transactional and relational marketing dichotomies. This focus on a narrow but important academic issue, with far-reaching theoretical implications, required the researchers to conduct an extensive review of the literature that underpins the relational approach and distinguishes it from the transactional approach. This review comprised six literature streams that all contributed to a view of marketing as an integrated activity emphasizing building and maintaining relationships through time (services marketing, inter-organizational exchange relationships, channels marketing, network research, strategic management/value chain research, and information technology research). Empirical research based on this theoretical scheme was widely published in *Journal of Marketing* and elsewhere (e.g., Coviello & Brodie, 2001; Coviello, Brodie, Danaher, & Johnston, 2002), and remains highly cited to this day. For example, one research stream developed an instrument to measure companies' use of four different purchasing practices, which companies then mix into four different configurations of practices ranging from transactional over interpersonal dyadic and interpersonal network to integrative relational configurations (Lindgreen, Vanhamme, van Raaij, & Johnston, 2013).

The corporate governance of the CMP research program can be stated in terms of six defining characteristics:

Creative tension between theory and practice: By emphasizing research-led teaching with managers, and using managerial practice as a unifying driver of research activity, CMP has been able to achieve a link between academic arguments and business relevance.

Pluralism in philosophy and method: CMP endorses a multi-theory approach, which is based on a variety of research streams, disciplines, and theories, and employs a multi-method approach combining qualitative and quantitative empirical research.

International emphasis: CMP has grown from its origins in New Zealand to include participating members from around the world, and empirical studies are similarly international in scope.

Lack of formal structure: The informal, loose structure of the CMP Group is suited to research flexibility and opportunism. Generally, the group functions using a project-based approach in which project teams with a common objective are formed.

Importance of research-led teaching: CMP Group members are largely academics with much experience teaching executive programs, which facilitates active discussion with managers. As a result, there is emphasis on both teaching-informed research and research-led teaching. Living case studies and action research are keys to this process.

Role of postgraduate research: Many CMP Group participants have completed their Ph.D. studies, and CMP research is often part of Ph.D. colloquia and research seminars. Postgraduate research activity has helped to maintain the conceptual rigor of CMP Group research.

NOTES

1. This section is largely based on the "About" page from the IMP website, https://www.impgroup.org/about.php.
2. This section is largely based on Brodie, Coviello, and Winklhofer (2008).

REFERENCES

Brodie, R.J., Coviello, N.E., & Winklhofer, H. (2008). Contemporary marketing practices research program: A review of the first decade. *Journal of Business & Industrial Marketing*, 23(2), 84–94.

Coviello, N.E. & Brodie, R.J. (2001). Contemporary marketing practices of consumer and business-to-business firms: How different are they? *Journal of Business & Industrial Marketing*, 16(5), 382–400.

Coviello, N.E., Brodie, R.J., Danaher, P.J., & Johnston, W.J. (2002). How firms relate to their markets: An empirical examination of contemporary marketing practice. *Journal of Marketing*, 66(8), 33–46.

Lindgreen, A., Vanhamme, J., van Raaij, E.M., & Johnston, W.J. (2013). Go configure: The mix of purchasing practices to choose for your supply base. *California Management Review*, 55(2), 72–96.

Appendix 2: Revising and resubmitting: Go configure: the mix of purchasing practices to choose for your supply base

Adam Lindgreen, Joëlle Vanhamme, Erik van Raaij, and Wesley J. Johnston

INTRODUCTION

Some 25 years ago, a purchasing and supply management revolution took place in North America and Western Europe. With it came a change in supplier relationships. No longer were these relationships only adversarial and arm's-length, many of those became instead much closer and more cooperative, and often embedded in a wider network of suppliers and their suppliers, customers and their customers, and other stakeholders.[1] The role of purchasing and supply management, as a business function, is to manage the organization's external resources and acquire inputs by the best means possible.[2] Traditionally, purchasing has revolved around single transactions or short-term contracts, with much of the emphasis being on low price. But manufacturing organizations typically spend 50–75 percent of their revenues on purchasing materials and services, and by the late 1990s, a growing need to improve quality and reduce costs in the face of international competition had led organizations to realize that purchasing and supply management offered enormous potential for more strategic management of costs, risks, and value.[3]

North America and Western Europe thus looked for inspiration to countries like Japan, where cooperative supplier relationships had been common practice since the 1960s.[4] Organizations such as Chrysler, Sony, Toyota, and Xerox reduced the number of suppliers for their components and raw materials, and their remaining supplier relationships became more cooperative and relational.[5] In transactional exchanges the buying organization and its supplier treat each other as adversaries in a zero-sum game, with no expectation of exchange beyond the current contract. By contrast, the new relational exchanges push the buying organization and its supplier to work together to increase mutual benefits, make dedicated investments, and develop expectations beyond the contract terms.[6] This shift toward more relational purchasing practices coincided with the emergence of a more strategic role for purchasing, which required purchasing managers to rely more on integrative partnerships with a limited number of key suppliers.[7]

Existing studies have assumed purchasing practices[8] are either transactional or relational.[9] Purchasing today, however, involves both transactional and relational practices, often through a mix of arm's-length transactional relationships and close cooperative relationships with suppliers.[10] Relational exchanges have attracted significant attention from academia in areas such as transaction cost economics, sociological approaches, and supply chain management,[11] and research has highlighted the advantages of cooperative relationships with suppliers. These can include, for example, reduced costs, improved product quality, and reduced lead times.[12] Yet cooperative relationships remain costly to manage and increase the buyer's dependence on the supplier.[13] Such relationships may therefore not be applicable in all situations. Because buyers engage in both transactional and relational purchasing, it is vital to understand more about how and why they decide which approach to take. That is, how do buyers choose, or mix, different purchasing practices, and how do different purchasing practices affect organizations' performance?

Evaluating how a specific choice of supply relationships relates to an organization's performance is only possible if the organization can measure the type and strength of its purchasing relationships and then judge those relationships against specific performance indicators. Managers thus need a toolbox.

For marketing practices, for example, a toolbox has led to a better awareness of "how firms relate to their [customer] markets in a manner that integrates both traditional and more modern views of marketing, and incorporates an understanding of both the antecedents and consequences of different practices."[14] This also includes an understanding of the role played by marketing. The marketing toolbox presents managers with a robust and well-tested way of evaluating what they are doing, using indicators based on the exchange and managerial aspects of marketing practices.[15]

Building a toolbox for purchasing requires purchasing to be categorized into transactional and relational practices. This chapter puts forward a new framework and a novel measurement instrument. What this proposed framework does in particular is:

- to identify fundamental aspects that distinguish different types of purchasing practices, especially those related to the exchange and management of purchasing rather than those related to differences in the purchasing function itself;
- to assess what different hybrid forms, or mixes, of transactional and relational purchasing are being used; and

- to relate the way in which purchasing is practiced to performance outcomes.

The framework addresses a range of important questions. What relative emphasis do organizations place on transactional and relational aspects of purchasing? Does relational purchasing occur across all types of organizations? Do organizations practice either transactional or relational purchasing, or is there a hybrid form that is more appropriate? Do purchasing practices depend on the materials and services being supplied? Are higher performance outcomes correlated with particular (mixes of) purchasing practices?

The proposed framework characterizes the key aspects of different purchasing practices, and has been used to examine the actual purchasing practices of 202 US organizations and what influence those practices have on performance outcomes. The framework captures the exchange and managerial aspects of purchasing, as they relate to four types of purchasing practices.

THE PURCHASING PRACTICES FRAMEWORK

Design of the Purchasing Practices Framework

One important distinction is between a supply management approach that is primarily transactional and one that emphasizes network coordination, including the supply chain.[16] Thus *transaction purchasing* refers to the use of aggressive sourcing (continuously searching for new suppliers) to obtain goods and services on the best terms possible,[17] whereas *network purchasing* involves positioning the organization within a wider organizational system or network.[18] Two additional practices are possible: *electronic purchasing*[19] and *interactive purchasing*.[20] With electronic purchasing, organizations use the internet and other one-to-one and one-to-many technologies to create and mediate data exchanges with suppliers; and interactive purchasing implies personal interactions between employees and individual suppliers.

It is important to note here that electronic purchasing as an approach to supplier management is not the same as electronic procurement. Electronic procurement refers to the collection of tools—usually based on internet technology—that support the purchasing function. Examples might include electronic auctions, marketplaces, or ordering systems.[21] But electronic auctions, for example, cannot serve as relationship management tools; they imply aggressive sourcing, or transaction purchasing.[22] In contrast, electronic purchasing as defined here uses the internet and other information technologies as a means of facilitating relationships with suppliers,[23] for example by using a supplier portal.

As reflected in the framework, all four purchasing practices are significantly different to one another in how the buying organization manages its exchange relationships with suppliers and interacts with them. For example, both the frequency of communication and the nature of the interdependency between an organization and its suppliers differ between transaction purchasing and the three relational purchasing practices (electronic purchasing, interactive purchasing, and network purchasing). Likewise there are also differences among those relational purchasing practices themselves.[24]

The proposed measurement instrument aims to investigate purchasing practices across a wide range of organizations and industry sectors. The measures used must therefore be general enough to have relevance across that range, yet the positions should also be specific enough to capture different practices of purchasing. Eight formative indicators are used to characterize transactional and relational practices, as summarized briefly in Table A2.1 and defined in more detail below; each purchasing practice can be determined by a combination of these formative indicators. Table A2.1 also includes a general indicator that captures the essence of each purchasing practice (and which is used when testing the external validity of the measuring instrument, see later in Box A2.1).

Purpose of exchange. In relational purchasing, buying organizations develop closer and more collaborative relationships with a smaller number of suppliers.[25] In each of the three forms of relational purchasing practices the aims are slightly different. In electronic purchasing it is about developing relationships that are facilitated by electronic data interchange systems;[26] for interactive purchasing, it is to develop interpersonal relationships with suppliers;[27] and in network purchasing, it is to develop relationships with all relevant parties in the wider organizational network.[28] Transaction purchasing is different again: here the aim is to obtain competitively priced components and raw materials and achieve cost savings through competitive bidding among many suppliers.[29]

Nature of communication. Although organizations with transaction purchasing interact with many suppliers and tend to use one-fits-all communication,[30] organizations that use relational practices reduce the size of their supply base and communicate more—at different levels, and in more complex relationships—with the suppliers that remain.[31] This can include technology-enabled communications in electronic purchasing,[32] personal interactions in interactive purchasing,[33] and senior managers interacting across organizations in network purchasing.[34]

Type of contact. Whereas transaction purchasing uses short-term, arm's-length relationships, relational purchasing involves longer-term, collaborative relationships. These are often at a strategic level, with a wider range of business partners.[35] Thus, transaction purchasing is characterized by impersonal contact, whereas relational purchasing is characterized by technology-enabled, interactive contact in electronic purchasing, interpersonal

Appendix 2   361

Table A2.1   Indicators pertaining to purchasing practices

Aspects	Transactional perspective	Relational perspective		
	Transaction purchasing	Electronic purchasing	Interactive purchasing	Network purchasing
Purpose of exchange: When dealing with our direct suppliers, our purpose is to:	achieve cost savings or other 'financial' measure(s) of performance (monetary transactions)	create information-generating dialogue with many identified suppliers	build a long-term relationship with specific supplier(s)	form relationships with a number of organizations in our supply market(s) or wider purchasing system
Nature of communication: Our communication with direct suppliers can be characterized as:	our organization using undifferentiated communications with all suppliers	our organization using technology to communicate with and possibly among many individual suppliers	individuals at various levels in our organization personally interacting with individual suppliers	senior managers networking with other managers from a variety of organizations in our supply market(s) or wider purchasing system
Type of contact: Our organization's contact with our direct suppliers is:	arm's-length, impersonal with no individualized or personal contact	interactive via technology such as the Internet	interpersonal (e.g. involving one-to-one interaction between people)	across firms in the broader network (from impersonal to interpersonal contact)
Duration of exchange: The type of contact with our direct suppliers is characterized as:	transactions that are discrete or one-off (i.e. not ongoing)	technology-based interactivity that is ongoing and real-time	interpersonal interaction that is ongoing	contact with people in our organization and wider purchasing system that is ongoing

Aspects	Transactional perspective	Relational perspective			
	Transaction purchasing	Electronic purchasing	Interactive purchasing	Network purchasing
Formality of exchange: When people from our organization meet with our direct suppliers, it is:	mainly at a formal business level	mainly at a formal level, yet customized and / or personalized via interactive technologies	at both a formal business level and informal social level on a one-to-one basis	at both a formal business level and informal social level in a wider organizational system / network
Managerial intent: Our purchasing exchanges are intended to:	continuously search for new suppliers to find the best deal (i.e., low prices)	create two-way, technology-enabled data exchanges with our suppliers	develop cooperative relationships with our suppliers	coordinate activities between ourselves, suppliers, and other parties in our wider purchasing and supply system (e.g., second-tier suppliers, key customers, service providers, and other organizations with which we interact through our purchasing activities)
Managerial focus: Our purchasing strategy is focused on issues related to:	the purchase item and its price	managing IT-enabled relationships with many individual suppliers	one-to-one relationships with suppliers, or individuals in supplier organizations we deal with	the network of relationships between individuals and organizations in our wider supply system
Managerial investment: Our purchasing resources (i.e. people, time, and money) are invested in:	specifying products, negotiations, ordering, and expediting activities	operational assets (IT, website, logistics) and functional systems integration (e.g., purchasing with IT)	establishing and building personal relationships with individual suppliers	developing our organization's network relationships within our supply market(s) or wider purchasing system

Appendix 2

Aspects	Transactional perspective	Relational perspective		
	Transaction purchasing	Electronic purchasing	Interactive purchasing	Network purchasing
General indicator: Overall, our organization's general approach to our direct suppliers (of product-related items) involves:	using aggressive sourcing (continuously search for new suppliers) to obtain purchase items at the most favorable conditions	using the Internet and other interactive technologies to create and mediate data exchanges between our organization and our suppliers	developing personal interactions between employees and individual suppliers	positioning organization within a wider organizational system or network

Notes: An additional aspect relating to the managerial level initially appeared in the framework ("In our organization, purchasing activities are carried out by: operational and tactical purchasers [transaction purchasing]; cross-functional buying teams, that is, purchasing specialists with technology specialists and possibly senior managers (electronic purchasing); many employees, that is, across functions and levels [interactive purchasing]; or the managing director or chief executive officer [network purchasing]"). This aspect was later discarded because (1) there was little support for such aspect in the literature and from discussions with practitioners and (2) it had poor external validity. As a complement to the support found in the literature, all practices were checked with both practitioners and academic experts.

contact in interactive purchasing, and inter-organizational contact across organizations in a wider network in network purchasing.[36]

Duration of exchange. Transaction purchasing has a focus on a single transaction or contract,[37] whereas relational purchasing focuses on an ongoing interaction, whether that is technology-based in electronic purchasing, interpersonal in interactive purchasing, or across a wider organizational network of purchasing relationships in network purchasing.[38]

Formality of exchange. Organizations with an arm's-length approach to purchasing limit their exchanges with suppliers to formal modes. The relational approaches, on the other hand, combine formal and informal modes, such that organizations become embedded in social interactions and networks.[39]

Managerial intent. Relational purchasing attempts to create technology-enabled exchanges with suppliers in electronic purchasing, build interpersonal relationships with specific suppliers in interactive purchasing, and coordinate activities in the purchasing network in network purchasing.[40] This is very different to transaction purchasing, where organizations continuously search for new suppliers in order to find the best deal.[41]

Managerial focus. Whereas transaction purchasing is preoccupied with purchase items and prices,[42] managing IT-enabled relationships with suppliers represents the heart of electronic purchasing, including automated data input and electronic data interchange between buyers and suppliers.[43] The relationships are fewer in number but more individualized in both interactive purchasing and network purchasing, and the latter includes relationships with partners from the organization's wider purchasing and supply network.[44]

Managerial investment. An organization that is pursuing relational purchasing invests significant and specialized resources to attract, develop, and retain strategic supplier relationships.[45] The investments and resources involved include information and communication technologies in electronic purchasing, personal relationships in interactive purchasing, and network relationships in network purchasing.[46] In contrast, to obtain lower prices from suppliers, an organization that uses transaction purchasing invests resources in specifying components and raw materials, as well as in negotiating, ordering, and expedition activities.[47]

The proposed purchasing practices framework enables an organization to score high, for example, on both transaction purchasing and electronic purchasing and low on the other two practices, or perhaps to score low on transaction purchasing and high on all three forms of relational purchasing practices. That is, the four practices of purchasing are not mutually exclusive. Frameworks that describe the organizational management of supplier relationships only as either type A or type B may fail to recognize all existing types of supplier relationships. For example, some organizations continuously search for new suppliers to find the best deal, whereas others believe that they can add value to their supplier relationships by combining that type of practice with relational practices, for example technologies that allow the organization to exchange data with suppliers and develop one-to-one relationships.

Surveying Organizations' Purchasing Practices

To get a better understanding of organizations' purchasing practices, this study used a nationwide survey of purchasing managers in US organizations. The survey was based on the proposed purchasing practices framework. From its databases, the Institute of Supply Management (ISM) provided contact details for 3,322 randomly selected members representing manufacturing, wholesaling and retailing, and service organizations (standard industrial classification codes: 20–39, 52–59, and 70–89). All respondents were contacted by regular mail; the packets contained a copy of the questionnaire (including the purchasing practices framework), a cover letter, a letter from ISM endorsing the study, and a pre-paid return envelope. Respondents could either return their completed questionnaire by mail or fill out an online version. This procedure produced 202 valid returned questionnaires.[48] It should be noted that the respondent sampling includes only ISM members, who are fairly representative of US organizations but might be relatively well-educated purchasing professionals,[49] and that for each organization only one individual was asked to complete and return the questionnaire.

The questionnaire consisted of six parts.[50] In the first part, respondents provided details of their organization, the degree to which technology was used in the organization and the part played by information technology. These questions recognize that technology is an important driver of change in the purchasing domain. All measures in this part of the questionnaire were taken from previous studies.[51]

In the second part of the questionnaire, respondents were asked to distinguish between suppliers of direct inputs (or "primary suppliers") and suppliers of indirect inputs (or "secondary suppliers"). *Direct inputs* are those materials and services that appear in the buying organization's final products or services such as wood for furniture; *indirect* inputs are those which do not, for example, office stationery.[52] Direct inputs are also known as revenue-generating, primary, or bill-of-materials inputs. Respondents also described the kinds of materials and services supplied by these direct and indirect suppliers, which helped them distinguish between the two types when answering questions about their organizations' purchasing practices. By making this distinction between relationships with suppliers of direct versus indirect inputs (not purchasing practices at the individual supplier level), this study is able to look at a broad range of organizations. It also ensures minimal respondent subjective bias. That is, one can distinguish relatively objectively between suppliers of direct and indirect input, which is not the case when asked to concentrate on "key" or "strategic" suppliers.

In the third and fourth parts of the questionnaire, respondents reported on their organizations' purchasing practices with direct and indirect suppliers. For suppliers of direct materials and services, 32 indicators reflected the eight exchange and managerial aspects of the purchasing practices (i.e., the framework), and 4 global indicators represented general descriptions of each practice (Table A2.1). For each of these 36 indicators, respondents indicated the extent to which it was currently practiced in their organization.[53] For suppliers of indirect materials and services, they were asked only about how the organization generally dealt with the suppliers, and only the 4 global indicators were used so as to ensure the questionnaire did not become too long.

The fifth part involved looking at three areas. Firstly, the organization's purchasing performance relative to its expectations about supplier lead time, on-time delivery, delivery reliability, and quality.[54] Secondly, its marketing performance relative to expectations with regard to customer attraction and retention, customer satisfaction, sales growth, and market share. Thirdly, its financial performance in terms of its expectations with regard to profitability.[55]

Finally, to judge whether the respondents provided an appropriate match for the study, the questionnaire solicited their personal data, including their position, how long they have held their current position, their tenure with the organization, and their formal purchasing qualifications or training. It also asked for gender and age information, consistent with previous studies of marketing practices and purchasing.[56]

Respondents from manufacturing, wholesaling and retailing, and services were well represented in the sample. Almost two-thirds of respondents came from large organizations (more than 500 employees). Sixty-five percent of the organizations were established more than 30 years ago, and most relied on a domestic market for their sales.

Because the vast majority of respondents hold positions in purchasing and at middle and upper levels in their organization, they probably have experience, knowledge of management policies, and access to operational and quality performance data.[57] With regard to marketing and financial performance outcomes, if respondents felt that they did not know the answer, the questionnaire encouraged them to seek this information from the appropriate departments. The average age of respondents was 47 years (minimum 21; maximum 66). The gender ratio was 57 percent men to 40 percent women; 3 percent left this question unanswered.[58] The data quality assessment and the psychometric properties (including a validity assessment) of the purchasing practices measurement instrument involved several checks, as reported in the "Methodology" section at the end of the chapter.

For each of the four purchasing practices (transaction purchasing, electronic purchasing, interactive purchasing, and network purchasing) the organization was scored against eight indicators (purpose of exchange, managerial intent, nature of communication, type of contact, duration of exchange relationship, formality of exchange, managerial focus, and managerial investment). The total score on all eight indicators for each practice was then converted into an index.[59] For each organization, four composite measures thus indicate the extent to which that organization practices transaction purchasing, electronic purchasing, interactive purchasing, and network purchasing. However, because these practices are not mutually exclusive,[60] each organization has its own particular mix of scores on the four purchasing practices.

Major Configurations of Purchasing Practices

Purchasing literature suggests that organizations traditionally practiced transactional purchasing but that relational practices have become more commonplace.[61] Not all organizations have made the transition to relational purchasing, however.[62] In reality, transactional and relational purchasing are not mutually exclusive and can be mixed in hybrid configurations. To reveal what kinds of configuration might be particularly common, this study incorporated a cluster analysis—described in more detail in Box A2.1—of the index scores to determine whether it is possible to identify meaningful groups of organizations in terms of their purchasing practices.

BOX A2.1 CLUSTER ANALYSIS

Before doing a cluster analysis, one needs to confirm that different variables do not suffer from substantial collinearity,[63] which would act as a weighting factor and bias the analysis (i.e., collinear variables are implicitly weighted more heavily[64]). The next step entails row centering the data to identify groups according to the relative importance of one construct (purchasing practice) to another and determine whether clusters with similar patterns can be identified. The hierarchical and nonhierarchical clustering methods are used sequentially to increase the validity of the solution.[65] Using Ward's hierarchical method and the recommended squared Euclidean distance, the most meaningful number of clusters was established and allowed a check of potential outliers.[66] Ward's method offers robustness, the ability to maximize within-cluster homogeneity and between-cluster heterogeneity, and the capability to recover known cluster structures.

No outliers emerged, so to determine the most appropriate number of clusters,[67] several steps were taken. The likely range of clusters was computed,[68] a dendogram was used to find any relatively dense branches,[69] and incremental changes in the agglomeration coefficient were analyzed.[70] Finally, managerial interpretability of the solution was sought.[71]

The analysis reveals four distinct clusters of organizations that differ markedly in their emphasis on the different purchasing practices (transaction purchasing, electronic purchasing, interactive purchasing, and network purchasing) and are easily interpretable and meaningful. A nonhierarchical K-means clustering method (with the cluster centers provided by the hierarchical results as initial seed points) fine-tunes these results, in a way less susceptible to outliers, the type of distance measure, or the inclusion of irrelevant and inappropriate variables in the analysis.[72] The results from the K-means clustering (i.e., the final results) are very similar to the previous results and are presented graphically in Figure A2.1.

One cluster (N = 38) consists of organizations that score high on the transaction purchasing index and low on electronic purchasing, interactive purchasing, and network purchasing (see Figure A2.1). This mix is labeled as a *transactional configuration*. Another cluster (N = 59) consists of organizations that score low on the transaction purchasing index and high on the electronic, interactive, and network purchasing indexes. This mix is labeled as an *integrative relational configuration*.

Two additional clusters are identified. Organizations in these two clusters achieve medium scores on the transaction purchasing index. The first configuration (N = 52)—labeled as *interpersonal dyadic configuration*—shows a high score on the interactive purchasing index but lower scores on the electronic purchasing and network purchasing indices. The second of these configurations (N = 53)—labeled as *interpersonal network configuration*—has a high score on both interactive purchasing and network purchasing but a low score on the electronic purchasing index.

The transactional configuration and the integrative relational configuration could, more or less, be seen as opposites of each other. With their medium scores on the transaction purchasing index, the interpersonal dyadic and the interpersonal network configurations could be regarded as intermediate ones.

Notably, relationships mediated by the Internet and other interactive technologies (i.e., electronic purchasing) reach high levels only when combined with the other two relational purchasing practices (i.e., interactive purchasing and network purchasing). In none of the clusters does network purchasing exceed interactive purchasing. Overall, in many organizations purchasing practices are pluralistic, with organizations mixing two or more different purchasing practices.

Appendix 2

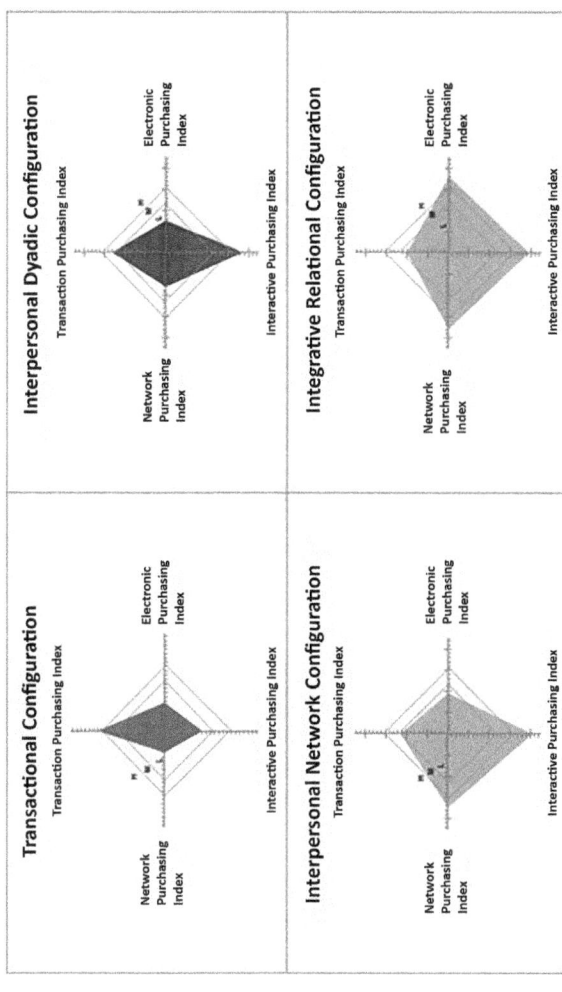

Notes: L: low ($< .63$); M: medium ([.63;.71]); H: high ($\geq .72$). Mean scores for all four clusters differ significantly (transactional (T) vs. interpersonal dyadic (ID): MANOVA $F(4, 85) = 35.962$, $p < .001$; T vs. interpersonal network (IN): MANOVA $F(4, 86) = 61.239$, $p < .001$; T vs. integrative relational (IR): MANOVA $F(4, 92) = 54.343$, $p < .001$; ID vs. IN: MANOVA $F(4, 100) = 38.820$, $p < .001$; ID vs. IR: MANOVA $F(4, 106) = 54.481$, $p < .001$; IN vs. IR: MANOVA $F(4, 107) = 37.678$, $p < .001$). Detailed technical information regarding how thresholds were defined and descriptive statistics are available from the first author.

Figure A2.1 Four purchasing configurations

So Which Mix of Purchasing Practices Should You Choose for Your Supply Base?

The purchasing practices framework has revealed different configurations that vary in their relational intensity. Several positive effects of relational purchasing practices appear in prior literature, often relating to the enhanced performance of suppliers and buyers. With organizations spending up to 75 percent of their revenues on purchasing, the performance of the buying organization depends increasingly on supplier performance.[73] A relational practice has positive effects on supplier quality, delivery reliability, lead time, and on-time delivery, as well as on the delivery- and quality-related performance of the buying organization itself. It also has effects on buyer performance in terms of cost and flexibility.[74] Improvements in cost-, quality-, and delivery-related performance as a result of close buyer–supplier relations also should enable a buying organization to serve its customers better with higher-value products and improved customer service.[75] Where an organization can deliver distinctive value to customers that should translate into better market performance.[76] Ultimately, such advantages in market and cost performance should lead, in turn, to higher financial performance by the buying organization.[77]

The findings of our study reveal that those organizations that have adopted an integrative relational configuration for their purchasing practices show the best performance. Figure A2.2 shows the comparison of the three clusters of organizations with transactional, interpersonal dyadic, and interpersonal network configurations with the cluster of organizations with an integrative relational configuration. This comparison highlights that the latter cluster performs better than any other cluster on the dimension of supplier quality. In terms of delivery reliability, organizations with an integrative relational configuration perform significantly better than those with a transactional configuration, but there is no significant difference between organizations with an integrative relational configuration and those with intermediate configurations. The integrative relational configuration outperforms the transactional configuration on supplier on-time delivery, but the performance differences with the two intermediate configurations are not significant. The four configurations are broadly comparable in terms of supplier lead time. With respect to marketing performance outcomes, the integrative relational configuration performs better than all other configurations for all marketing performance outcomes: customer attraction and retention, customer satisfaction, sales growth, and market share. This finding also applies to the financial performance outcome: profitability.[78]

Thus, organizations using all three forms of relational purchasing practices (i.e., integrative relational configuration) perform better on at least seven but up to nine out of 10 performance outcomes compared with organizations that

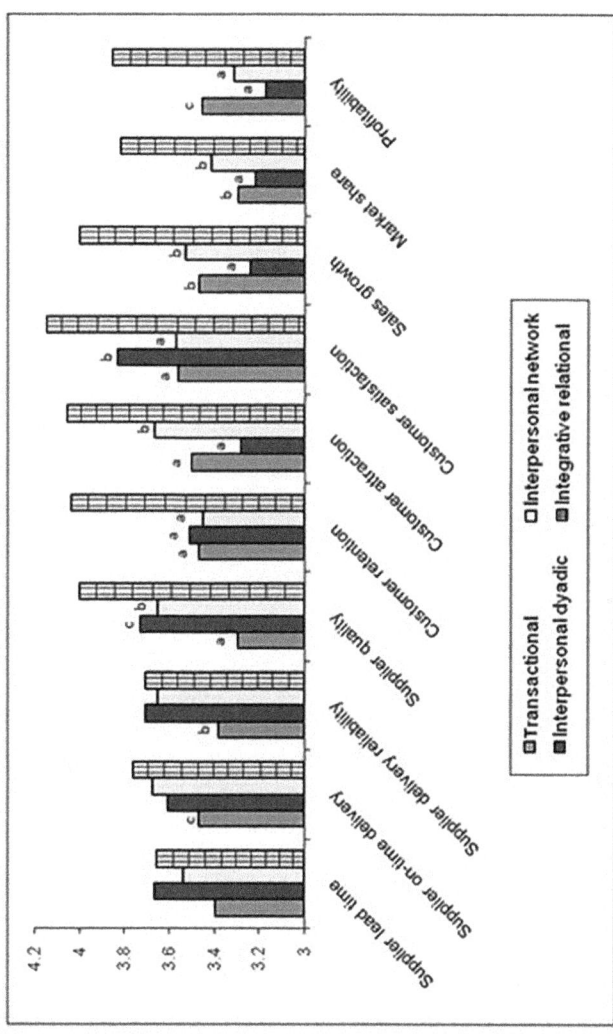

Notes: The labels a, b, and c at the tops of the bars indicate a lower performance for the marked configuration, compared with the integrative relational configuration (represented by the bar with squares on the right side of each set of bars); a: the difference is significant at $p_{\text{1-tail}} < .01$; b the difference is significant at $p_{\text{1-tail}} < .05$; and c the difference is significant at $p_{\text{1-tail}} < .10$. See note 76 for the specific statistical tests used.

Figure A2.2   Differences in performance outcomes between purchasing configurations

favor practices that are less relational (i.e., interpersonal dyadic, interpersonal network, and transactional configurations). This finding is true for all marketing and financial outcomes and up to three purchasing performance outcomes (Figure A2.2).

No significant differences were found across clusters in terms of the organizational demographics of cluster members (i.e., industry, organization size, age, and business activities). Some differences appeared in terms of the level of technology intensity and the role of technology in the organization. Organizations with an integrative relational configuration tend to be more technology-intensive than those with other configurations, and the role of information technology in the former organizations appears greater than in the latter organizations. For organizations with an integrative relational configuration, information technology acts not just to support current business activities but rather to redefine or drive such activities.[79]

Different Purchasing Practices in Relation to Direct and Indirect Suppliers

The survey results indicate that—across all clusters—organizations practice more relational purchasing with direct suppliers, and more transactional purchasing with indirect suppliers. When dealing with direct suppliers, organizations make significantly more use of interactive purchasing and network purchasing than they do with indirect suppliers. In contrast, with indirect suppliers they use significantly more transaction purchasing than they do with direct suppliers. There was, however, no marked difference with respect to electronic purchasing.[80]

DISCUSSION

The data indicate four configurations of purchasing practices, each characterized by a distinct mix of transaction purchasing, electronic purchasing, interactive purchasing, and network purchasing. Organizations with a transactional configuration (19 percent of the sample) and those with an integrative relational configuration (29 percent) generally represent the most extreme configurations. In between, intermediate configurations of practices are based on interpersonal relationships, either dyadic (26 percent) or network (26 percent). The emphasis on transaction purchasing, electronic purchasing, interactive purchasing, and network purchasing varies across configurations. Whereas interactive purchasing (based on interpersonal relationships) is pervasive and used to a great extent in all but the transactional configuration, transaction purchasing levels are generally medium to high, and used in all but the integrative relational configuration.

Thus, buying organizations manage portfolios of supplier relationships, some of which are more transactional in nature and others more relational. Transactional purchasing is not disappearing entirely, even as buying organizations move to more relational practices. Focusing solely on just two possible purchasing practices—pure transactional practice versus pure relational practice—is thus too simple a view of reality.[81] It also obscures performance outcome differences that reflect an organization's emphasis on particular mixes of purchasing practices. The integrative relational configuration outperforms all other configurations on the marketing and financial performance indicators, as well as on supplier quality. It also outperforms the transactional configuration on delivery reliability and supplier on-time delivery.

Purchasing practices relate to the type of supplier, such that more relational practices characterize relationships with direct suppliers, whereas more transactional practices are more common in dealing with indirect suppliers.[82] Quality or delivery problems with direct suppliers could result in disruptions to the buying organization's primary processes, so organizations often strive for close, cooperative relationships with critical direct suppliers. In contrast, the purchase of indirect materials and services receives far less management attention; the purchasing department may not even be involved in these purchases. Indirect supply purchases more often involve arm's-length transactions. Because indirect suppliers also lack critical relationships with the buying organization, the organizations may perceive less risk in letting price play a more dominant role when selecting this type of supplier. That is, they practice more transaction purchasing. Discussions with experienced purchasing professionals and academics confirm that when organizations purchase from secondary suppliers of indirect inputs, cost considerations are the most important factors. For primary suppliers of direct inputs, other factors, including supplier lead time, on-time delivery, delivery reliability, and quality, acquire greater importance.

Which organization selects which configuration cannot be explained by its size, age, or business activities. This finding contradicts what contingency theory suggests—namely, that the best approach to purchasing (relational or transactional) depends on the organizational context. Organizations are likely to make strategic choices regarding whether to focus on transactional or relational purchasing practices. However, respondents in the integrative relational configuration report that the intensity of information technology in their organizations is high and that they use information technology to redefine their business processes. These responses coincide with the finding that the main difference between the integrative relational configuration and the other configurations is that those in that first group make extensive use of electronic purchasing. To redefine an organization by extending its boundaries and to build, enhance, sustain, and align relationships with suppliers, customers, and other partners, strategic investments in information technologies appear necessary. This is because the involvement of partners enables organizations to market new products and services, gain operational efficiencies, and enhance revenues, amongst others. Especially when an organization has a complex manufacturing system, detailed interfaces with partners, and a dynamic market environment, information technologies may effectively enable that organization to develop, alter, and strengthen its relationships with partners in its purchasing system.[83]

Organizations that employ interactive purchasing use this alone or they combine it with either electronic purchasing or network purchasing. This observation supports arguments that suggest the primary feature of a relational practice is the level of trust between the buyer and supplier. Trust previously has been identified a key role in building successful personal interactions between employees and individual suppliers,[84] as well as in managing risks in an organization's supply base.[85]

Managerial Implications

Perhaps the key finding for managerial practice is how organizations with an integrative relational configuration performed significantly better than did organizations with other configurations. This was true on a variety of purchasing, marketing, and financial performance measures. The value-creation potential of purchasing and supply management has been noted before; the current study emphasizes the need to view purchasing and supply management as a strategic function that is internally aligned and integrated with other functions.[86] Organizations thus may find it more profitable to encourage mutual understanding and effective collaboration between marketing and purchasing; integrate technology-based interactions with suppliers; invest in interpersonal relationships across suppliers and the broader purchasing network; and consciously manage the marketing–purchasing interface.

In particular, the purchasing practices framework, depicted as a radar diagram (Figure A2.1), could be used as a form of scorecard. It provides a simple, easily accessible means to track and monitor the implementation of a purchasing configuration. For this study, the diagrams depict how four clusters of organizations compare in terms of the mixes of purchasing practices they employ. Each respondent answered the questions included in our measurement instrument (or 'toolbox') for all direct suppliers of his or her organization.

An individual organization could use the same measurement instrument in a slightly different way, asking each of its *buyers* to answer questions about the suppliers that they manage. All data for each purchasing practice (transaction purchasing, electronic purchasing, interactive purchasing, network purchasing) then could be aggregated into single scores. Therefore, for each buyer, there would be four scores—one per purchasing practice—that managers could plot on a buyer-specific radar diagram. On a different level, buyers often manage several *purchasing categories* (e.g., electronic components, spare parts, temporary labor, office supplies), so an organization could ask its buyers to answer questions for each purchasing category that they manage, then plot radar diagrams to compare how purchasing categories are managed. Similarly, a multi-unit business organization could plot and compare how *business units* manage (parts of) their supply base.

Applying the measurement instrument on these various levels requires that the questions be reworded slightly to make them applicable to the buyer, category, or business unit level. For example, in this study the measurement instrument asks how purchasing is practiced in a particular organization with its direct suppliers (see Table A2.1); this item could be reworded to query, "How is purchasing practiced when you deal with your *suppliers*?" (buyer level), "How is purchasing practiced with your *suppliers of product category A*?" (category level), or "How is purchasing practiced in your *business unit* with direct suppliers?" (business unit level). Other questions in the survey may need similar slight rewording, to reflect the level at which the survey takes place.

The four aggregate scores of purchasing practice—at the buyer, category, or business unit level—can be used to perform a cluster analysis, especially if the number of buyers, categories, or business units is large.[87] Although the number of buyers or business units may be limited in any one organization, such that radar diagrams can be constructed for each, organizations typically manage so many purchasing categories that clustering becomes opportune.[88] With the four scores, managers can devise a radar diagram per cluster, which in this case depicts how much of each purchasing practice gets used per cluster. The performance outcomes also could be evaluated per cluster.

A radar diagram of this kind then could be leveraged with target achievement levels. The gap between actual and target levels forms the basis for a focused discussion about how to bridge the gap. Over-achievement similarly could spark a discussion about whether some resources might be allocated more usefully elsewhere. Thus, the purchasing practices framework can help organizations track, monitor, and assess their purchasing practices across buyers, purchasing categories, and business units; it also can help determine the most appropriate configurations of purchasing practices to pursue.

With this performance outcome data on hand, organizations can specify their strategies, and managers can make informed decisions about the organization's relations with groups of suppliers. Objectives, in terms of purchasing practices and performance outcomes, result from the strategy specification. The next step involves tracking, monitoring, and evaluating purchasing practices, just as managers did when mapping the current situation. Finally, managers can reassess their strategy and take corrective action (strategy re-specification) if necessary. This process should be repeated periodically.

For analyzing purchasing practices at the industry level, the process is similar, except that further distinctions are necessary to assess the purchasing practices indicators, such as distinguishing direct from indirect suppliers or any other variable of interest. The supplier clustering then should be run separately for the chosen variables of interest, and the remaining steps of the process should be revised accordingly. An analysis at the industry level is likely to be carried out by groups, such as chambers of commerce, consulting companies, or industry representatives.

Further Research

Conventional wisdom suggests that the emphasis in purchasing is increasingly on relational aspects;[89] this study shows that an integrative relational configuration is also synonymous with increased performance. Yet the results indicate that when dealing with suppliers of direct inputs, almost a fifth of organizations still practice transactional purchasing. Are purchasing managers unaware of the performance implications of relational purchasing, or are these types of practices difficult to implement, perhaps because global sourcing initiatives have increased the physical distance between buyer and supplier?[90] To help uncover the drivers behind purchasing practices, further research should investigate when and why transactional and relational purchasing, and their different combinations, exist. If such research also predicted causal relationships, it would be possible to use structural equation models to achieve both the validation of the measures and the estimation of causal relationships. The use of structural equation models also would enable further fine tuning of the purchasing practices measurement instrument.

Further research could seek to adapt the instrument so that—within one organization—the type of practices used in relation to individual suppliers (i.e., one level lower than the buyer level) could be measured more easily. The instrument would need to be revised, to address the questions that are not suitable for the individual level (e.g., the question of "nature of communication" in regard to transaction purchasing and electronic purchasing), and then validated.

This study has revealed four configurations of purchasing practices. No claims, however, are made as to whether the interpersonal dyadic configuration (that makes high use of the relational interactive purchasing practice) and interpersonal network configuration (that makes high use of the two relational interactive and network purchasing practices) are merely transition states toward the integrative relational configuration (that makes high use of all three relational purchasing practices). Using a longitudinal design,[91] further research could capture the evolutionary patterns of purchasing practices, which would enhance greatly our knowledge of how relationships develop.[92] Longitudinal research also might help to determine whether purchasing develops progressively along a transactional–relational purchasing continuum (from the transactional configurations, via the interpersonal dyadic and the interpersonal network configurations, to the integrative relational configuration) or whether it can move in either direction.[93] For example, instead of traveling in a linear fashion through the four purchasing configurations, organizations may in fact employ any one at any given time, depending which specific mix of practices is felt to be most strategically advantageous. Examining the path-dependent nature of purchasing practices—that is, differences in the past lead to different purchasing practices in the future[94]—also could reveal the route that organizations follow to integrate their purchasing practices with suppliers.[95]

In conclusion, it is noteworthy that this study has provided significant findings regarding the measurement of purchasing practices. Additional fine tuning, using larger samples, could continue to improve the way purchasing practices are being measured.

METHODOLOGY

Checks of Data Quality

The assessment of nonresponse bias relied on a comparison of the demographics of the respondents with the demographic make-up of all ISM members,[96] which reveals that respondents are typical of ISM organizations. A time-trend extrapolation test can compare early and late responses on the key constructs; there were no significant differences. Nonresponse bias thus is not likely a problem in this study.[97]

Because the measures all rely on a single source, common method bias in self-reported measures could be a concern. Employing the widely used Harman's one-factor method,[98] a factor analysis was run on all measures to examine the likelihood of a single or dominant factor. The unrotated solutions show no evidence of a dominant common factor (13 factors had eigenvalues greater than 1.0; the first factor accounts for only 22 percent of variance). There is no indication that common method bias is a serious issue for this study.

Psychometric Quality of the Purchasing Practices Measurement Instrument

The indicators of the four purchasing practices constructs are treated as formative, because each indicator describes a different facet of the latent construct.[99]

In other words, transaction purchasing, electronic purchasing, interactive purchasing, and network purchasing each result from a unique combination of indicators. Changes to one indicator are not necessarily associated with changes to the others.[100] Although the indicators likely are correlated, they will not be highly correlated. For example, an organization's emphasis on transaction purchasing would be stronger if the organization were to increase its focus on achieving cost savings ("find the best deal"), even if it did not change its type of communication or contact with its direct supplier.

To verify the psychometric properties of the measurement instrument, the four critical steps are followed that Diamantopoulos and Winklhofer propose for constructing indexes based on formative indicators: content specification, indicator specification, indicator collinearity, and external validity.[101] These authors propose two methods for testing the validity of formative measures: the method used in the present study, which also is widely used in management studies,[102] and the method that relies on structural equation modeling (MIMIC model). The latter method cannot be used in the present study, which neither hypothesizes causal relationships between the formative constructs nor includes reflective indicators. Also, MIMIC models often require a larger sample size.

Content specification. The classification of purchasing into transaction purchasing, electronic purchasing, interactive purchasing, and network purchasing and the development of formative indicators of the exchange and managerial aspects of purchasing appear in our theoretical background section. All practices and indicators have been identified in prior literature and confirmed by purchasing professionals and academics.

Indicator specification. Unlike reflective indicators, formative indicators must cover all aspects of the construct.[103] The methodology used to develop the framework of marketing practices, which is similar in its purpose to the purchasing practices framework, is studied and a literature review is conducted to identify purchasing practices and their indicators. Discussions with experienced purchasing professionals and academics helped validate the practices and indicators. This method offered confidence that the indicators effectively describe the exchange and managerial aspects of transaction purchasing, electronic purchasing, interactive purchasing, and network purchasing.

Indicator collinearity. Indicators in formative constructs are not interchangeable. If an indicator represents an almost perfect linear combination of the other indicators, it contains redundant information and does not measure a different aspect of the latent construct.[104] To test for collinearity, a variance inflation factor (VIF) was calculated per type of practice for each indicator ($VIF_{ij} = 1/[1 - R^2_{ij}]$, where R^2_{ij} is the coefficient of determination for the prediction of variable ij by the other indicators of practice j[105]). Most VIFs are below 2.0, and the largest VIF is 2.8 (network purchasing, managerial investment indicator). Therefore, all VIFs are below the conservative VIF threshold of 3.3[106] and considerably below 10, the recommended cut-off value,[107] and there is no evidence of excessive indicator collinearity.

External validity. To determine the external validity of the indicators for each purchasing practice construct, a global indicator was used that summarizes the essence of the construct as an external criterion—that is, the organization's general approach to direct suppliers. Each indicator of a particular practice should be correlated with the global indicator of that same practice. Bivariate correlation analysis shows that all indicators are highly significantly and positively correlated with their respective external criterion ($p < .02$ or better).

Within-practice correlations and across-practice correlations also show that the indicators tend to be more highly correlated with their respective global indicator than with any other external global indicator (i.e., within-practice correlations higher than across-practice correlations), which confirms the quality of the measurement instrument. The only three exceptions are type of contact, indicator of transaction purchasing, and managerial intent and purpose of exchange, both indicators of electronic purchasing, but their correlations with the global indicator are still fine in terms of their size and significance. There is no reason, theoretical or statistical,[108] to delete these two indicators from further analysis.[109]

Thus, for each of the four practices, the organization's scores on eight indicators for that practice—purpose of exchange, managerial intent, nature of communication, type of contact, duration of exchange relationship, formality of exchange, managerial focus, and managerial investment—are summed and converted into an index, theoretically ranging from .2 to 1. As final evidence for the external validity of our formative constructs the correlation between the index and the external criterion was computed. Correlations range between .601 and .805, which indicates proper external validity.[110]

NOTES

1. J.H. Dyer, C. Dong Sung, and W. Chu, "Strategic Supplier Segmentation: The Next 'Best Practice' in Supply Chain Management," *California Management Review*, 40/2 (Winter 1998): 57–77; R. Terpend, B.B. Tyler, D.R. Krause, and R.B. Handfield, "Buyer-Supplier Relationships: Derived Value over Two Decades," *Journal of Supply Chain Management*, 44/2 (April 2008): 28–55. I.P. Morgan, "The Purchasing Revolution," *McKinsey Quarterly* (Spring 1987): 49–55.
2. B. Axelsson, F. Rozemeijer, and F. Wynstra, *Developing Sourcing Capabilities: Creating Strategic Change in Purchasing and Supply Management* (New York: John Wiley & Sons, 2005).
3. R.B. Handfield, G.L. Ragatz, K.J. Petersen, and R.M. Monczka, "Involving Suppliers in New Product Development," *California Management Review*, 42/1

(Fall 1999): 59–82; N. Capon and C. Senn, "Global Customer Management Programs: How To Make Them Really Work," *California Management Review*, 52/2 (Winter 2010): 32–55; J.H. Dyer and H. Singh, "The Relational View: Cooperative Strategy and Sources of Interorganizational Competitive Advantage," *Academy of Management Review*, 23/4 (October 1998): 660–679.
4. T. Nishiguchi and J. Brookfield, "The Evolution of Japanese Subcontracting," *Sloan Management Review*, 39/1 (Fall 1997): 89–101.
5. C.J. Corbett, J.D. Blackburn, and L.N. Van Wassenhove, "Partnerships to Improve Supply Chains," *Sloan Management Review*, 40/4 (Summer 1999): 71–82; W. Ulaga and A. Eggert, "Value-Based Differentiation in Business Relationships: Gaining and Sustaining Key Supplier Status," *Journal of Marketing*, 70/1 (January 2006): 119–136; B. Axelsson and F. Wynstra, *Buying Business Services* (Chichester: John Wiley & Sons, 2002); Capon and Senn, (2010); L.-E. Gadde and H. Håkansson, *Supply Network Strategies* (New York: John Wiley & Sons, 2001).
6. S.D. Jap and J.J. Mohr, "Leveraging Internet Technologies in B2B Relationships," *California Management Review*, 44/4 (Summer 2002): 24–38.
7. For example, see Capon and Senn (2010); A. Paulraj, I.J. Chen, and J. Flynn, "Levels of Strategic Purchasing: Impact on Supply Integration and Performance," *Journal of Purchasing & Supply Management*, 12/3 (March 2006): 107–122.
8. In this chapter, the term 'practices' refers to four theoretical purchasing practices (transaction purchasing, electronic purchasing, interactive purchasing, and network purchasing), as well as to how an organization goes about practicing purchasing (and this actual mix of the four purchasing practices is referred to as the organization's purchasing configuration).
9. A.S. Carr and J.N. Pearson, "Strategically Managed Buyer-Supplier Relationships and Performance Outcomes," *Journal of Operations Management*, 17/5 (August 1999): 497–519; Paulraj et al. (2006).
10. B.M. Bensaou, "Portfolios of Buyer-Supplier Relationships," *Sloan Management Review*, 40/4 (Summer 1999): 35–44; P. Kraljic, "Purchasing Must Become Supply Management," *Harvard Business Review*, 61/5 (September–October 1983): 109–117; R. Terpend, D.R. Krause, and K.J. Dooley, "Managing Buyer-Supplier Relationships: Empirical Patterns of Strategy Formulation in Industrial Purchasing," *Journal of Supply Chain Management*, 47/1 (January 2011): 73–94.
11. N. Gil, "Developing Cooperative Project Client-Supplier Relationships: How Much to Expect from Relational Contracts," *California Management Review*, 51/2 (Winter 2009): 144–169; S. Tadelis, "A Tribute to Oliver Williamson: Williamson's Contribution and its Relevance to 21st Century Capitalism," *California Management Review*, 52/2 (Winter 2010): 159–166.
12. Carr and Pearson (1999); D.A. Johnston, D.M. McCutcheon, F.I. Stuart, and H. Kerwood, "Effects of Supplier Trust on Performance of Cooperative Supplier Relationships," *Journal of Operations Management*, 22/1 (February 2004): 23–38; M.A.M. Primo and S.D. Amundson, "An Exploratory Study of the Effects of Supplier Relationships on New Product Development Outcomes," *Journal of Operations Management*, 20/1 (February 2002): 33–52.
13. P.D. Cousins, "A Conceptual Model for Managing Long-Term Inter-Organisational Relationships," *European Journal of Purchasing and Supply Management*, 8/2 (2002): 71–82; L.-E. Gadde and I. Snehota, "Making

the Most of Supplier Relationships," *Industrial Marketing Management*, 29/4 (July 2000): 305–316.
14. R.J. Brodie, N.E. Coviello, and H. Winklhofer, "Contemporary Marketing Practices Research Program: A Review of the First Decade," *Journal of Business & Industrial Marketing*, 23/2 (2008): 84–94. See p. 91.
15. N.E. Coviello, R.J. Brodie, P.J. Danaher, and W.J. Johnston, "How Firms Relate to Their Markets: An Empirical Examination of Contemporary Marketing Practices," *Journal of Marketing*, 66/3 (July 2002): 33–46.
16. M. Christopher, *Logistics and Supply Chain Management*, 3rd ed. (London: Financial Times Series, 2004); R.C. Lamming, T. Johnsen, J. Zheng, and C.M. Harland, "An Initial Classification of Supply Networks," *International Journal of Operations & Production Management*, 20/6 (June 2000): 675–691.
17. V. Kapoor and A. Gupta, "Aggressive Sourcing: A Free-Market Approach," *Sloan Management Review*, 39/1 (Fall 1997): 21–31.
18. G. Lorenzoni and A. Lipparini, "The Leveraging of Interfirm Relationships as a Distinctive Organizational Capability: A Longitudinal Study," *Strategic Management Journal*, 20/4 (April 1999): 317–338.
19. S.R. Croom, "The Impact of e-Business on Supply Chain Management: An Empirical Study of Key Developments," *International Journal of Operations & Production Management*, 25/1 (January 2005): 55–73; C.P. Holland, "Cooperative Supply Chain Management: The Impact of Interorganizational Information Systems," *Journal of Strategic Information Systems*, 4/2 (June 1995): 117–133.
20. I.D. Ford, "The Development of Buyer-Seller Relationships in Industrial Markets," *European Journal of Marketing*, 14/5–6 (May–June 1980): 339–354; R. Landeros and R.M. Monczka, "Cooperative Buyer/Seller Relationships and a Firm's Competitive Posture," *Journal of Purchasing and Materials Management*, 25/3 (Fall 1989): 9–18.
21. L. De Boer, J. Harink, and G. Heijboer, "A Conceptual Model for Assessing the Impact of Electronic Procurement," *European Journal of Purchasing and Supply Management*, 8/1 (March 2002): 25–33.
22. S.D. Jap, "Online Reverse Auctions: Issues, Themes, and Prospects for the Future," *Journal of the Academy of Marketing Science*, 30/4 (Fall 2002): 506–525.
23. Jap and Mohr (2002); A. Paulraj and I.J. Chen, "Strategic Buyer-Supplier Relationships, Information Technology and External Logistics Integration," *Journal of Supply Chain Management*, 43/2 (Spring 2007): 2–14.
24. Jap and Mohr (2002); M.J. Maloni and W.C. Benton, "Supply Chain Partnerships: Opportunities for Operations Research," *European Journal of Operational Research*, 101/3 (November 1997): 419–429; Terpend et al. (2011).
25. Bensaou (1999); R.E. Spekman, "Strategic Supplier Selection: Understanding Long-Term Buyer Relationships," *Business Horizons*, 31/4 (July 1988): 75–81.
26. Croom (2005); De Boer et al. (2002); Holland (1995).
27. Gadde and Snehota (2000); Spekman (1988).
28. Christopher (2004); Corbett et al. (1999).
29. B.B. Jackson, "Build Customer Relationships that Last," *Harvard Business Review*, 63/6 (November–December 1985): 120–128; Landeros and Monczka (1989); Spekman (1988).
30. Landeros and Monczka (1989); Maloni and Benton (1997).

31. Bensaou (1999); Cousins (2002); T.B. Lawrence, E.A. Morse, and S.W. Fowler, "Managing Your Portfolio of Connections," *Sloan Management Review*, 46/2 (Winter 2005): 59–65.
32. Gadde and Håkansson (2001).
33. G. Lorenzi and C. Baden-Fuller, "Creating a Strategic Center to Manage a Web of Partners," *California Management Review*, 37/3 (Spring 1995): 146–163.
34. Bensaou (1999).
35. Bensaou (1999); Spekman (1988).
36. Lamming et al. (2000); Lawrence et al. (2005); R.J. Trent and R.M. Monczka, "Purchasing and Supply Management: Trends and Changes Throughout the 1990s," *International Journal of Purchasing and Materials Management*, 34/4 (Fall 1998): 2–11.
37. Landeros and Monczka (1989).
38. Bensaou (1999); Jackson (1985); Spekman (1988).
39. Lawrence et al. (2005).
40. Holland (1995); D.B. Holm, K. Eriksson, and J. Johanson, "Creating Value Through Mutual Commitment to Business Network Relationships," *Strategic Management Journal*, 20/5 (May 1999): 467–486.
41. Landeros and Monczka (1989).
42. Spekman (1988).
43. Trent and Monczka (1998).
44. Lamming et al. (2000).
45. Bensaou (1999).
46. M. Naim, S. Disney, and D. Towill, "Supply Chain Dynamics," in S. New and R. Westbrook (Eds.), *Understanding Supply Chains: Concepts, Critiques, and Futures* (Oxford: Oxford University Press, 2004): 109–132.
47. Landeros and Monczka (1989); F.I. Stuart, "Supplier Partnerships: Influencing Factors and Strategic Benefits," *International Journal of Purchasing and Materials Management*, 29/4 (Fall 1993): 22–28.
48. Of the 256 questionnaires returned, 151 (59.0%) arrived through regular mail, and 105 (41.0%) were completed online. A multivariate analysis of variance (MANOVA) of the 40 purchasing practice items showed no significant differences related to response method ($F(36, 160) = .801$, $p = .512$), so all the responses may be pooled. The main reasons for nonparticipation were that the organization no longer trades, company policy did not allow survey participation, the respondent was no longer working for the organization, or the respondent lacked time to complete the relatively long questionnaire. The 54 questionnaires with substantial missing data were excluded from further analysis, so the final analysis used 202 organizations (effective response rate: 6.1%).
49. Paulraj and Chen (2007); Ulaga and Eggert (2006).
50. Details about the questionnaire are available from the first author.
51. Coviello et al. (2002).
52. A. Cox, D. Chicksand, P. Ireland, and T. Davies, "Sourcing Indirect Spend: A Survey of Current Internal and External Strategies for Non-Revenue-Generating Goods and Services," *Journal of Supply Chain Management*, 41/2 (Spring 2005): 39–51; L.M. Ellram, W.L. Tate, and C. Billington, "Services Supply Management: The Next Frontier for Improved Organizational Performance," *California Management Review*, 49/4 (Summer 2007): 44–66; Kapoor and Gupta (1997).

53. As recommended by J. Rossiter, "The C-OAR-SE Procedure for Scale Development in Marketing," *International Journal of Research in Marketing*, 19/4 (December 2002): 305–335, intensity-free Likert item-stems are used and the response intensity is built into the leaves of the item ('never' to 'always').
54. Scales adapted from T.C. Harrington, D.M. Lambert, and M. Christopher, "A Methodology for Measuring Vendor Performance," *Journal of Business Logistics*, 12/1 (Summer 1991): 83–104; and H. Shin, D.A. Collier, and D.D. Wilson, "Supply Management Orientation and Supplier-Buyer Performance," *Journal of Operations Management*, 18/3 (April 2000): 317–333.
55. Marketing performance and financial performance scales both from Coviello et al. (2002).
56. Including Coviello et al. (2002).
57. Shin et al. (2000).
58. Detailed descriptive statistics of the sample are available from the first author.
59. Coviello et al. (2002).
60. Pearson correlations between the different approaches show that electronic purchasing and interactive purchasing are significantly and positively correlated with network purchasing (.688 and .655, $p < .001$) but not with transaction purchasing (.081, $p > .05$); in addition, electronic purchasing and interactive purchasing significantly correlate with each other (.444, $p < .001$). This result is consistent with Coviello et al.'s (2002) finding that interaction marketing correlates with transaction marketing but not significantly with network marketing.
61. Axelsson and Wynstra (2002); Carr and Pearson (1999).
62. Bensaou (1999); D.M. Lambert, M.A. Emmelhainz, and J.T. Gardner, "Developing and Implementing Supply Chain Partnerships," *International Journal of Logistics Management*, 7/2 (Winter 1996): 1–17; J.K. Liker and Th.Y. Choi, "Building Deep Supplier Relationships," *Harvard Business Review*, 82/12 (December 2004): 104–113.
63. The variance inflation factors (VIFs) are below 2.0, except the transaction purchasing index, which is 2.9. These values are well below 10, the threshold limit, and confirm the absence of collinearity.
64. J.F. Hair, R.E. Anderson, R.L. Tatham, and W.C. Black, *Multivariate Data Analysis*, 5th ed. (Upper Saddle River, NJ: Prentice-Hall International, 1998).
65. Ibid.; M.T. Frohlich and R. Westbrook, "Arcs of Integration: An International Study of Supply Chain Strategies," *Journal of Operations Management*, 19/2 (February 2001): 185–200.
66. M.S. Aldenderfer and R.K. Blashfield, *Cluster Analysis* (London: Sage, 1984); P. Arabie and L. Hubert, "Cluster Analysis in Marketing Research," in R.P. Bagozzi (Ed.), *Advanced Methods in Marketing Research* (Oxford: Blackwell, 1994): 160–189.
67. Ibid.; Hair et al. (1998); R. Kathuria, "Competitive Priorities and Managerial Performance: A Taxonomy of Small Manufacturers," *Journal of Operations Management*, 18/6 (November 2000): 627–641.
68. This most likely number of clusters should lie between N/60 (or 3.5) and N/30 (or 6.5). See Kathuria (2000).
69. Aldenderfer and Blashfield (1984).
70. A relatively large increase would imply that dissimilar clusters merged together in step S, which means that the number of clusters at step S – 1 would be the most appropriate choice. See Hair et al. (1998).
71. Hair et al. (1998).

72. Hair et al. (1998).
73. Y. Dong, C.R. Carter, and M.E. Dresner, "JIT Purchasing and Performance: An Exploratory Analysis of Buyer and Supplier Perspectives," *Journal of Operations Management*, 19/4 (July 2001): 471–483; Handfield et al. (1999); Liker and Choi (2004); Paulraj and Chen (2007).
74. Shin et al. (2000).
75. L.L. Stanley and J.D. Wisner, "Service Quality Along the Supply Chain: Implications for Purchasing," *Journal of Operations Management*, 19/3 (May 2001): 287–306.
76. Ibid.; J.W. Stoelhorst and E.M. Van Raaij, "On Explaining Performance Differentials: Marketing and the Managerial Theory of the Firm," *Journal of Business Research*, 57/5 (May 2004): 462–477.
77. Carr and Pearson (1999); I.J. Chen, A. Paulraj, and A.A. Lado, "Strategic Purchasing, Supply Management, and Firm Performance," *Journal of Operations Management*, 22/5 (October 2004): 505–523; J. Gonzalez-Benito, "A Theory of Purchasing's Contribution to Business Performance," *Journal of Operations Management*, 25/4 (June 2007): 901–917; Paulraj et al. (2006); Paulraj and Chen (2007).
78. These results were based on a MANOVA with cluster membership as a between-subjects factor ($F(30, 516) = 1.578$, $p < .05$), followed by a contrast analysis (one-tail tests), which revealed the statistical significance of the hypothesized differences. See Hair et al. (1998). Directional (one-tailed) tests are used because, based upon the literature, a higher score is hypothesized for the relational integrative configuration compared to the other configurations. See G.A. Churchill, *Marketing Research: Methodological Foundations*, 7th ed. (Orlando, FL: The Dryden Press, 1999) for a discussion of one-tailed and two-tailed tests.
79. These results are based on analyses of variance (ANOVAs) for the level of technology intensity ($F(3, 198) = 10.304$, $p < .001$) and the role of technology ($F(3, 197) = 5.805$, $p < .001$), as well as post hoc difference tests (differences were significant at $p < .05$). Two-tailed post hoc tests are used because we merely explored the possible existence of differences across means for these variables (see previous note).
80. Using the four global indicators for both direct and indirect suppliers, a MANOVA used the type of supplier as a within-subjects factor and cluster membership as a between-subjects factor. Significant differences arose between direct and indirect suppliers in terms of purchasing practices ($F(4, 188) = 14.257$, $p = .0001$). The significance levels of the univariate ANOVAs for TP, IP, and NP ranged from .000 to .007.
81. Paulraj et al. (2006); Carr and Pearson (1999).
82. Cox et al. (2005), Ellram et al. (2007); Kapoor and Gupta (1997).
83. N.P. Greis and J.D. Kasarda, "Enterprise Logistics in the Information Era," *California Management Review*, 39/4 (Summer 1997): 55–78; B.R. Konsynski, "Strategic Control in the Extended Enterprise," *IBM Systems Journal*, 32/1 (Spring 1993): 111–142. See p. 112; S. Sivadasan, J. Efstathiou, A. Calinescu, and L.H. Huatuco, "Supply Chain Complexity," in New and Westbrook (2004): 133–163.
84. R.M. Morgan and S.D. Hunt, "The Commitment-Trust Theory of Relationship Marketing," *Journal of Marketing*, 58/3 (July 1994): 20–38; B. Nooteboom, *Trust: Forms, Foundations, Functions, Failures and Figures* (Cheltenham, UK and Northampton, MA, USA: Edward Elgar Publishing, 2002).

85. R. Spekman and E. Davis, "Risky Business: Expanding the Discussion on Risk and the Extended Enterprise," *International Journal of Physical Distribution & Logistics Management*, 34/5 (2004): 414–433; J.M. Whipple, D.F. Lynch, and G.N. Nyaga, "A Buyer's Perspective on Collaborative versus Transactional Relationships," *Industrial Marketing Management*, 39/3 (April 2010): 507–518.
86. C. Baier, E. Hartmann, and R. Moser, "Strategic Alignment and Purchasing Efficacy: An Exploratory Analysis of their Impact on Financial Performance," *Journal of Supply Chain Management*, 44/4 (September 2008): 36–52; Chen et al. (2004).
87. The minimum sample size for cluster analysis is at least 2^m, where m equals the number of clustering variables, that is, 4 in our case; $5*2^m$ is, however, the ideal situation (see Forman (1984), cited in S. Dolnicar, "Using Cluster Analysis for Market Segmentation: Typical Misconceptions, Established Methodological Weaknesses and Some Recommendations for Improvement," *Australasian Journal of Market Research*, 11/2 (November 2003): 5–12 and E. Mooi and M. Sarstedt, *A Concise Guide to Market Research* (Heidelberg: Springer, 2011).
88. See, for example, S. Kulp, T. Randall, G. Brandyberry, and K. Potts, "Using Organizational Control Mechanisms to Enhance Procurement Efficiency: How GlaxoSmithKline Improved the Effectiveness of E-Procurement," *Interfaces*, 36/3 (May/June 2006): 209–219, with an example of 49 sourcing categories for one organization.
89. Axelsson and Wynstra (2002); Gadde and Snehota (2000).
90. C. Steinle and H. Schiele, "Limits to Global Sourcing? Strategic Consequences of Dependency on International Suppliers: Cluster Theory, Resource-Based View and Case Studies," *Journal of Purchasing and Supply Management*, 14/1 (January 2008): 3–14.
91. Coviello et al. (2002); D. Narayandas and V.K. Rangan, "Building and Sustaining Buyer-Seller Relationships in Mature Industrial Markets," *Journal of Marketing*, 68/3 (July 2004): 63–77.
92. M.B Beverland and A. Lindgreen, "Relationship Use and Market Dynamism: A Model of Relationship Evolution," *Journal of Marketing Management*, 20/7–8 (July–August 2004): 825–858; R.F. Dwyer, P.H. Schurr, and S. Oh, "Developing Buyer and Seller Relationships," *Journal of Marketing*, 51/2 (April 1987): 11–27; M.K. Hingley, "Power to All Our Friends? Living with Imbalance in Supplier-Retailer Relationships," *Industrial Marketing Management*, 34/8 (November 2005): 848–858.
93. Terpend et al. (2008); P.F. Johnson, M.R. Leenders, and H.E. Fearon, "Evolving Roles and Responsibilities of Purchasing Organizations," *International Journal of Purchasing and Materials Management*, 34/1 (Winter 1998): 2–11.
94. P.A. Dabholkar, W.J. Johnston, and A.S. Cathey, "The Dynamics of Long-Term Business-to-Business Exchange Relationships," *Journal of the Academy of Marketing Science*, 22/2 (Spring 1994): 130–145.
95. Frohlich and Westbrook (2001); C. Claycomb and G.L. Frankwick, "Buyers' Perspectives of Buyer-Seller Relationship Development," *Industrial Marketing Management*, 39/2 (February 2010): 252–263.
96. ISM, *ISM Membership Demographics* (Tempe, AZ: Institute for Supply Management, 2004).
97. J.S. Armstrong and T.S. Overton, "Estimating Non-Response Bias in Mail Services," *Journal of Marketing Research*, 14/3 (June 1977): 396–402.

98. A.S. Carr and H. Kaynak, "Communication Methods, Information Sharing, Supplier Development and Performance: An Empirical Study of Their Relationships," *International Journal of Operations & Production Management*, 27/4 (April 2007): 346–370; Gonzalez-Benito (2007); M. Howard and B. Squire, "Modularization and the Impact on Supply Relationships," *International Journal of Operations & Production Management*, 27/11 (November 2007): 1192–1212; Paulraj et al. (2006); P.M. Podsakoff and D.W. Organ, "Self-Reports in Organizational Research: Problems and Prospects," *Journal of Management*, 12/4 (Winter 1986): 531–544. The amount of common method variance is an issue when either a single factor emerges from the factor analysis or one general factor accounts for the majority of covariance among the measures.

99. A. Diamantopoulos and H.M. Winklhofer, "Index Construction with Formative Indicators: An Alternative to Scale Development," *Journal of Marketing Research*, 38/2 (May 2001): 269–277; Rossiter (2002). It should be noted that the formative measurement approach has gained increased attention in response to arguments that measures treated as reflective in many empirical management studies probably have been misspecified. See for example A. Diamantopoulos and J.A. Siguaw, "Formative Versus Reflective Indicators in Organizational Measure Development: A Comparison and Empirical Illustration," *British Journal of Management*, 17/4 (December 2006): 263–282; Rossiter (2002). Because knowledge of formative measures is relatively less advanced though, the debate regarding their properties, advantages, and limitations continues. See J.B. Wilcox, R.D. Howell, and E. Breivik, "Questions about Formative Measurement," *Journal of Business Research*, 61/12 (December 2008): 1219–1228. One of the most controversial issues remains the appropriate validity assessment of formative measures. See A. Diamantopoulos, P. Riefler, and K.P. Roth, "Advancing Formative Measurement Models," *Journal of Business Research*, 58/12 (December 2008): 1203–1218.

100. Diamantopoulos and Winklhofer (2001).

101. Ibid.

102. See for example N. Coviello, H. Winklhofer, and K. Hamilton, "Marketing Practices and Performance of Small Service Firms: An Examination in the Tourism Accommodation Sector," *Journal of Service Research*, 9/1 (August 2006): 38–58; Ch. Homburg, O. Jensen, and H. Krohmer, "Configurations of Marketing and Sales: A Taxonomy," *Journal of Marketing*, 72/2 (March 2008): 133–154; C.S. Katsikeas, D. Skarmeas, and D.C. Bello, "Developing Successful Trust-Based International Exchange Relationships," *Journal of International Business Studies*, 40/1 (January 2009): 132–155; R.W. Palmatier, L.K. Scheer, M.B. Houston, K.R. Evans, and S. Gopalakrishna, "Use of Relationship Marketing Programs in Building Customer–Salesperson and Customer–Firm Relationships: Differential Influences on Financial Outcomes," *International Journal of Research in Marketing*, 24/3 (September 2007): 210–223.

103. Ibid.

104. Ibid.

105. Hair et al. (1998).

106. Diamantopoulos and Siguaw (2006). All condition indices are also largely below 30, further confirming the absence of collinearity problems (Hair et al., 1998). Confirming that condition indices are below 30 is a complementary check of dependence between indicators.

107. Ibid.

108. Rossiter (2002). Note that the relatively small sample size might be the cause of these less clear patterns of correlations encountered in the present study. See also Palmatier et al. (2007) and Katsikeas et al. (2009).
109. Details regarding the size and significance levels of correlations are available from the first author.
110. J. Cohen, *Statistical Power Analysis for the Behavioral Sciences*, 2nd ed. (Hillsdale, NJ: Lawrence Erlbaum Associates, 1988).

Index

abstract
    in academic search 306, 307–8
    length 254
    main types 239
    purpose 253
    recommended content 239–40
    for research funding applications 106–7, 109
    serving as advertisement 239
    when to write 240
academic article citations *see* citation
academic career advice
    dilemmas and their resolution 25–8
    for early-career researchers 28–35
    interviews with thought leaders 13–14
    mistakes to avoid 20–25
    recommendations 14–20, 35–6
academic journal article writing
    abstract 239–40
    acknowledgement section 255
    conclusions 253
    convincing editors of publication deservedness 254–5
    discussion 252
    findings 250–252
    hypothesis section 242–4
    introduction and literature review 240–242
    keywords 240
    length 254
    publishing success and rejection rates 236–7
    research methodology 244–50
    scientific message 254
    selecting appropriate journal 253–4
    title 238
academic life
    advantages 49
    as difficult to explain to non-academics 48–9
    see also balancing act

Academic Search Engine Optimization (ASEO) 305–10
academic writing
    first impressions 289–90
    style differences with funding applications 105
    see also academic journal article writing; case study methodology section; manuscript framing; manuscript review; revising for premier academic journals
academics
    balancing act 38, 42–9
    business collaborations
        challenges 135–9
        engaging successfully 139–44
        inside perspective 130
        motivations and expectations 131–5
    collaboration with 14–15, 36
    differences with practitioners 182–3, 185, 207
    as evaluated by publication performance 132
    mimicking 21–2, 36
    tasks of 38–41
    see also academic career advice
acknowledgement section 255
action research
    abductive 136
    CMP Group 83, 181, 356
    interaction and collaboration 324
    under-representation 136, 182
affirmation citations 298–9
analysis of manuscript
    construct measures and definition alignment 286–7
    interaction terms 288
    methodology section 246–50
application citations 298
applied theories

in CMP research program 75
concept 119–20, 206
conditions for drawing on
    theories-in-use 121
interface with general theories 205,
    207, 223
article recognition *see* manuscript
    recognition
article writing *see* academic journal
    article writing
aspiration 20–21, 26, 160
assessment
    of CSR compliance 227
    data quality 377
    impact 173, 325
    one-size-fits-all 317, 342
    for research funding 104–5
    of societal value 317, 325–7,
        340–341
    for success 65–7, 295
    of validity and reliability 232, 285
assumptions
    challenging 56–7, 125, 141, 276,
        350
    of methods 245
    shared 225
    validity of 193
authorship, sequence of 26
avenues for future research
    inclusion in manuscript 170, 189,
        245, 303
    purchasing practices example 376–7

balancing act 38, 42–9
black box analogy 257–8
British Academy of Management 114–15
brown-bag sessions 36, 41, 47, 64, 99,
    101, 103
business marketing
    OBC (observe, bridge, challenge)
        model for 52–8
    research devoted to 51, 58
business schools
    journal rankings 39, 295, 352
    pursuing research funding 40, 97–8,
        350–351
    recognition and ranking 173–4
    and relevance of academic research
        24, 303
    and societal value 336–8, 340–342

strategies for research success 61,
    63–7, 86
translating research into teaching
    173–86
see also academics; Cardiff Business
    School; Copenhagen
    Business School
business-to-business (B2B) marketing
    advantage in classroom 185
    classes designed around use of cases
        180
    dilemmas and their resolution 25–8
    early-career researcher guidelines
        28–35
    examples of conceptual framework
        development styles 211–21
    great teaching 177–9
    as grounded in realistic, strategic
        managerial decision-making
        278
    interviews with thought leaders
        13–14
    mistakes to avoid 20–25
    recommendations 14–20, 35–6
    relativism ontology 225
    research funding application cases
        111–15
    typified as design science 122
    typified by high degree of
        stability in buyer–supplier
        relationships 71
    see also conceptual frameworks
businesses
    engagement with 15, 41
    and government-backed funds 101
    inclusion in research and teaching
        46
    surveying purchasing practices
        365–7
    viewing research as worthy of
        financial support 338
    see also university–business
        collaborations

capabilities
    dynamic, of for-profit hybrids
        214–16, 336
    need to develop collaborative 139
    Ph.D. students 154, 159–61, 166
    Ph.D. supervisors 162–4

research 67–8, 77–8, 153, 301
  team 202
Cardiff Business School 41, 67, 152, 164
career advice *see* academic career advice
career transition 153–4, 159–60, 171
case method research 247–9
case study methodology section
  analyzing data 229, 232
  background and context 225–6
  best practice examples 232–3
  case selection 226–7
  crafting instruments and protocols 228–9
  validity and reliability
    addressing concerns 232
    securing design tests of 230–231
citation
  background and context 295–6
  CMP Group 74, 85, 95–6
  creating recognition
    offline 303–5
    online 305–10
  ethical considerations 310
  IMP Group 77, 82, 84, 85, 94–5
  as increasingly important measure of research quality 65–6
  measuring societal impact 326
  potential for, as top factor in manuscript assessment 237
  preparing for 300–303
  readily accessible metrics 311
  reasons for
    article types 42–3, 296–8
    citation types 298–300
citizenship 41, 42, 349
clarity in expression 68, 78–9, 301
clash of theories 53, 55, 57
cluster analysis 217, 367–8, 375
CMP Group
  activity history 73–7
  articles and citations 95–6
  charter example 354–6
  clarity in expression 79
  corporate governance characteristics 355–6
  getting research accepted 84
  getting research recognized 85
  initiating research stream 78
  living case studies 83, 181–2, 184–5

platform to consolidate knowledge 81
research problems leading to research opportunities 78
role of theory and theorizing 81–2
sustaining leadership and innovation 83, 86–7
teamwork within network of scholars 80
tenacity and resilience 86
co-creation
  interaction and collaboration 323–4
  of learning 174–6
  of value 176, 177, 321, 324
co-poiesis 138
collaboration
  academic 14–15, 36
  basic aim of 129
  building network for 45–6
  for cross-disciplinary research 124–5, 127
  dropping those that don't work 46
  importance of 32–3, 36
  lack of 161
  Ph.D. student/supervisor 164, 168–9, 170
  via co-creation, action research and learning 323–4
  see also practitioner collaboration; university–business collaborations
collaborative competences 139, 141–2
commercial activities 318, 322–3
conceptual articles 204, 205, 209–11, 221, 298, 299
conceptual development 205–6, 221, 223, 301–2
conceptual frameworks
  background and context 204–6
  guidelines for developing 221–3
  role of theory vs. empirical data in developing 204–5
  styles for developing 209–11
    examples from B2B marketing 211–21
  theory-generative approach to developing 336
  theory informing development of 206–9
conclusions

Index

in academic journal articles 253
benefits of 34
clear, for presenting research 303
length 254
manuscript framing 198–200
manuscript review 288–9
construct definition 281–2, 286–7
construct measures 286–7
consultants/consulting 131–2, 318, 321–2
Contemporary Marketing Practices Group *see* CMP Group
contract research 318, 321–2
contributions
in conclusion 26, 198, 281
and desk rejection 261
to the field, strong 300–301
figures, diagrams and tables for summarizing 201
in introduction 167, 193–5, 276, 279, 290
of Ph.D. thesis 166–7
theoretical and managerial 276–8
unrecognized 328
contributions section
manuscript framing 193–5
manuscript review 274, 276–8
presenting research 300–301
in research funding application 110
Copenhagen Business School 124, 126, 152, 153–4, 156, 158
corporate social responsibility (CSR) 212–14, 297
courageous ideas
developing 52–8, 350
lack of 51–2, 58
creative tension between theory and practice 355
criticism
accepting in positive light 265–6
building on 190, 289–90
coping with 34–5
responses to 292
cross-disciplinary research
barriers to breaking 118–19, 122–4
practical steps to undertaking 127
steps to undertaking 124–6, 351
theorizing processes for 119–22, 127, 221
value of 126–7
curiosity-driven dialogue 138–9

Danish regional research funding 111–14
data analysis 229, 232
data quality assessment 377
definition alignment 286–7
design
ex ante and *ex post* approaches 246–7
increasing heterogeneity in research 132
multi-method research 81–2
optimizing articles for search 307–8
of purchasing practices framework 359–65
research 195–7
in research funding case 111–13
tests of validity and reliability 230–231, 232
design science research 122
dimensionality 281–2
directional hypotheses 244, 282–3
discussion
classroom 176–7, 178, 180–181
of overall research process or model, in methodological considerations 245–6
of societal value, journals requesting 314
of theory, in setting case framework 248
discussion section
in academic journal articles 252
length 254
manuscript review 288–9
presenting research 302–3
separating from 'Findings' section 250–251
dissemination
as academic task 40–41
broad 317
dimensions of 329–30
as element of research funding application 109, 110
of knowledge 318, 320–321, 354
platforms for 296
duration of exchange 75, 217, 218, 361, 364, 367, 379

e-mail management 45
e-mail signatures 304
early-career researchers

academic search 305–10
advice 28–36
   B2B guidelines 28–35
   continuous learning 165
   dilemmas and solutions 25–8
   mistakes to avoid 20–25
   recommendations 14–20
   for research funding *see* research funding
editors
   building visibility and reputation with 33
   convincing about value of paper 26–7, 254–5
   decision 'rules' 270
   looking for clear research objectives 300
   manuscript desk rejection 261–3
   preferring well-known ideas, constructs and theories 298
   and reviewers 263–72, 291–2
   role in prioritizing research influencing management practice 339
   role in supporting emerging research streams 87
   selection of reviewers 240, 259, 261
   wishing for more original research 52, 58
education
   as academic task 39–40
   university and executive training 318, 321
efficiency
   in managing emails 45
   in managing time 44–5
electronic purchasing 217–20, 359–65, 367, 368, 372–9
engagement
   as academic task 41
   common forms of 317, 320
   customer 67, 68, 121, 299
   dimensions of 328, 329–30
   two modes of 138
enthusiasm
   abstract conveying 107
   author communicating to reader 194–5
   working with people who lack 20–21

ex ante research design 246, 247
ex post approaches 246–7
executive training 318, 321

Field Wright Citation Index 295–6
findings/results
   in abstract 239–40
   in academic journal articles 250–252
   in case study methodology 228, 231
   compelling, for presenting research 302–3
   discussion of 288
   dissemination, IMP Group 354
   length 254
   relevance of 198–9
first impressions
   importance of 289–90
   title creating 238, 253
focus
   maintaining 19
   manuscript framing 190–192
for-profit hybrids 214–16, 336
formality of exchange 75, 217, 218, 362, 364, 367, 379
fun 20
functional silos 118, 122–4, 127, 153
funding *see* research funding
future pipeline 27–8

general theories
   CMP typology 74–5, 83
   commonly used 118
   concept 119, 206
   domains of knowledge 120, 208
   foundations in many different disciplines 118, 351
   integration to develop midrange theory 119–22, 127, 182
   interfaces 121, 205
Goodhart's Law 310
Google Scholar 17, 65, 67, 74, 236, 295, 304–6, 309, 310, 316
graphics 107, 275–6, 308

hypotheses
   clearly written and well-supported 280–281
   conflicting predictions 282–3

construct definition and
  dimensionality 281–2
directional 282–3
as element of research funding
  application 109
framing counterintuitive 277
poor quality leading to rejection
  237
use of correct measures 287
hypothesis section
  in academic journal articles 242–4
  length 254
  manuscript review 280–283

ideas
  developing original and courageous
    52–8, 350
  lack of original and courageous
    51–2, 58
  screening 46–7
IMP Group
  activity history 70–73
  books, articles and citations 94–5
  charter example 353–4
  clarity in expression 78–9
  getting research accepted 83–4
  getting research recognized 84–5
  initiating research stream 78
  platform to consolidate knowledge
    80–81
  research problems leading to
    research opportunities 77
  role of theory and theorizing 81
  sustaining leadership and innovation
    82–3, 86
  teamwork within network of
    scholars 79
  tenacity and resilience 85–6
implications *see* managerial implications
  statement
Industrial Marketing and Purchasing
  Group *see* IMP Group
Industrial Marketing Management
  aim to promote best research 97
  fostering academic–practitioner
    collaboration 340, 342
  IMP Group 82, 83, 85
  increasing impact factor 51, 85
  more longitudinal work published
    in 233

quality of qualitative case analyses
  published in 247
readership of 13, 51
reasons for continued increase in
  quality and influence of 236
recommendation to prioritize
  conceptual work
  development 204
resubmissions 190, 290
review and revision process 258–71
and societal value 313–14, 340,
  341–2
special issues 73, 80, 297
students publishing in 160, 166
as top B2B marketing journal 180
usefulness of studies published in 1
innovation
  abduction approach and scientific
    method 136
  collaborative 130, 131, 143
  open 129, 287
  performance, in university–business
    collaboration 135
  societal value 326
  speed of, as reason for universities
    seeking links with businesses
    133
  sustaining 69, 82–3, 86–7, 302
  universities acting as co-producers
    of 131
inspiration
  avenues for future research 104
  from experts 47
  learning from colleagues 103
  from own realities 157
  for writing riveting introduction
    191–2
instrumental collaborative exchange 138
interaction and collaboration 319, 323–4
interaction terms 288
interactive purchasing 217–20, 274,
  359–64, 367–8, 372, 376, 378
interdisciplinary research *see*
  cross-disciplinary research
international emphasis of CMP Group
  356
international networks 65, 68, 102, 353
international students 158, 161, 177, 185
internationality problem 326
internationalization 41

introduction section
    in academic journal articles 240–242
    benefits of 34
    clear statement of research objectives in 26, 303
    as element of research funding application 109
    hook/positioning 275–6
    length 254
    manuscript framing 191–5
    manuscript review 274–9
    statement of theoretical and managerial contributions 276–8
    structured 278–9
    three main objectives 252

jargon 106, 185, 240, 286, 290
journal article writing *see* academic journal article writing

keywords
    in academic journal articles 240
    in academic search 306–7
knowledge
    co-production 323–4
    contribution of Ph.D. thesis 166–7
    dissemination of 318, 320–321, 354
    domains of 119–20, 207–8, 221, 223
    platform to consolidate 68, 80–81, 301
knowledge exchange 334–6

leadership
    and CSR 212–14
    for research funding 98–102, 115
    as strategy for success 64
    strong research groups 350
    sustaining 69, 82–3, 86–7, 302
    teams 126
learning
    co-creation of 174–6
    from colleagues 103
    curiosity-driven dialogue 138
    interaction and collaboration 319, 323–4
    personal, constant 18, 143–4, 165
    processes of 175–6
    from work experience 184–5

length of manuscript 200–201, 254
licensing 318, 322–3
limitations of research
    in abstract 239
    in academic journal articles 245, 252, 253
    manuscript framing 199–200
    and media 321
    in methodology 283–4
    presenting research 303
    in published articles, quoting 195
literature
    accumulating broad knowledge of 29
    gap-spotting method 155, 157, 167, 193
    identifying gaps in 56, 277, 278
    immersing oneself in 15
    introducing new concept or method to 194
    outside main research area 126
    purchasing 216–17, 367, 378
    'slice of literature' approach 157, 275
    staying current 30
literature review
    in academic journal articles 241–2
    and citation 297, 298
    CMP Group 355
    critical 279–80, 301
    length 254
    manuscript framing 195
    manuscript review 279–80
    tables 291
living case studies 16, 83, 181–2, 184–5, 356

managerial contributions 26, 276–8
managerial focus 75, 217, 219, 362, 364, 367, 379
managerial implications
    in conceptual framework 213, 215, 220–221
    purchasing practices example 374–6
managerial implications statement
    common fault in 129
    in conclusions 253, 288, 303
    to increase relevance 339
    manuscript framing 198–200, 203

Index 395

managerial intent 75, 217, 219, 362, 364, 367, 379
managerial investment 75, 217, 219, 363, 364, 367, 378–9
manuscript framing
    conclusions and managerial implications 198–200, 203
    contributors' remit 189–90
    framing 202–3
    introduction, research focus and contribution 190–195
    length 200–201
    literature review and research design 195–7
    methodology and methods 197–8
    revision 202
    visualizations 201–2
manuscript major revision 265–71
manuscript recognition
    offline creation 303–5
    online creation 305–10
manuscript rejection
    editors 261–3
    reviewers 263–5
manuscript review
    analysis 286–8
    background and context 273–4
    discussion and conclusions 288–9
    first impressions 289–90
    hypotheses 280–283
    introduction section 274–9
    literature review 279–80
    methodology 283–6
    readability 290–291
    webpages of targeted journal 293
    working with reviewers 291–2
measurement
    academic impact 315–17
    construct 286–7
    of contribution of Ph.D. thesis 166–7
    Goodhart's Law 310
    of purchasing practices 216–17, 355, 360, 361–79
    of research quality 65–7, 295–7, 311, 315, 338
    societal impact 316
    of societal value of research 318–20, 324–31, 333, 340–341, 342

meetings 152–3
mentoring
    access to 126, 127
    discussing strategy for research funding 100–101
    engaging in 30, 41, 163
    Ph.D. program example 171
    purpose of 100
    via collaboration 352
metadata 309
methodological pluralism 155, 250
methodology
    and methods 197–8
    purchasing practices example 377–9
methodology section
    in academic journal articles 244–50
    analysis considerations 244–50
    manuscript framing 197–8
    manuscript review 283–6
    methodological considerations 244–6
    qualitative 247–50, 285–6
    quantitative 246–7, 249, 284–5
    readability and jargon 286
    see also case-study methodology section
midrange theories
    as bridging body of theory 207
    characterized by abductive reasoning 75
    concept 119, 206
    domains of knowledge 120, 208
    integration to develop 119–22, 127, 182
    interfaces 121, 205
    managerial practice informing research process 223
    multiple pathways to develop 120, 121, 221
    use by CMP research program 76, 83, 87
monographs 164–5

narrative-based style 209, 210, 211, 214–16, 222
nature of communication 75, 217, 218, 360, 361, 367, 379
negation citations 298
network practice 75

network purchasing 217, 218–20, 359–64, 367, 368, 372, 374, 378–9
networks
    for collaboration and support 45–6
    for cross-disciplinary research 126
    for Ph.D. students 163
    for research funding 102–4, 115
    of scholars, teamwork within 68, 79–80, 301
    and theory 56–7, 120, 208

OBC (observe-bridge-challenge) model
    bridging disciplines 55–6
    challenging assumptions and theories 56–7
    concept 52
    golden quadrant 57–8
    observing the world 53–5
    as Venn diagram 53
offline recognition creation 303–5
online platforms 69, 176–7, 295–6, 326
online recognition creation 305–10
online teaching 176–7
original ideas
    developing 52–8, 350
    lack of 51–2, 58

passion 31–2, 164
patents 318, 322–3
perfunctory citations 298–300
personal learning, constant 18, 143–4, 165
Ph.D. students
    capabilities 154, 159–61, 166
    challenges faced by 156–9
    characteristics of less capable 161–2
    contract research example 322
    questions asked of supervisors 150–151
    rankings attracting 173
    supervision of 151–5, 166–71
Ph.D. supervisors
    career transition to research and teaching 153–4
    characteristics of good 162–4
    questions asked of 150–151

    role in developing student publishing and teaching skills 164–5
    supervision of Ph.D. students
        conventional 154–5
        and meetings 152–3
        overview 151
        reflections on 166–71
Ph.D. thesis
    contributions to knowledge 166–7
    finishing 159
pipeline, future 27–8
pluralism
    methodological 155, 250
    in philosophy and method 355–6
policy
    contributions to public 319, 323
    as strategy for success 63–4
positioning
    align with methodology 283
    cross-disciplinary research 125, 127
    manuscript introduction 34, 275–6
    network purchasing 359, 363
    research 21, 26–7
    visualizations 201
postgraduate research role 356
practitioner collaboration
    academic career advice 15–17, 22
    co-production of knowledge 207, 323–4
    common forms of engagement 317, 320
    constant learning for 143–4
    conversation with practitioners 140–141
    incorporating into research process 332
    Industrial Marketing Management fostering 340, 342
    interactional expertise 142
    necessity of 351
    as occasionally irrelevant 338–9
    university–business 134–6
practitioners
    article highlights written for 308
    differences with academics 182–3, 185, 207
    dissemination of knowledge 320
    feedback from 290–291

Index 397

involvement in socially relevant
 research 332
 theorizing with 182
 use of theory 183–4
predictions, conflicting 282–3
premier academic journals *see* academic
 journal article writing; revising for
 premier academic journals
presenting research 300–303
prioritization
 of importance of tasks 42–3
 of urgency of tasks 43
problems with no practical relevance
 21–2
professionals, experienced
 Ph.D. programs attracting 171
 supervision of 155–6
 working with 167
project management skills 202
prolepsis 192–3
proposition-based style 209–10, 211,
 212–14, 222
psychometric quality of purchasing
 practices measurement instrument
 377–9
public policy 319, 323
publication process 272
publication success rate
 guidelines for improving 237–55,
 300–303
 of *Industrial Marketing
 Management* 236
publishable articles 164–5
publishing
 as academic priority 134
 assessing for success in 65–7
 in highly-ranked journals 352
 monograph vs. publishable articles
 164–5
purchasing practices
 avenues for further research 376–7
 background and context 357–9
 conceptual framework 217, 220
 design of framework 359–60, 364–5
 discussion 372–7
 four kinds of 217
 framework 359–72
 indicators pertaining to 218–19,
 361–3

major configurations of 367–9
 diagrammatic representation
 369
 differences in performance
 outcomes 371
 managerial implications 374–6
 measurement of 216–17, 355, 360,
 361–79
 methodology
 data quality checks 377
 psychometric quality of
 purchasing practices
 measurement instrument
 377–9
 in relation to direct and indirect
 suppliers 372
 selection of mix for supply base
 370–372
 surveying organizations' 365–7
 transactional/relational 216–20,
 358–9, 361–4, 367–73, 376–7
 typology-based style applied to
 216–21
purpose of exchange 75, 217, 218, 360,
 361, 367, 379

qualitative analysis 247–50
qualitative methodology 285–6
quantitative analysis 246–7, 249, 250
quantitative methodology 284–5

readability 286, 290–291
reading
 about company successes or failures
 176
 editorials 258
 establishing routine 29
 expanding in targeted way 56
 for exposure to different writing
 styles 291
 five Cs of 'first-pass' 193
 topics outside main research area
 126
 webpages of targeted journal 293
recognition of research
 achieving 69, 84–5, 302
 creating offline 303–5
 creating online 305–10
 scholarly 173

references 229, 241, 254, 259, 262, 284, 290
regularity 29–30
relationship practice, traditional 75
relationships
    building components 16
    buyer–supplier 71–3, 248
    cause–effect 209–10, 222, 339
    in hypotheses 243–4, 277, 288
    new paradigm for marketing based on 76
    purchasing 357–65, 368, 372–4, 376–7
    for research funding 102–4, 115
relativism 225
relevance
    of manuscript subject 237, 275–6, 279, 286, 288–9
    of relational marketing 74, 78, 87, 355
    of research 21–2, 24, 40–41, 180–181, 196, 303, 310
    research–relevance gap 97, 115
    rigor–relevance gap 129, 132, 197–8
    and search terms 306
    of university–business collaboration 134
    see also societal relevance
repository 309
"requisite variety" 184–5
research
    as academic task 39
    capabilities 67–8, 77–8, 153, 301
    career transition to 153–4, 159–60, 171
    devoted to business marketing 51, 58
    getting accepted 69, 83–4, 302
    getting cited 295–311
    model for generating original, courageous 52–8
    originality as biggest challenge 52
    positioning 21, 26–7
    with practical significance 35–6
    role of postgraduate 356
    setting up and presenting 300–303
    strategies for success 63–7
        reflections on 77–86
    translation into teaching 179–86, 351–2

unsuitable 27
    see also recognition of research; relevance: of research
Research Assessment Exercise (RAE) 173
research community, offline 303–5
research design 195–7
Research Excellence Framework (REF) 23, 41, 173, 314, 317, 325, 326, 337
research funding
    as academic task 40
    application 104–11, 115–16
    case studies 111–15
    current trends 97
    from industry 100, 102–3, 107, 338
    leadership 98–102, 115
    pursuit of 'good' 350–351
    relationships and networks 102–4, 115
    research groups 64, 100
    research support office 104
    societal value 111, 325, 337, 352
research funding applications
    abstract, importance of 106–7, 109
    attributes sought by reviewers 104–8
    balance between technical jargon and simplicity 106
    budget predictions 108
    elements of 109–11, 116
    evaluation criteria 104–5
    following exact guidelines 106
    layout 107
    outcomes 108
    starting from scratch 105–6
    successful cases 111–15
    target readers 106
    time predictions 107
    writing style 105
research groups
    building 61–87
    developing strong 350
    reputation 66
    see also CMP Group; IMP Group
research-led teaching 181, 355, 356
research problems
    addressing for research funding 115
    borrowing methodology from different fields to investigate 245

Index 399

identifying new, important 69, 350
and interdisciplinary work 123,
    124–5, 127, 138, 351
leading to research opportunities
    67–8, 77–8, 296, 301
research question
    align interview questions with 286
    align with methodology 155, 245,
        246
    allowing to emerge from practical
        problem 155
    analysis section appropriateness
        246, 250
    constructing clear 125–6, 127, 278
    findings section congruence with
        302
    fulfilment of shown in conclusions
        253
    gap-spotting method 155, 157,
        276–7
    hypotheses clearly related to 281
    importance of 33–4
    introduction focusing reader on 240,
        252
    practitioners' ability to develop 134
    and research design 196
    in research funding case studies 113,
        114
    single 266
    'slice of life' approach to identifying
        157, 275
    stating in abstract 239–40
    of wide interest to relevant field 263
research repository 309
research stream
    collaboration for building 32
    conditions for success 67–70,
        77–87, 301–2
    distinction with school of thought 62
    editor's role in supporting emerging
        87
    IMP and CMP groups establishing
        successful 77–87
    initiating 68, 78, 301, 350
    meta-analysis in 297
    well-established 61
research support office 40, 99, 103, 104,
    116
resilience 70, 85–6, 302
results *see* findings/results

review citations 298–9
review process 258–71, 273–93
    black box analogy 257–8
    funding 115–16
    for *Industrial Marketing*
        Management 259–61
    negativity seemingly related to 35
    preventable mistakes in 272
    and project management skills 202
    role in improving manuscripts 70
    similarity bias 69
    strategizing role in 274
    support for students undergoing
        157–8
    tenacity and resilience for 86
reviewers
    comfort zones 123, 136, 298
    common problems with 25
    general agreement amongst 292–3
    on hypotheses 243
    major revision of manuscript
        265–71, 291–2
    on manuscript framing 189–203
    manuscript rejection 263–5
    red flags 285, 293
    research funding applications
        104–11
    similarity bias 69, 84
    working with 291–2
reviewing manuscripts *see* manuscript
    review
reviews
    editors' role 261
    handling 25, 35, 267
    informal 290
    re-reading 257
    value of thorough and critical 36
revising and resubmitting case study *see*
    purchasing practices
revising for premier academic journals
    background and context 257–8
    publication process 272
    review and revision process 258–71
revision process
    background and context 258–9
    editors' desk rejection 261–3
    for *Industrial Marketing*
        Management 259–61
    obvious mistakes 271
    and project management skills 202

reviewers
   manuscript rejection 263–5
   manuscript revision 265–71, 291–2
revision and review decisions 261
typical results per 100 submissions 271
rigor–relevance debate 129, 132, 155, 197–8, 286

scientific contributions 193–5, 276, 298–9
scientific message 254
scope 157, 190–192, 241, 298–9
search 305–10
self-citation 254, 304, 310
service dominant (S-D) logic 83, 87, 120–121, 122, 174–5, 176, 179–80, 185, 351–2
'slice of life' approach 157, 275
social media
   analytic results from data 326
   dissemination via 320–321
   interactive content 309–10
   requiring additional tasks from authors 305
   role in citation building 296
   and societal value 333
societal impact
   comparison with societal relevance 316
   and CSR 213
   definition 316
   as inadequately recognized by universities 137
   as increasingly important motivator for academics 132
   of individual's research 329–30
   metrics 325, 326
   national governments seeking measures of 314
   in research funding application 111
   as sub-component of societal value 313, 316
   of universities 132
societal relevance
   achieving 352
   comparison with societal impact 316
   as component of excellent research 315
   definition 316
   and Hong Kong government 325
   of individual's research 329–30
   national governments seeking measures of 314
   as sub-component of societal value 313, 316
societal value
   academic journals supporting research with 338–40
   activities and measures 318–19
   activities applied in research 333
   beneficiaries and involvement of practitioners 332
   business schools supporting research with 336–8
   context 313, 352
   defining 315–16
   demonstration and documentation 333
   emergence in universities 314
   frameworks for understanding 325–7
   and global challenges 314–15
   identifying relevant 316–17, 320–324
   in *Industrial Marketing Management* 313–14, 340, 341–2
   knowledge exchange supporting 334–6
   measurement of 324–31, 333, 340–341
   recommendations for increasing 329–30, 331–40
   sub-components of 313, 316
   support for researchers 331–2
standing up for your work 26–7
strategy, as strategy for success 63–5
stress 48–9
structure
   atomistic 71
   governance 64
   informal, CMP Group 356
   introduction section 278–9
   optimizing articles for search 307–8
   organization 118
   of Ph.D. students 169–70
success
   celebration of 20

strategies for 63–7
supervision
   benefits and drawbacks 167–9
   characteristics of good 162–4
   of experienced professionals 155–6
   of Ph.D. students
      conventional 154–5
      and meetings 152–3
      overview 151
      reflections on 166–71
   role in building publishing and
      teaching skills 164–6
support networks 45–6

tasks
   of academics 38–41
   looking for synergies between 43–4
   prioritizing by importance 42–3
   prioritizing by urgency 43
teaching
   building skills in 166
   career transition to 153–4
   evaluating 173–4
   nature of great
      actions to facilitate learning
         processes 175–6
      applying S-D logic principles
         174–5
      in business-to-business
         marketing 177–9
      occasional adjustments 177
      use of technology to best
         advantage 176–7
   translation of research into 179–86,
      351–2
Teaching Excellence and Student
   Outcomes Framework (TEF)
   173–4
teamwork within network of scholars 68,
   79–80, 301
tenacity 70, 85–6, 302
theoretical contributions 26, 134, 193–5,
   276–8
theoretical development
   conditions determining success of
      221
   hypotheses derived from 243, 244
   as part of manuscript 241
   presenting research 301–2
   relating to findings 252, 302

theories-in-use (TIU) 119–20, 121, 122,
   182, 206–7, 211, 221
theorizing
   for conceptual frameworks 208–9,
      211, 223
   interfaces for 121
   "lazy" 206
   mid-range processes 75–6
   post hoc 196
   with practitioners 182
   role of 69, 81–2, 296, 302
theorizing processes 75–6, 119–22, 127,
   182, 206, 207–9, 221, 223
theory
   challenging 56–7
   contingency 373
   vs. empirical data, role in
      developing conceptual
      frameworks 204–5
   incorrect 243
   informing development of
      conceptual frameworks
      206–9, 221, 223
   levels of 119–20, 207–8
   lost in translation 134
   practitioner use of 183–4
   relevance 53, 54
   role of 69, 81–2, 296, 302
   theory-based case method, need for
      more research 248
   theory–practice 132, 182, 355
   see also general theories; midrange
      theories
theory adaptation 209, 211, 215
theory development 23, 182, 204, 222–3,
   299
theory-generative approach 215, 336
theory synthesis 209, 211
thoroughness 33–4, 36
time management 23–5, 36, 44–5
title
   of academic journal articles 238
   in academic search 306, 307–8
   manuscript review 290
   reviewers recommending
      improvements to 262
transaction purchasing 217–19, 359–64,
   367, 368, 372–3, 378, 379
transactional practice 75, 373
"travelling off the beaten path" 18–19

type of contact 75, 217, 218, 360, 361, 364, 367, 379
typology-based style 209, 210, 211, 216–21, 222

UK funding agency 114–15
uniqueness 31–2
universities
    cross-disciplinary research 122–7
    demanding research funding 97
    education 318, 321
    leadership 98–102, 115
    research repositories 309
    research support office 104, 116
    societal impact of 132
    and societal value 314, 315, 327, 328, 335, 341, 352
    see also university–business collaborations
university–business collaborations
    challenges
        business perspective 135–6, 339
        discussion 138–9
        university perspective 136–8
    engaging successfully
        collaborative competences 141–2
        constant personal learning 143–4
        conversation with practitioners 140–141
        direct approaches 324
        need to develop collaborative capabilities 139
    and knowledge exchange 334–5, 337
    motivations and expectations
        business perspective 130–132
        discussion 133–5
        university perspective 132–3
    recommendations 223, 351

v-index 327–31
validity and reliability
    addressing concerns 232
    for quantitative studies 247
    reviewers searching for evidence of testing 285
    securing design tests of 230–231
vector graphics 308
visibility
    building with editors 33
    for citations 296
    creating offline 303–5
    creating online 305–10
    of IMP Group 84
    managerial implications section 303, 339
    need for awareness of ways to increase 305–10
    research bringing 39, 69
    of research stream 302
vision
    articulation by business school deans 338
    clear, for cross-disciplinary research 126, 127
    common, in Danish regional partners 112
    defining 342
visualizations 201–2, 291

webpages of targeted journal 190, 259, 293
work colleagues
    celebrating success with 15, 20
    collaboration with 32–3, 46
    lacking enthusiasm and aspirations 20–21
    learning from, as inspiration 103
work–life balance 48, 349
wow factor 47–8, 49, 170, 192

"zone of mutuality" 181, 185